Gateway to Vacationland

Gateway to Vacationland

THE MAKING OF PORTLAND, MAINE

JOHN F. BAUMAN

UNIVERSITY OF MASSACHUSETTS PRESS

Amherst and Boston

Copyright © 2012 by University of Massachusetts Press
All rights reserved
Printed in the United States of America

LC 2011050379
ISBN 978-1-55849-909-6 (paper); 908-9 (library cloth)

Designed by Sally Nichols
Set in Garamond Premier Pro by House of Equations, Inc.
Printed and bound by Thomson-Shore, Inc.

Library of Congress Cataloging-in-Publication Data

Bauman, John F., 1938-
Gateway to vacationland : the making of Portland, Maine / John F. Bauman.
p. cm.
Includes bibliographical references and index.
ISBN 978-1-55849-909-6 (pbk. : alk. paper)—
ISBN 978-1-55849-908-9 (library cloth : alk. paper)
1. Portland (Me.)—History. I. Title.
F29.P9B28 2012
974.1'91—dc23 2011050379

British Library Cataloguing in Publication data are available.

To Barbara,
my loving wife,
companion,
and
research assistant

Often I think of the beautiful town
That is seated by the sea;
Often in thought go up and down
The pleasant streets of that dear old town,
And my youth comes back to me
And a verse of a Lapland song
Is haunting my memory still:
"A boy's will is the wind's will,
And the thoughts of youth are long, long thoughts."

I remember the black wharves and the ships,
And the sea-tides tossing free;
And Spanish sailors with bearded lips,
And the beauty and mystery of the ships,
And the magic of the sea.
And the voice of that wayward song
Is singing and saying still:
"A boy's will is the wind's will,
And the thoughts of youth are long, long thoughts."

I can see the breezy dome of groves,
The shadows of Deering's Woods;
And the friendships old and the early loves
Come back with a Sabbath sound, as of doves
In quiet neighborhoods.
And the verse of that sweet old song,
It flutters and murmurs still:
"A boys will is the wind's will,
And the thoughts of youth are long, long thoughts."

Strange to me now are the forms I meet
When I visit the dear old town:
But the native air is pure and sweet,
And the trees that o'ershadow each well-known street,
As they balance up and down,
Are singing the beautiful song,
And sighing and whispering still:
"A boy's will is the wind's will,
And the thoughts of youth are long, long thoughts."

And Deering's Woods are fresh and fair,
And with joy that is almost pain
My heart goes back to wander there,
And among the dreams of the days that were,
I find my lost youth again.
And the strange and beautiful song,
The groves are repeating it still:
"A boy's will is the wind's will,
And the thoughts of youth are long, long thoughts."

—LONGFELLOW, "My Lost Youth"

Contents

Maps and Illustrations

Acknowledgments

An author owes a debt of gratitude to many people. This book originated as my presidential address given in St. Louis at the 2003 biennial meeting of the Society for American City and Regional Planning History (SACRPH). That address explored Portland, Maine's Parkside neighborhood. I next studied another Portland neighborhood, Bayside, before examining the impact of Model Cities in shaping the Forest City. From there I turned to the city as a whole, and the role, inspired by Longfellow, that beauty and tourism played in making Portland. The University of Southern Maine, and the Muskie School, where I have been a visiting research professor since 2000, generously supported this project in diverse ways. Not only did the school provide travel funds, but the graduate courses that I taught there in Housing and in Historic Preservation helped deepen my understanding of both the city and its long history. Student research projects focusing on places such as Munjoy Hill and the city's Jewish community proved extremely useful. A Muskie School research grant and a Muskie graduate assistant, Sara Devlin, proved invaluable. Sara did time-consuming and deeply appreciated research for me at the Maine Historical Society, combing through year after year of Portland's *Board of Trade Journal* and copying key articles. Professor Kent Ryden of USM's New England Studies Program invited me to teach a summer course on Portland History; doing so further broadened my knowledge of the city. New England Studies faculty Donna Cassidy and Joseph Conforti, and the USM History Department's Joel Eastman, all distinguished scholars, shared their great knowledge and insight about Portland and its history. I also thank the Muskie School's Anne Edwards, who did yeoman service in taking a three-hundred-page manuscript, rife with typos, undecipherable endnotes, and other nonconforming features and producing a presentable, publishable manuscript.

The staff of USM's Glickman Library always cheerfully helped me. My research took me to many other libraries as well, including USM's Osher Map Library, which adjoins the Glickman. There Yolanda Theunissen and her staff helped me with historic maps of Portland and its region. I found their collection of early guidebooks for automobilists especially useful. At the Portland Public Library I worked closely with Abraham Schecter, the librarian in the Portland Room, whose always friendly demeanor and wide knowledge of contemporary Portland history made working there not only enjoyable but very rewarding. Likewise, the staffs of the Hawthorne-Longfellow Library at Bowdoin College, the Folger Library at the University of Maine in Orono, the Maine State Library and Archives in Augusta, the Boston Public Library, the Gorham Public Library, the Edmund Muskie Archives at Bates College, the Baker Library at the Harvard Business School, and the Frances Loeb Library at Harvard's Graduate School of Design graciously assisted me with important collections and my requests for books, records, and other documents. As usual, the capable staff at the Library of Congress, especially Jeffrey Flannery, proved very helpful and friendly.

Over the past decade I have spent many hours at the Maine Historical Society, located next to the Longfellow House on Congress Street in Portland. I did considerable research in that venerable institution and also across the street in the basement of the old Benoit's Department Store building, to which the society moved its collections during major renovations in 2009–2010. The extremely knowledgeable, accommodating, and friendly archival staff of the society, Nicholas Noyes, William Berry, and Jamie Kingman Rice, made research—as always, but especially during that difficult period—highly enjoyable. Dani Fazio at MHS provided extensive help and guidance in my search for illustrations. No history of Portland could be possible without the society's loving stewardship of Maine and Portland history.

I also found a rich trove of Portland history in the library of the Portland Planning and Urban Development Department, where, despite their busy schedules, Lee Urban, Alex Jaegerman, William Needelman, and Deb Andrews found time to afford me access to their historic records and to answer questions. In the midst of my Portland research in 2007 I chaired the biennial meeting of SACRPH in Portland, cohosted by USM and Portland's Planning Department, to which I owe much of the success of that meeting.

Both Deb Andrews and State Historic Preservation Officer Earle Shettleworth Jr. have served on the board or in other leadership roles of Greater

Portland Landmarks, today headed by Hillary Bassett. Deb, Hillary, and Earle, who was born in Portland and possesses encyclopedic knowledge of the city, played vital roles in making this book possible, as did Don Nicoll, a Washington, D.C., aide to the late Edmund Muskie. I interviewed both Don and Earle at length for this book.

I wish to extend special thanks to the University of Massachusetts Press, especially to senior editor Clark Dougan, who guided the development of this book almost from the beginning. Clark proved wonderfully supportive, as did other press staff members, including managing editor Carol Betsch.

The book also owes much to the friends, colleagues, and family who have been so supportative and encouraging over the years. I am particularly indebted to Edward (Ted) Muller, David Schuyler, and Charlie Colgan, who read earlier versions of the manuscript and made extensive, constructive, and highly valuable comments. I am grateful as well for the friendship and encouragement of dear colleagues Jill Pearlman, Roger Biles, Kristin Szylvian, Chris Silver, Alex Von Hoffman, and Ray Mohl. Much of this book was written while my wife and I lived in a picturesque little town in southern France called Collobrières. After a day of feverish writing there, I eagerly looked forward to a glass of wine and good conversation with my wife and our good friends Frank Wirgis and Bruce Lashley. I thank them, my brother, a former manuscript librarian at the Libary of Congress, Fred Bauman, and especially my wife, Barbara Baker Bauman, who spent hours with me in those aforementioned archives and libraries taking notes, photographing and copying documents, and just being with me. This book about a city that we both love is dedicated to her.

Acronyms

AAA	Agricultural Adjustment Administration
CCC	Civilian Conservation Corps
CNR	Canadian National Railroad
CPC	City Planning Commission
CPB	Citizens Planning Board
CWA	Civil Works Administration
DSCUR	Division of Slum Clearance and Redevelopment
E&NA	Europe and North America Railroad
FERA	Federal Emergency Relief Administration
GNRP	General Neighborhood Renewal Plan
GPL	Greater Portland Landmarks
GTRR	Grand Trunk Railroad
HHFA	Housing and Home Finance Administration
KKK	Ku Klux Klan
LWV	League of Women Voters
MERA	Maine Emergency Relief Administration
MICAH	Metropolitan Council on Affordable Housing
NRA	National Recovery Administration
NES	New England Shipbuilding
PHA	Portland Housing Authority
P&R	Portland and Rochester Railroad
P&O	Portland and Ogdenburg Railroad
PPB	Portland Planning Board
PRA	Portland Redevelopment Authority
PWA	Public Works Administration
PWAC	Portland West Advisory Committee
SCRAP	Slum Clearance and Redevelopment Authority of Portland
UDG	Urban Design Group of Newport, Rhode Island
WPA	Works Progress Administration

INTRODUCTION

Of Longfellow, Portland, and long, long thoughts on the "beautiful town seated by the sea"

Come now, join an 1893 delegation of the Portland Board of Trade high atop the Observatory on Munjoy Hill. Look leftward, please, over Casco Bay and then just to the right toward Commercial Street see the vast Grand Trunk Railroad yards, the roundhouse, and the giant grain elevator. Those steamships—the one loading Canadian winter wheat and tied by great hawsers to the Grand Trunk pier, the others anchored at rest in the harbor—fly flags from England, Germany, Belgium, and Brazil and arrive from ports such as Liverpool, Bremen, Antwerp.

Portlanders, such as the Board of Trade members gathered at the Observatory in 1893, spoke of their city as a gateway, an appellation surely deserved. The Board of Trade took enormous pride in Portland's being a doorway to commerce. Since the 1850s the Grand Trunk Railroad had carried Canadian winter wheat (blocked from Halifax or Saint John by a frozen St. Lawrence River) from Montreal to Portland. International steamers then bore that Canadian wheat to Liverpool and Bremen. Other steamers carried Portland-made locomotives, Maine lumber, and Maine canned lobster and on return brought Irish, Swedish, Italian, and English immigrants. In addition to marketing locomotives built by the city's Portland Company, and other locally made products such as chewing gum and artificial legs, Portland beginning in the 1870s marketed itself, its beauty, its healthy air, and its role as the "Gateway to Vacationland."

Newly elected mayor James Phinney Baxter has just joined us in the Observatory and, as he so often does, ponders freely the past and the future of his verdant urban peninsula jutting into Casco Bay and once eloquently described by the city's favorite son, Henry Wadsworth Longfellow, as "the beautiful city by the sea." But Baxter's Portland has a complex urban history. As early as the 1840s, the city's civic and business elite inaugurated a long urban conversation about how best to balance the social and cultural needs of a city reputed for its beauty yet having the economic demands of a regional center geographically blessed by a deep, ice-free harbor and eager to establish itself commercially and industrially. The conversation shifted constantly between the imperatives of commerce and industry and those promoting health, aesthetics, and tourism: parks, tree-shaded streets, the building of attractive promenades. That same conversation still raged on that Observatory platform atop Munjoy Hill in 1893; it continues in 2011.

In many ways, as this history undertakes to make clear, the Portland of 2011 retains much of the character and tempered vibrancy of Baxter's 1893 city. Because, in the 1960s, Portland tempered its appetite for bulldozer-style urban renewal and launched an aggressive historic preservation program, much of its nineteenth- and early twentieth-century architecture and neighborhood charm remain, including not only the McLellan Mansions on High and Spring Streets but the Victoria Mansion on Danforth. Even the brick edifices of the 1846 Portland Company, the firm that ushered in the city's railroad age, still stand staring out over Casco Bay. Although urban renewal, the construction of Interstate 295, and land reclamation and park development around the Back Cove have greatly altered the character of Bayside—the working-class neighborhood that sloped down toward the earlier industrialized Back Cove and once Portland's Lower East Side—still, in 2011, a junkyard, traces of old triple-decker tenements, and faint vestiges of once busy railroad sidings and switching yards that earlier served stove works and tanneries all exist. And just west of the Cove, beyond the Forest Avenue exit of 295, stands Longfellow's Deering Oaks, the emblem of Portland historic beauty. Although freeway construction reduced its size, "Deering's Woods," to quote Longfellow, "are [still] fresh and fair." Indeed, on July 1, 2010, Portlanders beheld a wandering moose splashing playfully in the Deering Oaks pond, disturbing, no doubt, the chickadees and other birds that roost in the pond's mansion-sized birdhouse. Lombard poplars and elms still line many of the city's streets, helping Portland retain the nickname "Forest City." The name originated in the 1850s when the city purchased sixty-three acres of land in Cape Elizabeth (now South Portland) for the Forest City Cemetery, a municipal burying ground which, like Evergreen Cemetery

(1852, located in Westbrook), doubled as a "rural cemetery" and quiet, parklike retreat, or place of "refinement," for summer strolling.[1]

Yet Portland hardly escaped the inexorable forces of change. Like most larger and smaller cities in the 1960s, 1970s, and 1980s, it endured deindustrialization and emerged as a postindustrial city with an economy structured largely around financial, real estate, and corporate management services as well as culture, health care, higher education, and—crucial for this study—tourism. South Portland's busy terminal for tankers carrying Canadian-pipeline-bound petroleum and natural gas keep the Port of Portland's tonnage volume high, yet outside of lobstering, some unloading of chemicals for the state's dwindling paper industry, and some boating, fishing, and other maritime-related enterprises, the city's "working-waterfront" activities steadily diminish. Cruise ships loom in importance as driver's of the city's waterfront economy. Portland officials have talked seriously about building an offshore international pier to accommodate the behemoth tourist vessels and heatedly debated changing the 1987 ordinance that zoned the city's waterfront piers for primarily marine-related business.

Another profound modern change affecting Portland concerns the city's demographic profile. In 1893 a Yankee City with a large Irish neighborhood, a few Italians, Germans, Scandinavians, Russian-Jews, and a sprinkling of blacks, by 2010 Portland flaunted racial and ethnic diversity. It was even reputed for its sprightly gay population, giving it in sociologist Richard Florida's language the ingredients for an emergent "creative economy." The city's rich array of high-quality restaurants (by 2010 featuring "locavore" fare: i.e., Maine-grown meats, vegetables, fruits, wines, and dairy goods), and the recent presence of national, upscale grocers such as Whole Foods and Trader Joe's in the parvenu Bayside locations, give impetus to Florida's assertions.[2]

Its diversity aside, Portland in the year 2011, as in 1893, cherishes beauty while simultaneously addressing the challenges of modernity. Indeed, during much of the city's history, in setting urban priorities, Portland's civic and business leadership strove to balance the demands of economic growth with the urgency of preserving its image as a place blessed by a healthy environment and natural beauty.

Of course, other cities too—Seattle, Washington, for example, with its majestic Puget Sound setting and Mt. Rainer backdrop—boasted natural beauty. In his *Emerald City: An Environmental History of Seattle,* Matthew Klingle interprets its nature as, among other things, a "messy" mix of biological and human (cultural) elements, a culmination, so to speak, of human and environmental forces. Natural beauty, one could argue, derived from that same complex, since in Seattle just as in Portland, Anglo Americans ("Bostons," Klingle calls them), bent on commercial success, to borrow another quote from Klingle, never hesitated to complete "the work which nature had left undone."[3]

Portlanders, however, seemed more mindful than Seattle's business elites of the commercial benefits of beauty, perhaps because of the Forest City's particular economic history. From the moment of its European settlement in the 1630s, Portlanders cleared forests, built roads, canalized rivers, filled in marshlands, graded hills, and reconfigured coves, aiming not only to make what was already stunningly beautiful even more splendid to behold, but also to make it more useful. Enterprising Yankee Portlanders in the eighteenth and ninteenth centuries transformed a glorious wooded peninsula at first into a booming port for furs, masts, and lumber, then a shipbuilding center, and next a port for the West Indian molasses trade. By 1900 they had converted Portland into a modestly industrialized railroad center. They never discounted the importance of the city's natural beauty, however. Preserving this balance between beauty and economic growth, the task of such distinguished business and civic leaders as Mayors Charles J. Chapman and James Phinney Baxter, created an enduring tension between nurturing the city as a verdant, beautiful place of sparking ocean views and establishing it as a busy hub of industry and rail and maritime commerce. This tension within the city's social and ethnic relations pitted Portland Irish longshoremen, Italian laborers, and Jewish peddlers seeking a foothold in Portland's shaky opportunity structure against a Puritan-rooted English and Scots-Irish Yankee establishment determined to uphold both order and hallowed tradition.

There are very few general histories of Portland, Maine, and none that explore its long courtship with the idea of beauty. William Willis's monumental *History of Portland* chronicles its growth from 1632 to 1864 and does it lane by lane, street by street, house by house, and reverend by reverend.[4] Typically, it is a Whiggish story of progress from the town's origin as an isolated seventeenth-century trading post, through the adversity of the Indian wars, to its destruction by the British in 1775, and finally to its glory as a seaport and shipbuilding center in the mid-nineteenth century. Edward Elwell's *Portland and Vicinity, 1876,* and John T. Hull's edited *Handbook of Portland* (1888) more modestly embody a similar triumphant story.[5]

Recently, historian Joseph Conforti, in his edited *Creating Portland: History and Place in Northern New England* (2005), joined together a number of insightful essays that grappled with Portland as a particular place over time.[6] Chronologically ordered, the essays explore distinctive facets of the city's history (its seventeenth- and eighteenth-century struggles for survival, its West Indian commerce, its art and architecture, its black, white, and female working class) which collectively inform and make Portland a unique place.

Yet none of these works develop a unifying theme or argument illuminating why or how Portland evolved as it did and how Portland's place, its geographic or its natural setting on the frontier's edge and within the orbit of the Canadian Maritime Provinces, operated in tandem with its social and political culture to shape the city's destiny. The historian who wrestled most thematically with Portland's rise and fall as a major North Atlantic port was University of Maine historian Robert Babcock. An economic historian, Babcock treated Portland as part of the Maritime Provinces, a connection tightened by the forging of a railroad link between Portland and Montreal in the 1840s, making the city the major winter port for Canadian grain and, argued Babcock, for all intents and purposes a Canadian city. However, unlike Halifax or St. John, Nova Scotia, in the late nineteenth and early twentieth centuries, Portland allowed its maritime infrastructure of wharves and piers to languish while its tourism infrastructure of parks and promenades blossomed.[7]

Following Babcock, this book vastly broadens the Portland story by viewing the city's exquisite geographic setting and consciousness of its beauty as vital parts of its history. Beauty thus unfolds as an important element of the social and political context for the transformation of the Forest City from a thriving shipbuilding center and port for West Indian molasses, to a railroad hub and winter port for Canadian wheat, to a gateway for Maine vacationers, and finally into a modern financial center and culinary Mecca, whose bustling Old Port and working waterfront attract ships and tourists alike.

Although in many ways paralleling the process of urbanization that shaped many American cities, large and small, Portland's history is special. In addition to its Longfellow mystique and its historic dalliance with beauty, several other factors make Portland's history unique. As noted, for over seventy-three years the city's destiny was closely wedded to Montreal and to the Canadian winter-grain trade. As some historians have argued, the city in 1893 was conceivably as closely linked to Canada and to the Maritime Provinces as it was to the United States. Its geographic position as a northern international port and railroad hub, albeit distinct from the mainstream of U.S. urban industrialization, saved Portland from experiencing the full ugly brunt of industrialization, and from the heavy burden of immigration that shaped Boston, Providence, Worcester, Hartford, New Haven, Philadelphia, and other American cities. Whereas in New York's Manhattan and other cities, business houses, city halls, mansions, and other architectural treasures caught in the path of rampant commercial progress and rising urban land values were regularly and with impunity creatively destroyed, by the 1950s much of the nineteenth-century Victorian architecture that had escaped Portland's disastrous fire of July 4, 1866, remained unscathed. Indeed, Portland long carefully cultivated both the Longfellow mystique and the city's reputation for nurturing a rich Yankee heritage and superb architecture. Finally, Portland avoided the teeming, impoverished immigrant slums and black ghettos that festered in many cities. Although a small African American community formed in early nineteenth-century Portland, and a large Irish neighborhood emerged in the 1830s and 1840s, periods of sluggish urban growth and the absence of a thriving industrial base—and therefore opportunity—for unskilled labor kept both the population of European immigrants and the tide of black migration relatively small. After the Civil War, Yankee civic leadership strove to preserve the Forest City as a unique place unblemished by urban industrialization, as a place ripe for a new clean industry: tourism.

Although this book focuses on Portland's nineteenth- and twentieth-century history, the roots of any city's history, and its mystique as a place, reside in its beginnings. After briefly sketching Portland's seventeenth-century origins as George Cleeve's fishing and trading post called Machigonne, the story moves quickly forward to its epiphany as Falmouth, a thriving British mast port, a place where the tall white pine selected for His Majesty's Navy was shipped to England. Forces of rebellion swept Falmouth up in the American Revolution and in 1775 the town was burned to the ground by a vindictive British commander, Henry Mowatt. But Portland arose—as it had after King Philips War (1675–76)—from the ashes. Following the Revolution, and especially after Maine's statehood in 1820, Portland developed into a prosperous center of shipbuilding, of West Indian trade, and of rum and sugar production. At midcentury, 1850, the glorious age of sail, Longfellow's biographical poem "My Lost Youth" bequeathed to the city a legacy of beauty and romance forever etched on Portland's civic memory and, thus, as is argued here, a force shaping the city's history.[8]

Ironically, Longfellow's influence burgeoned at the very moment that railroads linking Portland to Boston, and Portland to Montreal and the Canadian grain trade, transformed the city from a shipbuilding and West Indian trading port into a railroad hub and a center of international and coastal trade. It also made Portland after the Civil War, and after it burned to the ground in 1866, the "Gateway to Vacationland." With resurgent post–Civil War trade, and an architectural renaissance in the hands of great masters such as Francis Fassett and John Calvin Stevens, emerged also nascent industrialism, the Portland Company foundry, marine hardware firms, James Phinney Baxter's canneries, Portland Stoneware, carriage-making, and other modest industries. This book argues that Portland's late nineteenth-century commercial boom put commerce and the vision of industrialism into conflict not only with Longfellow's dreamy images of boyhood frolics in Deering Woods and of the beautiful town seated by the sea but also with the new and growing economic engine of tourism. Since the 1870s, in additional to its deep-water port, Portland capitalized on its unique geographic setting on the rocky Maine coast, on Longfellow's popularity, on Winslow Homer's art, and on the curative powers of Maine air.

In the twentieth century the promise of industrialism became increasingly elusive, and the city's famed commercial greatness slowly faded. These developments left Portland highly vulnerable to the Great Depression and, in the post–World War II era, to the vagaries of suburbanization, deindustrialization, blighted housing, downtown decay, and urban renewal. Portland's postwar struggles with neighborhood blight and downtown obsolescence fueled a vision of modernism, pro-growth politics and the great burst of federally funded renewal activity in the late 1960s and early 1970s. That burst produced the urban renewal Maine Way project, modern downtown offices, and Portland's modern service economy. As the book explains, however, with the demolishing of the Falmouth Hotel, the Old Post Office, and other architectural gems, it also engendered countervailing pressures to save and restore the city's architectural heritage. Historic preservationists such as Edith Sills, John Calvin Stevens II, Pamela Plumb, Frank Akers, and Earle Shettleworth saw that just as Longfellow's dreams drove nineteenth-century tourism, so a similar nostalgia, embodied in the splendors of the Victoria and McLellan Mansions and in the enchanting ways and byways of the Old Port, could revitalize the city's tired heart, restore tourism, and energize the urban economy. The whole story of Portland's remarkable post–World War II transformation and many rebirths ("Resurgem" is Portland's motto) as "the beautiful town that is seated by the sea" form the bone and sinew of this history.

CHAPTER ONE

From Beleaguered Outpost to Booming Port City, 1632–1860

"In all of New England there is no pleasanter town than Portland, in the State of Maine." Thus begins Samuel Longfellow's *Life of Henry Wadsworth Longfellow.* It is an appropriate opening for a book about Samuel's father, Henry Wadsworth, which includes the poet's diaries, where Longfellow ceaselessly extols the spectacular beauty of his birthplace and island-studded Casco Bay. He describes Portland as the "beautiful city by the sea," where foaming waves crash against Portland Head and where, from the Western Promenade, the sun sets brilliantly over distant snowcapped Mount Washington. Free of sandbars, safe for the largest vessels at all stages of the tide (once periodically dredged), Casco Bay and the Fore River docks made Portland in the nineteenth century not only beautiful but—together with Boston, New York, Philadelphia, Baltimore, Charleston, Savannah, and New Orleans—one of America's premier harbors. Fellow poet, historian, and six-term mayor of Portland, James Phinney Baxter, shared Longfellow's ecstasy at Portland's natural beauty. "Thus, this beautiful peninsula," wrote Baxter in the "Story of Portland," an article for an 1895 issue of *New England Magazine,* "rising above the blue sea, adorned with sheltering groves, and verdant glades, kept fresh by perennial springs, in due time became the abode of man."[1]

Baxter's 1895 words captured a central truth about Portland, and one that has exerted a driving force shaping the city's history into the twenty-first century: paramount among its many natural assets was beauty itself. Among the early voyagers drawn to the beauty of Portland, Baxter counted Norse kings, Henry Cabot, Samuel Champlain, and Christopher Levett of York, England. But, explained Baxter, it was the fur trader George Cleeves who in 1632 planted the first settlement in an area that the natives called Machigonne or The Great Knee.[2]

By 1658, the year the Massachusetts Bay Court, empowered by Puritan Oliver Cromwell's victory in England, proclaimed authority over Maine and renamed Cleeves's settlement Falmouth, forty families lived there.[3] In the late seventeenth and first half of the eighteenth century, Falmouth became a theater in a larger, worldwide conflict that historians have called the Great War for Empire. In the form of King Philip's War, which allied the French and the Wabanaki Indians against British settlers, the conflict in 1676 reached Falmouth and reduced the small but flourishing British trading outpost to ashes. A few Falmouth residents returned in 1681 and, under the command of Governor Thomas Danforth, built Fort Loyal near the foot of India Street, then called King Street.

Six hundred people lived in Falmouth by 1688. But no sooner had it regained population and prosperity than the long British-French struggle for empire doomed it a second time. In 1690, during King William's War (1688–1697), the French under Louis de Baude Frontenac and his Abenaki Indian allies laid waste to Falmouth once more, so desolating it that no townspeople returned until 1715.[4] Again, Falmouth resurrected itself, not only as a shipping port for fish and lumber but as a favored mast port for the British navy.

It was not alone as a northern port vying with Boston to achieve prominence; Providence, Rhode Island; Nantucket, New Bedford, and Newburyport, Massachusetts; Portsmouth, New Hampshire; and York and Kennebunkport, Maine, all entered the lists. All those places, like Falmouth, had deep, ice-free harbors. For example, Portsmouth in the eighteenth century thrived as the main center of settlement and government of colonial New Hampshire. By the 1770s the Strawbery Banke riverfront of Portsmouth at the mouth of the Piscataquis River had developed a lively European and West Indies trade in lumber, flour, fish, and other local products—trade that would continue to expand.[5]

In 1774, on the eve of the American Revolution, more than 2,000 people inhabited Falmouth Neck (as the peninsular landform was called), which steadily loomed as an important part of the Atlantic World. As it had earlier, the heart of the local economy involved timber, cut by farmers in the richly forested hinterland and floated or carted to coastal sawmills where white pine,

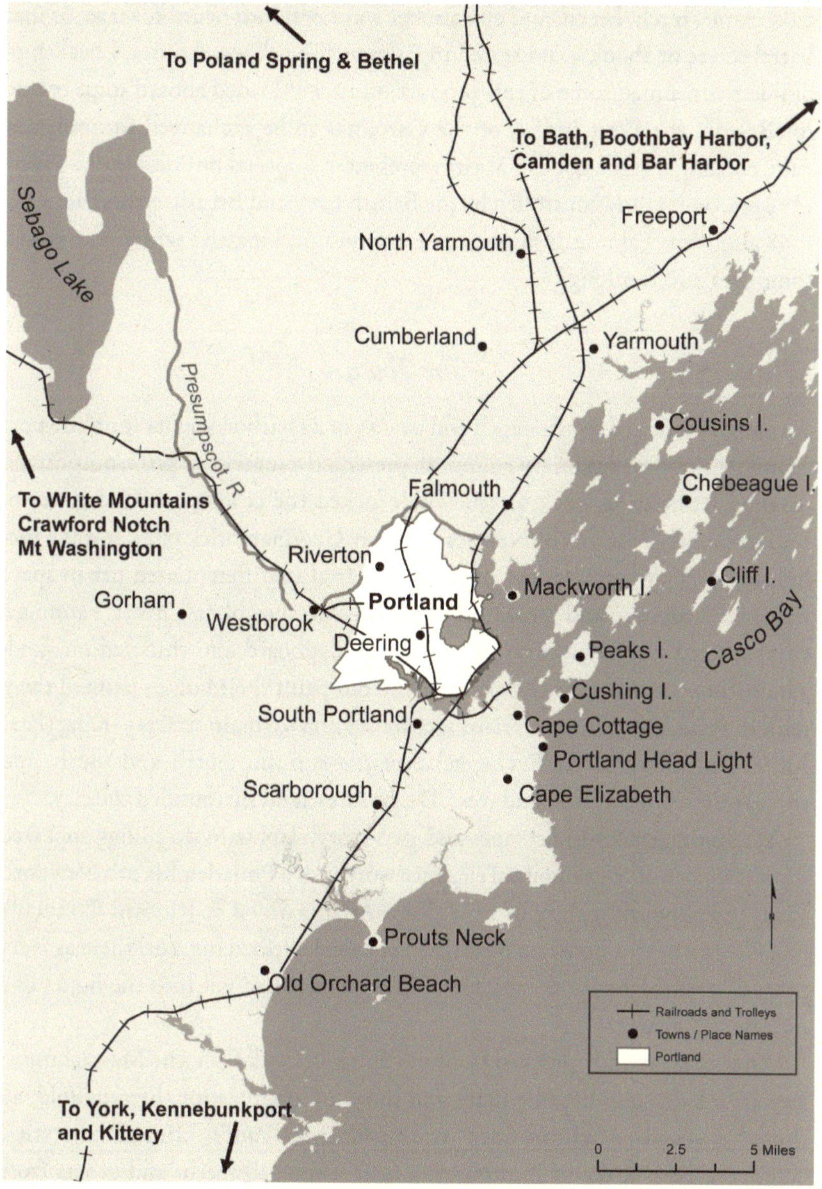

Map of the Portland region showing islands, suburbs, and important sites of hotels and tourist attractions ca. 1900–1940. Drawn by Rosemary Mosher, Orbis, LLC.

oak, maple, birch, beech, and elm timber was sawn into board footage, or into barrel staves or shooks, and stored in Falmouth Neck warehouses. Local shipbuilders consumed some of this product; most was loaded aboard ships bound for Boston, the West Indies, or the Carolinas to be exchanged for molasses, rum, cotton, or trade goods.[6] Masts represented a special business in the 1720–1774 era, one tightly controlled by the British navy and British agents. Between 1768 and 1772, Falmouth shipped to England 1,046 massive white pine masts, some over 200 feet long.[7]

The Town

Although sustained by the depth and beauty of its harbor, and its sprightly port economy, pre-Revolutionary Falmouth presented a somewhat grim, outpost demeanor. Its housing stock on the whole lacked the cosmopolitan elegance of Philadelphia's, Boston's, or Newport's stately Georgian brick piles. It was a preindustrial city where wealthy merchants shared undifferentiated urban space with their artisan and unskilled working-class neighbors. Most Falmouth citizens lived unpretentiously in unpainted clapboard and shingled one-and-a-half-story cottages (the few citizens who did paint their houses painted them red). In form, the town comprised 230 houses on two main streets—King (later India) and Court (later Exchange) Streets—running north and south, and three streets running east and west. Dense forestland surrounded the city.[8]

Yet among the ordinary one- and two-story clapboard dwellings appeared some evidence of cosmopolitan elegance worthy of a Philadelphia or a Newport. Visiting Falmouth in July of 1774, John Adams dined at Richard Codman's fine Georgian-style home on Middle Street; he described his meal there as "very genteel" and the house as "spacious:" "I thought I had got into the house of a nobleman," he wrote.[9]

After 1658, steadily peopled by hearty Puritan stock from the Massachusetts Bay area, Falmouth became more and more a Congregational stronghold, although a sizable Anglican flock worshiped at St. Paul's. Hinterland settlers across the Fore River in Purpooduck, near Cape Elizabeth, and others from Pemiquid through Boothbay and Topsham and into Cumberland, the land of the Scotch-Irish McCobbs, McClintocks, Campbells, and McFarlands, favored Presbyterianism. Influenced by the Great Awakening movement of Jonathan Edwards, Scotch-Irish preachers like Boothbay's Antrim-born John Murray infused reformer John Knox's staid Calvinism with a revivalist passion

Map of Portland (that original part of the city once called, in the eighteenth century, "Falmouth Neck" and now in 2011, "Downtown Portland"). The map identifies important streets, neighborhoods, and historic and modern landmarks, including the region burned in the fire of 1866. Drawn by Rosemary Mosher, Orbis, LLC.

that after the 1775 battles of Lexington and Concord likewise enflamed hinterland patriotism. Scotch-Irish patriots such as Brunswick's Captain Samuel Thompson and his compatriots in the Boothbay and Topsham regions resented the tepid Yankee patriotism of Falmouth's merchant class with its too intimate links to British factors and business houses as much as they disliked the Toryism of its Anglicans.

By 1775, that festering hinterland resentment at the Falmouth merchant class bore bitter fruit. Throughout the Stamp Act crisis of 1766, the Townshend Duties of 1767, the nonimportation movement, the 1770 Boston Massacre, and the 1773 Boston Tea Party, Falmouth's merchant leadership—fearful of royal wrath, distrustful of mob behavior, and harboring a visceral dread of social disorder—had distanced itself from patriot radicalism. Patriot passions intensified in 1774 with the Intolerable Acts and the closing of the Port of Boston. Falmouth merchants duly denounced the Intolerable and Coercive Acts but feared to oppose the Crown and thereby disrupt their profitable port commerce.

Thus things stood in March of 1775 when a British sloop sailed into beautiful Casco Bay bearing a cargo of rigging and other supplies from England, which in defiance of the colonial nonimportation agreements would enable Falmouth merchant Thomas Coulson to complete building his new ship. The royal governor of Massachusetts, Thomas Gage, dispatched HMS *Canceaux* under the command of Captain Henry Mowatt to protect Coulson's ship.[10] As Mowatt strolled along the Fore River shoreline, local patriots led by Brunswick's Thompson seized him as their prisoner. Thompson ultimately released him, but the insult left its mark. On October 16, 1775, Mowatt's fleet arrived in Casco Bay, and following a sustained bombardment and torching by British seamen, more than three-quarters of Falmouth—from India to Congress Street to the foot of Exchange Street and the entire Fore Street waterfront—lay yet again in ashes.[11]

Mowatt's vengeance forced residents to abandon the Neck, including Henry Wadsworth Longfellow's father, Samuel, who fled to Gorham. Not until the Peace of Paris in January 1783 did Falmouth rise again, this time no longer as an outpost but as one of the urban pearls dotting the North American coastline. Indeed, by the late 1790s, Falmouth, after 1786 renamed Portland, flaunted impressive Georgian architecture and a somewhat rich cosmopolitan culture. It had become very much part of the Atlantic World. This new prosperity and elegance, however, hardly disguised the port's traditional function. Portland remained an entrepôt (a commercial port where export goods such as lumber, cordwood, and ice were shipped and commodities received for distribution), only now a more exuberant one, led by a new generation of merchants, many from non-Falmouth families, who brought to the town a more cosmopolitan vision.[12]

Some of the new merchant generalists, entrepreneurs who traded in a variety of goods, arrived from Boston as newcomers armed with much-needed capital. Those men, such as Asa Clapp, joined a throng of post–American Revolution newcomers, mainly from the Boston area, seeking cheap land and opportunity in Maine. The influx pushed Maine's population from 56,000 in 1784 to 96,000 in 1800. Other Falmouth residents who had fled Mowatt's destruction returned: men such as Joseph and Hugh McLellan, Daniel Tucker, Enoch Ilsley, and Lemuel Moody.

A millennial,Whiggish spirit, a heady belief in the unbounded possibilities of the new nation, infused this largely Federalist, soon to be politically Whig, merchant class. With Alexander Hamilton, and later Henry Clay, they favored strong, positive government, and despite the lurid memory of Mowatt's revenge, they maintained close ties with British business houses after 1784. In fact, this circle of merchants would shortly be enlarged by a new generation of traders from London, such as Abraham Osgood from Axminster, who opened a store on Fore Street, and Stephen Codman, whose general merchandise business sat on Titcomb's Wharf. Collectively, these merchants sought to transform late eighteenth-century Falmouth Neck into a major American port.

Several things gave verve and substance to their vision. First, in 1786 the Massachusetts Court had approved the petition of Joseph and Hugh McLellan, Lemuel Moody, James Deering, Daniel Tucker, and twenty-five other prominent citizens—half of whom owned ships—to disconnect Falmouth Neck from the broader Deering, Westbrook, Falmouth, Cape Elizabeth region and to create a new separate town called Portland. Next, in 1791, with George Washington's approval, the Portland Head lighthouse opened, enhancing the safety and commercial prominence of Portland's harbor. Two years later, in 1793, Portland's prospects brightened even more. Thanks to the French Revolution and then the rise of Napoleon Bonaparte, France and Britain resumed their historic struggle for world power. At war, they banished each other's ships from their colonial ports. American merchant fleets—Portland's for one—gladly filled the vacuum. To facilitate enlarged trade with the West Indies and European markets, Portland's merchant leadership quickly erected the 2,000-foot Union Wharf and, for capital in 1802, created both the Portland Bank and the Maine Bank. In 1800 the Maine Fire and Marine Insurance Company opened its doors.

From fiery ruins in 1775, phoenixlike Portland had arisen commercially strong and vigorous. The nation's first census takers counted 2,240 people in 1790; ten years later they found over 3,700. The handsome, newly built city overlooking shimmering Casco Bay and its islands thrived at the turn of the new century; the billowing sails of Portland-built vessels, large ships (square-rigged with three or more masts), square-rigged, two-masted barks, hermaphrodite brigantines, and fore-and-aft-rigged sloops, passing Cushing Island to port or departing Hussey Sound, Peaks Island, to starboard—bound for Charleston, Havana, Liverpool, or other American and foreign ports—attested to its resurgence. In 1807, indeed, Portland rivaled Boston as one of America's busiest seaports, and to underscore its eminence, a consortium of seafarers led by merchant Lemuel Moody raised money to build an eighty-foot high observatory atop Munjoy Hill. Using a flag system, an observer stationed there alerted city folk to the daily arrival of vessels and their cargoes.[13]

Portland in the New Nation

Portland's post-Revolution economy broadened its historic entrepôt mission: that is, the city's busy retail and wholesale houses, its shipbuilding, and its thriving carrying trade in lumber, ice, bricks, pearl ash (or refined potash used in baking), and salted fish. Between 1790 and 1807, Portland with its large fleet of ships—barks, brigs, and sloops—greatly expanded the town's carrying trade. Much of that trade involved farmers from the rural Deering, Westbrook, Gorham, Cumberland, and Falmouth hinterland, and operated largely on a barter basis: general merchandise (pots and pans, ribbon, gewgaws, for example) in exchange for lumber (harvested in the winter) and for potash and pearl ash, flaxseed, and the like to be shipped to Europe and the West Indies and the Carolinas. In addition to lumber (the principal export) and bricks, pearl ash, and ice, salted cod and mackerel made their way south in the holds of Portland ships. Casco Bay and other Gulf of Maine fishermen carried their catch of cod and mackerel to Portland to be salted and transported southward. In fact, the West Indies, especially Cuba, occupied a vital position in the town's growing post-Revolution economy. When in 1783 the British Parliament barred the new nation's ships from Caribbean ports, Falmouth merchants personally traveled to London to plead for entry. In 1787, observed historian Willis, "out of the eighty-nine [ship] entries [into Portland Harbor] seventy-three were from the West Indies, and the same number were cleared for the West Indies."[14]

That snug relationship continued into the nineteenth century. In 1826, noted Willis, the tonnage of vessels entering the Port of Havana from the United States was 117,776; 11,619 tons hailed from Portland, while Boston had fewer than 11,000 tons, and New York a bare 8,000. Portland ships returned from Havana and other West Indies ports loaded with rum, or molasses that could be converted to rum. The city operated seven distilleries and shipped its excess rum to Boston, a city that despite Portland's surge, still viewed its northern urban neighbor as a satellite. Portland merchants, however, vowed to establish the city's prominence with its larger southern rival, and they competed aggressively in this carrying trade, despite the fact that their city's much more modest size, and accordingly its limited market for imports, kept Portland merchant vessels, such as those bearing rum, ultimately destined for Boston. This meant, explained Willis, that "while the store houses of Portland are neglected, the goods which might be bought and sold here, at a more reasonable rate, are bought by the people of this neighborhood at an exorbitant price at Boston."[15]

Shipbuilding constituted the final piece of Portland's economic equation. The business had long flourished in Clay Cove and at other points along the Fore River, and it expanded well into the 1850s, employing a host of shipwrights, joiners, and other craftsmen and supporting sailmaking, ropewalks, chandleries, and other ship-provisioning businesses.[16]

Amid its late eighteenth- and early nineteenth-century boom, Portland had shed its more modest outpost physiognomy, and its appearance brightened considerably. The French Duke de la Rochefoucault toured the city in the late 1790s and extolled it as "handsome, with houses of very good appearance." Those few dwellings that had survived Mowatt's bombardment, however, he maligned as "a parcel of mean houses, the habitations of the poorer people."[17]

Fueled by the infusion of fresh capital, Portland's building boom surged in the mid-1780s, and by 1803 close to 600 dwelling houses lined the city's streets, mostly clapboard but many with brick ends and twenty-six all brick—such as Peleg Wadsworth's fine Georgian-style home (1785) on Back (Congress) Street, the first all-brick house in the city. Among other stately brick piles soon enhancing urban Portland were Nathaniel Dyer's fanlight-entrance-adorned Georgian dwelling (1803), Hugh McLellan's Federal-style mansion (1800) at High and Spring Streets, and Stephen McLellan's grand Federal-style home—like its mate designed by the young John Kimball Jr.—fronted by a stunning pillared portico, highlighted above by a classic Palladian window. By the early 1800s a whole new section of the town had opened west of the old India, Pearl, Market, and Fore Streets settlement, such as Joseph Holt Ingraham's new State Street development. To design his own home at number 51 on the newly laid-out State Street, and thus engender settlement there, Ingraham retained a young Massachusetts-born architect, Alexander Parris, who had just moved to booming Portland. Ingraham's home reflected the influence of Boston's Charles Bulfinch on the young architect. Most of the early nineteenth-century houses built on or near State Street, however, were not Federal-style palaces but sturdy homes for working-class families, shopkeepers and tradesmen.

Still, Portland in 1803 reflected an exuberant cosmopolitanism that lured ambitious architects like Parris and his new wife. Hugh McLellan decorated his Federal-style home with wallpaper, mirrors, and fabrics from Boston and Europe. Furniture came from Philadelphia's Thomas Chippendale–influenced William Savery and from Boston cabinetmakers. Abigail May, a Bostonian who visited her Portland aunt in 1796, reported that the friends she made there lived in "Elegant Style" and reveled in "every species of enjoyment such as dancing, backgammon, journal writing, and painting." Portland's common-school-educated young men furthered their education at Harvard, at Yale, and after 1802 at Bowdoin College. The seacoast town boasted a newspaper by 1785, the *Falmouth Gazette*, and in 1805 a museum and waxworks.[18]

But the economic pall of the Napoleonic Wars bore down upon Portland as they did on Boston, New York, and Philadelphia. Portland's renaissance halted abruptly with President Thomas Jefferson's 1806 Non-Importation Act, followed by his Embargo Act of 1807. Among the twenty-four Portland merchants ruined by the embargo that closed British and French ports to American shipping were John Taber, Dr. Stephen Cummings, Joseph McLellan, and Portland's biggest land developer, Joseph H. Ingraham. Another casualty of the embargo was the Portland Bank, its building also designed by Parris. In fact, by 1809 the city's homebuilding business had ceased, and Parris left Portland for Richmond, Virginia. Poverty gripped the city, forcing officials to set up a soup kitchen in Market Square to feed the indigent. Portland's once flourishing entrepôt economy did not fully recover until 1818, after the Peace of 1815 ended the War of 1812. Meanwhile, Portland privateers carrying letters of marque and reprisal sallied forth to wreak havoc upon British merchantmen and to trail their prizes into port amid throngs of cheering Portlanders. (A wartime naval engagement fought off Monhegan Island would be memorialized in

Longfellow's poem "My Lost Youth.") Significantly, the failure of Massachusetts to supply militia aid to end the British wartime occupation of Castine, a town down east of Portland, fueled a seething resentment of the Bay State and a separatist movement. As part of the Missouri Compromise of 1820, Maine became the twenty-third state in the union, and Portland its capital.[19]

Longfellow's City

The poet Longfellow belonged to a distinguished Portland family (fig. 1). His grandfather, Peleg Wadsworth, who in 1786 had built the stately brick dwelling on Back Street (now Congress), had commanded the Northern Massachusetts patriot forces during the American Revolution. Peleg's daughter Zilpah married a young Harvard-educated lawyer, Stephen Longfellow, and the attractive couple ultimately made their home in Peleg's Congress Street dwelling.

In 1807 Zilpah and Stephen had a son, Henry Wadworth. Born not on Back Street but in his uncle Captain Samuel Stephenson's house at the corner of Fore and Hancock streets next to Clay Cove, in the year of Jefferson's devastating embargo, as a youth Henry pondered little the advent of economic hard times marking his birth. Instead, in his poetry, he mused about the beauty and energy of a resilient, resurgent Portland. During the 1820s the future Bowdoin graduate, poet, and Harvard professor wandered Deering Woods and from still-verdant Munjoy Hill gazed out over Casco Bay to the sleek merchant ships, barkentines and brigs, furling and unfurling their glorious white canvas sails.

After Bowdoin, Longfellow's father, a trustee at the college, secured his son a professorship in modern languages at his alma mater. In preparation, Longfellow traveled abroad in 1826, in the process learning seven languages. In 1834 he moved to Harvard. His first wife, Mary, died in 1835, but his second wife, Frances (Fanny) Appelton (whom he married in 1843), bore him six children, and the blissful life they shared in Cambridge, raising their large family, ultimately became a model for Victorian domestic love. It was his Cambridge years, 1836 to 1855, which produced Longfellow's principal body of work including, *Voices of the Night* (1839), *Evangeline* (1847), and *Song of Hiawatha* (1855), written a year after he retired from Harvard. Fanny's tragic death in 1861 thrust the poet into despondency.

Longfellow had departed Portland in 1826, but he returned there periodically to visit his parents in their fine brick home on Congress Street, just down from the First Parish (Unitarian) Church, where the Longfellows doled out

1. Portrait of a youthful Henry Wadsworth Longfellow, ca. 1843. Courtesy of Maine Historical Society.

pew rent. His journal entries in 1840, and his 1877 "My Lost Youth" reflected the poet's enduring love for Portland and its beauty. "How lovely," he wrote in one diary entry, "the view of the harbor, the pearly sea with its almost irresistible attraction, drawing me into it. A whole fleet of vessels on the horizon looking in the distance like the spires and towers of a great city."[20]

After his father, Stephen, died in 1849, Henry rarely visited the city of his youth. But the poet's paeans to his birthplace endured eternally in his prose and pentameter, and most important, served to cloak Portland in a romantic hue in an age of rapid urban industrialization when, as historian David Schuyler has observed, American cities forged a "new urban landscape." Standing at this urban threshold, perched on Congress Street, the spine of the Portland peninsula, Portlanders in the 1840s, as Longfellow reminded us, had but to gaze southward over Casco Bay to see the romance of the seas, and the glorious clipper ships that endowed the age with their name. Alternatively, Portlanders might peer northward toward the mighty oaks of Deering Woods, or on some balmy late fall evening from the heights of Bramhall Hill and the Western Promenade—a narrow swath of land presciently purchased by the city in 1837—they might glimpse in the distance the sun just setting over snow-covered Mount Washington.[21]

Between 1820 and 1855, Portland enjoyed general (though not unbroken) prosperity marked by solid but not exceptional growth in population. Between 1790 and 1800 it grew 65 percent, from 2,240 to 3,704, then leaped 94 percent to 7,169 by 1810. Moderating somewhat with the embargo, it grew only 20 percent from 1810 to 1820 but jumped almost 50 percent between 1820 and 1830 to 12, 601, then up another 37 percent to almost 21,000 at midcentury. Although that was solid growth, Portland's population increased slowly compared with that of other cities. Its 1860 population of 26,341 ranked it thirty-second among American cities of 10,000 or more, behind Allegheny, Pennsylvania, Hartford, Connecticut, Mobile, Alabama, Lowell, Massachusetts, Richmond, Virginia, and Troy, New York, but just ahead of Cambridge, Massachusetts. Irish immigration accounted for much of the city's population rise. Early Irish immigrants came through Halifax, Nova Scotia, but in the 1840s the sons and daughters of Erin sailed directly from Liverpool and other English ports.[22]

Brisk port activity and new business ventures must be considered factors in the city's prosperity, as should be the city-building process itself, especially new homes and business and urban infrastructure. Next to mariners, joiners—the backbone of the nineteenth-century home and commercial building construction industry—constituted the largest occupational category in Portland's city directories. Wealthy midcentury Portlanders, such as John Bundy Brown, John Mussey, John Neal, and Thomas and Nathaniel Warren invested heavily and safely in real estate—explaining, perhaps, the wide streak of conservatism endemic among the city's mercantile elite.[23]

Not surprisingly, much of the capital investment during the period appeared along Fore Street, Portland's pre-1850 waterfront. In addition to the Union Wharf, ships entering Portland Harbor in 1836 now docked at one of the growing number of waterfront piers: Commercial Wharf, Crabtree Wharf, McLellan, Sturdivant, Railway, Wood, Burnham, Fox, Widgery, Merrill, and Walker wharves among others. Fine public buildings now embellished the Portland urban landscape. In 1833, the successful Portland merchant Charles Q. Clapp, whose own magnificent Greek Revival home on Spring Street added considerable luster to the city's nineteenth-century architectural heritage, employed the McLellans' architect John Kimball Jr. to remodel the market house at Market Square into a Greek Revival–style city hall, its front portico supported by four massive Ionic columns. Clapp's generosity was timely and commemorative. By act of the state legislature, Portland in 1832 had received a city charter under which it would be governed by a mayor, seven alderman, and a common council of twenty-one, three councilmen from each of the city's seven wards. The new government met in Clapp's Greek temple.[24]

In a port city sheltering the largest merchant fleet on the East Coast, it followed that Portland's Merchant's Exchange would exceed Clapp's City Hall in splendor. Completed in 1839 and located at Middle and Exchange Streets (the current location of Post Office Park), the Greek Revival Merchant's Exchange occupied an entire city block. Like City Hall it was fronted by massive Ionic pillars, eight of them, but unlike City Hall it was topped by a magnificent gilded dome. The stunning building evoked the exalted place of commerce in the city and expressed the importance that Portland's merchant class ascribed to their enterprising little metropolis. Likewise, the city prided itself on its ecclesiastical architecture, including the new granite, high-spired Greek Revival First Parish Church, the Gothic Revival State Street Congregational Church, the Park Street Congregational Church, and St. Paul's Episcopal (originally on School Street, but after being destroyed by Mowatt's cannons in 1775, rebuilt first in 1787 at Middle and Church Streets, and after 1803, of brick back on School street). The new St. Dominic's Catholic Church on State Street arose to the city's growing Irish community at Gorham's Corners.[25]

Portland's antebellum renaissance owed much to the character of its merchant elites and their commitment to the continued expansion of the city as an entrepôt, a gateway for lumber, ice, barrel staves, ice, and other regional products to be shipped on Portland bottoms to the West Indies, New York, Philadelphia, Charleston, or New Orleans in return for molasses, rice, grain, cloth, tools, and other imported goods for distribution to the towns and small cities of New Hampshire and Maine. It reflected as well the Yankee city's devotion to "Whiggish public policy." Once a stronghold of Federalism, after the December 1815 Hartford Convention debacle which, perhaps unjustly, tainted Anglophile Federalism with the indelible stain of disloyalty, Federalists in Portland and elsewhere decamped to the National Republican Party of John Quincy Adams and Daniel Webster, a political affiliation that like its successor, the Whigs, was deeply infused with the optimism and spirit of revivalist perfectionism preached alike by the Presbyterian minister Charles Grandisson Finney and Congregationalist divine Lyman Beecher. Finney's and Beecher's Second Great Awakening sought to rekindle an emotional evangelicalism within a New England Yankee Protestantism made too tepid by Enlightenment rationalism. Portland National Republicans championed not only Henry Clay's system of state-sponsored internal improvements and "Manifest Destiny" in foreign policy but also, in the millennial spirit of perfectionism, philosophical positivism: the belief that through the nurture of children, temperance, prison reform, banishing wife abuse, and ending chattel slavery lay the best possible future for all. Portland with America marched forward toward the millennium.

But these Yankee social reformers, although embracing the republican virtues of simplicity, self-reliance, and community stability dear to their colonial forebears, clutched just as tenaciously the emerging values of the marketplace. Indeed, Portland merchants eagerly seized the Whig vision of an expansive American capitalism buttressed by an orderly, morally secure, and deferential social structure, one clearly at odds with the leveling tendencies of Andrew Jackson's new democracy.[26]

Upon Republican candidate Henry Clay's defeat in 1832, these vehemently anti-Andrew Jackson proselytes of reform and proponents of the use of government to promote America's manufacturing destiny emerged as Whigs, Portland's dominant pre–Civil War political party. New England's and Portland's merchant elite subscribed to what historian Philip Ethington has called Republican liberalism, "a belief that men of civic virtue should and would act on behalf of a singular good, i.e., the General Welfare." Portland Whigs evinced devotion to the common good in their support for the construction of the Munjoy Hill Observatory, the Union Pier, City Hall, and the Portland Merchant's Exchange.[27] Other public works were even grander. To facilitate the movement of lumber from the constantly retreating virgin forests of the city's rural hinterland, as well as the shipment of potash and other rural products from the Sebago Lake area north of the city, Portland merchants led by Woodbury Storer and Joseph Noyes, and also by the recently formed Canal Bank (1826), undertook the construction of the Cumberland and Oxford Canal, which followed the Presumpscot River through twenty-seven locks from Sebago Lake to the sea at Portland. Chartered in 1803 but not completed until 1830, the $206,000 canal, for which users paid tolls, did boost commerce and manufacturing in the city but, unfortunately, not to expectations. Railroads replaced it in the mid-1840s.[28]

Holding the vision of their city as a world-class port, its leaders in the years 1832–1855 expanded Portland's fleet and enlarged its fisheries, helping to confirm its dominance in the West Indian and Carolinas carrying trade of lumber, ice, and salted fish. Thanks to entrepreneur John Bundy Brown, who in 1845 built the city's first sugarhouse, the third in the country, Portland became a national sugar-refining center (fig. 2). Shipbuilding also flourished in an era when at least thirteen yards, mainly along the Fore River, engaged in the business of building and launching wooden sailing vessels: large ships, barks, brigs, schooners (fore and aft rigging on main and mizzen masts), and sloops, many of them sizable. In 1845 the Thurston Yard at Fish Point launched the 158-ton brig *Henrietta*. A year later the 708-ton *Cordelia* slipped off the ways at Dyer's busy Clay Cove yard. At the corner of York and Maple Streets near the Titcomb, Long, Central, and Widgery piers (the heart of the city's West Indian commerce), the Robert Knight yard built such fine sailing ships as the 536-ton *Astarche* and the 392-ton *Ozark*. Nearby, in 1849, Ralph Kelly launched the 497-ton *Dirigo*. Farther up the Fore River, G. W. Lawrence built the 1,258-ton *Sebago* in 1854 and the 1,019-ton *Emily Hall* in 1855. Across the Fore River in Knightville, the Nathaniel Blanchard yard in 1850 turned out the magnificent 1,484-ton *Phoenix*. Between 1845 and 1848 alone, Portland yards produced twenty-four ships, seventy barks, forty-seven brigs, and forty-one schooners.[29] At least one of Portland's earlier-built ships, the *Greyhound*, found its way into the slave trade. In 1800 it was found awash and abandoned off the coast of Florida, its gratings fore and aft a testimony to its history as a slaver.[30]

2. John Bundy Brown's Portland Sugar House, ca. 1850. The factory was a key link in Portland's lively antebellum West Indies trade. Courtesy of Portland Public Library.

Some of the sloops and schooners entered the Gulf of Maine fisheries, an industry driven in the years 1830–1860 by both the growth of the nation's immigrant population, flowing from Catholic Europe, and the expanding slave population in the American South and the West Indies. By 1850, Maine dominated the American cod fisheries, and although some schooners sailed directly for the West Indies from Maine ports such as Boothbay Harbor, most of the fish, once salted, departed from Portland. National policy established in 1792, to support American fisheries but also to enhance naval strength, instituted the cod bounty. By subsidizing the individual vessel based on ship tonnage, the bounty benefited smaller ships. Payment went to the ship owners and crews on the basis of share of catch; thus it assured the toilers in Maine's cod and mackerel fisheries stable incomes and protected them, as one writer put it "from the worst effects of nineteenth-century monopoly capitalism." Sadly for Maine, the critical subsidy was discarded in 1865.[31]

Though not subsidized, Portland's mackerel and herring fisheries proved equally lucrative. Like cod, salted and dried mackerel, loaded aboard Portland ships, headed southward for Charleston and Havana, to be exchanged for cotton and hogsheads of molasses. The bulk of the molasses shipped northward to Portland went to John Bundy Brown's Portland Sugar House. Starting business in 1828 as a grocer, Brown in 1840 concentrated his tireless business energies on sugar, owning ships, wharves, piers, and mills as part of a vertically integrated business enterprise. Between 1845 and 1848, at York and Maple Streets in Portland's Gorham's Corner, he built two massive, ninety-foot-long sugarhouses, one four stories high and one six stories, where he transformed West Indies molasses into high-quality brown sugar and thus founded one of the city's great family fortunes. Devoted to the city and enchanted by its haunting beauty, Brown after the Civil War poured his wealth into Portland real estate (fig. 3).[32]

Unlike Providence, Fall River, Lowell, Philadelphia, and so many other young American cities, Portland had no swift-flowing river for waterpower and inland transportation. The Presumpscot lacked sufficient depth and current. Therefore, Brown's sugar business, like all early Portland manufacturing, employed heavier inputs of labor than capital, mostly linked to the maritime trade. Though not all of Portland's antebellum enterprises like Brown's were wedded to the city's West Indies–linked economy, many found the West Indies market attractive, even for factory-made furniture. Clearly, some of the lumber shipped to Portland over the Oxford and Cumberland Canal remained for the city's furniture industry. As evidenced in Portland, as well as in places such as Boston and Philadelphia, furniture-making in the 1830s evolved from a craft into an industry. In 1836, Portland's Walter Corey mass-produced and marketed furniture at his Market Street plant, turning out chairs sold both in Maine and in the West Indies. Portland remained chiefly a regional trading center; the city's global ambitions notwithstanding, business enterprise there reflected national trends toward greater specialization, differentiation of labor and management, artisanal skill erosion, and greater capitalization—the same trends found by historian Stuart Blumin in Philadelphia, Boston, and New York as part of his seminal study of the emerging American urban middle class. By 1850, seventeen of Portland's largest firms, like Corey's, boasted capital investment of more than $10,000 and, understandably, half employed steam presses, planes, and drills.[33]

In 1836, the same year Corey began to mass-produce furniture in Portland, Thomas S. Laughlin launched his marine hardware business. Both firms fit

3. John Bundy Brown, founder of the Portland Sugar Company, builder of the Falmouth Hotel, and developer of Portland's Bramhall Hill. Courtesy of Portland Public Library.

nicely into Portland's entrepôt economy, as did the host of wholesale grocers such as Weston F. Milliken and George Burnham, who—with a young partner, James Phinney Baxter—entered the canning business. Capitalizing shipbuilding, canning, and sugar-refining ventures—as well as underwriting shipping—required capital, and Portland by 1840 had nine banks. The depression of 1837 struck hard, however; by the Civil War years only seven banks survived, including Canal, Casco, Manufacturers and Traders, and Mechanics and Merchants, collectively capitalized at $2,675,000. Most of the banks, insurance offices, and brokerage houses in that 1840–1850 era were located on Exchange Street, the Wall Street of Portland.[34] Retail businesses as well as dry goods, and hardware houses stood on Middle Street, the city's principal pre–Civil War commercial thoroughfare.

Albeit bustling, the scale of the city's downtown remained modest by contemporary urban standards. Portland journalist and theater critic John Neal observed that before the Civil War and the devastating fire of 1866, despite brisk commercial activity, only a fifth of the town's commercial buildings were built of brick. Most, as Neal described them, were "low studded, seldom over eighty or ninety feet on the ground floor, dark, narrow, and never more than 28 or perhaps 30 feet up to the eaves."[35]

The hub of Portland commercial activity in the 1840s centered on the port itself, especially Fore Street, the locus of the West Indies trade. Bowsprits of great ships, tied fore and aft at the wharves, jutted across busy Fore Street, where the steady clatter of the iron-sheathed wheels of drays, carts, wagons, and other conveyances on the cobblestone paving produced an unremitting and deafening roar. Here huddled the cheap boardinghouses crowded with mariners and common seamen; and here, before 1851, stood the ubiquitous, boisterous, and brawling rum shops, groggeries, and saloons that outraged the city's decorous Whig reformers. Evidence of the West Indian trade abounded not only in the stacks of shooks piled high on the wharves ready for shipment to Havana but in the faces of the seamen themselves and the longshoremen—many West Indian, some black. Longfellow, however, remembered this port scene as delightful rather than hectic, describing "the Spanish Sailors with bearded lips, and the beauty and mystery of the ships, and the magic of the sea."[36] By 1855, as a lithograph of the town revealed, Portland appeared a thriving and handsome maritime city (fig. 4).

Groggeries aside, members of Portland's merchant class hardly ignored the natural attractiveness of Longfellow's charming city. Their architect-designed

4. View of Portland seen from ship launching in South Portland, ca. 1855. Note the volume of Fore River maritime activity and the absence of development on Munjoy Hill, where the Portland Observatory is visible. Courtesy of Osher Map Library, University of Southern Maine.

brick homes, the Merchant Exchange, and City Hall all attested to that fact. As early as 1826, long before New York created a Park Commission and retained Frederick Law Olmsted to design Central Park, Portland's mayor, Levi Cutler, proposed a system of promenades and marginal ways, a foot and wagon roadway encircling the then flourishing Portland peninsula.[37] Two years later, acting on a proposal for breathing spaces, the city purchased twelve acres of land on Mount Joy (now Munjoy) Hill for an eastern promenade, and land on the Bramhall Hill in the West End for a cemetery and a western promenade. In 1836 the Portland newspaper, the *Eastern Argus,* referred to the two sites as "locations surpassing any other in New England. . . . Let the road[ways] be ornamented with four rows of young elms so arranged as to accommodate both carriages and promenades." Only one year later, both promenades had been constructed, the Eastern Promenade from Fore Street to Washington Street. Although the national economic depression that struck that year halted further beautification efforts, it was Portland's penchant for lining all its major streets with elms that gave rise to its alternative name, the Forest City.[38]

Neither the city nor its merchant leadership in the pre–Civil War era dismissed the city's need for cultural education or social welfare. In addition to

Longfellow, its favorite son, Portland nurtured, among others, Sarah Payson Willis (known as Fanny Fern), the poet-journalist Nathaniel Parker Willis, the art critic John Neal, and the artist Paul Akers. As for public education, the city claimed to rival Boston. In 1821 it joined Boston in becoming the first two American cities to establish tuition-free high schools. For the care of its poor and needy, Portland built a second almshouse in 1805 and founded the Portland Benevolent Society the same year. By midcentury the town had thirty different charitable organizations, among them an orphan asylum, the Home for Aged Women, the Seamen's (Church) Institute (which provided reading rooms as a refuge from the rum shops), and in 1854 to abet thrift, the Portland Provident Association, whose president was John Bundy Brown.

Portland's 1805 almshouse, or poor farm, located just off Portland Street in the shadow of Deering Woods and at the foot of Bramhall Hill (where Hadlock Field now stands), signified that not all Portlanders prospered. Indeed, like New York, Boston, and Philadelphia, Portland sheltered another half. Historians Thomas Bender and Paul Boyer have reminded us that in antebellum urban America, evolving institutions such as the urban police, asylums for the poor, and even public schools responded not only to the reform impulse but to rising fears about a growing and potentially dangerous urban-immigrant working class.[39]

Mechanics, Seamen, and Longshoremen in Portland's Golden Age

Robert Corey's chair factory revealed that in Portland, as in other cities, pre–Civil War industrialism engendered specialization and task differentiation. Factories separated management from labor, transformed journeymen into wage earners, and undermined the Craftsmen Empire earlier envisioned by those who in 1790–1820 had envisioned a new republic of labor. In 1841 Portland "house wrights, joiners, shipwrights, riggers, and sail makers, craftsmen all, paraded their trade banners through the city streets shouting slogans such as 'Artisan Republicans, the Tyrant's Foe, and the People's Friend!'" But industrial capitalism, especially in the wake of the Depression of 1837, soon shattered that vision and with it the Jeffersonian dream of a nation of small farmers, artisanal independence, and a "decent competency" for all.[40]

A few displaced Yankee apprentice cabinetmakers in the 1840s may have gravitated to Portland's teeming waterfront, where they would have confronted not only ethnic but racial rivalry. A few black Americans and West Indians, slave and free, had worked on the waterfront in the eighteenth century: according to Willis, there were twenty-one slaves in Falmouth in 1749. In the early nineteenth century, argues historian Marcus Rediker, blacks appeared frequently in American seaports, either as seamen—a brutal, dangerous, and demeaning occupation—or as longshoremen. This was true of Portland between 1813 and 1840; Longfellow remembered Sunday morning churchgoers along Fore Street pausing to hear the rhythmic chanting of black longshoremen busily loading cargo into ships' holds. A small black community took form on Munjoy Hill, still thinly settled in the early 1800s. Black families there, relegated to the gallery of Portland's Second Parrish Church, in 1835 built their own Abyssinian Congregational Church at the corner of Mountfort and Newberry Streets. African American Portlanders such as Enoch McLellan, John Siggs, and William Butler toiled on the city's waterfront.[41]

After 1822, however, Portland's black waterfront labor faced stiff competition from the city's burgeoning Irish workforce. Early in the nineteenth century a few Irish families, the Mahoneys and Driscolls, had settled in Portland. Beginning in 1815 the flow of Irish to America and Portland surged. Between 1815 and 1845 (before the Great Hunger) some 800,000 to 1 million Irish left Ireland. The numerous potato blights that preceded the famine of 1845, plus periodic outbreaks of typhus, dysentery, and cholera, rendered it harder and harder for poor Irish cotters to pay rent on their little stone cottages and small plots of barely arable land. British landlords seized on the famine as an ideal opportunity to rid themselves of these lowly cotters and more profitably raise cattle instead. Indeed, British laissez-faire policy treated the potato blights as God's just punishment for perceived Irish sloth. Since the Irish subsisted chiefly on a potato diet and sold their grain and livestock to pay land rent, these chronic potato failures devastated the cotters as well as their artisan and tradesmen neighbors.[42]

Often unskilled and with few if any resources, the incoming Irish nonetheless possessed information about America from relatives who had earlier emigrated. Therefore, more Irish immigrated to Portland in the 1820s, when the city's port expanded and canal jobs were plentiful, than in the late 1830, when a severe American economic depression slowed growth. Irish immigration increased in the Famine Forties but never matched the 1820–1830 tide. Because British legislation imposed restrictions on immigrants who boarded United States–bound vessels, the Irish in these early years crowded Canadian-bound lumber ships and thus entered North America through Quebec rather than Portland or Boston. When Bishop John Chevrus arrived in Portland in 1822, he discovered 160 communicants eager to build a church. Despite nativist grumblings, Portland merchant John Fox sold land on State Street to the Catholic parish, and Saint Dominic's opened on the site in 1833.[43]

Saint Dominic's stood near what became the center of Portland's Irish community. Though some Irish families lived on Munjoy Hill, the heart of the antebellum Irish community centered on Gorham's Corner, not far from Saint Dominic's, at the intersection of Pleasant, Danforth, York, and Fore Streets. The neighborhood included streets such as Free, Center, and Union, where Irish families crowded into red brick and clapboard tenements. To squeeze more large Irish families into these hovels, landlords simply added ramshackle additions. It was to police this practice that the city in 1853 passed an ordinance forbidding "the erection of any wooden building in said city . . . of more than 16 feet in height from the ground or foundation thereof."[44]

By 1850 the Irish made up 11 percent of Portland's population of 20,819 persons, most concentrated at Gorham's Corner, an area by then notorious for gangs of "rowdy Gorham's Corner Boys," for shillelagh-wielding interfamilial street warfare, for keeping pigs, for crime, and for excessive consumption of the cheap rum called the "cratur" sold in swill shops and low dives. Mortality for children under five years of age exceeded 44 percent in 1850 (fig. 5).

Nativists such as Portland's Neal Dow in effect declared war on Gorham's Corner, on the neighborhood's Roman Catholicism (Dow called it the whore of Babylon), and on its surfeit of groggeries and street brawls. At the local level, Dow led a nationally organized nativist movement given political form in the 1850s as the "Order of the Star Spangled Banner" and better known as the "Know-Nothings." In 1851, Dow succeeded in having the State of Maine enact the Maine Law, which prohibited "the manufacture, sale, and possession of alcohol with the intent of sale." Born in 1804 on Congress Street in Portland, son of Josiah Dow, who owned a tannery, Neal Dow was a maverick Whig and later a maverick Republican who had fought the so-called liquor interests since the 1840s. In that era, temperance advocates like Dow, together with the antislavery forces, believed in the power of moral suasion. The Maine Law, however, like earlier efforts at enacting licensing laws, signified a shift from moral suasion to active enforcement. Dow, moreover, aimed his law not only at the rum industry but at the Irish he regarded as foreign scum. All the while, wealthy Portlanders, enabled by local authorities, continued to import fine wines and liquors from Boston. Indeed, the law utterly failed to dry up the

5. Photograph of Gorham's Corner, ca. 1904. This was the heart of Portland's large Irish community in the nineteenth and early twentieth centuries. Courtesy of Maine Historical Society.

antebellum city, as Dow admitted in 1857, when more than 400 grogshops were operating in the Forest City.[45]

Portland nativism never reached the same level of violence as in Philadelphia and Boston, but it did exist. Anti-Irish and anti-Catholic "riots" broke out on Fore Street in 1848, 1849, and 1854. In 1854, Know-Nothings circulated a rumor that secret Irish militia companies were forming, and that Saint Dominic's Father John O'Donnell had taken a trip to Boston and brought back "heavy boxes overflowing with poison that Irish servant girls would use to murder families." Father O'Donnell feared to walk the streets, and in a formal letter printed in the city press he assailed "bigotry in the City of Elms." That summer, Know-Nothings hurled stones through Father O'Donnell's study window and smeared horse manure on the doors of his church.[46]

Poor's Vision: Portland on the Eve of the Civil War

Although Longfellow may have waxed rapturous about the parade of ships, their staysails and topsails unfurled, reaching gloriously past Cushing Island or through Hussey Sound, bound for Havana and other romantic ports,

Portland—as its somewhat sluggish population growth in the 1830s testified—failed to attain first-class status as a city. It's economy waxed and waned as a regional but not a national urban power. The Forest City proved unable to utilize canal technology to efficiently exploit a lumber-potash-ice-and-limestone-rich hinterland. But John Alfred Poor, a lawyer born in Andover,Maine, had an answer: railroads. He saw railroads connecting Maine with Montreal and the St. Lawrence, and binding Maine, New Hampshire, Vermont, and the Maritime Provinces into a regional economic powerhouse. As a North American common market, a kind of American Hanseatic League, the region connected by rail would trade directly by sea with Europe, bypassing the bullying giants of Boston and New York.

From his first glimpse of a locomotive in 1834 to his witnessing the opening of the tiny Bangor and Piscataquis Railroad in 1836, Poor, a disciple of Henry Clay's American System, believed that the railroad would revolutionize and energize what he saw as Maine's not inconsequential lumber, fishing, shipbuilding, and West Indian–dependent carrying-trade economy (fig. 6). After his wife and daughter died tragically, Poor moved to Portland, by then the center of Maine capital formation, and there launched his campaign to weld the state's economic future to railroading. In particular, Poor sought to use the railroad to link Portland to Montreal and the St. Lawrence trade, and to make Portland the winter port for Canada during those cold months when thick ice made the St. Lawrence impassable. Such a road, reasoned Poor, would make Portland the winter port not only for western Canadian grain but also for commerce from the Great Lakes, the rising metropolis of Chicago, and west to the Pacific. It would connect Portland to American Manifest Destiny.

Poor imagined Portland seated at the apex of a railroad system independent of rival Boston. Not only would this system bind Portland into a Northern New England/Maritime Province Common Market, it would also, by geographical imperative, establish Portland as the favored port for Europe-bound cargoes. Poor preached the gospel of magnificent Portland-crowned Casco Bay: a glorious, nature-blessed Maine harbor, capacious, deep, ice-free, and half a day to a full day and a half closer to Liverpool than Boston was.[47]

Although Portland capitalists in the 1830s and 1840s feared that railroad technology favored Boston over the Forest City, after the Panic of 1837 had eased, they listened intently to Poor's argument: that railroads would resuscitate the city's wilting economy. Railroads, preached Poor, were superior to canals in getting rural timber and agricultural products to market; railroads would spur

6. John Alfred Poor, ca. 1860. Poor was instrumental in founding the Portland/ Montreal railroad nexus and the Portland Company, which serviced the Atlantic and St. Lawrence Railroad (later the Grand Trunk). Courtesy of Maine Historical Society.

population growth and halt the outmigration of Maine youth and capital to the West. Not only would Portland blossom as a world-class port, proclaimed the evangel of railroading, but "Maine will present at some future day, along our bays and harbors, a line of cities, surpassing those which are now found upon the shores of the English Channel or the Baltic Sea." Here was a global vision long before the twenty-first century invented the term globalization.[48]

Before 1840, Maine had a handful of tiny narrow-gauge railroads (the rails less than the standard-gauge 4 feet, 8.5 inches apart) such as the Bangor and Piscataquis, whose opening Poor had witnessed in 1836. At that date, Maine and Portland merchants feared the technology as a threat that would divert commerce southward to Boston. Nevertheless, in 1837, one group of Boston investors began building the Boston and Maine Railroad, and another the Eastern Railroad, which in 1842 reached Portsmouth, New Hampshire, where it merged with the Portland, Saco, and Portsmouth (chartered in 1837) offering rail service into the Forest City. Boston investors looked not only eastward into Maine for profits but, like Poor, also northward to Montreal and the Canadian winter grain trade, fully aware of Maine's designs on that Canadian market. In fact, in the economically dismal year 1837, the Maine legislature created a Board of Internal Improvements to study and outline a policy for a system of state-aided canals, roadways, and railroads. As part of the study, state engineers surveyed a railroad route to Quebec. But the 1837 Panic, plus squabbles among Maine towns competing to be the terminus of a Montreal line, squelched the plans.[49]

After 1840, Poor and his cadre of Portland promoters, Judge William Preble and David A. Neal, resumed railroad lobbying with a vengeance. They funded another survey, this time by engineer James Holt, which identified a viable route, involving both modest grades and tunneling, through Dixville Notch to the Canadian border, thence to connect with a projected Canadian road to be built from Montreal. Next, the group sought and, in 1845, won from the State of Maine a charter for the Atlantic and St. Lawrence Railroad.

News in February 1845 that the Montreal Board of Trade would imminently select either the Boston or Portland route forced Poor in a howling winter blizzard, and in a historic and spectacular act, to race by sleigh to Montreal, using the Holt route and thus dramatically demonstrating its efficiency. A week later, Judge Preble arrived with the charter for the Atlantic and St. Lawrence in hand. Montreal decided in Poor's favor not only for his heroics but for his logic as well. Portland with its snug, deep, ice-free harbor not only sat closer to Liverpool but, politically, offered less of a threat to Montreal than Boston did when negotiating the tax, permission, land-use, and other issues involved in establishing a major foreign depot for winter grain business.[50]

As with all large-scale engineering ventures, unforeseen physical obstacles arose, and construction costs unexpectedly soared. Portland floated over $2 million in bonds for the broad-gauge, Atlantic and St. Lawrence line, a wider track width meant to afford greater stability over rugged mountainous terrain but also to bar Boston's standard-gauge competition. Portland's financial support, noted historian Edward Kirkland, inaugurated in Maine a "liberal state-supported system of internal improvements." It proved, alas, insufficient. Three weeks after the Atlantic and St. Lawrence arrived in Portland, July 18, 1853, to a jubilant welcome, the railroad line, having cost twice what had been originally estimated, was leased for 999 years to the Canadian Grand Trunk Railroad. Thus, Poor's railroad, designed to declare Maine and Portland's independence from Massachusetts and Boston, was now firmly lodged under Canadian control. Moreover, as historian Robert Babcock has persuasively argued, until 1923, Canada, when it shifted its winter grain shipments to Halifax, Nova Scotia, exerted considerable influence over Portland development.[51]

But the Grand Trunk/Atlantic and St. Lawrence represented only the main spine of a larger Poor-proposed system. As work got under way on the Montreal line, Poor quickly proceeded to complete it, branching off the Androscoggin and Kennebec line (chartered in 1845, the same year as the Atlantic and St. Lawrence) to Waterville in 1849, then the Penobscot and Kennebec to Bangor in 1855. Meanwhile, the rival, narrow-gauge Kennebec and Portland Railroad, promoted by the so-called Augusta Group and piqued that Poor's Androscoggin and Kennebec had shunned Augusta, Maine's capital city, reached Waterville in 1855 via Augusta with a branch to Bath and Brunswick. This battle between the rail lines raged until resolved by state legislation in 1856, at which time the Kennebec and Portland was leased to the Androscoggin and Kennebec; then both "consolidated and merged in 1862 as the broad-gauged Maine Central. Another road, the York and Cumberland, chartered in 1846 and reorganized as the Portland and Rochester, gave ready access to southern New Hampshire.[52]

Poor pushed as well for a system to link Maine and Portland to Halifax and the Maritime Provinces. He dreamed of a Maritime trading region connected almost directly to Europe by a railroad from Portland to Halifax, a ferry across the Atlantic to nearby Galway Bay, thence to London, a trip he advertised as two days closer by rail than by steamship. The railroad apostle hosted a Portland Conference in 1850 to unveil his plans for the Europe and North American Railway (E&NA). He also saw military advantages to the road. Maine chartered the line, but the Civil War intervened. Poor died in 1869, and by 1871, when construction from Bangor to the New Brunswick border had been completed, the faster speed of screw-propeller steamships had already rendered plans for the E&NA obsolete.[53]

The failure of the E&NA aside, Poor's Grand Trunk Railroad, as he had predicted, changed the history of Portland, Maine. In 1853 it became the sole winter port for all of eastern Canada. At least for the fall and winter months, October through April, Portland enjoyed direct transatlantic steamship service to Liverpool. In September 1853, Portlanders gathered in throngs to witness the arrival of the steamship *Sarah Sands*. Her arrival from Liverpool inaugurated regular steamship service for the city. Meeting her was a large delegation from the newly formed (1853) Portland Board of Trade, comprising the city's leading merchants. That evening at Lancaster Hall, over sumptuous food and with numerous toasts (can we assume wine?) the board feted the captain and officers of the *Sarah Sands* and celebrated the city's new status as a world port. The ship's arrival reinforced as well Portland's self-image as Longfellow's city, a world-class trading port but one devoid of the squalid slums and human despair of such places as London and New York.[54]

Significantly, in the wake of the Grand Trunk and the *Sarah Sands*, Portland's new Board of Trade focused its initial efforts not on luring factories but on strengthening the port. In fact, the work had begun earlier in anticipation of the completion of the Portland-to-Montreal connection of the Atlantic and St. Lawrence. In order to link the A&StL terminal at the foot of Munjoy Hill in the eastern end of the city with the city piers that historically stretched along Fore Street and the Fore River westward to the foot of Bramhall Hill and the terminal of the Portland, Saco and Portsmouth Railroad, Portland's officialdom undertook a massive engineering tour de force to reconfigure and modernized its entire port complex.

Nineteenth-century American cities brutally remade the urban landscape to suit commercial ends. Seattle toppled hills to convert the tidelands of Puget Sound's Elliot Bay into buildable real estate, and Boston severed hilltops to fill in the Back Cove fenlands. So, too, Portland cut down a sizable portion of Munjoy Hill, using the fill to transform its existing Fore Street piers into foundation pilings supporting a new, 100-foot-broad by 5,993-foot-long waterfront thoroughfare called Commercial Street. A 26-foot rail corridor occupied the center of the new commercial avenue, giving rail access to an array of new, modern piers.[55]

With scheduled service to Liverpool, access to Detroit, Chicago and the West via Montreal and a tubular, mile-long Victoria Bridge (called the "Wonder of the World"), Portland and its bumptious Board of Trade reveled in an apparent triumph over its nemesis Boston. In 1858 the city next expected to berth another wonder of the world: the British-built leviathan *Great Eastern*, with its 112 furnaces and carrying capacity of 4,000 passengers. To prepare, in the eastern end of the city beneath the Eastern Promenade, Portland in 1857 built the massive Great Eastern wharves. But that ship never arrived, choosing New York instead. The disappointment never dimmed Portland's pre–Civil War radiant optimism, however. For one thing, the city now was doing unprecedented business. As historian Edward Kirkland has observed, Portland became a Canadian city for weekly steamship service to Liverpool, subsidized by the Canadian government. Now Portland, not Boston, handled the business in bonds for the Liverpool-to-British-Canada trade, and products of the American West actually reached Boston through Portland. Poor's once-deemed-extravagant promises seemed fulfilled. In 1858 Maine's senator and Portland's son, William Pitt Fessenden, tried to make Portland the center for transatlantic mail service. Like Poor, he contended that Portland could handle the mails more efficiently and more quickly—but he failed to convince his nationalistic colleagues that they should allow American mail to sail on British ships.[56]

As part of Poor's Grand Trunk enterprise, Portland did acquire a sizable industrial venture, albeit one in the city's commercial/entrepôt mold. In 1846 Poor and his business colleagues had founded the Portland Company, a metal foundry, to manufacture and service railroad equipment initially for the Atlantic and St. Lawrence Railroad Company. Located at 58 Fore Street, strategically in proximity to the planned terminus of the Montreal to Portland rail line, many of its brick buildings dating to the late 1840s and early 1850s remain today. The company's first officers, including the president, John A. Poor, were Portland merchant elites who had pressed for railroads. Poor turned to the City of Philadelphia for expertise, specifically to the Norris Locomotive Works. Norris supplied the $13,500 in machinery and tools necessary for building the first locomotive: the cylindrical mills, the bearing mills, lathes, and planing machinery. Norris also supplied Septimus Norris, the Philadelphia firm's chief engineer, who in the company's early days directed the building and operation of the works. By 1848 the Portland Company had severed its intimate relationship with Philadelphia's Norris Works but retained Norris's Benjamin Horace Felton as plant superintendent.

Naturally, the Portland Company concentrated its early energies on railroad stock for the Atlantic and St. Lawrence: locomotives, rails, rail cars, and other equipment. By 1849 the company employed over 100 workers, many Irish, and had already produced ten locomotives and seventy-nine freight and passenger cars. One year later, after enlarging its Fore Street complex, the company broadened its product line to include snow plows, stationary steam engines, and boilers. In 1852, a year before the completion of the Atlantic and St. Lawrence line, Portland Company employees loaded a locomotive aboard a Portland ship bound for Panama and the new Isthmus Railroad. In 1860, the Portland Company valued its annual business at $333,376. It was Portland's largest company.[57]

Poor's Atlantic and St. Lawrence Railroad, which soon became Canada's Grand Trunk Railroad (GTRR), connected Portland to Canada's grain trade and to Detroit, Chicago, and the West. It expanded Portland's market for canned goods, furniture, marine hardware, and other products, while the Portland Company gave the city a little niche in the locomotive and steam engine market. Thanks, however, to the GTRR, the Portland, Saco and Portsmouth, and the city's other railroads, along with its burgeoning steamship service, another market opened for the bustling little port: tourists.

Tourism did not spring up in Portland full grown. Like everything else, it evolved. While some nineteenth-century tourists took the fashionable or grand tour to Niagara Falls or Saratoga Springs, others in the 1830s—like Henry David Thoreau, Nathaniel Hawthorne, and the Hudson River School artist Thomas Cole—ventured to the more rugged, dizzying, but romantically sublime natural beauty of the White Mountains, that part of the Appalachian chain, mainly in New Hampshire, which features 6,288-foot Mount Washington and such other scenic wonders as Franconia Notch, Crawford Notch, the Flume, and the Old Man of the Mountain, a natural rock outcropping (tragically for New Hampshire tourism, the craggy visage fell off in 2003). These writers and artists converted their encounter with the scenic splendors of the White Mountains into salable art and literature which was eagerly consumed by a cosmopolitan public anxious to escape the stain of burgeoning urban industrialism. But as historian Dona Brown has argued, Cole, Hawthorne, Thoreau, and the other Yankee elites who visited Ethan Allen Crawford's White Mountain Inn and gazed rapturously at the cliff-face visage of the Old Man of the Mountain believed that only those possessing refined taste could truly appreciate such scenic wonders. By the 1850s, however, the railroad had opened those vistas to a broader, less refined middle-class viewership. Railroad companies established hotels and, through guidebooks, transformed scenic wonderlands into summer retreats.

The railroad that opened the White Mountains to middle-class tourism was Poor's Atlantic and St. Lawrence, making Portland not only the doorway or gateway to the delights of Crawford's Notch, Franconia Notch, and Mount Washington but also to the delights of the Maine coast, Boothbay Harbor, Squirrel Island, Camden, Bar Harbor, and Portland itself.[58] In the 1850s, Longfellow's city could be reached by both railroad and steamship lines. Organized in 1844, the Portland Steam Packet Company did a fairly brisk business carrying passengers between Boston and Portland as did the Maine Steamship Company between New York and the Forest City. By 1863, Portland Steam Packet estimated that it had transported as many as 1,500,000 travelers to and from Boston. Many who came as tourists preferred the steamship to the uncomfortable early railroads. In fact, the comparative ease and comfort of steamship travel versus the often crude, park-bench-style seating on railroads before the (post–Civil War) advent of the Pullman car, favored both steamship travel and Maine's coastal towns, such as Portland.[59]

Drawn by gazetteers, writers, and artists such as Thomas Cole—who, in addition to extolling the sublime White Mountains, raved about Maine's beauty—tourists in the 1840s and 1850s began discovering places such as Kittery Point, York Harbor, the Kennebunks, Old Orchard Beach, Bar Harbor, Camden—and Portland. Closer to Boston, southern Maine offered tourists not only history but wide, sandy beaches. Early on, these tourists often boarded in guesthouses such as Ebenezer Staples's farm in Old Orchard Beach. In 1840, Staples named his simple ocean-front lodging the Old Orchard Beach House. Towns north of Old Orchard Beach offered few beaches and traded mainly on their charm, their scenery, and their seafood. Portland in the 1840s advertised several seasonal or vacation hotels, including the Verandah, located in the East Deering section of Portland, and Cape Cottage on Cape Elizabeth, described by its owner as "the most romantic spot on the shore of New England." Four years later, in 1850, also surrounded by Cape Elizabeth's dazzling scenery, Ocean House opened.[60]

But tourism was hardly confined to the White Mountains and to the Maine coast's breezy hotel verandas. Some travelers, including Henry Thoreau—who regularly visited Maine between 1846 and 1856 and whose ventures there were chronicled in his posthumously published *Maine Woods*—roughed it. Moosehead Lake attracted hunters and fly fishermen, some of whom stayed at the lake's Kineo House, others in much cruder lodges.

As a hub of middle-class railroad excursions to both mountain and coastal summer retreats, Portland soon established its niche in the emerging tourist marketplace. Through aggressive marketing the Maine Central and other railroad companies would soon loudly trumpet the glories of Portland's lighthouses, of island-studded Casco Bay, of Cape Elizabeth, of sunset views from the Western Promenade, as well as the joys of cooking freshly caught brook trout—all thrills available in Portland or just a few hours away by rail.

A romantic poet, Longfellow well understood the lure of the Maine coast, the Maine woods, and his city. The author of *Hiawatha* also understood Portland's long history of resurgence in the wake of cataclysm. With direct connections to Montreal, Detroit, and the American West, with the arrival of the *Sarah Sands* and scheduled biweekly service to Liverpool, and with one of America's largest sugar refineries plus a first-class foundry and producer of locomotives, elm-adorned Portland in 1855 seemed poised to become one of North America's premier ports without, miraculously, the urban squalor found in Dickens's London or New York's Five Points. Significantly, when Longfellow visited Portland in 1848, at a time when the Portland Company operated around the clock to supply stock for the Atlantic and St. Lawrence Railroad, the poet saw nothing of the foundry's fiery furnaces or its smoke and grit. Rather, "How lovely the view of the harbor," he wrote, "the pearly sea with its almost irresistible attraction drawing me into it. A whole fleet of vessels [rested] on the horizon." At sunset he walked by his father's house on Congress Street and strolled down to Fore Street, where the "gurgling of the sea among the wood piers was the only other sound" than the clip-clop of a horse or the distant rumble of a carriage. The smoky Portland Company never appears. In 1848, it was but one of a handful of factories secreted in the crevices and odd corners of what was otherwise a shimmering sun-, breeze-, and surf-splashed city by the sea. Some dissonance, however, lurked in the corners of that idyllic place.

CHAPTER TWO

Civil War, the Great Fire, and Reshaping Portland's Urban Image

In 1855, with its deep, ice-free harbor, its bay studded with furled and unfurled white sails, its rail link to Canada secured, and early tourist arrivals from Philadelphia, Boston, and Montreal, Portland readied itself to compete with Boston for commercial supremacy. John Alfred Poor's vision of his city supplanting Boston as the center of New England commerce actually seemed believable. That would not happen, however. Ultimately, it was Longfellow's beguiling boyhood dream of the "beautiful town," of Deering Woods, and of "Spanish Sailors," and the "magic of the sea," that would forever resonate, while Poor's vision faded.

Social, economic, and political events preceding, during, and just following the Civil War challenged the capacity of modest Portland to become a premier, first-class commercial city in the Age of Industrialism. That fateful verdict forced Portland to turn from industrialism and to capitalize on its strengths—not only on its enviable role as Canada's winter grain port and its historic role as an entrepôt, a center for the distribution of goods to Maine and New Hampshire, but also on its natural assets as a port of entry for tourists seeking the beauty and health of Maine's rocky coast, its unpolluted air, and the region's fabled mountains. By the 1870s, Portland boosters had unveiled a theme rivaling "Resurgem" as the city's motto: "Gateway to Vacationland."

Five critical events between 1855 and 1874 rendered Poor's dream ultimately impossible. First, the prelude to the Civil War revealed political fault lines in what seemed to be the cultural hegemony of the city's Yankee merchant elite. Second, events in the 1850s uncovered social class cleavages that shattered the illusion of Portland as having generally escaped the street rioting and turmoil that erupted from the bowels of urban slums in Boston, New York, and Philadelphia. Third, the Civil War itself, although propelling Portland's infant industrialism, marked a watershed in the city's economic history, leaving deep scars on its fishing, shipbuilding, and entrepôt economy.

Fourth, and perhaps most significant, the Civil War inaugurated a new era of large-scale corporate capitalism: from the bloody conflict sprang the Andrew Carnegies, the Cyrus McCormicks, the Daniel Drews, the Henry Clay Fricks, the Jay Goulds, and the other moguls that journalist Matthew Josephson once famously branded "Robber Barons." This new age of urban industrialization involved massive capitalization, and the restructuring of industry and enterprise both vertically and horizontally. But though Poor may have imagined the dawning of this era, his Portland colleagues seemed unprepared and, moreover, unwilling to play in this national urban arena. In 1874 Portland would surrender its pretentions to competition with Boston and New York as a major American transatlantic port.

Fifth and finally, years before the holocausts of Chicago in 1871 and Boston in 1872, on July 4, 1866, flames destroyed three-fourths of the City of Portland. As in the case of Boston and Chicago, the fire, albeit costly, proved cleansing, enabling the city's leaders to digest the changes transforming the national economy and to consider how Portland might adapt. During this critical period in Portland history, not only the Civil War, the fire, and the new national economy impacted the city, the social, economic, and political vision of Portland's postwar business leaders—John Bundy Brown, James Phinney Baxter, and others—shaped late Victorian Portland more toward Longfellow's dream of the beautiful city by the sea than toward Poor's grand design for a world city.[1]

The Five Crises

New England, especially Portland, approached the impending crisis of the Civil War with almost millennial fervor. Noontime revivals filled downtown churches in the late 1850s, and Neal Dow's temperance crusade gained momentum. Dow saw the enactment of a state law banning alcoholic beverages as bringing law and order to Portland and lessening the need for police patrols along grogshop-lined Fore Street, which catered to inebriate seamen. His 1851

"Maine Law" would also, promised Dow, empty crowded jails and bring domestic tranquillity to rum-shattered households. But socially and politically, Dow's crusade opened fault lines. Portland's Catholic hierarchy backed temperance; priests at St. Dominic's preached temperance; the Catholic Church sponsored a temperance organization; and clergy regularly trudged from the State Street rectory down Danforth Street to Gorham's Corner to quell rum-enflamed brawls. Portland's Irish community, however, viewed itself as the target and victim of Dow's crusade, not its beneficiary. In the 1850s, Portland's nativist toughs and anti-Irish Know-Nothings made this view explicit. To make matters even worse for the city's Irish, in 1852 Portlanders elected Dow mayor of the city.[2]

If Portland's working-class Irish sided with grogshop owners against Yankee scolds, they were equally aligned against the city's millenarian Whigs on the critical issue of slavery. Politically fervent Jacksonian Democrats, the Irish showed little sympathy for the antislavery, abolitionist views of William Lloyd Garrison, Henry Ward Beecher, or the Tappan brothers, New England firebrands who periodically harangued Portland crowds at local churches. In the 1850s, even while Irish longshoremen increasingly ruled the waterfront, many black and West Indian workers, as Longfellow noted, still hoisted cargoes aboard West Indies–bound ships.[3]

Yet similar battle lines—tolerance for strong drink versus temperance or abstinence; antislavery and abolitionism versus gradualism or states' rights—took form in Yankee neighborhoods, on the streets of Bayside, and in those elm-shaded enclaves of Park Street, Deering, and State. In the spring of 1855, anger over the operation of the Maine Law led to a night of rioting and the death of a Deer Island seaman, John Robin, a bystander drawn to the riot scene by chance. It began when Mayor Neal Dow, for reasons unexplained, on his own ordered a large cache of spirits to be stored in the city's Liquor Agency, located in the basement of the City Hall, which fronted Market Square. Hearing about the stash and convinced that Dow, "the temperance man" but very much part of the city's elite, wished to profit from the stored liquor, a crowd gathered at City Hall demanding it be "spilt" into Portland Harbor. Dow let the mob seethe all day until at nightfall, according to John A. Poor (another bystander whose hat would be pierced by one of the bullets fired in the ensuing melee), the angry crowd pummeled the hall with rocks. Dow at last ordered out the city militia (mainly youthful recruits) to be stationed at City Hall. Shots were fired; Robin was killed. Dow suffered politically for the riot and was not reelected. The Maine Law would never be effectively policed, and its uneven enforcement—the poor arrested, the wealthy free to enjoy their cabernet, chablis, and brandy—endured as a festering sore on the body politic. The 1855 incident exposed latent social and economic tensions surfacing in the apocalyptic years preceding the Civil War. Indeed, these tensions refashioned national, state, and Portland city politics.[4]

Portland, given its intimate trading partnership with the slaveholding West Indies and the Cotton South, had remained sorely divided on the issue of involuntary servitude, especially before 1837, when a pro-slavery mob in Alton, Illinois, murdered Elijah P. Lovejoy, a graduate of Waterville College (now Colby) for printing antislavery literature. As with most New Englanders, Portland's Yankee Whigs tended to oppose slavery on moral grounds but abjured abolitionism as meddling with Cotton Kingdom freedom. They viewed southerners as generous and righteous people who, once "enlightened"—that is, "perfected" religiously—would gradually emancipate their chattel. In their minds, abolitionists and antislavery activists, people such as Theodore Parker, William Lloyd Garrison, and George Thompson—all of whom from time to time Portland Quakers and antislavery activists such as Nathan and John Winslow and Harriet and Emma Dow invited to speak at City Hall and in local churches—merely stirred up unnecessary trouble.[5]

Lovejoy's lynching changed the discourse. It forced Portlanders to view the antislavery debate as an issue less of moral choice than of free speech. Portlanders such as Samuel Fessenden and his son, William Pitt Fessenden, who served terms in both the United States Congress and the Maine legislature, now spoke forcefully against the South and its "peculiar institution," especially after the Mexican War deepened the prospect of slavery expanding into the western territories. The Kansas-Nebraska Act of 1854 negated the Missouri Compromise, which had given birth to Maine statehood, and instituted "popular sovereignty," outraging most Portlanders. The act triggered open warfare between pro- and antislavery forces, those for "Free Soil, Free Labor, and Free Men" versus those sympathetic to the South. In 1852, Portland's Whig Party split between Free Soilers (opposed to "popular sovereignty") and those clinging to southern gradualism. Portland's Jacksonian Democrats likewise, fragmented into Woolheads (who opposed slavery and popular sovereignty) and Wildcats (who were for the Compromise of 1850).[6]

By 1854 the political realignment involved temperance as well as slavery. Nativists or Portland Know-Nothings joined Free Soil Whigs and Democratic

Woolheads to form the new Republican Party, consequently branding the opposition Democratic Party the party of "freedom to drink and to own slaves." Ex-Whig William Pitt Fessenden became a Republican and, in 1864, Abraham Lincoln's secretary of the treasury. Meanwhile, Maine's long-term Democratic standard-bearer (rural Maine had been largely pro–Andrew Jackson and Democratic since the 1840s) and Fessenden's political foe, Hannibal Hamlin, switched from the Democratic to the Republican Party to become Lincoln's vice president in 1860. Thus, the Civil War made Maine a solidly Republican state and Portland—Whig before 1854—rabidly Republican after 1860. Nevertheless, those deep strains of Whig political moralism and fierce individualism, which feared political corruption and championed small "r" republicanism, from time to time produced Democratic mayors in post–Civil War Portland.[7]

Portland and the Civil War

In the turbulent, premillennial milieu of the late 1850s, with "Beecher's Bibles," cries of "bloody Kansas," and the wrathful specter of John Brown rending the land, John Poor's ecstatic vision of railroads and Portland's destiny dissolved; following Lincoln's election as president in 1860, the attack on Fort Sumter, and the first Battle of Bull Run, they all but vanished. The bombardment of Fort Sumter found Portland not only in the throes of political restructuring and millennial fervor but in the midst of a periodic economic slump as well. Britain, with its cotton-dependent textile economy, sided with the South, compromising Canadian–U.S. financial relations and rendering the Grand Trunk Railroad unable to pay the Portland Company for the delivery of an almost-completed, sizable order of twenty-five freight cars and a locomotive. That failure forced the foundry to float a large loan to pay its bills. The fiscal crisis lingered into 1863. By June 1862, however, the Portland Company had a bevy of new contracts from the federal government, and it busied itself constructing lathes for tooling and rifling fifty cannon, the rifling making them a novel and deadly feature on the field of battle. Meanwhile, a new order arrived for two 200-foot-long gunboats (with thirty-five-foot beams), the *Agwan* and the *Pontousuc*, to be built in partnership with Portlander George Lawrence's shipyard. Both of these formidable, steam-powered naval platforms carried on deck an array of twenty-four howitzers and other weaponry. The Portland Company far exceeded its cost estimates for producing the two double-ended warships, however, and as late as May 1874 its lawyers were still battling the federal government in court and in Congress to be indemnified for its heavy losses.[8]

The Portland Company's federal contracts suggested that perhaps the Civil War presaged an industrial future for the city. The conflict siphoned off over 5,000 blue-uniformed young men from Portland's labor supply, opening up opportunities galore for those workers left behind. Moreover, it also suddenly terminated Portland's historic and vital trade with the South and the West Indies, forcing the young Board of Trade to emphasize industrial in lieu of port activity.[9]

As Maine's numerous Civil War monuments attest, the state's towns, villages, and cities, including Portland, lost many of their fathers and sons in battles such as Antietam, Fredericksburg, and Gettysburg. They also produced heroes such as Joshua L. Chamberlain, a future governor and president of Bowdoin College. Portlanders Francis Fessenden and Major John Mead Gould of the Tenth Maine Infantry served in numerous campaigns. Fessenden lost his leg; Gould, the diarist and historian of the 1-10-29th Maine Regiment, for the remainder of his life suffered malaria attacks. There were other great costs to the city as well. For one, the South actually dispatched a squadron of Confederate corsairs northward to attack Portland Harbor, which sank several ships before being captured. Then, too, in addition to the cessation of the city's West Indian and Charleston commerce, Portland suffered Britain's shift of much of its transatlantic trade from Portland to British bottoms.[10]

Moreover, by discouraging foreign immigration, the Civil War shrank Portland's population growth from a significant 37 percent in the 1840s, and a still respectable 26 percent in the 1850s, down to just 19 percent in the 1860s. Most important, the closing of the West Indies ports, combined with Dow's Maine Law, effectively padlocked Portland's seven distilleries. It also undermined the city's historic molasses trade, and with it John Bundy Brown's flagship Portland Sugar Company (see fig. 2). After the war, Brown still imported molasses from Havana and other West Indian ports, most for the much smaller Eagle Sugar Refinery that opened in 1866. But the Portland fire that same year halted Portland sugar operations, and although Brown rebuilt his Gorham's Corner refinery and experimented briefly and unsuccessfully with beet sugar, by then his superannuated refining technology, stiff competition with refined white sugar, and the emergence of giant sugar combines ended the little Brown sugar dynasty. In 1887 H. O. Havemeyer was able to merge seventeen sugar refineries into the American Sugar Refining Company, but by the mid-1870s, Portland's sputtering sugar trade with the West Indies lingered only in a greatly diminished form.[11]

Finally, the Civil War inflicted on Portland less obvious but still onerous additional costs. Since not all Mainers willingly enlisted in the Grand Cause, upon Lincoln's institution of the draft, July 2, 1862, Portland was authorized to pay a bounty of $100 to each recruit who counted toward its quota of draftees. Or the bounty could be paid to a substitute; during the war Portland paid over $150,000 in bounties. Ultimately, the state repaid much of that, but during the war the bounties, rising costs, and the city's bonded debt for railroad loans forced taxes upward.[12]

Portland soldiers who did return, whole or, like Gould and Fessenden, maimed, bore with them lasting memories and deep emotional scars that often made it difficult for them to readjust to their previous life—in Gould's case, as a bank clerk (fig. 7). With his deep Christian convictions, and hoping to take part in southern Reconstruction, Gould lingered on in the South, in the Georgetown District of South Carolina's Sea Islands, at Yankamma Ferry. He started a small sawmill to cut cyprus boards, to be shipped by brig back to Portland. That venture collapsed utterly, and in 1867 Gould returned to Portland a "Failed Man. . . . A Man that got euchred, a man that can't pay his debts." He married, and after working briefly as an accountant for J. B. Brown's Portland Sugar Company, and then part time for the Kimball Carriage Company, he returned to his prewar position as a bank teller at the Manufacturers and Traders Bank, where his father, Edward, worked as head cashier. Gould, like many Civil War veterans, perpetually sought to recapture the exhilaration of the battlefield and the camaraderie of the campfire. A loyal member of the Tenth Maine, he wrote a regimental history and rarely missed a Grand Army of the Republic reunion, picnic, or meeting, especially those that dealt with erecting in Portland a commemorative Civil War monument. Toward that end, in October 1873, the city's Civil War veterans formed a Soldiers and Sailors Monument Association, designating Market Square as the site. Francis Fassett, John Calvin Stevens, and even James Phinney Baxter submitted proposals, but the battle over exactly what form that monument would take (see chapter 3) raged well into the late nineteenth century.[13]

If the Civil War's legacy was costly in lives, in government debt, and in psychological stress, it also bequeathed some financial benefits. City chronicler Edward H. Elwell concluded that Portland "came out of the Civil War without great loss."[14] During the war businessman James Phinney Baxter won a highly

7. John Mead Gould, Civil War veteran, bank clerk, regimental historian, and Portland diarist. Courtesy of Maine Historical Society.

lucrative contract to supply canned corn to the Union Army. Despite its later case against the federal government, the Portland Company's contract with Uncle Sam for cannon and double-ended gunboats kept business humming at the city's largest foundry. In general, therefore, the war enhanced the city economically. City real estate valuations of almost $10 million in 1853, the year of the Grand Trunk's arrival, reached almost $14.5 million in 1863. The war also forced an increase in the millage rate, however, from 7 percent in 1853 to 14.4 percent in 1863. Portland raised almost $147,000 from real estate in 1860 but almost $421,000 in 1865, up over 186 percent.[15]

Portland in the New Age of Industrialism

Most profoundly, for Portland and for every American city, the Civil War transformed the national economy. Without the South as a countervailing social and political force, impelled by congressionally enacted federal land grants and grants-in-aid, railroads, as Poor had imagined, followed by people, swept across rivers, plains, deserts, and mountains, binding the nation together in twin bands of steel. An expanding national marketplace attracted international capital and restructured business away from the old individual firm or partnership form toward new larger and more complex corporate entities, including monopolies and giant trusts. As historian Philip Scranton explained in his study of Philadelphia's textile industrialism, *Figured Tapestry,* older and more traditional business forms survived in "specialized" markets, but increasingly—as in the case of Portland's J. B. Brown Portland Sugar Company—such firms withered and were absorbed by larger companies. Wider, networked markets unleashed other social and economic forces whose ultimate impact on Portland was rarely for the good. After 1880, with the rise in demand for newsprint and other paper products and the growing importance for their manufacture of wood pulp over rag content, timber-rich Maine became a papermaking center. The state had twelve mills in 1880 but thirty-seven in 1899, several located near though not in Portland. In the 1890s, papermaking had a positive impact on the port of Portland. Many traditional port enterprises, such as fishing and shipbuilding, fared less well after the Civil War. Historian Jackson Lears has argued that advertising, primitive before the Civil War, acquired much greater sophistication in the latter nineteenth century, appealing to subconscious "felt" needs and thus establishing the concept of "taste" and a proclivity for the modern. These national trends had ramifications for Portland. For example, in modern, railway-laced America, refrigerated rail cars could transport fresh fish, rendering Portland's salted cod and salted mackerel—even for the urban poor of New York, Boston, and Philadelphia—now unappetizing.[16]

Just as seriously, the Civil War shifted the locus of America's shipbuilding industry away from Maine and New England, where—with the exception of the Portland Company's gunboat contract and some work at the Sewell and Hyde yards at Bath, Maine—shipbuilders clung to wood and sailcloth and continued to produce wooden-hulled, four-, five-, and six-mast "down-easters" for the coal trade into the twentieth century. The war, however, had demonstrated the superiority of propeller-driven, iron- and steel-hulled vessels built in Scotland's Clyde yards, in Philadelphia's and Camden's Sun and Cramp shipyards, New York's East River yards, and Baltimore's Bethlehem yards, where Andrew Carnegie supplied plate for modern steel-hulled warships.

Likewise, political as well as technological changes eviscerated Maine's and Portland's once buoyant fishing industry, which in 1861 had ranked first in the nation. Wartime inflation and Republican protective tariffs sent the prices soaring for cordage, sail canvas, chain, and other marine hardware vital for the industry. In 1866 a laissez-faire Republican Congress repealed the cod bounty that had produced Maine's sizable fishing fleet of independently owned boats. By 1870, only a small fleet of fishing vessels anchored in Portland Harbor (though a few still did a salt-cod business in the West Indies). The New England fishing industry, once centered as much in the Boothbay Harbor, Portland, and York regions as in Boston, Portsmouth, and Newburyport, had shifted southward to Gloucester, Massachusetts, where new, highly capitalized firms adopted the latest fishing technology and where large, steam-powered side or eastern-rig trawlers dominated.[17]

Modern American capitalism spawned not only larger but more clearly specialized cities, often stamped by a single process or product: for example, Milwaukee beer, Chicago meatpacking, Pittsburgh steel, Hartford insurance. Portland, however, lacked either the strategic geographic position, the access to critical resources (except forest products, such as wood pulp), or the verve to exploit this new age of enterprise. Pittsburgh with its nearby rich coal resources, its existing iron and glass industries, and its Henry Clay Fricks, Thomas Mellons, and Andrew Carnegies, stood poised for steelmaking. Chicago had not only superb rail connections but the Great Plains at its doorstep. Providence, in addition to rivers, railroads, and a port, had also a long history of diversified manufacturers, textiles, tools, and steam engines: the

Corliss steam engine, for example, the centerpiece of the 1876 Philadelphia Centennial Exhibit, which dazzled the young Civil War veteran John Mead Gould.[18]

Although Portland boasted the Grand Trunk and Maine Central rail systems which, running through Montreal, Detroit, and Chicago, gave it access to western markets, its entrepreneurial energies seemed exhausted in the 1870s. Evidence appeared in the case of the Brown sugar empire's failure to innovate, in the city's shipbuilding stasis, in its canneries and other enterprises that, unlike the "endless novelty" Philip Scranton found in other cities, largely clung to established technologies.[19] In addition to the Portland Company, post–Civil War Portland supported a cluster of small manufactories: a chewing-gum factory, a boots-and-shoes industry, canneries, artificial-limb-making, a stoneware company, and a major producer of marine hardware. But the bulk of its leading merchants, consistent with the city's historic entrepôt role, engaged in wholesaling dry and fancy goods and groceries. The economic configuration confirmed Portland's status as a regional rather than a national port. When the city's civic and economic elites in the period stared into their proverbial crystal balls, looking for a niche in the national corporate/capitalist marketplace, what they beheld was what Longfellow and other earlier tribunes of the people had seen: the city's Casco Bay seascape, its Deering Oaks, its tree-lined and architecturally bejeweled streets.[20]

In 1866, wide, rail-laced Commercial Street with its piers and warehouses, where tall ships and modern steamers loaded and unloaded cargoes, had formed the heart of Portland's busy maritime economy. Railroad tracks connected the Grand Trunk's terminal at India Street with the Portland, Saco and Portsmouth's station at the western end of the busy, mile-long waterfront thoroughfare. Rail sidings branched off to allow loading and unloading at various piers, such as the Grand Trunk, the Atlantic, Galt, Central, Union and Brown, and Sturdivant's and Hobson's wharves at the foot of High Street. It was there, at approximately 5:00 o'clock in the evening of July 4, 1866, in a boat builder's shed located but a stone's throw from John Bundy Brown's gigantic sugarhouse and just above Commercial Street on York Street, that a young boy eager to celebrate the holiday set off a firecracker.

The tiny explosion ignited a pile of wood shavings. Within minutes, flames from the burning shed, fanned by a stiff southwesterly breeze, reached the sugarhouse, setting off a violent explosion and, in John Neal's words, "a hurricane of fire." The inferno swept through the city, engulfing every building on

8. Photograph taken in 1866 of Portland in ruins following the great July Fourth fire of that year. Courtesy of Maine Historical Society.

the north side of Commercial Street and most if not all of the residential and commercial buildings (brick and stone) on York, Maple, Danforth, Congress, Temple, India, Cumberland, Oxford, Fore, and Exchange, as well as a host of smaller streets and alleys. The fire, which did not extinguish itself until reaching the Eastern Cemetery on Munjoy Hill, consumed three-fourths of the city, including the recently completed $264,000 City Hall (1863), eight churches, every Portland bank and insurance office, and most law offices, plus the 1826 Portland Athenaeum, the hall of the Portland Society of Natural History, the library of the YMCA, several fine hotels, and numerous business blocks such as the large granite Mussey, Fox, and Thomas blocks (fig. 8). Journalist John Neal estimated the total cost of the insured losses at $6 million dollars. The conflagration, which blazed for over fifteen hours, left 10,000 people homeless. Some, like Second Parish Church's Reverend Payson and others, fled to Gorham, to Cape Elizabeth, or even Bethel. Irish longshoremen and other less affluent Portlanders, denizens of decimated places such as Gorham's Corner, or on Cumberland, Pearl, and Washington Streets, found shelter in a tent city erected on Munjoy Hill or in temporary barracks quickly built on unscathed Fore Street land leased for a "nominal" fee from the Portland Company.[21]

At John B. Brown's fire-consumed sugarhouse, insurance covered half of the sugar tycoon's $522,532 loss, but many who were uninsured lost everything. Others, like the federal employees of the Portland Customs House, endured the steep rents and high prices for the necessaries of life that marked the fire's aftermath. They forthwith petitioned Senator William Pitt Fessenden for a raise to cover these added costs, but apparently to no avail.[22]

Once again, Portland recovered, helped by an outpouring of aid (estimated at $600,000) that came from Boston, New York, Philadelphia, Chicago, Cleveland, St. Louis, Albany, Hartford, Saco, Lewiston, and other cities, including Montreal and Halifax. In two years, Portland—like Chicago after its 1871 fire, Boston following its Great Fire of 1872, and Baltimore and Newburyport after similar infernos—rebuilt. In the city's larger historical memory, however, the tragedy of the fire and its hardships became easily confounded with the national hard times triggered by the so-called Panic of 1873. This economic buffeting in the wake of the 1866 fire kept Portland's struggling economy depressed throughout the 1870s.

Resurgem: *Portland in the Not-So-Gilded Age*

Having supplied tents and barracks shelter for the city's many homeless, and policed what the mayor described as the "multitude of rough and desperate characters who considered the confusion . . . favorable for their operations," Portland proceeded to enact stringent new fireproof-building standards within the downtown burn area, and it organized a National Board of Fire Underwriters to streamline the handling of claims in future disasters.[23] The city undertook rebuilding determined that in the new downtown, wholesale, retail, and professional businesses would be transacted in more modern, commodious, architecturally distinguished space. The city's small but acclaimed cadre of architects, Fred H. Fassett in particular, led the architectural effort. Fassett made his goal to rebuild Portland as not only a fashionable and architecturally commendable but also a more beautiful place.

Fassett and the rebuilders conducted the task most admirably. Middle Street arose as the city's new central retail and dry goods corridor lined with stately, three-story brick commercial buildings with Connecticut freestone and Albert stone trim, and bearing the wide bracketed cornices, mansard roofs, and hooded windows typical of the then fashionable Italianate and Second French Empire styles of the late 1860s and early 1870s. Exchange, another street totally obliterated by the fire, was likewise reconstructed in Italianate and Second Empire garb. Market Square, fronted by the old City Hall and surrounded by the fine U.S. Hotel, the Preble House, the Clapp and Deering blocks, stood at the heart of the rebuilt city; in Elwell's words it represented Portland's "Roman Forum."[24]

John Bundy Brown delivered the pièce de résistance: to crown the post-fire rebuilding of the city's commercial core, in June 1868 he opened the Falmouth House, a grand hotel located at Middle and Union Streets, close to Market (now Monument) Square, the heart of the newly rebuilt city. Covering a lot of nearly 27,000 square feet, measuring 153 feet fronting Middle and 174 feet on Union, the elegant six-story, 225-room hotel cost $300,000 to build. Italianate in design, it was lavishly ornamented with Albert stone, and its brick Middle Street facade had an ornate bracketed cornice, pillars, and pilasters. Brown appointed the interior sumptuously with a grand dining room, a marble-tiled, black-walnut-paneled, and brocade-wall-papered lobby, ladies' parlors, billiard halls, and telegraph office, all illuminated by dazzeling gas chandeliers. The Falmouth's curtained, carpeted, and fine-furnished rooms equaled the best found in New York or Boston. Its June 29, 1868, opening matched in splendor the grand edifice itself: by special train, the sugar merchant transported 1,500 dignitaries from Boston to the gala opening of the Falmouth—as much a testimony to and celebration of Portland's new potential future as a spa, as it was a farewell to the city's past as a premier manufactory of brown sugar (fig. 9).[25]

The population fully shared Brown's vision of post–Civil War, post-fire Portland as a place to behold, a tourist spectacle. Indeed, immediately after the fire, while the city still smoldered, thousands had come to gawk at the smoking ruins. Now Portland would present the glory of a risen phoenix. In fact, for a new city hall and county office building, architect Fred H. Fassett designed a magnificent Greek Revival temple, built at an estimated cost of $200,000; the impressive edifice had galleries seating over a thousand persons. At Middle and Exchange Streets the federal government in 1867 built another temple, a stunning Greek Revival (Parthenon-like) post office designed by Alfred B. Mullett, matched blocks away by an equally grand Second Empire/Renaissance Revival customs house. Elsewhere, the city replaced its destroyed fire stations and schools with fine, substantial, architect-designed Victorian and Queen Anne–style buildings. Portland prided itself on its well-designed schools and the quality of its education. It had both public and Catholic schools, but in the 1860s and 1870s no private school system. Graduates of Portland's public schools—such as Percival Baxter, James Phinney's son and a future governor; and John Mead Gould's children—joined their college-bound classmates at Bowdoin, Harvard, Yale, and Mount Holyoke.

The city's sick or injured were not ignored in the rebuilding process. After five years of planning, on Bramhall Hill and within view of Brown's mansion

9. John Bundy Brown's Falmouth Hotel, ca. 1890. Courtesy of Maine Historic Preservation Commission.

the State of Maine built the large brick, forty-bed Maine General Hospital of Second French Empire design, which was dedicated in October 1874.[26]

But rebuilding Victorian, post–Civil War, post-fire Portland into a truly beautiful city involved more than fine, fireproof architecture. Portland's rebirth transpired in the shadow of cholera epidemics and—thanks to the work of Joseph Lister, Louis Pasteur, and Robert Koch in the 1870s and 1880s—at the dawn of germ theory and the bacteriological sciences. Guided earlier by the fear of dreaded "noxious exhalations," London sanitarians such as Edwin Chadwick (1842) had clearly recognized the significance for public health of overcrowded tenements and human squalor. In America, Frederick Law Olmsted, Andrew Jackson Downing, and Calvert Vaux argued for urban parks and greenswards, emphasizing the need for open spaces, trees, and grass to function, among other things, as the health-giving "lungs" of the city. Thus, in an age of the new sanitary sciences, Portland officials addressed not only new city halls, schools and firehouses but also new streets, new water systems, new parks, and new sewers.[27]

In 1866 most Portland streets had remained unpaved, relying on the city's natural drainage to keep the mud at bay. Residents rejoiced when on October

12, 1863 the Portland and Forest Avenue Horse Railway provided rail service as an alternative to perambulating on foot the city's dirty, unevenly graded streets, or being jostled unmercifully on an omnibus. In 1865 the line renamed itself the Portland Railroad Company, and when electrified in 1895, it possessed over eleven miles of rails, fifty cars, and 225 horses. Portland's post–Civil War horsecars ran from India down Middle Street onto Congress and Preble and then Portland Street onto Forest Avenue and at last all the way to Morrill's Corners. The system inaugurated Portland's first suburbs. Nineteenth-century Europeans and Americans recognized the hazards of urban overcrowding. Charles Dickens's novels reeked with the stench of squalid rookeries and the acrid, polluted Thames. Before the Civil War, some Portland elites had found a healthful refuge from the Forest City's modest density in places such as Deering, Cape Elizabeth, and Falmouth. After the war Portlanders such as bank teller John Mead Gould purchased land at Willard Beach in South Portland, where he built a rude but pleasant summer cottage and raised a substantial garden crop.[28]

But urban congestion and the costs of sanitary urban growth concerned Portland. In the face of periodic epidemics, public officials (fiscal conservatives all, whether Republicans or Democrats) scorned penuriousness when confronting the cost of public health; as historian Jon Teaford has noted, late nineteenth-century urban public servants, faced with rising city populations and issues of public health, often cared for the interest of the commonweal quite well. Portland's Mayor Moses M. Butler in 1878 made the case eloquently and explicitly in stating the limits of urban thrift even in the face of serious debt: "Consistently with the true interests of an enlightened, progressive community like our own," explained Butler, "whose aim is to keep abreast of the times in all that makes for the comfort, health, and well-being of the citizen, it cannot be expected that this course of retrenchment can go on indefinitely, or indeed much further. It is not according to the spirit of our people that economy should degenerate into parsimony and penuriousness. Our schools, drains, and sewers, police, and public health, fire department, are matters of necessity, and must be provided for."[29]

Street improvement progressed, based on assessing individual Portland homeowners for the cost of paving, laying culverts, and installing curbing. The whole process proved laborious and difficult, and collecting the assessments both very inconsistent and inefficient. Nevertheless, as the record shows, street after street, whether large or small, whether commercial or residential, with rich owners or poor tenants, one by one, Commercial, Clark, Deering, Elm, Green, Free, and Fore, after hours of labor, thousands of feet of grading, and tons of granite and curbstone set and reset, were all beautifully paved.[30]

Unlike Chicago, Philadelphia, or other such large places as New York's Manhattan (where urban densities reached 272 per city block in 1850 and 986 persons to an acre in Gotham's thirty-two-acre sanitary district in 1894), Portland's densities were modest with the exception of the relatively small Gotham's Corner. Water issues arose not over quality, but over accessibility for fighting fires in times of drought and over the feasibility of tapping water from Sebago Lake, twenty miles distant, as opposed to the closer Cumberland and Oxford Canal or Presumpscot River. In 1866 the state legislature chartered the Portland Water Company (headed by John B. Brown, Samuel Spring, and Jacob McLellan) "for the purpose of conveying to the City of Portland a supply of pure water, for domestic and municipal purposes, including the extinguishing of fires." Water was to be furnished to City Hall, the public schools, and the city's fire hydrants without charge.[31]

The 1866 fire added urgency to the water supply issue, and although consulting engineers agreed on the difficulty of laying pipe in Maine granite, the city chose a pipeline to Sebago Lake as the solution. Portland contracted with the Portland Water Company, and on July 4, 1870, "to the beat of drums, horns, and a military and civic parade," water arrived via a twenty-inch main from Lake Sebago to a 12-million-gallon reservoir on Bramhall Hill. Then, by gravity, Sebago water reached the city's principal streets.[32]

With a fresh water supply and the increasing popularity of indoor plumbing (the U.S. Patent Office issued numerous patents for water closets in 1870), and with stricter city ordinances against outdoor privies, Portland's esteemed city engineer and apostle of efficiency William A. Goodwin urged the development of a modern, combined sewerage system that would carry away together both storm and waste water. In fact, more paved streets and better surface drainage by gutters and culverts made improved sewerage imperative. Mayor George Wescott in 1873 agreed with Goodwin, stating that "the welfare of city and the citizens to be benefited . . . demands the adoption of some definite plan of sewerage for the whole city."[33]

The sewerage issue threatened the city's claim to be not only a beautiful but also the "healthiest city." Under the cover of darkness, Portlanders often took rubbish and night soil to the Commercial Street docks, as Londoners did to the Thames, and dumped them in the Fore River. Indeed, a city ordinance enacted in 1878 prohibited Portlanders from "empty[ing] or remov[ing] the contents of any privy vault within the city limits"; it licensed individuals charged with removing night soil.[34] The Back Cove presented a more serious problem for the city.[35] Portland citizens such as John Mead Gould, who lived in Bayside near Pearl and Cumberland Streets overlooking the cove, complained about the offensive odors wafting up from the Back Cove, especially on hot summer evenings. Some, like Mayor Moses Butler, blamed the effluvium on trapped sewer gas that backed up, at night and at high tide, from the Bayside sewer and into homes. He recommended that offended homeowners ventilate their sewer connections via a pipe connected to the chimney flue.[36]

Butler admitted, however, that the city's first sewer, on Middle Street, dated to the early 1850s and that otherwise the city lacked any accurate record of its sewers. The sewer on the northwesterly side of the city, he reported, discharged directly onto the foul mud flats of the Back Cove "to the detriment of public health and on the easterly side into the docks of the harbor, filling them up to the extent of injuring the right of navigations." Butler regretted that the problem required the construction of costly interceptor sewers along the shores of the Back Cove and along Commercial Street, but that meanwhile, scows and small dredges must remove the sewage. In some grim cases, "notably the millpond above Deering Bridge [the Duck Pond at today's Deering Park], the garbage and other waste, human and from tan yards, have produced a pestilential slough and an intolerable nuisance."[37]

The following year, Chief Engineer Goodwin hired a worker to monitor the Green Street sewer that emptied into the millpond above Deering Bridge. Goodwin wrote that in addition to his daily labor of cleaning the drains, the employee "ha[d] buried below the high tide water mark, 4 hogs, 50 dogs, 101 cats, 35 hens, and 11 heaps of rotten meats and fish, which but for disposal would have done their pestilential work and their stench would have been attributed to the sewers."[38]

Offensive sewers rebuked Portland's claim to health and beauty. But Goodwin, a highly competent professional in the tradition that historian Jon Teaford has described as prevailing among many late nineteenth-century city engineers, served Portland as a distinguished civil servant, one committed to making it a more healthy city. Butler observed in his 1877 annual message that "before the introduction of sewerage and Sebago water, the [Portland] death rate in some years rose to as high as twenty-eight [per] thousand inhabitants." Statistics, explained Butler, show that "about fifteen to a thousand is about the lowest death rate obtainable in cities as an average. Portland, from its natural, healthful situation and means of good drainage and its immunity from pestilence and epidemics, ought to be one of the most salubrious cities in the World." Butler found the city ordinances with few exceptions "ample." The Back Cove posed a problem, as did a "few overcrowded tenements and unpoliced privy vaults." Otherwise, Portland moved toward its goal: World's Healthiest City.[39]

A theme emerged: Portland was not only a beautiful but also a healthy city of elms, parks, and good (if not yet perfected) drainage. Indeed, an important step had been taken in August 1867, when a committee of City Council reported in favor of purchasing for $83,000 the fire-devoured tract bounded by Congress, Franklin, Federal, and Pearl Streets (once densely developed with flimsy wooden structures) and to convert it into Lincoln Park. The parcel adjoined the destroyed but soon-to-be-rebuilt City Hall. Lincoln Park would double as a fire break and as a garden for strolling and enjoying the fresh Maine air. As its first act toward creating this new urban landscape, Portland created a Department of Parks and voted an additional $15,000 for the construction of a decorative iron fence and stone work to adorn the new parkland.[40]

Considerations of health and urban beautification also motivated the decision to replant the many destroyed elm trees that had graced and shaded city streets and had earned Portland the name Forest City. Portland also planned to "carry the forest" into the West End and into the new Parkside neighborhood, which in the wake of the fire now arose between Cumberland and Portland Streets, west of State Street and at the edge of Deering Woods.[41]

At the promontory of Bramhall Hill, where the West End culminated in the Western Promenade with its Fore River and White Mountain views, stood John Bundy Brown's mansion surrounded by a large wooded estate. The estate, with its garden-fronted Victorian mansion facing the promenade, port cochère, and stables, occupied eleven impeccably landscaped acres. It was the J. B. Brown and Sons Company that had built the fabulous Falmouth Hotel, and it was the very same company that now proceeded to subdivide its verdant but urbane West End acreage into attractive streets, including Bowdoin Street, for upscale residential development.[42]

By the late 1870s and early 1880s, the West End, the area adjoining Western Cemetery, the Western Promenade, the Brown estate, and such fashionable, upper-class and upper-middle-class streets as Vaughn, Chadwick, Neal, Bowdoin, and Thomas, had become the Main Line or Gold Coast of Portland, lined with the richly ornamented Italianate and Queen Anne homes of Israel

Washburn, Charles Chapman, George True, T. C. Hersey, the artist Harry Brown, and architect John Calvin Stevens.[43] It was in the late 1870s that Mayor Butler further enhanced the fashionability of the West End. Butler lamented in 1878 that the two promenades had now "an uncared for and neglected appearance entirely unworthy of their natural beauties as if unappreciated by the city they so much adorn. Nature bountifully has done her part," he wrote; "*let cultivation and art do theirs* [original emphasis]." Butler suggested that the city make "a small appropriation," and that the landscape architect of New York City's Central Park, Frederick Law Olmsted, be consulted.[44]

The western end of the city received the lion's share of the modest, $1,000 appropriation. Aided not by Olmsted but by Olmsted's former partner and New York landscape architect Calvert Vaux, and possibly by relief labor, the city extensively graded the Western Promenade, planted flowerbeds, shrubs, and thirty elm and maple trees, producing the fashionable spaces that drew Gilded Age strollers and carriages in the spring, summer, and fall and sleighs in Portland's harsh, snowy winter season (fig. 10).

Hard Times

Behind Mayor Butler's concern for penuriousness and his emphasis on a small appropriation for parks and promenades lay a singular harsh truth: Portland in the 1870s endured hard economic times that lasted for the duration of the decade. Early in 1872 John Mead Gould mourned that "business is quite dull of late. Portland is wilting. There is no shipbuilding and no commerce except what little the British steamers do. . . . We rarely see a ship in the harbor now. Hardly any vessels of the immense West Indian fleet. . . . We are so behind-hand at manufacturing that we can hardly ever get on an even footing with other towns now."[45] A few years later in reviewing the events of 1876, including his trip to the Philadelphia Centennial Exhibition, Gould remarked that "tramps abound in great numbers; we never knew them as a great half-organized class of good for nothings before last winter."[46]

The cost of the fire clearly contributed to the city's growing plight; but so did the worldwide Panic of 1873 (brought on by the collapse of Barings Bank in London, the failure of Jay Cooke's American financial empire, and the ensuing national economic plunge).[47] Many Portlanders blamed the city's exuberant monetary backing of railroad ventures for the hard times, specifically its overindulgence in underwriting with city bonds the building of the Portland and

10. The Western Promenade, ca. 1900. Portland obtained the land in 1829, and in 1937 laid out a carriage drive there. Ultimately, the "Prom" became part of the Olmsted firm's plan for Portland's Emerald Necklace. Courtesy of Maine Historic Preservation Commission.

Ogdenburg (P&O) and the Portland and Rochester (P&R) roads. In 1867 the Maine state legislature had passed legislation enabling cities to raise money by taxation or bonds (up to 5 percent of the city's assessed valuation) for the purpose of underwriting the construction of railroads. Portland acted quickly by approving in 1867 a $700,000 loan to the P&R, secured by a mortgage on the line. Before 1865, Portland had known the P&R as the Portland and Cumberland (a poor project), at which time bank foreclosure forced its reorganization. It finally opened as the P&R in 1875, linking Portland to New York City and western markets.

The P&O in 1868 had promised Portland a direct route to the scenic White Mountains, thence to the American West. The city voted to invest $750,000 in the venture, and to coax even more money from Portland, the P&O in 1872 offered free rides to North Conway, New Hampshire. One customer who accepted, John Mead Gould, remained skeptical. On the eve of the June 1872 vote, he wrote that the loan would probably be approved because "those opposed . . . feel as if they will be spotted and lose something by their opposition. . . . Principally, the road will do its best with the riff-raff." By "riff-raff," Gould of course meant the Irish, who saw jobs at stake in the vote. And, as Gould predicted, the loan passed, making Portland owner of 7,143 shares in what many saw as a dubious enterprise.[48]

The P&O vote took place just one year before the Panic of 1873, a national event that had sent tremors rolling through the city's business community. Although Gould insisted that solid, conservative business institutions like his Exchange Street National Traders (formerly Manufacturers and Traders) Bank had weathered the crisis, other firms such as the Kimball Carriage Company, where Gould had worked for a number of years as a part-time bookkeeper, failed, as did the P&R, which in 1873 reneged on its interest payment, forcing the city to lend the line more money to keep it afloat. Soon thereafter, the P&O slumped into receivership. And in 1875 the Bank of Portland, a venerable institution, crashed.[49]

Frances Fessenden, mayor during the Centennial Year, 1876, preferred "depression" rather than "panic" to describe the dismal economic climate but acknowledged "the great increase in expenses which must be met [by the city] this year . . . owing to the failure of railroads constructed upon city credit to meet the maturing interest of city bonds." Fessenden added that the pain of the "depression" had fallen "on every kind of business and labor."[50] In 1878, Mayor Moses Butler shared both Gould's and Fessenden's diagnosis that despite the fall of the house of Cooke, the blame for "hard times" lay with "the reckless financial management of large railroads and the political influence of railroads in general." Like Butler, Gould observed powerful railroad interests behind the panic, decrying in particular the excessive political influence of the Boston and Maine, the Grand Trunk, and the Portland and Ogdenburg.[51] But Butler was unsparing in his indictment of civic imprudence for backing railroad ventures. The "chief evil," he wrote, "is that modern [state] legislation has clothed municipalities with powers foreign to their nature. . . . [It is] most pernicious legislation . . . which authorizes a majority, however large, of a municipality to vote away the money of a minority for extra-municipal enterprises of doubtful issue. . . . Our city ought not be the owner of the Portland and Ogdenburg Road now in receivership."[52]

Past railroad extravagances notwithstanding, in the face of economic hardship Portland's mayors in unison joined the city business community in preaching economy and retrenchment. Economy! Economy! Economy! Indeed, the whole drama of the Panic of 1873 and the enduring economic crisis of the 1870s played out against the backdrop of the so-called Greenback Controversy. During the Civil War, to help pay for the conflict, Congress had issued unsecured paper currency (greenbacks). After the war, New England Republican conservatives like Portland's William Pitt Fessenden immediately called for withdrawing that paper currency and for the "resumption of specie payment." Moses Butler referred to the issue in his 1877 mayoral address when he observed that "the dollar whether in gold, silver, or paper, cannot be acquired without work, or retained without prudence and frugality. In view of the present shrinkage of value," he continued, "the stopping of the wheels of industry, the distrust in all channels of business . . . [one would be bold to] predict [any] recovery or restoration of business prosperity in the present municipal year."[53]

Fessenden, Butler, Gould, John B. Brown, and James P. Baxter, plus Portland's Mayor George Walker in 1879, constituted a solid phalanx of conservative Republicans who, though once enraptured by Poor's prewar vision of Maine and northern New England as a railroad-armored economic bastion, ideologically abjured risk in favor of staid, biblically grounded, sound (hard) money principals. Walker told Portlanders in 1879 that "the people demand and justice requires that you (city council) should exercise economy in every department."[54]

Portland's urban economy, as Elwell pointed out, though buffeted, had in essence changed little since the 1850s, the Civil War, and the 1866 fire. The city remained a trading or entrepôt economy with a modest mix of manufacturing. It still boasted a sizable fleet; Portland shipowners had regularly registered their vessels and in 1871 enrolled in the city fleet 20 large, three- and four-masted, square-rigged ships, 49 barks, 56 brigs, and 114 schooners. The principal owners of Portland tonnage were S. C. Blanchard, J. S. Winslow, and Charles P. Ingraham. Those many vessels plying the eastern coast (though now less frequently West Indian waters) kept Portland active in the carrying trade, despite the decline in shipbuilding. Ships still arrived and cleared the Port of Portland throughout the late nineteenth century, but the Panic of 1873 took its toll. During the hard times, John Mead Gould—who regularly visited the harbor on Sunday mornings seeking to escort drunken tars back to God by leading them to services at his Fore and Exchange Streets Bethel Church—reported fewer and fewer ships in the harbor.[55]

Some Portlanders, like Mayor Benjamin Kingsbury Jr. (1870–1872), urged manufacturing, but such pleas aside—and despite the creation of a Board of Manufacturing and the distribution of a circular lauding Portland's unique advantages for manufacturing—few new manufacturers were attracted—not surprising, considering the dull business climate of the 1870s.[56]

Portland's business leadership, the core of the city's Board of Trade, engaged largely in the wholesaling of dry goods. Such wholesale houses as Deering, Milliken and Company kept large warehouse stocks of duck, grain bags, oil cloth, and carpets, sold by Deering and Milliken salesmen in the Canada, Maritimes, and New York markets. From Richardson's Wharf, Twitchell, Champlin and Company did a brisk wholesale business in beef, coffee, roasted peanuts, tobacco, soap, stockings, and canned goods in New York, Boston, and all of Maine.

As in the past, many Portland manufactories catered to the city's railroad and maritime enterprises—not only the Portland Company but also the Portland Rolling Mills, which specialized in rails; A. E. Stevens (on the Atlantic Wharf), which supplied goods for both railroads and shipbuilders; and the Thomas Laughlin Company (founded in 1836), a marine hardware producer that specialized in galvanized anchors and block tackle. Laughlin had clients in Russia, England, and other European nations as well as the United States. But Portland boosters also tirelessly stressed the diversity of the city's small industrial base. Curtis and Sons, with its workforce of 100 (mainly women), produced spruce chewing gum, which was sold as far away as Mexico and Hawaii. Portland's Allen Company employed 250 women making boys' clothing, which company salesmen sold in towns and villages all along the Grand Trunk line. Star Matches lit gas stoves and cigars nationwide. John T. Winslow's Portland Stoneware Company supplied American towns and cities with drainpipe, firebrick, and other kiln produced goods, including giant vases.[57]

Their grip on certain niche markets aside, all these firms were relatively small, owned individually or in partnership, and modestly capitalized compared with firms like Philadelphia's Disston Saw, or Morrill Meats and McCormick Reaper Works in Chicago, or Carnegie Steel mills or the Heinz Pickle factory in Pittsburgh. To exploit growing national markets, these larger firms were integrated vertically or horizontally. When capital dried up in Pittsburgh and New York in the 1870s, Carnegie personally pounded on the doors of European banking houses.[58]

But in Portland, much of the city's vibrant pre–Civil War entrepreneurial energy seemed drained by the mid-1870s, especially in the wake of the Panic of 1873 and then after 1874 when the Grand Trunk Railroad switched from broad gauge to standard gauge, signaling the denouement of Portland's bid to eclipse Boston as the Gateway to Europe. John Bundy Brown before the war had pioneered the manufacture of brown sugar, while also investing heavily in John A. Poor's railroad schemes. Brown's Portland Sugar Company loomed nationally, and his large city pier infrastructure enabled him to convey annually thousands of hogsheads of West Indian molasses aboard ships like the *Matanzas* to his Portland docks and thence to his giant York Street refinery. After the 1866 fire, Brown had rebuilt his refinery, and experimented with beet sugar, but only a few years later, in 1872, he sold Portland Sugar for $84,752, a fraction of the cost of rebuilding. After that, he turned his energies to J. B. Brown and Sons, his real estate and private banking firm, through which for some time he had been converting his sugar profits into Portland Company bonds, Atlantic and St. Lawrence shares, gold, and real estate. By 1867–1868, as his ledgers testify, fewer and fewer of Brown's transactions involved sugar; more and more were investments in his Bramhall Hill mansion and the rebuilding of his Middle Street properties, especially the Falmouth Hotel. J. B. Brown and Sons' decision to focus on Portland real estate rather than sugar refining underscored the city's shift away not only from its historic West Indian trade but also from heavy manufacturing. Although a smaller sugar refinery remained for a while in the city, after Brown's sugarhouse disappeared, only the Portland Company survived as a large-scale manufactory, and it supported the city's vital railroad link to Canada and Portland's all-important winter grain business.[59]

Real estate, especially luxury real estate, attracted many Portlanders whose wealth had once flowed into shipbuilding and trade ventures with the South and the West Indies. Brown's opulent Falmouth Hotel, like the Brown Block and his mansion, reflected Portland's business elites' deep attachment to their city. Whereas Carnegie generously bestowed colleges, libraries, and a natural history museum on Pittsburgh, the steel magnate spent little time in smoky Pittsburgh, preferring the luxury of New York or his castle in Scotland. John Bundy Brown, however, rarely left the Forest City. He counted his civic engagement in the great buildings adorning Portland's cityscape and bearing his stamp: the Brown block, the Falmouth, and Bramhall Hill. And although he sat on many boards of directors, he never formally entered politics. By contrast, James Phinney Baxter, who succeeded Brown as the city's prince of enterprise, regularly dabbled in city politics. And Baxter was hardly alone. Charles H. Randall, George P. Wescott, John W. Deering, and Charles J. Chapman all came from the world of business, and each one served as city mayor. Baxter had first made a fortune in canned lobster. During the Civil War, his Portland

Packing Company had supplied canned corn to the Union Army, another testimonial to the momentary boost that the war had given the Forest City's economy. After the war, taking advantage of Portland's excellent rail and steamship connections, Baxter made his Portland Packing Company—headquartered in the city but with scattered plants—into one of the world's leading canneries, with agents in all the major European and American cities (fig. 11). Like Brown, Baxter adored Portland. He traveled extensively, drumming up business in Boston, New York, Chicago, Saint Louis, San Francisco, and other cities. He also toured for pleasure, sometimes taking his entire large family with him for a month in the western United States, or five months in Europe and the Middle East. Yet his heart and his home remained in Portland, especially his summer home on Macworth Island in Casco Bay, just a rowboat ride away from the Union Pier. Baxter devoted himself to the city and to its history and its welfare. He researched and wrote both Portland and Maine history, spent six years as mayor of Portland, and among his many philanthropic gestures he underwrote the building of the city's beautiful public library on Congress Street.[60]

Baxter exemplified the tradition of elite civic involvement witnessed in the lives of many Portland business and professional people. He served not only as mayor but also as a member of the Board of Trade and a host of charitable committees, as well as president of the Maine Historical Society. By 1880, with the hard times somewhat in retreat, many of these civic-minded Yankees, Baxter for one, joined Elwell in seeing Portland's future not necessarily in expanded manufacturing but in building upon its "unequaled facilities and attractions—having the seashore at its feet, the mountains at its back, bay islands and inland lakes on either hand." For Elwell and Baxter, the railroads—the Grand Trunk, the Boston and Maine, the Portland and Ogdenburg—economic problems notwithstanding, "open[ed] new routes of pleasure travel." They confirmed Portland's proper place as a gateway to vacationland, a theme that would thenceforth boldly resonate in the city's promotional literature.[61]

Enhancing the city's attractiveness, beauty now competed with business expansion as Portland's mission. Reflecting much later on the Forest City's nineteenth century past, Baxter mused that "while Portland is well situated for many kinds of manufacturing industries, requiring small plants, it can never become a large manufacturing center. A commercial and residential city, however, is the best kind of city and this is what Portland is to be. Hence," he wrote, "to extend her commerce and to make her attractive to residents . . . [must] be

11. James Phinney Baxter, ca. 1896. Prominent canned corn and canned lobster entrepreneur, Baxter served six terms as mayor of Portland and was an avid historian and distinguished benefactor of the city. Courtesy of Maine Historical Society.

the aim of the citizens, . . . by beautifully adorning streets, and improving her park system."[62]

The work Baxter solicited had already begun. In 1878, as noted, at Mayor Butler's and City Engineer William Goodwin's request, New York architect and former Olmsted partner Calvert Vaux visited Portland to consult with the city's chief engineer on the promenade work. With Vaux's advice, grading, tree planting, and carriageway development proceeded at the Western Promenade; under Goodwin in 1879, similar work got under way at the Eastern Promenade, where the city laid out ten-foot wide elm-tree-lined esplanades along a forty-foot roadway. That same year, Portland acquired Deering Oaks, the oak and evergreen forest memorialized as "Deering Woods" in Longfellow's "My Lost Youth." Deering Oaks was part of the Deering farm that belonged to James Deering, the wealthy nineteenth-century Portland businessman popularly hailed as the first suburbanite. His farmhouse stood on the present site of the University of Southern Maine's Portland campus. A gentlemen farmer, James Deering chose to keep his land in a natural state as the pasture and rugged stands of oak celebrated in Longfellow's verse. Before the Civil War, City Council had authorized the mayor to offer $50,000 for the Deering and Preble forest lying between Portland Street, Green Street, and Forest Avenue, but the Deering family refused the deal. In 1871, the town of Deering was incorporated, splitting the considerable Deering acreage between two political jurisdictions and so complicating any real estate transaction. Finally, in 1879, the Deering heirs deeded their half of the 44.62-acre parcel to the city for a nominal sum, and the Preble heirs their half for $9,000. Mayor William Senter rejoiced that Portland now owned the "noble ornament of our city." Curiously, however, he dismissed the health aspect of the purchase and emphasized another facet of the nineteenth-century urban parks movement. Portland, he argued, didn't need parks "from necessity as regards health." It was surrounded by water, had broad streets, and was "well open to light and air." Rather, declared Senter, "the effect of the ownership [of Deering Woods] will be to improve the value of the surrounding land, making it desirable for a better class of buildings; removing the fear of its ever becoming an unsightly portion of the city."[63]

Nevertheless, Senter clearly saw the park as a boon to more than real estate values. In his 1880 report he indicated that planning was under way to landscape a park that "will not only be ornamental, but healthful, where our citizens will spend many pleasant hours in health-deriving exercise—and though the leaves have their time to fall, and flowers to wither, 'still may those brave old

12. Deering Oaks Park in the winter, ca. 1890. Courtesy of Maine Historic Preservation Commission.

oaks' be spared the woodman's axe and grow and thrive to show the wisdom of the purchase (fig. 12)."[64]

Portland and its Yankee merchant leadership had embraced Longfellow's vision of the city. As he prepared for bed on a wintry Portland evening in January 1881, John Mead Gould jotted in his diary that he had just learned that John Bundy Brown had fallen on the ice in front of his Bramhall Hill estate. Brown died at 5:00 o'clock in the morning of January 10, 1881. His mantle fell to James Phinney Baxter of Deering Street and idyllic Macworth Island.[65]

CHAPTER THREE

James Phinney Baxter's City, 1882–1896

Portland never became a New England mill town. Instead, by 1880, Portland—within sight of Thoreau's Maine woods, and the rugged, wave-battered, pine-tree-studded Maine coastline hallowed in Longfellow's poems and in young Winslow Homer's art—enshrined itself as the antidote to industrialism, a tree-lined, beautiful place lauded by its boosters as the "healthiest city."

South of Portland, York Harbor and the Kennebunks had for decades attracted summer visitors, and in the 1870s wealthy Philadelphia, New York, Boston, and Canadian rusticators (along with Mainers from Augusta and Lewiston) discovered Boothbay Harbor, Camden, and Bar Harbor and commenced the reshaping of Maine as a vacationland. Portland in the 1880s and 1890s increasingly capitalized on its natural and manmade beauty, its superb harbor facilities, and its excellent rail connections in order to fashion itself into the port of call: a gateway for tourists seeking Maine's salt-air breezes, the state's spectacular rockbound coastline, its mountain lakes, and its fishing and other adventures in the North Woods.

Tourists in the 1880s traveled from Philadelphia or New York to Boston and thence by steamship to Portland and from Portland by rail or steamship to Bath, Camden, Boothbay Harbor, Bar Harbor, or other down-east destinations. Hotels and seaside inns sprang up near or in Portland, and tourism became big business. Even though the city's international commerce, its Portland

Company, and its palette of small manufactories employed a sizable workforce, in the later nineteenth century tourism became a highly distinguishable part of the Portland's economy. This chapter first looks at Portland's chronically sputtering, too Canadian-dependent and railroad-mortgaged late nineteenth-century commercial economy. It next profiles the neighborhoods of the city's ethnic working class, whose lives were rarely on display to nineteenth-century summer visitors. Finally, and importantly, it examines how Portland made beauty and tourism a vital part of its economic mix and how that decision affected the landscape of the Forest City.

Is Portland Wilting?

Although Portland's economy brightened somewhat in the 1880s, the cant that the city was wilting (a vestige of the hard times of the 1870s) lingered. In October 1888, following another recession between 1884 and 1885, an introspective item in the *Board of Trade Journal*, though titled "Doing Better Now," despaired that "the trade of the port does not grow much, and there is a certain stagnation about the place which seems impossible to remove. The city looks busiest during the season of summer travel, but from its location it ought to have an active and growing trade throughout the year."[1]

It would not be until the decade of the 1890s, however, after investors from Wall Street and elsewhere had pumped dollars into Maine's rural paper mills, granite quarries, and lumber industry, and after Canada had invested new money in its Portland Grand Trunk Railroad complex, that the city's economy again blossomed. Indeed, with economic revival, Portland's population in the Gay Nineties soared 37 percent.[2] Portland shaped its late nineteenth-century boom more around trade expansion and the cultivation of beauty than around manufactures. More and more, during this late Victorian era, tourism invigorated Portland's sluggish economy in those balmy summer months when the city's income from the Canadian grain trade vanished.[3]

In truth, the basic nature of Portland's maritime economy changed very little in the wake of the dire 1870s. Conceding the post–Civil War decline in two key sectors, shipbuilding and fishing, the city in the 1880s remained a commercial port anchored by international and regional steamship service, by the carrying trade in Portland bottoms (increasingly coal, limestone, and ice), by its Grand Trunk, Maine Central, and Boston and Maine rail systems, and by its sizable and respected cadre of wholesale merchants, as well as its medley of small industries—many, like the boys' clothing and boot and shoe factories, producing for a regional market and with small company sales forces. Obvious exceptions, such as the Portland Company, the Portland Machine Works, and the Portland Foundry, existed to serve the city's maritime and railroad industry.[4]

A handful of examples highlight Portland's economic mix. Agents from George True's wholesale grain company traveled to the Maritime Provinces as well as to Vermont and New Hampshire, as did salesmen representing many other wholesale houses. Portland Packing, James Phinney Baxter's canning enterprise, boasted a national and international market penetrating both Russia and China. So did Portland Star matches. Most city companies, however, such as Portland Stoneware and Zena Thompson's carriage works and L. F. Pingree's prosthesis company, embraced fairly narrow regional markets. An 1877 Portland business publication listing almost every one of the city's leading businesses afforded a general overall picture of the Portland economy for that year; however, since it ignored the city railroad infrastructure, the picture appears somewhat distorted. From the extensive list of Portland area enterprises (mainly confined to those within the city) certain general, useful categories can be identified, including heavy industrial (Portland Company), light industrial (hats, clothing, matches, book publishing, carriage-making, and steam laundries), marine (chandleries, ship stores), fishing, hotel and other hospitality businesses, the trades and professions (including carpenters, plasterers, bricklayers, architects, civil engineers, doctors, nurses), and, last, finance (banking and brokerage houses). The list ignored many of the hotels, boardinghouses, and summer lodging houses located outside Portland in suburban Cape Elizabeth, Falmouth, and Gorham, and on the Casco Bay islands. Nevertheless, it identified 376 "leading [Portland] businesses" of which a mere six (1.6 percent) could be classified as "heavy," and seventy-seven (20 percent) as "light." Portland's wholesale and retail sector—especially dry goods merchants—made up 48 percent of its businesses; the trades and professions accounted for 14 percent; the commercial fishing industry only 1.6 percent; banking, brokerage, and insurance houses barely 8 percent. Interestingly, for booster purposes the Board of Trade often proclaimed that Portland had over 300 manufactories, but that figure encompassed the greater region that included Westbrook, Gorham, Deering, South Portland, Cumberland, and other nearby towns, an early expression of what is today called metropolitan statistical area (MSA).[5]

Nineteenth-century portraits of Portland's leading businesses therefore highlighted a commercial economy dominated by wholesale houses and light industry, not heavy manufacturing. Portland industrialism paled before the New England urban industrialization undergirding such places as Providence, Rhode Island; Manchester, New Hampshire; and Fall River, Lowell, and Worcester, Massachusetts—all of which required heavy inputs of capital scarce in the tight, gold-standard-driven national economy of the late nineteenth century. Unlike Pittsburgh's Andrew Carnegie, who shopped European cities for capital, James Phinney Baxter rarely ventured farther than Boston or New York. Moreover, Portland in this era no longer dueled for supremacy with Boston but with Halifax, guaranteeing that London capitalists in the late nineteenth century would most likely have regarded any request from Baxter to capitalize Portland industry as threatening imperial interests.[6]

Instead, Portland entrepreneurs in the 1880s found themselves shopping for local capital in a city whose business community took pride in being hyperconservative, staunchly wedded to sound money and fiscal prudence. It was a city where the valuation of taxable wealth, real and personal, barely inched forward from $30,185,000 in 1879 to just under $33,000,000 in 1885, and where Mayor John W. Deering's annual address in 1884 lamented that "our high taxes prevent many from making Portland their home."[7] Throughout the 1880s and into the 1890s, every mayor pleaded with City Council to reduce the rate of taxation. And while the Board of Trade, as historian Robert Babcock has noted, ceaselessly urged the city to encourage manufactures, reality always intruded, nudging the city back to its entrepôt roots, as it did in March 1890. Assessing "Portland's Possibilities" that year, the Board of Trade reminded readers of its *Journal* that Portland was "a natural seaport," that "Europe is 400 miles nearer Portland than New York, 200 [miles] nearer than Boston, and equidistant with St. John. Halifax is the only rival. . . . Portland is the nearest and in all ways the most available port for European shipment." If destiny would triumph, the *Journal* imagined ships from all over the world cramming Portland's harbor, and "the stretch of rolling country below the Western Promenade and reaching to the Fore River . . . becom[ing] one vast railroad yard."[8]

Every member of the city's Board of Trade realized that Portland's late nineteenth-century economy rested on two mighty pillars: first, its deep, ice-free port located at least one day closer to Europe than the larger American cities; and second, the network of railroads connecting it to Halifax, St. John,

Montreal, Quebec, Detroit, and points west, but also, Boston, New York and Philadelphia. Yet in the nineteenth century, as the preceding chapter suggested, railroads could be as much a curse as a blessing.

In 1884, in addition to the Canadian-owned Grand Trunk, the largely Boston-owned Maine Central dominated railroading in the Forest City and the state. The Maine Central—a consolidation of the Kennebec and Portland, the Saco, Portsmouth and Portland, the Penobscot and Kennebec, the Androscoggin and Kennebec, and other lines, and leased to the Boston and Maine—controlled 524 miles of track, the most in New England, and emerged as one of the nation's principal regional railroad systems. In fact, it was able to shed much of its debt, paying 6 percent interest on its bonds. Behind this latest glimmer of success, though, lay a long history of past warfare over gauges and an economic battlefield littered with bankruptcies, defaults, and reorganizations. The bitter controversy over broad versus standard gauge had pitted John Poor and Judge Preble (who saw the broad gauge as a wall against Boston competitors) against other Portland businessmen who viewed the gauge wars as patently wasteful and a barrier to good business. In 1872, the Maine legislature approved the standard gauge for the Maine Central, and by 1874 the Grand Trunk had shifted to standard gauge, creating a unified standard-gauge railroad system in New England and effectively dismantling Poor's idea of barring Boston.[9]

One of the rail lines that the Maine Central ultimately absorbed was the embattled Portland and Ogdenburg. Both the P&O and the P&R had originated as controversial railroad schemes to reduce the Forest City's dependence on the Grand Trunk and to open wider western and eastern markets to Portland merchants. In 1868 J. B. Brown, for one, had pushed the idea of building a Portland railroad through the White Mountains to Ogdenburg, Vermont, and thence west to Chicago.[10] Others deplored the scheme as of "doubtful expedience," fearing that it would trigger warfare with Montreal and the Grand Trunk. Moreover, they argued, Portland "has not the money to build such a line."[11]

In the same way promoters viewed the Portland and Rochester (formerly the Portland and Cumberland) as "an additional outlet to the Atlantic for products of the West." Portland in the 1870s had lent $700,000 in aid to both the P&O and the P&R, so by the mid-1870s the P&R ran to Worcester, Massachusetts, with connections to New York City; the P&O into Vermont, with western connections to San Francisco. Both lines faced severe economic difficulties, since both had defaulted on their bond obligations to the city, and neither generated the promised volume of business. By 1882 the Portland and Ogdenburg was in receivership, and Portland held a mortgage on the dubious road as collateral for its debt. Five years later, still under receivership, the P&O was reorganized as the smaller and more local Portland and Ogdenburg Railway.[12]

Despite setbacks, Portland railroad visionaries dreamed on. In 1883, with the nearly completed Canadian Pacific Railroad seeking a location for its Atlantic terminus, Portland imagined itself "destined to serve" in that capacity. As Mayor Charles J. Chapman phrased it, "Not only has the Canadian Pacific been completed from Minneapolis and Lake Superior to the Pacific Coast, but also into the British possessions, draining an immense territory . . . which should naturally seek an outlet through our city."[13] Portland coupled its Canadian Pacific vision with its P&O problems, imagining that a merger of the Grand Trunk and the P&O would provide the ideal facilities for the new line's grand terminus. Unfortunately but almost predictably, political opposition arose from Canadians who favored Canadian ports for Canadian railroads. The idea died.[14]

Profitable or not, in receivership or not, by the mid-1880s through the P&O, the P&R, the Maine Central, the Boston and Maine, the Europe and North America (all by 1900 part of the Maine Central System), Portland entrepreneurs could access East Coast cities such as Philadelphia and New York, as well as Chicago, Quebec, Montreal and the Maritime Provinces. Portland had become a railroad city, a fact pronounced on the urban landscape. Railroads encircled the city, following Marginal Way. The Grand Trunk occupied busy Commercial Street; its depot and terminal facilities dominated the eastern end of the city, adjoined by the red brick multi-edifice complex of the Portland Company, historically linked to the Atlantic and St. Lawrence line, which was leased to the Grand Trunk. In addition to the Grand Trunk's passenger depot and its roundhouse, blacksmith shops, freight house, coal shed, and car shops, the 144,281-square-foot Atlantic Wharf, and, of course, its giant grain elevator (to be matched in 1890 by a second leviathan), Portland's whole Grand Trunk complex covered more than three-quarters of the city's eastern waterfront, from historic India Street to Fish Point beneath the Eastern Promenade (fig. 13).[15] Nor did the city ever ignore the vital role of the Canadian-owned Grand Trunk Railroad and its importance to Portland's economy. When Congress in 1889 considered rescinding Canada's bonding privilege on the 2,250,000 barrels of Canadian flour annually shipped to Europe through Portland, the Board of Trade stormed to Washington in protest. "It is almost a prescriptive right to us, this bonded system. Any disturbance of the existing system would destroy

13. The Grand Trunk Railroad Yards, ca. 1890. Munjoy Hill and the Portland Company are visible in the background in this wintry scene. Courtesy of Maine Historical Society.

it. The whole political force of the Dominion of Canada is thrown in favor of the port of Halifax as against Portland. . . . If Congress meddles with the Canadian roads they will turn our traffic through Canada and deprive us of our business. . . . Adverse legislation would not only place an arbitrary tax upon our food but would drive the ocean steamships to Canadian ports and deprive us of this source of gain."[16]

For much of the nineteenth century the separate rail terminal facilities of the Boston and Maine and of the Portsmouth, Saco and Portland Railroads greeted visitors at the western end of Commercial Street. Then in 1888 the city opened its resplendent Union Station, a monumental, turreted, red granite Victorian pile fronted by a soaring bell tower befitting a tourist-beckoning city. "Here," announced the Board of Trade, "passengers will take divergent routes. The station is reached from all parts of Portland by horsecars and makes the city now very easy and cheap of access for passengers stopping off at Portland."[17] Indeed, by 1888 the Portland Railroad Company (formerly the Portland and Forest Avenue), with multicolored cars reflecting different routes, had extended its horse-railway system well into the West End, where the new Union Station stood on St. John Street. Congress and Middle Streets had been double-tracked, and "suburban lines" now extensively served the city's Deering section, Westbrook, Gorham, Falmouth, South Portland, and Cape Elizabeth.[18]

If Portland thrived as a railroad center, it existed as a port; the two coexisted symbiotically. As Robert Babcock has argued, however, although on the one hand the city loved and hated its railroads, held bonds and mortgages on them, vilified them editorially but honored them with magnificent terminals, on the other hand it benignly neglected its port, its economic lifeline. Simultaneously, it engaged in an endless albeit fruitless quest for a clean, light industrialism that would engage an intelligent, respectable Yankee workforce.[19]

On one very pleasant but chilly Tuesday afternoon in early September 1895, after a particularly busy day at the bank, a now middle-aged John Mead Gould strolled down Pearle, over to Exchange Street, crossed noisy Commercial, then sauntered onto Portland's Long Wharf. Gazing dreamily out over busy Casco Bay, Colonel Gould decided to count "some of the steamers that we see now-a-days." He spotted a handful: the *Tremont*, just launched with boilers produced at the Portland Company; the *Forest City*, about to be scrapped after forty years of service "with hardly a serious mishap"; the *Portland*, the *State of Maine*, and the *New Brunswick* of the International Steamboat Company; the fire department's *Foreside*; and a couple of steam-powered tugs and ferry boats. All the other vessels in Portland's busy harbor that early fall day in the late nineteenth century were sail, not steam powered. That picture soon changed.[20]

The size of the Portland fleet actually grew slightly (15 percent) during the harsh economic times of the 1870s, from 238 vessels in 1870 to 275 by 1880. Shipbuilding survived, if barely, in the East Deering and South Portland yards, and in nearby Yarmouth and Brunswick. Steamships gradually transitioned from side- and stern-wheel-models to faster and more efficient screw-propeller types.

But the profile of Portland-owned vessels changed dramatically in the last twenty years of the nineteenth century, and with that change the passing of an era that had once inspired Longfellow, Melville, Joseph Conrad, and many others. Between 1880 and 1900 the size of Portland's fleet decreased by half, from 275 vessels (not including yachts and small fishing smacks) to a modest 138. The steamships that Gould had counted constituted less than 1 percent of the 1890 fleet, but steamships made up 35 percent of the city's 1900 fleet. Now gritty coal smoke darkened and beclouded the billowing white sails that in 1850 had enchanted and inspired Longfellow. Whereas large 1,200-ton ships and 500 ton barks led Portland's 1880 fleet, only four Portland-owned ships and thirteen barks (under 1 percent) anchored in the city's Fore River port in 1900.

Over half were schooners or down-easters, mainly engaged in hauling bulky ice, coal, and limestone.[21]

With Canada's winter grain trade, twice weekly transatlantic steamship service to Liverpool, regular steamship service to Boston and New York, and the coastal carrying trade in coal, lumber, ice, and limestone, the Port of Portland in the 1880s kept busy. In addition to being ice-free and deep, Portland's Fore River offered twenty-nine wharves, most served by rail sidings, cranes, and other loading and unloading machinery. As the trajectory of Portland-owned ship tonnage and the slippage in volume of non-Canadian commerce indicated, however, ominous signs darkened the Casco Bay horizon. Robert Babcock convincingly argues that these gloomy signs persisted unaddressed. Therefore, by 1892, before the banking collapse that triggered the severe national economic depression of that year, Portland's Board of Trade, speaking of the city's maritime economy, lamented that "the business of Portland has not come up to the anticipation of her businessmen, but has been disappointing, and but a few have made any money." The Board of Trade blamed "tramp steamers" from Boston and New York for "stealing" Portland's shipping business; but the problem proved too chronic for that explanation. First, Portland never dealt with the lack of inbound cargoes which had historically contracted its commerce and siphoned off business to Boston and New York. Despite Portland's dominance in Maine, Vermont, and New Hampshire, that market proved too small to lure oceangoing commerce away from the larger coastal metropolises, especially after fast, propeller-driven steamships made Portland's geographic proximity to Europe meaningless.[22]

Portland might have, as John A. Poor had once imagined, become the center of a regional maritime trading economy, a little Hanseatic League. Here, too, it faced an awesome problem, a rising opposition from Canadian nationalists who resented both the Forest City's control over the Dominion's winter grain trade and Portland's ever covetous eye on the Canadian Pacific Railroad traffic. Urged by Canadian nationalists, asserts Babcock, Ottawa in the late nineteenth century sought as a national policy to lure Britain's "Fast Atlantic Service" steamers away from New York to ice-free Halifax, Nova Scotia, and to Saint John, New Brunswick. To make those two Canadian ports more attractive to transatlantic commerce and a reasonable alternative to Portland for Canadian-bound cargoes, Ottawa in 1895 subsidized winter steamship service and that same year invested public monies in extensive harbor improvements. At the turn of the century, Canadian nationalists intensified their lobbying for "Canadian Ports for Canadian Commerce," a slogan that boded ill for the future of the Portland-Montreal grain business.[23]

Meanwhile, signs of doom notwithstanding, Portland grew steadily more dependent upon the Canadian grain trade, which accounted in the late 1890s for the bulk of the city's exports. Portland by itself exported in 1898 a trifling 3,202 net tons of goods. Imports that year amounted to a mere 24,028 net tons. While the volume of imports and exports increased with the growing nineteenth-century prosperity, the adverse balance between imports and exports barely budged. In 1900, Portland exported $31,106,455 worth of goods, mainly Canadian wheat, but it imported goods valued at only $8,204,500. Only a small percentage of those exported goods came from Portland—machinery from the Portland Company bound for South America, apples, peas, bales of hay, lumber, cordage, and, of course, fish, salted and fresh.[24]

Portland's Board of Trade, joined by the longshoremen's union, constantly pressed Washington to keep the Fore River and Casco Bay harbor dredged, and to preserve the bonding and other tax advantages that kept the Canadian trade, which sustained the port. Then, too, in late 1888, dry goods, grocery, and other commission merchants—faced with scarce capital and high taxes—campaigned for either federal, state, or city funds to modernize the aging city piers. In 1888, Mayor Chapman pleaded in vain with Washington for federal subsidies to entice steamships to stop in Portland. Not only was Washington deaf to Chapman's plea, but, unlike those of Halifax or Saint John, there is no evidence that Portland's local officials or its politically powerful congressional delegation successfully wrung any important harbor improvements from the government.[25]

Some of Portland's aging wharves berthed the city's fishing fleet, an industry that continued to languish in the 1890s. The Board of Trade looked back longingly in 1892 to the decade of the 1870s when 500 to 1,000 mackerel smacks (many of them Portland owned) sought harbor haven during a gale. That fleet had disappeared by 1892, and most Portland fishermen concentrated on lobstering. Although diarist John Gould observed that in season, Maine smelts, flounder, and mackerel still found their way into New York's Fulton Fish Market, lobstering alone did impact the city's economy. The Board of Trade estimated in 1892 that over two million large lobsters arrived on the Portland piers, which at eight cents each added $160,000 to the city coffers. Nevertheless, the Board discounted the significance of the industry as a key sector of the economy.[26]

As they had so often before, Portland business leaders resumed their litany on behalf of increased manufacturing. But the plea seemed too mechanical and too fainthearted. Portland's manufacturing sector in the late nineteenth century had changed little from the hard times of the 1870s. According to the Census of Manufactures for the year 1880, Portland's $3,018,999 net value of product ranked it 63rd, just behind Evansville, Indiana (61st), and Erie, Pennsylvania (62nd) and also behind Utica, New York, and Scranton, Pennsylvania. In New England, Bridgeport, Connecticut, and New Bedford, Massachusetts, ranked higher. Despite increasing the net value of its industrial product to $5,085,000, Portland fell to 71st in 1890. Again, between 1880 and 1890 Portland's industrial profile had altered little. While the city continued to employ both men and women in the production of male and female clothing and in dressmaking and in millinery, the firms were very small, and the capital investment in them small as well. But these tiny dressmaking and millinery operations continued to be part of Portland's industrial economy into the twentieth century. Until driven from the scene by the automobile at the turn of the century, carriage-making firms such as Zena Thomas's, capitalized at around $50,000, employed some eighty men and produced a variety of carriages and sleighs. Portland's boot and shoe industry still performed well in 1880: several firms, such as Shaw and Gooding, employed as many as 210 men and women. The number of boot and shoe firms rose to eight in 1890 and employed well over 700 men; then, because of strikes by the Knights of Labor in the 1890s, the firms fled the city to less unionized and less hostile rural locations in Maine. Only two boot and shoe firms remained in Portland by 1910, when Portland Shoe employed 100 men and 50 women. The city had also hosted a lively printing and book publishing sector in 1880—which declined only slightly in 1890—as well as cabinet- and furniture-making, the latter comprising fifteen firms employing 162 men in 1880, which dropped to ten firms and eighteen employees in 1890.[27]

While Portland's carriage, shoe, stoneware, stove, chewing gum, and artificial limb firms provided jobs and tax ratable, it was the city's flagship foundry, marine hardware, and machinery industries, all wedded to railroading and Portland's maritime economy, that undergirded the Forest City's industrial base. Thomas S. Laughlin's huge Commercial Street marine hardware complex of three large three-story brick buildings housed an array of forges, lathes, and rolling mills. Like the Portland Company's waterfront panorama of machine shops and foundry, car, blacksmith, and boiler shops, it also dominated Portland's modest industrial landscape. These firms, like the Milliken Machine Shop in the 1890s, expanded and attempted to adapt to major late nineteenth-century capital inputs from New York and Boston financiers by boosting Maine's papermaking capacity. Milliken joined the Portland Company in producing machinery such as wood digesters; it also built pulp-screening equipment. Thomas Laughlin not only outfitted steamships but also moved into equipping yachts for the upcoming world of summer leisure.[28]

Pulp screens and digesters aside, the essential pattern of Portland's historic port-based commercial economy remained intact in 1890. Nevertheless, behind talk of emerging boom times and some innovation lurked the reality of a vanishing shipbuilding industry, a greatly reduced fishing fleet, and the diversion of shipping to New York, Philadelphia and Baltimore. Portland also fretted over persistent rumors that Halifax and St. John harbored designs on its Canadian winter grain business. And in good years and bad, like the changing seasons, with the arrival of Portland's first snowfall the somber, recurrent query arose: "What's the matter with Portland?" The editors of the *Board of Trade Journal* asked it again in October 1891, bewailing the city's failure yet to find a replacement for its lost West Indian trade. "We still have the most favorably located port and the best harbor for commerce," professed the *Journal*. "It seems to be a generally accepted opinion with our businessmen that manufactures should be encouraged so as to draw operatives and their families to settle here to help populate the city, build up waste places, and to occupy the houses and business places now comparatively unproductive. . . . The question then naturally raised is, what manufactures are best adapted to Portland?" To that rhetorical question the editors of the *Journal* readily responded: "small manufactures . . . such as demand small measures of mechanical power, as require comparatively small amounts of heavy, bulky raw materials, and as call into requisition the service of *comparatively intelligent operators* [italics added]." To attract such clean, blithe manufactures, the *Board of Trade Journal* urged a policy of "tax remission to approved enterprises."[29]

The *Journal* was, however, a voice crying in the wilderness. Less than a year later the same publication was in despair at the "disheartening apathy among our capitalists to give any encouragement to manufactures so much needed now." Such apathy left the editors querulous: the city had so much to offer; why had they not come? "As a place of residence, Portland has made good progress. New and elegant residences, stores, and public buildings have been erected, fine new streets, parks, and lawns laid out, monuments erected; . . . many wealthy tourists have come among us this past year to enjoy the unrivaled scenic beauties of our situation, . . . to enjoy the delicious climate of the city by the sea, having realized that the air . . . is about as pure and healthy as can be had." Here again was Longfellow's paean to Portland: above all, the "beautiful city by the sea."[30]

In truth, in addition to wealthy tourists, many others had come, but not all were the comparatively intelligent operators so desired by the city's Yankee business elite. Portland's largely Maine-born, Yankee-stock New Englanders lauded their Forest City for its history of affording opportunity and for its creative, energetic, civic-minded citizenry. Most of the city's business and professional community, people such as James Phinney Baxter and John Mead Gould—though energetic and civic-minded, classically educated, and devoted to Handel oratorios and Bach and Mendelssohn choral music—despised risk, worshiped the gold standard, and favored low taxes and economy in municipal affairs. Although mayors such as Francis Fessenden, George Wescott, and Charles J. Chapman feared that Portland's steep housing costs (most workers rented) discouraged skilled artisans and operatives, for most upper- and middle-class Portlanders, like the National Traders Bank teller John Mead Gould, the city proved an oasis. On his $1,800 annual income—in an age when factory operatives earned $600-$800 annually—Gould not only owned a respectable, three-story clapboard home at 167 Pearl Street—at the corner of Pearl and Oxford, one block from City Hall—but sent his sons Oliver and Theodore to Bowdoin and his daughter Annie to Mt. Holyoke College, where she studied to become a missionary. (Annie would teach in a mission in China and there die tragically—indeed, hideously—in the Boxer Rebellion.)[31]

At Work in Longfellow's City by the Sea

Until the late nineteenth century, Portland's working class—those who labored on the city's waterfront, laid railroad track, moved freight, paved the city's streets, dug its sewers, forged its anchors, and toiled in its chewing gum factories—hailed mainly from rural New England, Ireland, and Canada. Indeed, from 1870 to 1900 Portland consistently drew a large portion of its immigrant population from Canada: both French Canadians and second-generation Irish as well as British-born Canadians. Twenty-nine percent of the city's population in 1870 had been born in Canada, 45 percent in 1880, 42 percent in 1900. Unlike residents of Philadelphia, Baltimore, and New

York, few—just 1 or 2 percent, in Portland—called Germany home. English- or Welsh-born immigrants accounted for 8 to 10 percent in the 1870–1900 era; and although the Goulds and Baxters from time to time had Swedish maids, fewer than 8 percent of the city's population had emigrated from Stockholm or other Scandinavian ports. By 1900 Portland's ethnic variety had been enriched by Italian peasants, Jews fleeing Russian pogroms, and Armenians escaping the Greek slaughter. Overwhelmingly, Portland in the 1870s and 1880s harbored an ethnic population of first- and second-generation Irish.[32]

The Forest City's chronically sluggish industrial economy, void of the giant steel mills, the deep, maze of coal mines, the grisly slaughterhouses, and the oily carpet, cotton, and wool mills of Chicago, Pittsburgh, and Philadelphia, proved uninviting to that great tide of late nineteenth-century East European immigration flooding out of Italy and the collapsing Austro-Hungarian Empire. This storied "restless refuse of your teeming shores," in Emma Lazarus's words, followed a chain of personal information (from relatives and fellow villagers) to places in America (and the world) where jobs were plentiful and rewarding enough to fulfill the dream of one day returning to Calabria, Croatia, Serbia, or Herzegovina with money to purchase a speck of arable land. Portland most often failed the test.[33]

Nevertheless, beautiful Portland did afford a small niche that allowed a number of immigrants who steered a course into the city to find modest opportunity. This was especially true of the Irish. In truth, by 1870 56 percent of the population had fled places like Connaught and County Galway for a home in Portland. The Irish population increased minimally to 57 percent in 1880 before slipping to 40 percent in 1890; however, combining the foreign-born and those of foreign-born parentage shows that Portland's Irish population actually rose slightly to 58 percent in 1890 at a time when the city's foreign-born German (sixty-seven persons), and Italian (thirteen persons) population remained negligible. Next to the dominant Irish, English-speaking Canadians, and British-born residents, the only significant ethnic group in 1890 comprised the city's seventy Russian Jews and the Armenians, the first of whom settled in Portland in 1896.[34]

Deeply troubling for Portland's Yankee Protestant majority, the city's Irish created a cohesive community around strong Catholic parishes (St. Dominic's and the Cathedral of the Immaculate Conception), around loyalty to the Democratic Party, and around a host of Irish organizations. Some of these, like the Fenians, translated folk memory of past and present British brutality in

Ireland into rabid support for Irish nationalism, repeal of the Act of Union, and Irish Home Rule. Other organizations—the Hancock Democratic Club, the Cleveland Guards and Cleveland Zouaves, and the Irish American Relief Association—evidenced not only Irish ethnic cohesion but Irish endeavor to mold patrimony into political power. In the 1880s and 1890s the Irish community regularly elected members to City Council. The Irish failure to achieve any level of political hegemony in late nineteenth- and early twentieth-century Portland, however—as they did in Boston—attests to entrenched Yankee authority in Longfellow's, Brown's, Baxter's, and Gould's Portland.[35]

Still, Portland's Irish in the late nineteenth century did rule the waterfront. There, organized as the Portland Longshoremen's Benevolent Association (PLBA), they represented an emerging political force and even from time to time won important battles, much to the chagrin of the city's Yankee elite. Membership in the PLBA (whose charter forbade blacks) reached a high of 868 in 1895. The society, which became affiliated with Samuel Gompers's American Federation of Labor (AFL), not only provided social benefits for irregularly employed waterfront workers but also organized leverage against Portland employers who sought to cut labor costs, to speed up the pace of work, or to replace manpower with technology. Moreover, to regularize employment, the PLBA tirelessly fought, though in vain, to make Portland a year-round rather than only a winter port.[36]

Historically, Portland's Irish supplied brawn for the city's workforce, rather than capital or journeymen skills. John B. Brown hired Irish labor for his sugar refinery, and John Poor employed unskilled Irish labor for his Portland Company foundry. By 1900 the Portland Company listed a handful of Irish in skilled positions (such as blacksmiths) earning $15 a week or $600 annually, but only if they worked steadily—something they rarely did, given the turbulent economy. In fact, few of Portland's Irish in 1890 toiled in the skilled trades such as carriage-making or shoemaking, vocations that remained the province of Yankee Mainers and New England–born workers.[37]

Women made up an important part of the unskilled workforce. A sizable number of women worked at the Portland Match Company, sewed at the boys' clothing factory or in small millinery shops, or performed tasks in other unskilled or semiskilled industries. Unmarried Irish women ordinarily shunned factory employment and instead worked in domestic service.[38]

During most of the second half of the nineteenth century, the Irish in Portland did the hauling, digging, and other backbreaking labor, but by the late 1880s, rivals had appeared. In the 1890s it was Armenians who inherited the hard, unskilled jobs in the Portland stoneware industry, and foreign faces showed up elsewhere as well. On May 23, 1895, rushing down Exchange Street to his job at the Trader's Bank, John Mead Gould encountered a group of about 100 Italian laborers digging and dressing the roadbed for the new electric trolley lines; Portland's electric trolley service started the next day. That evening Gould bitterly scrawled in his diary that "another hundred Irishmen stood by and growled because they were not hired."[39]

Relatively small numbers of African Americans and Italian families lived in Portland in 1900, but most of the employed black or Italian heads of resident households worked as cooks, porters, or laborers for the railroad and steamship lines. A community of black cooks, Pullman porters, and redcaps employed by the Maine Central lived off St. John Street just above the Union Terminal. Other black cooks and porters who toiled aboard Portland-based steamships such as the *Portland* made their homes in the historic old African American community centered near the Abyssinian Church on Munjoy Hill. The tragic sinking of the steamship *Portland* off Cape Cod during a horrible blizzard in November 1898 devastated the city's black Munjoy Hill neighborhood: nineteen black workers perished with the ship.[40]

Portland's Working-Class Neighborhoods

In the late nineteenth century, Portland harbored three identifiable working-class neighborhoods: Gorham's Corner, Munjoy Hill, and Bayside. Only Gorham's Corner (the Irish enclave scorched in the 1866 fire but rebuilt with some brick but mainly clapboard tenements) and Munjoy Hill (unscathed in 1866, but where many of those made homeless found refuge) resembled in any way the ethnic districts found in such cities as Boston, Pittsburgh, or Philadelphia. Yankee Bayside, however, evidenced the beginnings of an ethnic influx.

Gorham's Corner was just south of Spring Street, where York, Danforth, Center, and Fore Streets converged, and where J. B. Brown's giant sugar refinery had once dominated the landscape (see fig. 5). In the 1890s it remained a working-class neighborhood, teeming with Irish families. As noted in chapter 1, since the 1820s, Portland's Yankee establishment had decried Gorham's Corner as an Irish pesthole, a nest of groggeries and hooliganism. One Sunday morning in 1872, on his usual lookout, for unchurched derelict sailors, John Mead Gould "started up through Gorham's Corners. I never saw so many villains out screaming," he wrote, "smoking and loafing, indifferent to all things. They are mostly second generation Irishmen."[41]

Time only deepened the Corner's scurrilous reputation. A dozen years later, in the mid-1880s, the neighborhood had changed little. It remained a mixed residential and industrial district, with Brown's rebuilt sugarhouse intact, bakeries, bookbinders, a planing mill, cheap hotels, and numerous boardinghouses and tenements, including some surviving and moldering 1820s- and 1830s-vintage Greek Revival–style double houses converted into three- and four-family flats. Interspersed throughout the neighborhood on tiny streets such as Cotton, Union, South, and Dunphy's Lane, and in defiance of Neal Dow's ordinances, stood hardly disguised groggeries. And here were the Feeneys, the Connollys, Delanys, Currans, and Mulhearns, large six-, seven-, and eight-person families, often extended by relatives or collateral kin, and headed by longshoremen, draymen, railroad workers, and other laborers—although in the 1880s the more frequent listing of skilled molders and boilermakers attested to modest upward mobility.[42]

Many Irish also lived on Munjoy Hill. Lower Munjoy Hill, east of India Street and the site of the city's origin, had been a Yankee stronghold and the birthplace of Henry Wadsworth Longfellow, who in 1849 commented on "the wonderful views from the eastern hill. There ought to be a hotel built here." By 1882 the Irish McGlinchy family ran a saloon on Fore Street in the shadow of the Portland Company, and the Burkes, Kenneys, Doyles, Sweeneys, and Nolans lived nearby on Adams and Newberry Streets. Many of these Irish heads of household worked as machinists, boilermakers, and patternmakers for the Portland Company. In 1882, however, despite this significant incursion of Irish into the India, Monument, Newberry, Fore, Federal, and Mountfort Street area, Munjoy Hill, including the Congress Street artery and the neighborhood around the Observatory, was still a Yankee world.[43]

Ethnic change came rapidly to Munjoy Hill in the next decade. In 1890 the neighborhood housed an ethnically diverse population. It had historically sheltered Portland's small but fairly stable population of African Americans. In the late 1860s a handful of Jews moved into the area where Hampshire Street crosses Middle, and by 1877 the neighborhood had a small synagogue. Portland's "Jewish Quarter" in 1880 supported not only a synagogue but a Hebrew Benevolent Society. Pogroms in Russia in the 1890s unleashed a flood of Jewish immigrants to America. The 1890 census showed seventy Russian-born Jews living in Portland, mostly on Munjoy Hill, many engaged in peddling. Portland Jews established the Shaarey Tphiloh Synagogue on Newberry Street in 1904, and a Young Men's Hebrew Association opened soon after. Over 1,300 Russian Jews lived in the city in 1910.[44]

Portland's Jewish population at the turn of the century lived cheek by jowl with the city's small but growing Italian community. Italians first came to Maine in significant numbers in the 1880s, brought to the state by the New York Italian Labor Company to work on the railroads and in the granite quarries. Most came from Sicily, Sardinia, Apulia, and Calabria. Their numbers, however, remained very small in Portland until after 1900.[45]

Devoid of the ethnic flavor of Gorham's Corner or Munjoy Hill, Bayside between 1880 and 1900 nevertheless bore the markings of a working-class neighborhood. Largely spared by the Fourth of July fire of 1866, thickly settled Bayside sprawled across the eastern end of the Portland peninsula east of Preble Street as it sloped northerly down from Cumberland Avenue past Lincoln and across the Portland and Rochester railroad tracks into the Back Cove. The neighborhood's modest two- and three-story clapboard housing revealed much of the distinctive character of the city's nineteenth-century Greek Revival and Italianate architectural heritage. Some plain infill triple-deckers dotted the streetscape along tree-lined Chestnut, Pearl, and other byways of Bayside. Here lived a medley of working-class families headed by seamen, shipbuilders, clerks, mechanics, mill operatives, draymen, police and firemen, and day laborers. Few of these largely working-class residents of Bayside owned real estate: 82 percent rented, and 11 percent boarded. One exception to this pattern of renting was John Mead Gould, who in the 1880s purchased a three-story clapboard, Italianate home at Pearl and Oxford Streets, just down the block from his parents' home at Pearl and Cumberland. The Goulds' pre–Civil War presence in Bayside as a solidly Yankee, Congregationalist family recalls the middle-class roots of the neighborhood, which in 1890 was only blocks from City Hall and Portland High School and a short walk from Exchange and Commercial streets.[46]

Gould, however, watched the neighborhood change—and not phlegmatically. Irish families joined the mix of renters and boarders sharing the divided space in what had once been respectable middle-class homes. By 1900, Bayside's Lancaster, Oxford, Cedar Streets and others became the center of a small but growing Armenian community, which by 1904 had its own grocery and real estate company. In 1908 it had grown to twenty-five families, most working for either Portland Stone Ware or the Portland Leather Tannery.[47]

As a bank clerk, Gould was part of Portland's and urban America's mushrooming white-collar and corporate managerial sector, stemming from the organizational restructuring of late nineteenth-century capitalism, which spawned hundreds of new job opportunities for clerks, accountants, bookkeepers, office managers, typists, and salesmen. That new white-collar class found housing in a new neighborhood, Parkside, located off Portland Street between State and Mellen Streets, platted and developed in the 1880s by the Deering family heirs as part of the agreement deeding Deering Oaks Park to the City of Portland. Here, along Grant and Sherman Streets, builders erected a number of attractive, upscale Queen Anne–style triple-deckers, each story of which was equivalent in space to a Chicago-style bungalow. Though Gorham's Corner was known for its tenements and groggeries; Bayside (according to Gould), for the noxious odors of the Back Cove; and Munjoy Hill, for the essence of the melting pot, none of the three neighborhoods matched in scale, population density, or sheer wretchedness New York City's Lower East Side, as described in Jacob Riis's *How the Other Half Lives*. Portland had none of Manhattan's notorious, fetid, six- or seven-story railroad or dumbbell tenements. Neither did it produce the teeming, largely African American slums of Chicago's South Side, or the execrable rookeries described by historian Oscar Handlin in his study of Boston's Irish South End and Fort Hill neighborhoods. Portland, indeed, advertised the fact. Portlanders lived on tree-lined streets, not in slums.[48]

Portland and the Seeds of Tourism

Travelers such as Thoreau had discovered the natural beauty of Maine and Portland long before the Civil War, when a few summer hotels had opened at places such as York Harbor, Kennebunkport, and Old Orchard Beach. The age of industrialism, urbanization, and modernization, however, gave a new impetus to tourism in Maine and, in particular, Portland. Travel before the Civil War had been unstructured, unreliable, unpretentious, and usually uncomfortable. Train passengers crowded into unheated, crude, and socially unsegregated rail cars, the rich democratically sharing the dirt and discomfort with the poor. Similarly, American hotels provided a democratic experience: under the "American Plan," all meals came with the room, and guests ate at a common table. After the Civil War, thanks to George Pullman, extra-fare cars enabled rail travelers to ride in comfort, in luxury, and socially apart from hoi polloi. European-style hotels like Brown's Falmouth featured luxurious, chandeliered dining rooms where guests paid separately for meals (see fig. 9). Thus traveling became a pleasure, not an ordeal. More important, as Portland illustrates, cities and their boards of trade came to recognize travel as a lucrative new industry, a critical epiphany for the Forest City, desperate to generate economic activity during the sluggish summer months when Canadian grain ceased flowing. As part of this industrialization of travel, argues historian Catherine Cocks, cities became commodified like soap, breakfast cereal, and a host of other consumer products. In other words, boosters constructed for their cities salable personalities to explain to the traveling public why they were worth visiting beyond just their beautiful commercial buildings and mansions or their stunning parks and boulevards.[49]

As its selling point, Portland and its Board of Trade appealed to an important phenomenon in late nineteenth-century American culture: the quest for rugged, real, authentic, natural beauty. Historians Thomas Bender and Jackson Lears have both pointed out that many middle-class, late Victorian Americans, watching the nation grow physically soft and unmanly, awash in luxury and the gadgetry of civilization, searched for real or visceral experience. Like New York City police commissioner and later American president Theodore Roosevelt, they wished to rough it, and Casco Bay with its islands, its rugged coast, its rough clapboard or cedar-shingled cottages and hotels, perched high on sheer, granite cliffs overlooking the Atlantic, offered that immediate connection to nature and real experience. Portland professed to be the antidote to an overcivilized, smoggy metropolis. Ignoring Gorham's Corner and the Portland Company, Board of Trade boosters habitually portrayed the city as clean, with but modest industry, without slums, with tree-lined streets and thoroughfares, cooling breezes, verdant parks, and unsurpassed views—a veritable part of nature itself.[50]

And in the late 1870s, with the end of the railroad gauge wars, Portland could advertise that it was more accessible than ever: travelers might leave New York City, Boston, or Philadelphia and reach Portland without transferring from one rail system to another (steamships also provided uninterrupted service). By 1890 the Boston and Maine Railroad called itself the "Great Tourist Route," and the Maine Central, the "Favorite Pleasure Route to all principal cities and summer resorts in Maine and the Maritime Provinces."[51]

Above all, as before, Portland boosters expounded upon the city's spectacular beauty and, especially, its healthfulness. In 1874 John Neal had called Portland not only one of the most beautiful "but one of the healthiest cities in the world."[52] Advertising itself as the "Gateway to Maine," Portland in the 1880s exalted its healthfulness as a summer resort: "the brightest, the cleanest, and the most attractive city in New England as the *New York Mail and Express* has called it."[53] Wrote another apostle, "Ocean breezes whisper and tired ones come eager for [Portland's] life-giving breath. . . . The loveliness and beauty of the city beckon with a thousand graceful hands."[54]

Throughout the 1880s, under William A. Goodwin, Portland labored to upgrade water delivery and its sewerage and drainage systems to deserve the accolade "healthful." It especially strove to relieve the so-called "Back Bay nuisance, and to modernize its streets and gutters." The city's decades-long battle to solve the Back Cove problem of foul odor traceable to drainage issues underscored its commitment to healthfulness. But the problem would not be rectified until the 1920s, when much of the Back Cove had been filled in to create Baxter Boulevard.[55]

Portland boosters naturally kept the Back Cove off the tourist itineraries. In fact, in 1890 the city freely and perhaps disingenuously boasted its freedom from "the noisome characteristics peculiar to most cities." It focused instead on the "health-giving sea breezes tempered by the piney, balsamic zephyrs . . . that quicken the sluggish blood and restore . . . wasted energies and give . . . exhilaration to depressed spirits . . . worn down and enervated from . . . the crowded marts of great cities or the rush and crush and irregularities of modern life."[56] Citing Portland's location aloft on a high bluff overlooking the Atlantic, the Board of Trade contended in 1890 that "no city could be more favorable to health." It called Portland "the handsomest and most picturesque city in the world," the "threshold to the great play-ground of North America . . . [situated] in the midst of island seas, mountain streams, and the sparkling, healthful, springs of Maine, the very fountain of health."[57] In an age when many urbanites still subscribed to theories linking sewer gases and miasmas to illness, the Board of Trade pressed the health resort theme as far as possible. It became a vital part of the Portland brand. "Portland for Health," proclaimed the *Journal* in 1893. "Sea vapors make the Forest City the ideal resort for the 'real cure' . . . especially in cases of insomnia."[58]

In the 1880s, Portland no longer advertised just its fine hotels, like the Falmouth and the Ottawa, but stressed the suitability of its islands and other oceanfront property for summer homes and seaside estates. The Board of Trade in 1891 reminded its readers that "many seashore estates are occupied by people of means and taste, and have upon them beautiful cottages with extensive and highly cultivated grounds." Thus, "cottages furnished or unfurnished in most excellent neighborhoods are to be leased for the season on favorable terms . . . and [businessmen coming from the great centers] will appreciate the advantages of Portland's location over that of many resorts, [for] if necessity arises, they can so quickly reach Boston, New York, Philadelphia, Albany, Chicago, and other prominent points."[59]

Many of those businessmen took the *Journal*'s advice, to the benefit of Portland's economy. Prominent city architects such as John Calvin Stevens were kept busy in the 1880s designing magnificent (now National Register–listed) shingle-style "cottages" on the Cape Elizabeth shore and especially on Cushing Island, one of the 365 idyllic little islands dotting Casco Bay. The Boston Group, a New York syndicate operating as the Cushing Island Company, purchased Cushing Island in 1883, built the Ottawa House, and secured the help of famed landscape architect Frederick Law Olmsted to lay out home lots, carriageways, and parks. During the spring of 1883, Olmsted, Sr. with his stepson John C., landscape architect and Olmsted partner Charles Eliot, and architect Francis H. Fassett toured the island. His report to the Cushing Island Company recommended homes no higher than thirty feet, of local stone, and "free of 'jig-saw or other extremities and puerile ornaments." Olmsted then helped promote the Boston Group's real estate enterprise, touting Cushing as "the finest and most picturesque locality East of New York."

It was John Calvin Stevens who from 1883 to 1910 would design most of the Cushing cottages.[60] Aided by the Boston Group and real estate tycoons such as Portland's E. A. Strout, the city during the 1880s enjoyed a real estate boom, encompassing much of the Maine coast, which extended into the 1890s. At Chicago's 1893 Columbian Exposition, the great Chicago fair, Maine's Board of World's Fair managers distributed a very popular Portland-published souvenir booklet promoting Maine's summer resorts. Nearby, the Maine Central Railroad passed out 50,000 leaflets hawking a similar message.[61] At the century's end Portland's tourist infrastructure rivaled its commercial and industrial plant. Branded as the most beautiful and most healthful city on the continent, Portland shaped its cityscape accordingly—albeit perhaps in conflict with another lingering but somewhat flagging vision of itself as a premier port on the Atlantic Coast.[62]

Although the 1880s and 1890s saw more and more summer cottages built, Portland still boasted fine hotels with good food, easily accessible by horsecar to the port and to railroad terminals. The city directory listed fifteen hotels in the mid-1870s and that number had changed little by the end of the century. Portland's Falmouth called itself not only the largest but "the most beautifully furnished and modern hotel east of Boston." Likewise, the Preble House, the St. Julian, and the Swett House on Temple Street traded on their modernity and fashionability.

American hotels long regarded themselves as homes away from home, and the American Plan, including meals in the room fee, underscored that view. Although by 1900 most hotels had switched to the European Plan, Portland's Lafayette, at the corner of Park and Congress, and the West End still clung tenaciously to the American Plan. Several hotels, the Colonial on fashionable High Street and the Chadwick near Monument Square, specialized in tourists. In fact, in 1897 the Board of Trade pleaded for more summer hotels, arguing that "Portland is the only city on the coast where one can be sure of keeping cool the whole summer." Every hotel advertised fine cuisine and by all reports (and to the consternation of an apoplectic and aging Neal Dow) equally fine cabernet sauvignon.[63]

Portland occupied the center of a vacation region. Its principal summer hotels were built off the urban peninsula on South Portland's rocky promontories or, like Cushing's Ottawa House or Peak's Island Peak House, on islands. On Prout's Neck, south of Portland in Scarborough and the home of Winslow Homer, stood the magnificent Checkley with its "broad verandas, dainty music room, pure spring water, perfect sanitation, and a reputation for the excellence of its cuisine." Prout's Neck also featured the Willows and the Jocelyn, up-to-date establishments thirty to sixty minutes away from Portland aboard the Boston and Maine. Portland also considered the 1890 Glen House, located on White Mountain, New Hampshire, and owned by Portland businessman Charles Milliken, as within its orbit, as well as the 250-room Poland Spring House (located north of Portland, in Poland Spring, Maine), owned by the Rickert family and famous for its medicinal waters.[64]

Mayor Charles J. Chapman clearly saw Portland's future as the Gateway to Vacationland and captured the vision in his exceptionally long annual address of 1887, which meticulously painted the boosters' sanitized portrait of the city—with its Gorham's Corner, Munjoy Hill, and unsightly little industrial plants deftly removed from view. Chapman devoted a key section of his address to "Portland as a Summer Resort," where he appealed for "due encouragement . . . to such projects as will bring Portland and vicinity into prominent favor as a place of summer resort. Undoubtedly there is no locality offering superior natural advantages in this respect to our own, with its wholesome summer breezes, picturesque islands, charming suburban drives, and numerous accessible points of interest. But it is our duty . . . to supplement natural attractions with the added improvements of man's art. Our islands, from their accessibility, and desirableness for summer homes, are a growing factor in the city's resources. . . . Considering the investment being made there it seems highly important that complete surveys should be had of their territory, by means of which streets can be laid out systematically, and development proceed with some regard to the laws of symmetry. . . . When we fully avail ourselves of our opportunities, we may confidently look for such an increase of summer residents as shall enliven our summer months, infusing new life into the otherwise languid trade of that season, and dotting our bay and coasts with beautiful cottages, in unmistakable token of their healthfulness and charm."[65]

That the Boston engineer George Herring was consulted on a sewer design to address the Back Cove nuisance; that in 1885, pursuant to state legislation, Portland appointed three commissioners of cemeteries and public grounds; and that in 1894 the city undertook a "careful survey" of its street system all strongly suggest that before the advent of the City Beautiful Movement and the early twentieth-century dawn of formal city planning, Portland engaged in the systematic shaping of the urban environment with the business of tourism in mind. The 1885 law empowering the mayor to appoint three commissioners who "shall have charge and control of all cemeteries, other than Evergreen Cemetery, together with the parks, promenades, squares, and other grounds, which are or may hereafter be reserved for ornamental uses, belonging to the city."[66]

Chapman chose the Honorable George Walker, Captain J. S. Winslow, and Dr. A. W. Smith to be commissioners of cemeteries and public grounds. Smith led the body—later renamed the Commission of Parks, Cemeteries, and Public Grounds—and it was he who in 1896 recalled that it had "laid out a system of improvements" which transformed Portland's public lands beyond "the crude and limited condition of [the] parks and public grounds" that existed in 1885. Portland's Board of Trade, in recognizing the commission's tenth anniversary, applauded Smith and his commissioners and, in doing so, sealed the connection between beauty and tourism. It noted that "with limited appropriations," the commission had "secur[ed] desirable additional tracts and territory for picturesque and historical preservation, and for future adornment, that have been made already beauty spots of marked attraction, not only to our citizens, but to tourists from all parts of the country."[67]

Immediately, at Chapman's behest, the commission undertook work beautifying the Western and Eastern Promenades by planting more trees and building new walls and flowerbeds. It also enhanced the attractiveness of Lincoln Park and launched major improvements to Deering Oaks, beginning with the construction of an impressive granite gateway and several rustic stone bridges. Begun in 1888, by 1896 Deering Oaks Park displayed a variety of flowering shrubs; for summer boating a beautiful and popular lake bejeweled with an ornamental spray fountain, swans, and a small but ornate Victorian duck house atop a petite island in the center of the lake; and a small zoo holding deer, bears, monkeys, peacocks, and other birds (see fig. 12).

Embellishing the tree-lined streets, establishing ornamental flower and shrubbery plantings at the two promenades, and dutifully replanting the elms lost in the 1866 fire represented an ongoing post-fire endeavor to restore Portland's reputation as the Forest City. John Neal had commented in 1874 that among the "most beautiful and characteristic features of Portland are the forest avenues; long, wide streets with large trees on both sides, over-arching the distant perspective," and Portland's late nineteenth-century city planning strove to propagate that special feature throughout.[68]

Like American cities nationwide, Portland in the 1880s and 1890s experienced a building boom, in which arose the Whitney Block, the Jose Block and the Baxter Buildings on Congress, and at Oak and Free Streets—in 1895 Maine's largest business blocks. Here, too, downtown Portland undertook to nurture its beautiful and healthful cachet. Plans for both a Victorian fountain in Lincoln Park and a Longfellow statue at Longfellow Square (by the sculptor Franklin Simmons) received popular accolades. Another scheme to demolish the old City Hall and erect a monument to the city's Civil War dead did not, at first.

Conversation about a memorial to Portland's Civil War dead had begun immediately after the war, and as earlier observed, a Monument Association had been formed that included Francis Fessenden and John Mead Gould, who proudly never missed a Grand Army of the Republic reunion. What emerged over the years was a controversial plan to demolish the old City Hall, a landmark structure, and convert historic Market Square into Monument Square, there to erect the memorial to the city's Civil War heroes. Calling the old City Hall "unsuitable for armories [or] drill halls," Mayor John Deering in 1885 heartily recommended to City Council that it approve conveying the Market Square site to the association for the Civil War monument.[69]

Franklin Simmons (who designed the bronze image of the poet for Longfellow Square) submitted one entry for the monument, a thirty-foot column with iconographic symbols at its base and topped by a statue of Our Lady of Victories. Neither the Simmons design nor the idea of demolishing City Hall won broad popular approval. Francis H. Fassett and John Calvin Stevens each submitted drawings, as did New York architects Clarence Luce and Henry Avery. Even James Phinney Baxter weighed in with a design to convert City Hall into a Greek temple which—as the Lincoln and Jefferson Memorials in Washington, D.C., do—would shelter a symbolic statue: in this case, a statue of Lady Liberty. Baxter's reconstructed City Hall and Civil War memorial would preserve relics of the war and accommodate a large public auditorium.

Sides formed, for and against the City Hall demolition and Monument Square idea. Neal Dow, Gen. Francis Fessenden, and John Mead Gould led the opposition. Dow circulated a petition opposing the demolition, and Gould wrote antimonument diatribes for the press, for which Dow and ex-Mayor King thanked him. After a noisy referendum on the issue where GAR members, aligned on both sides, screamed at one another, the Dow, Fessenden, Gould forces lost, and sculptor Franklin Simmons with his original design triumphed. The cornerstone of the monument was laid on Memorial Day 1889, and the grand edifice dedicated October 28, 1891 (fig. 14).[70]

A city that had lost so many of its sons in places such as Antietam and Gettysburg, had been burned in the French and Indian Wars and bombed in the American Revolution, had fought a naval engagement in the War of 1812, and had given the literary world a Longfellow and politics a Fessenden, a James G. Blaine, and a Thomas Reed, could proudly make its history part of its personality. The Longfellow statue, Monument Square, the Thomas Reed statue on the Western Promenade, the Cleeve statue on the Eastern Promenade, all added history as a vital element of the Portland mystique. Accordingly, in 1896 the park commission commenced placing tablets in the parks and elsewhere marking "conspicuous historical localities or objects of interest to the general public or to visiting strangers or tourists." One such tablet appeared in 1896 mounted on the pedestal of a lone Ionic column in Deering Oaks Park, atop which stood a model of a Greek Revival building. The inscription read: "Above is a Model of Market Hall. Built in 1825. From which this Column was Taken When It Was Removed From the Spot Now Occupied by the Soldiers and Sailors Monument in 1886 [*sic*]."[71]

14. Monument Square in the early 1930s. Note the trolley tracks, the automobile traffic, and the Fidelity Trust and Chapman Bank buildings, the tallest in the city. Courtesy of *Portland Press Herald* Still-Film Negative Collection, Portland Public Library Special Collections and Archives.

Significant architecture on display in the 1890s included the new Francis Fassett–designed public library, a gift of James Phinney Baxter. The city also proudly unveiled for tourists its palette of historic and architecturally distinguished homes. Here "by the sea" was "Fair Portland," a "Garden Spot" where "people live happily and contentedly," according to a *Portland Telegram* article, circa 1895, and probably penned by James Phinney Baxter himself. Baxter's encomiums applied most especially to Bramhall Hill and streets such as Deering, where he and his large family happily dwelt. Baxter unabashedly described Bramhall Hill as "the fashionable quarter . . . spared by the great fire of 1866 [which] now contains the choicest mansions as well as the newest and most elegant residences. The streets here are all shaded by stately elms and the houses surrounded by well kept gardens and lawns—not as formerly shut into seclusion by high . . . fences, but thrown open to the public view by low ornamental hedges." Deliberately or unintentionally oblivious to certain dismal parts of Gorham's Corner and Munjoy Hill, Baxter's article insisted that the "people of Portland have not yet been persuaded that it is desirable to pack a few square miles of territory with block on block . . . of five-story dwellings and eight-story stores and tenement houses, saloons, dives, and theaters and occasional churches, an area that seethes with restless, nervous, artificial, unwholesome life. No! this result has been attained elsewhere, but Portland does not aspire to this manner of prosperity."[72]

Baxter's Bramhall Hill—"Fair Portland," in his words—had been developed, as formerly noted, in the 1880s after John Bundy Brown's death. In conjunction with William A. Goodwin's extensive landscaping of the Western Promenade in the 1880s—grading, wall building, and tree and shrubbery planting—the Brown subdivision, which included Bowdoin Street, made the West End the most highly desirable neighborhood. John Calvin Stevens purchased a Bowdoin Street lot in 1884 and built a magnificent three-story, shingle-style home. In time, Bowdoin Street became itself a monument to Stevens and his architectural style, and home to prominent city lawyers such as Harry Verrill, as well as architect-engineers such as John J. Cunningham.

Fearing that the building of Union Station on St. John Street and that the subsequent appearance of an unseemly and spreading neighborhood of redcaps, Pullman porters, and other railroad workers opposite the terminal on the escarpment below the Western Promenade would obstruct the view and reduce land values on Bramhall Hill, Stevens in 1888–1889 proposed to block further expansion of the working-class neighborhood with Bramhall Park, a system of verdant, tree-lined walks and carriageways. City Council rejected Stevens's park plan as too costly but did award him the contract to build beautiful shingle-style shelters on both the Eastern and Western Promenades.[73]

Portlanders viewed their historic homes such as the Longfellow House on Congress Street, the two McLellan mansions on upper High Street, and the Italianate Villa Morse-Libby (Victorian) mansion on Danforth Street—together with their many Fassett- and Stevens-designed treasures—as tourist sites rivaling their parks, monuments, and sweeping viewscapes. In 1896 Portland considered—albeit briefly—constructing an arch spanning Congress Street at Railway Square and bearing words of welcome to city visitors. Such an arch, explained the Board of Trade, would encourage tourists to stop "if only for a day . . . to make [our] acquaintance and see [our] homes."[74]

For tourists who looked for more than historic sites, stately homes, and spectacular ocean views, Portland offered a mix of entertainments, from daily rail and steamship excursions, island clambakes, and fishing trips to yachting and yacht-racing, the latter hosted by the Portland Yacht Club located at the tip of Merchant's Wharf. Also, after 1895, the Portland Electric Railroad furnished daily trolley excursions that by 1896 included Riverton-on-the-Presumpscot. Riverton followed a national trend for urban railroad companies to build entertainment parks meant to promote lucrative suburban real estate development. New York's Coney Island, Philadelphia's Willow Grove Park, and Pittsburgh's Kennywood Park are three examples. Located at the terminus of the street railroad's Prides' Corner extension and on the banks of the Presumpscot River, Riverton's well-landscaped amusement park featured a John Calvin Stevens–designed casino, shady picnic groves, boating, tennis courts, a merry-go-round, and as part of the casino a spacious dining room, a bowling alley, and a large meeting hall with a rustic fireplace.[75]

At the turn of the century, the Maine Central Railroad, the Boston and Maine, and the International Steamship Company, among others, promoted the mystique of New England. They celebrated New England's Puritan Heritage, its manicured town commons, white-steepled churches, and white-picket-fenced homes. Maine had not only the church steeples and commons but a rugged Yankee individualism that had presumably survived intact. Travelers were advised to spend at least two days in Longfellow's "the beautiful town . . . seated by the sea." Robert Carter, author of *Along the New England Shore,* barely mentions Portland's still-busy port; instead, following Longfellow, he lauds the view of Deering Woods from Bramhall Hill, the city's many shade trees, its resurgence from the 1866 "tornado of fire," its Cleeves, its Fort Lloyal, Commodore Preble, and other history, as well as its beautiful homes and, of course, its "perpetual feast of scenic beauty." Here, exhorted the tourist-city boosters, was an urban place without the smoke, the grit, and the Homestead Strike labor violence of a Pittsburgh, or the sordid stockyards drama of Upton Sinclair's Chicago. Gorham's Corners existed, however, and beneath its cloak of beauty, Longfellow's city harbored some of the same problems troubling the rest of urban America.

CHAPTER FOUR

City Growth, City Problems, City Beautiful, 1893–1915

A tourist on a sunny day in 1890 atop the Observatory on Munjoy Hill, gazing out over sparkling, sail-studded Casco Bay, might easily have basked in the beauty of the place. Prevailing southwesterly winds whisked away the relatively little sulfurous smoke from the Portland Company foundry. Bayside alone suffered the noxious stench wafting at low tide from the Back Cove's polluted flats and emanating all day from the cove's tannery, slaughterhouse, and stoneware manufactory.

Like all late nineteenth-century American cities, Portland exhibited the growth pains attending urban industrialization. Beneath the stunning hilltop vistas lurked many of the same urban problems found in larger and more notorious cities such as Boston, Philadelphia, and even New York: housing decay, immigrant poverty, crime, insanitation, and, of course, the machinations of the political machine. For many late nineteenth-century Americans the sheer density of the big city, the clatter and clamor of its congested narrow streets, and the evidence of squalor, provoked alarm at the uncomely character and quality of modern urban life, and the impotence of politics to uplift the other half and produce a safer, more salubrious environment for the growing middle class.

Turn-of-the-century reform embodied the nation's great outrage at these distressing shortcomings of urban industrialization. It was a rancor expressed by a highly diverse segment of Americans, from businessmen like Portland's Baxter to middle-class teachers, lawyers, ministers, physicians, social workers, and other professionals, as well as clubwomen, union leaders, and even some ward politicians. Despite its modest population, 36,425 in 1890, and the unpretentiousness of its industrialism, Portland exquisitely illuminates the varied economic and aesthetic concerns of the Progressive movement as it unfolded in the late nineteenth and early twentieth centuries.

Portland had early spawned a brand of Yankee reform focused largely on the Social Gospel concern for human brotherhood and for the physical and moral well-being of the less fortunate. It also emphasized honest, efficient government in which the best men would serve the whole city, rather than the narrow, corrupt needs of a few machine-controlled ethnic wards. Finally, it reflected the civic improvement, civic art, and city beautiful side of urban reform, the urge to better the appearance and livability of the emerging metropolis. Accordingly, Portland reformers espoused aesthetic as well as social and economic reform, the efficient delivery of street, sewer, water, park, and other infrastructural services, and the adornment of the city with decorative street lamps, horse troughs, and monuments.

Undergirding Portland's largely Yankee-led reform movement lay deeper cultural undercurrents manifest in the life of James Phinney Baxter, the central actor in the drama of late nineteenth-century Portland reform (see fig. 11). Baxter, like many in the city's Yankee establishment, endeavored to restore Portland's earlier moral and creative energy. He fought to recapture the lost spirit of Portland's fabled Augustan Age when proud Yankee entrepreneurs like John Poor built railroads, when John Bundy Brown refined shiploads of West Indian molasses into sugar, when majestic Portland-built ships ruled the seas, and when a youthful Longfellow wandered Deering Woods thinking "long, long thoughts." By 1905, this reform impulse, magnified by the diverse concerns of a host of other social and political reformers, morphed into the Progressive Movement focused even more rigidly on making Portland and its government efficient. That movement—aimed at parks, street paving, sewers, and other forms of city beautification and public health—underscored the Forest City's increasing dependence on tourism as an economic driver.[1]

On a smaller urban scale, Portland harbored some examples of execrable, congested housing conditions similar in places to those found in Boston's Fort Hill and Philadelphia's Seventh Ward. Although post-fire ordinances dictated brick building construction in the downtown fire area, by 1880, weak code enforcement in the Irish Gorham's Corner area and dense residential construction in other neighborhoods peripheral to the downtown had resulted in block after block of frame, usually clapboard, one-and-a-half-, two-and-a-half-, and three-and-a-half-story gable-end structures housing three, four, or sometimes six or seven families.[2]

Indeed, most of Portland's working-class neighborhoods—Munjoy Hill, Gorham's Corner, and Bayside—consisted of two- and three-story gable-ended houses interspersed with infill triple-deckers: the much maligned New England tenements where ideally one family occupied each of three floors that included minimally a parlor, dining room, kitchen, three bedrooms, and a small rear porch. More typically in Portland, working-class families lived in two-and-a-half-story clapboard tenements where the gable end abutted the street and was accessed by a side entrance and a little door yard. These vernacular structures—mostly frame, some brick—devoid of any architectural ornamentation, abounded in Portland even on Fore Street east of the Customs House. On Munjoy Hill the addition of Queen Anne bay windows and Italianate bracketed window hoods and cornices afforded some architectural embellishment in a neighborhood that by 1914 featured a diverse mixture of Irish, Italian, and Russian Jewish families.

In densely settled Irish Gorham's Corner, along Center, Cotton, and Pleasant Streets, nineteenth-century speculators had erected three-and-a-half-story tenements, each crowded by 1900 with four and five families. Often, as on Center Street, the first floor served as a paint, carpentry, or furniture store, and the second and third story housed tenant families. Owners frequently occupied one of the three or four floors; a coal or wood stove supplied heat for both cooking and winter warmth; an outdoor, often foul, privy provided inadequate sanitary facilities.[3]

Mayor George Walker in 1879 had attested to the wretchedness of Portland housing, blaming much of the city's tuberculosis on the "poor hygienic conditions . . . [of] some of the tenements in which people live." Walker called them "abominably filthy," and he bemoaned the fact that "it is not an infrequent occurrence to find a family of six or seven living in two rooms; indeed, I have seen a family of five all packed into one bed, like so many sardines, breathing vitiated air eight or ten hours at a time."[4] Such conditions endured year after year in the congested areas of Gorham's Corner, Bayside, and Munjoy Hill, where inspectors continually found unsanitary privies, filthy cellars, dirty yards, and other unhealthy spaces.[5]

In 1905 "Mac," from the Portland Board of Trade, accompanied the city's district nurse on one of her periodic calls on "our less fortunate brothers and sisters in the great human family." Together they visited tenements where Portland's "other half" lived. Here, as Mac discovered, "families cooked, ate, and slept in the same room." These were "noisome" places, he wrote, "where running water and bath tubs are luxuries unknown." Like Mayor Walker a quarter-century earlier, Mac and the nurse in 1905 beheld lodgings "where there was not a room in the house in which lived fewer than four persons. Not a man, woman, or child could boast the exclusive use of a bed." In one filthy hovel with broken windows, these social sleuths uncovered a "Russian [woman] lying on the floor. In one corner on an old bed slept the father and four children. There was no fire and through a broken window the snow blew making a white mound on the bare floor." Mac and the nurse journeyed on through a "narrow, dirty alley, . . . through . . . dark, ill-smelling passageways, . . . up steep, dark stairways with an atmosphere sometimes stifling into crowded rooms, some with the greatest disorder, others surprisingly clean."[6]

These urban voyeurs discovered cases of grinding poverty beneath Bramhall Hill. City officials knew of it. Portlanders had endured hard times during the Panic of 1873 and again through the long depression of 1893–1896, although the latter was described as less severe in Portland than elsewhere. Other events had produced sundry hardships for city dwellers: ships lost at sea, frequent business failures, industrial accidents (especially common among the city's many railroad and maritime workers), the insecurity of old age, and widowhood. Additional economic vagaries—low and uncertain wages for longshoremen, for example—assured that poverty, especially among the city's immigrant class, remained entrenched. Carefully, meticulously, as good Victorians, the city's Board of Overseers had carefully separated the "deserving" from the "undeserving" poor. Those undeserving, tramps in particular, whose numbers rose steadily in the 1870s until state law in 1877 proscribed vagrancy under threat of imprisonment, were barred from assistance. Deserving families received either "indoor" (asylum) care or "outdoor" (home) care. Portland's outdoor poverty cases—widows, wives of the imprisoned, women deserted by their husbands, as well as the aged, sick, and unemployed—involved many Irish families. Assistance took the form of firewood and commodities such as pork, fish, rice, flour, oatmeal, sugar, and molasses. Indoor relief meant the almshouse. Before the city annexed Deering in 1898 and merged almshouses, Portland's almshouse and poor farm, together with the city's Greely Hospital for the poor and insane, were located just off Portland Street, the present-day site of Hadlock Field (the home of Portland's minor league baseball team, the Sea Dogs). In the 1880s and 1890s these facilities cared for 125 to 180 persons (including young children) whose age, health, or dire poverty rendered them homeless and desperate. The eighty-acre poor farm adjoined the almshouse and produced a hay crop, apples, pears, beets, cabbage, beans, pork, milk, eggs, and corn valued annually in the 1880s at over $5,000, and used mainly for the poorhouse and Greely Hospital residents. Almshouse inmates not only tilled the fields and harvested the crops but, for their room and board, toiled side by side with sanitation department personnel collecting city manure and garbage to fertilize the farmland and feed the pigs.

Not everyone in Portland rejoiced at the presence of a Dickensian workhouse in their midst. Its existence, together with Gorham's Corner, belied the Longfellowian idyll, but it also affronted the spirit of modern charity organizing, which stressed professionalism. An 1894 article in the *Eastern Argus* titled "The City Poor" questioned whether the almshouse was "suitable." It suggested that both the almshouse and hospital "are not in proper condition . . . and that the entire system of dealing with the poor of Portland is sadly in need of marked, if not immediate change."[7]

Mac and the district nurse were not alone in investigating the dark side of late nineteenth-century urban America. In the 1890s Jacob Riis, a Danish immigrant and Manhattan newspaper reporter, accompanied the young New York City police commissioner Theodore Roosevelt on nocturnal excursions through Gotham's foul East Side courtyards and alleys, and into dark fetid places such as Mulberry Bend and Robber's Roost. Riis discovered that vice and crime flourished there together with poverty and epidemic disease. Portland's middle class dreaded that Gorham's Corner's rookeries, like New York's, harbored so-called dangerous classes. Indeed, the city's crime statistics seemingly confirmed these fears, as did screaming headlines in Portland's yellow press, such as "WAS IT MURDER?" when Patrick H. Flaherty was found dead on Holyoke's Wharf.[8]

The Irish and other ethnic denizens of Gorham's Corner, Munjoy Hill, and Bayside starred in the city's annual crime statistics, especially those for drunk and disorderly conduct and larceny. But setting those misdemeanors aside, in harmony with the desirable tourist image purveyed by the Board of Trade, the data portray Portland as relatively safe, especially when one considers that the arrest numbers included young boys collared for playing marbles or baseball in the streets or caught throwing snowballs, sledding, or racing sleighs on a cold winter's evening. Portland experienced very few murders, only eight between 1878 and 1890. The 100 to 125 annual assaults (most the result of brawls) proved disturbing, but robberies accounted for fewer than two or three arrests each year.[9]

Moreover, Yankee fears aside, the data also indicate that Portland's Irish became either less prone to alcohol, and as a result more law-abiding, or that between 1876 and 1900 the increasing number of Irish policemen refused to make formal arrests of Irish tipplers. In fact, during those years, crime in Portland diminished slightly, and the 60 percent of Irish among the 2,440 arrested in the fiscal year 1877–1878 had dropped by 1894 to 17 percent. Meanwhile, the percentage of crime committed by Portlanders born in the United States *rose*, from 21 percent in 1877 to 68 percent in 1894. Not only had the Irish enlarged their foothold in Portland society economically and politically, but the ethnicity of those arrested reflected increasingly greater diversity by the 1890s to include Italians, Russians, Poles, Scots, Norwegians, and even Chinese.[10]

Thus, like other nineteenth-century cities, Portland suffered slums, poverty, and crime—tell-tale signs of urban industrialization—socially convulsive enough to disturb the domestic tranquillity of the Yankee middle class placidly ensconced on State and Deering Streets and on Bramhall Hill. Conservative Yankee Portland also felt the sting of labor unrest, if only mildly. Graphic verbal and visual images of the Great Railroad Strike which in 1877 paralyzed the cities of Baltimore, Pittsburgh, and Chicago, were carried in the *Evening Argus* and the *Press*. They conjured apocalyptic images of the violent Paris Commune of 1871 and reminded Portlanders of the dreaded consequences of class warfare. While railway workers in Portland remained on the whole quiescent in 1877, the July "Epidemic of Violence," as the *Argus* branded it, had negatively impacted Portland's crucial summer tourist trade. The same happened seventeen years later during the Pullman strike of 1894. According to the Board of Trade that year, all the city's resorts suffered from the "crazy warfare that has been carried out against the transportation companies without any apparent justification. . . . Here," rejoiced the Board, iterating conservative theory about the natural harmony between capital and labor, "there has been very little sympathy with lawlessness. Men have been well disposed toward their employees and have attended to their business."[11]

Portland Yankees clung to the classic belief that wage levels were the result of workers' individual contracts with employers. From their plush niches on Bramhall Hill, Yankee Portlanders observed workers enjoying "good circumstances" and not prone "to incite or encourage strikes. . . . [It is] the shiftless, indolent and lazy class," incanted the Board of Trade, "that labor with their tongues more than their hands, that demoralize or incite discontent." Portland capitalists "did not wish to depreciate the value of trade unions in promoting the best interests of fellow craftsmen, except, of course, when they interfere with the right of any person to fix a price for his own labor."[12]

Contrary to the Board of Trade's discourse, as early as 1860 Portland workers such as Irish longshoremen, plasterers, and carpenters had organized to seek shorter hours and better wages. The Knights of Labor entered Maine in 1882 and reported 27,900 members by 1887. Portland in 1890 had a Central Labor Union, which petitioned Senator Thomas Reed on several labor issues, such as efforts to prohibit the practice of blacklisting union organizers, and to overturn Maine's Conspiracy Act of 1889, which criminalized union activity.

Vigorously opposed by employer agencies such as the Portland Builders Exchange (which fought the 1890 building trades union campaign for the nine-hour day) and the Master Bakers Association (which battled the Portland Bakers and Confectionery Workers), the city's labor movement, albeit the state's largest, weakly stumbled along. The plasterers, who in 1882 had won a wage increase to three dollars a day, suffered a grievous defeat in 1900 when they struck unsuccessfully against a Builders Exchange scheme to replace a daily rate beneficial to workers with a prejudicial hourly rate. Similarly, in 1900, Portland's disunited Grand Trunk Railroad workers met defeat when they attempted to protest unfair labor practices on the Gorham-Portland line. The Amalgamated Association of Street Electric Railway Employees fared no better against the Portland Street Railway Company.[13]

Thwarted at every turn by superior business organization and wealth, and by the power of government and the courts, which held labor unions to be in restraint of trade, Portland's union movement faltered. Unionism proved countercyclical, much stronger during prosperous times, weakest during the numerous nineteenth-century economic troughs. And during much of the last twenty years of the nineteenth century, Portland's maritime economy proved lackluster, beset by periodic bank and business failures (some caused by the centralization of businesses brought about by the rise nationally of giant trusts), by a lethargic fishing and shipping industry, by a failure to upgrade port facilities, and by the Damoclean threat that Canada would cease shipping its grain through the Forest City.[14] Although Portland weathered the depression of the 1890s without the agony suffered by larger manufacturing cities, its lumber, ice, railroad, and foundry enterprises sputtered.[15]

The city's economy boomed again after 1896, however. Steamers once more crowded Portland harbor, and the city's freight sheds in 1897 were bursting with merchandise. Part of this new commercial bonanza, imports as well as exports, involved not only Canadian grain but also cargoes of pulp wood and china clay feeding the region's new papermaking industry. Fifty-four steamships departed Portland Harbor in 1897, while over a thousand railroad cars crowded the spacious new Grand Trunk yards in East Deering. In his journal for May 1, 1898, James Phinney Baxter mused that the city was finally "recovering from the long depression, and every boy was hopeful of an era of prosperity"—although, he added, in light of the war with Spain, "people are filled with apprehension of the future."[16]

The revival of Portland's maritime economy in the late nineteenth century did in fact energize the city's labor movement. Membership in the longshoremen's union peaked at 868 in 1900. That year the Central Labor Union received a charter from Samuel Gompers of the American Federation of Labor, compelling the *Evening Argus* to exclaim that "labor has never been so strongly organized in this city."[17] By 1903 the city boasted twenty-two unions with over 2,629 members. Portland's socialist-influenced union movement burgeoned in the early twentieth century, and finally notched some victories. When the Amalgamated Association of Streetcar Workers walked out in 1916, they won support among Portland's citizenry and even some local merchants, forcing the streetcar company finally to concede to the union's wage and hour demands.[18]

The Reverend Mr. Clymer of the Pine Street Methodist Church stood as something of an exception in late nineteenth-century Portland. In concert with the emerging Social Gospel movement, led nationally by Washington Gladden and Walter Rauschenbusch, Clymer viewed Portland's changing society organically. He preached that the low wages, poor housing conditions, and gnawing misery of the working class "effected [*sic*] the whole of society." Most of Clymer's comfortable Yankee neighbors like John Mead Gould, however, viewed the labor turmoil of the 1890s as part of the larger upheaval battering America. Portlanders added the labor problem to all the other urban problems unhinging the staid Yankee milieu of the past: Irish hooliganism, fetid slums, and above all the problem of the corrupt political machine, a notorious ring rooted in the bowels of Irish Gorham's Corner. These Yankee anxieties, coupled with concern about the sustainability of Portland's maritime economy, the durability of Yankee culture, and the future of respectable society, nourished a belief among many that Portland needed to be reformed.[19]

The changes transforming Longfellow's city into a petite, ethnically plural metropolis tormented Portland's Yankee establishment, which feared being swept into obscurity by the forces of modern, immigrant-fueled urbanization. Old New England families like John Mead Gould's bridled at the specter of Irish longshoremen and upstart Irish politicians such as Thomas E. Coyne and James McGlauflin, who in 1889 sat on the Portland City Council and could conceivably challenge the cultural supremacy of families rooted in the storied Puritan past. "We are fast becoming an Irish Catholic City," lamented Gould in 1893, "and soon will be unable to control anything that will unite with them."[20]

Heroic Civil War veterans like Gould, whose family life epitomized the Victorian domesticity portrayed in the literature of Henry Ward Beecher and Harriet Beecher Stowe, preserved a prewar Calvinistic moral fervor, but one bereft of the earlier faith in perfectionism. The Whiggish belief in a cyclical rise and fall of civilizations still survived, however, together with a nagging dread that political corruption was inexorably eroding the fabric of the commonweal and that the nation's overexhausted, overcivilized modern urban society lacked the moral fortitude, the manly vigor, that would enable it to cope with social decay. Not only had a rum-swilling President Ulysses S. Grant disgraced the presidency of the United States, but an uncouth, venal business class—the Daniel Drews and Jay Gould—had monopolized the great railroads and money itself, and, closer to home, the rise of the Armour and Swift meat trust imperiled the livelihood of Portland's smaller packing houses.[21] Gould's diaries documenting life in late nineteenth-century Portland chronicled his wife Amelia's constant battle with "her illness," an immobilizing "exhaustion," and his own loss of faith in the Republic, a republic eviscerated by a "political corruption engulfing both parties." His descriptions of psychic malaise, his wife's and his own, tempt the diagnosis of "neurasthenia," which historian Jackson Lears found rampant in late nineteenth-century America. With each national and local election in the 1880s and 1890s Gould prayed for the "beginning of better times in our political life as a nation. In the army," he wrote, "I always believed we should win. . . . In this battle I have had no such faith."[22]

The perceived withering of the fabric of the autonomous community provoked, in Robert Wiebe's words, a "search for order" which assumed a multitude of forms, including the buttressing of religious faith among single male newcomers to the city through the Young Men's Christian Association (YMCA); the expansion and enforcement of public education; for Gould and his comrades, the Grand Army of the Republic; and for his wife Amelia, the Daughters of the American Revolution. Stated succinctly, the quest for order to restore cohesion within and control over an increasingly fragmented society demanded societal reform. Beginning in Portland among the city's clergy, for the education and moral welfare of the poor; among middle-class women for more effective charity; and among the city's Yankee business class for a more efficient and boss-free city government, reform in urban America in general unfolded as a broad, all-encompassing movement for a more rational, scientific-bureaucratic approach to solving all urban problems. It involved not only ministers and clubwomen but physicians, teachers, lawyers, social workers, engineers, and other professionals. Portland reforms in the late nineteenth century and early twentieth century blossomed into an urban Progressivism that sought to apply the modern, scientific-bureaucratic method to making the Forest City a more useful, more efficient, and, yes, more beautiful city.

If Portland canning tycoon, diarist, historian, and artist-turned-politician James Phinney Baxter viewed government efficiency as part of a larger crusade to purge Portland of sin—especially sinful, ring-ruled government—his daughters, college-educated Emily and Madelaine, blended a deep social conscience with their knowledge of modern, scientific methods into what historian Roy Lubove called "professional altruism": that is, social work. As the headworker at Fraternity House, Portland's only settlement house in 1899, Emily's story in particular would become an integral part of the Forest City's age of reform."[23]

Fraternity House, the Social Gospel, and Portland's Age of Reform

Fraternity House opened in 1871, preceding by thirteen years the planting by several Oxford students of Toynbee Hall in the heart of East London. In Portland a group of about forty Unitarians and Universalists, responding to an appeal by city street urchins to learn to read and write, had gathered in the vestry of the Unitarian Park Street Church and founded Fraternity House. Beginning as a free evening school first located in the Preble Chapel vestry, Fraternity House moved next to small rooms on Congress Street and then, after incorporating in 1876, to Free Street before relocating to quarters on the grounds of Portland's school for the deaf. Fraternity House evolved into a settlement house modeled somewhat on Chicago's famous Hull House, founded in 1889 by Jane Addams and Ellen Gates Starr, both influenced by London's Toynbee Hall and Robert Wood's South End House in Boston. In 1895 the trustees of Fraternity House purchased the John Smith House on the fashionable corner of Spring and Oak Streets. Staffed by volunteers and exuding a Social Gospel faith in the power of human love, the brotherhood of man, and the potency of education, Fraternity House offered to Portland's young Irish, Italian, Canadian, and Jewish youth "wholesome" and elevating instruction, as well as "self improvement and healthful recreation." It furnished a warm amusement room for "innocent games . . . to attract boys and girls from the street and worse places," and a reading room with a good library and daily newspapers. In 1887, Fraternity House's roster of officers, presided over by E. C. Jordan, read like a list of Portland's Yankee illustrious—Edward Noyes, Mrs. Charles H. Kimball, Mrs. Frank Woodin, and Mr. James Phinney Baxter, who served as treasurer. Five years later the names of Mrs. Zena Thompson and Rev. John Carroll Perkins had been added to the roll of directors.[24]

In the last decade of the nineteenth century, Portland's largely voluntary altruism manifested itself in diverse ways, from the fuel, clothing, and shoes dispensed by the Portland Benevolent Society and Provident Association to the Portland Seamen's Friend Society, the Female Charitable Society, the Widow's Wood, and the Children's Christian Club (which each year treated the city's poor youth to a free holiday dinner at City Hall). Portland's many churches, High Street Congregational, for example, supported a host of charitable endeavors which grew with each major downturn in the economy: the Diet Mission, founded in the harsh 1870s, the Mary Brown Home and Samaritan Aid Society for destitute children in the 1890s. The latter leased cottages in the Deering suburbs to accommodate ten homeless boys.[25] This outpouring of uncoordinated charity could prove exasperating for some middle-class Portlanders, even those deeply involved in the city's philanthropic impulse. With business slumping in 1884, one organization after another beseeching him for cash, and his wife Hetty busily at work cutting garments for poor women, a clearly aggravated J. P. Baxter, seated at his desk on Deering Street one cold January evening, scribbled in his diary that "this constant begging is getting oppressive."[26]

Portland's High Street Congregational Church at Congress Square, like Baxter's wealthy State Street congregation, generously supported charity. But in harmony with its Yankee membership, it opposed socialism and trade unionism, chided the poor for their intemperance, and viewed the general state of society with alarm. Most Portland churches had historically migrated westward toward more affluent Bramhall Hill. As the High Street neighborhood lost residential population, church membership dwindled and, before closing in 1922, High Street Church merged with the State Street Church. State Street, however, was no more sensitive to Portland's poor than High Street had been. On State Street's fiftieth anniversary, Rev. Smith Baker of Williston Congregational Church upbraided its worshipers for the church's lack of mission to the city's poor. Evidence of a Social Gospel in Portland came mainly from Methodist clergy such as the Reverend Clymer and especially, after 1891, from the First Parish (Unitarian) Church and its Harvard Divinity School–educated assistant pastor, John Carroll Perkins. When First Parish Church's minister, Rev. Thomas Hill, died in November 1891, Perkins inherited the prestigious pulpit of what had been the Longfellows' church.

Described as a "scholar and brilliant exemplification of religious modernity . . . [and] always worth hearing in his flowing Geneva gown of black silk and velvet," Perkins reflected the influence of Boston's dynamic Unitarian, Social Gospel preacher and author, Edward Everett Hale. For his 1893 sermon before the Portland Provident Association, Perkins quoted Paul's "Letter to the Galatians" on "remembering the poor," and its insistence that "we must love God and love men." Perkins's preaching and his civil activism as a board member (and librarian) of Fraternity House, and numerous other reform organizations, expressed an intense moral zeal both for his own personal salvation and for that of the whole community that he viewed as organic and united by Christ. Perkins's activism also harkened to his enormous trust in "the human capacity for brotherhood" and his faith that evil could be vanquished and good nurtured. As a disciple of Edward Everett Hale, Perkins subscribed to Christian socialism, the vision of a coming Christian Commonwealth where youth—and he probably had in mind Emily Baxter and Fraternity House—freely and unselfishly devoted themselves to raising up the poor.

Perkins's zeal may not have inaugurated a heady Social Gospel movement in Portland; it did, however, intensify the reformist impulse there. In November 1900 the State Street's Rev. J. L. Jenkins joined High Street's Rev. Rollin T. Hack in forming the Pastors' Committee on Social Betterment to "improve social conditions, press for more suitable playgrounds, discuss shorter working hours for men and women retail workers, "and to conduct a house to house canvass to ascertain the actual conditions of the poor."[27]

A few years later, Perkins helped create the Economic Club of Portland, a group of prominent citizens, including F. H. Fassett and John Calvin Stevens, who met regularly to "discuss the great economic and political questions of the day." The next year, Perkins, as pastor of First Parish and treasurer of Fraternity House, joined in founding the Liberal Ministers Association.[28]

Fraternity House and Professional Altruism in Portland

Organized in 1871 as just one part of Portland's galaxy of charitable institutions, Fraternity House had by the 1890s evolved into the city's first and only settlement house and, with its college-educated leadership, a model of professional altruism. Moreover, it fit historian Allen Davis's description of what he called a "Spearhead for Reform." In 1896, a year after Fraternity House had purchased and moved into the Smith House at Oak and Spring Streets, the city launched a free evening school staffed by trained teachers—an action that forced Fraternity House to reconsider its historic educational mission. Staffed increasingly by women "of strong character and refinement . . . [who strove] to implant higher ideals of living in the minds of young boys and girls," Fraternity House retained its library and reading room as well as its wholesome amusement activities but discontinued traditional classes and instituted instead an expanded line of practically oriented clubs meant to uplift the city's immigrant poor by building skills. By 1912, Fraternity House offered over thirty clubs, half of them "practical or industrial" in nature, such as sewing, machine work, cooking, and hat making. Other clubs, in the settlement house tradition, elevated the mind and inculcated middle-class values, especially an appreciation of Portland's Anglophilic past. For example, the roster of club choices featured English history, English literature, poetry, music, dancing, and cooking. The Victorian Club involved "ten small boys in need of supervision who were helped to acquire the spirit of brotherhood."[29]

Increasingly, however, Fraternity House balanced the spirit of Christian brotherhood with the practical needs of managing a core of activities and meeting the social service needs of its neighborhood clients. In 1889, W. D. B. Bliss had already described Fraternity House in his authoritative *Encyclopedia of Social Reform* as a settlement house. With the hiring in 1900 of the New York–trained, albeit unpaid, Miss Ellen Barker to manage and systematize the work of the house, the agency moved forthrightly from the age of amateur philanthropy into the age of scientifically trained, professional social work. Barker's replacement, Emily Baxter, continued the new emphasis. Wellesley College–educated, Emily had been sojourning in Paris in May of 1900 when her father, James P.

Baxter, and mother, Hetty, discovered that she had converted to Catholicism. Horrified and distraught, they quickly dispatched brothers Percival and Rupert abroad to rescue their wayward daughter. Emily returned to America but never renounced her Catholic faith. By December she had found a new refuge: University Settlement in New York City's Lower East Side, the home from time to time of such distinguished Progressives as Robert Hunter, Walter Weyl, and William English Walling. A year later, in 1901, Emily joined Fraternity House as head worker. She brought to the agency a honed professionalism; her sister, Madelaine, was soon engaged in the same work at Boston's College Settlement.[30]

Convinced that the club activities, visiting nurse, counseling, and truant-hunting services of Fraternity House warranted a full-time, paid staff member, in 1903 the trustees hired Miss Ethel Clark Nutt, formerly of the Lewiston Settlement. Under Nutt, by 1907–1908 Fraternity House was part of a broad, organized, middle-class assault on Portland poverty and of the city's larger effort, launched as early as 1879, to organize charity. Founded in 1879 by J. P. Baxter, headquartered in City Hall, the city's Associated Charities (AC) listed a board of familiar Yankee elites such as State Street Church's Raymond Calkins and businessman Zenas Thompson. AC functioned as a social service exchange to streamline altruism, bureaucratically, prevent overlapping charity, and lift clients from the muck of the almshouse. All of Portland charity, public and private, from the Benevolent Association and the Home for Friendless Boys to the Overseers of the Poor, cleared requests for assistance through the Associated Charities.[31]

Protesting that it was not a charity, Fraternity House, which received many calls for help, responded with brotherly compassion to some needy but referred most cases to the AC. Fraternity House also worked closely with the Portland Civic Club, a Progressive organization concerned with making the city more attractive. Through its Tenement House Commission, the Civic Club was also deeply concerned about public health: tuberculosis, the need for urban cleanliness, public baths, and playgrounds. During the summer of 1907 the club worked tirelessly to "provide a place of amusement to which children may resort at any time . . . in which the surroundings may be attractive and with places for recreation of various kinds."[32]

Fraternity House never ignored the importance of recreation. By 1907, that concern had blossomed into a national movement for urban playgrounds, part of America's response to Frederick Froebel's gospel of creative play, which spawned kindergartens as well. The playground movement compelled Fraternity House to confront the lack of play space at its Oak and Spring Street location.

Moreover, that location seemed too distant from Gorham's Corner, the locus of need and clients for the burgeoning settlement house. That May, 1907, Fraternity House received a written offer from an "anonymous benefactor" (probably J. P. Baxter), presenting the land he owned at the heart of Gorham's Corner near the Center Street (Staples) School. The offer included a cash donation of $1,500 toward the purchase of the adjoining building. The city, explained the benefactor, "is now hiring a room on Center Street for a kindergarten, which might be greatly enlarged and transferred to the new building proposed." Fraternity House accepted the offer.[33]

The building at 52 Center Street, between Spring and Pleasant Streets, a three-and-a-half-story vernacular brick pile formerly owned by Peter Gill, had housed a tenement and store. The Staples School stood on one side of it, Cobb's Court and the benefactor's empty lot on the other. Fraternity House demolished the few moldering tenements on Cobb's Court and turned that lot into a playground. As planned, the city promptly permitted the settlement the use of the Staples School basement for indoor recreation (fig. 15).[34]

At the new Gorham's Corner location, under the leadership of Elsie Nutt, Fraternity House focused not only on urban recreation, accompanying new immigrants to the milk station and the hospital, and "going to court to rescue small boys" but also, as in the past, on teaching practical skills preparing its poor Irish but also its Polish, Jewish, and Italian neighbors to fit into the city's workforce. In 1913 some sixty young girls were learning sewing skills, while the young boys mastered shoe repair. Girls above the age of fourteen learned how to prepare for their "working husbands . . . inexpensive, wholesome dishes." Fraternity House radiated the professional settlement worker's creed: that, in Nutt's words, "social life may be so organized as to be a benefit to all who share it, [and] . . . to change the environment and conditions of life so the former may be more wholesome." In other words, it sought to bring the beauty and healthfulness of Portland into the lives of its ethnic working-class families as well as its tourist summer visitors. By 1893, in order to counter the harsh social and environmental consequences of urban industrialism, the reform agenda of people and groups such as Perkins and Fraternity House had entered the political arena.[35]

James Phinney Baxter and Progressive Era Politics in Portland

James Phinney Baxter, mayor from 1893 to 1896 and again in 1904–1905, symbolized Yankee yearning for the revival of an imagined, purified, New

15. Located in Gorham's Corner, the fraternity house was Portland's only settlement house. Image found in *Portland 1924 Re-Assessment.* Courtesy of Department of City Planning Library.

England Commonwealth, the restored "civil body politic" that undergirded much of Portland's late nineteenth-century age of reform. Baxter's post–Civil War corn and canned lobster fortune had enabled him to become a Portland civic luminary, a philanthropist, and ultimately an important reform politician. By 1893 his credentials radiated prestige: founder of Associated Charities: president of the Benevolent Association, the Maine Historical Society, and the Longfellow Statue Society; builder and benefactor of the Portland Public Library, the Baxter Building, and the Maine Historical Society Library (see fig. 11).

He was born in 1831, the son of a Gorham physician who in 1841 had moved his family to Portland. Comfortable but not rich, educated by a stern private school instructor, young James early turned from formal schooling to the world of business and of Portland dry goods merchants, first with his brother William and then as a dry goods clerk for William Atkinson and Company. Without the means for college, Baxter next traveled to Boston to study law under Rufus Choate. Choate shortly returned Baxter to Portland, however, advising his pupil to read history and the classics and to study French, Latin, and German. Baxter's self-education produced a renaissance man: a historian, poet, artist, and entrepreneur—a truly public man. With $3,000 from his father and instructions to seek a lucrative career, Baxter dabbled in the jobbing business, finally partnering with William G. Davis in canning. Rejected for military service in the Civil War (because of "my general health, which at the time, was not good"), Baxter instead laid the foundation for his fortune by entering the canned green corn business.

Already affluent in the 1870s, the canning giant and his growing family settled on Deering Street in Portland, where he built a safe and stable Victorian home, a quiet, familial haven in a frenetic, urban-industrializing world. Tragically, his first wife, Sarah, who bore him three children, died in 1872, and a year later he married Mehetable (Hetty) who bore him four more children, including Emily, Madelaine, and Percival. Baxter took great pride in his family, in his family travels, often abroad, and in his summers on Macworth Island in Casco Bay, surrounded by his wife, his children, and his dogs. He yachted on Casco Bay, spent evenings reading Jane Austen to Hetty, and every Christmas entertained poor children in his large, picturesque Victorian-style Deering Street home.[36]

A devout Congregationalist who weekly attended State Street Church, though without serving as a church officer, Baxter clung stoically to his belief in mankind's redeemability through education and through individual grit and determination—a conviction he saw nourished by organizations such as Fraternity House. But as with other virtuous Portland Yankees, while his personal fortune waxed in the post–Civil War years, his optimism about America's future waned. He subscribed to a Whiggish interpretation of America and Portland as the history of heroic men such as George Cleeves, John Adams, John Bundy Brown, and Joshua Chamberlain, who led the nation and the city toward a glorious destiny. But as in ancient Rome, in his view, luxury and excess sapped the nation's moral fiber; venality and corruption threatened the republic. Weak, immoral leaders in both political parties—Grant, Cleveland, and McKinley alike—men unduly influenced by powerful and ruthless schemers such as Jay Gould and by the rise of giant corporations such as the New York Central Railroad, Standard Oil, and the Sugar Trust debased politics and imperiled democracy.[37]

Although Baxter remained a steadfast but independent-thinking Republican, he branded uncritical partisanship as offensive and saw detestable, ring-led politics corrupting both parties. At the heart of that corruption in Portland were the railroad and the liquor interests. In collusion with corrupt, low-born city ward leaders and their property-less, immigrant minions, powerful interests such as the Portland and Ogdenburg and the Boston and Maine Railroads had unscrupulously wrested from Portland's respectable citizens one extravagant bond issue after another.

Republican ring-rule in Portland derived not only from the monstrous railroad power, and the debt burden it piled upon the state and the city, but also from rum power. Baxter imagined a whole corrupt rum-and-railroad-perverted political complex—the ring—headed in Maine by James G. Blaine who, like an octopus, possessed evil tentacles, plunging deep into City Councils. In 1889, having just lost a battle to have the Maine State House restored to Portland, Baxter wrote that "a worse despotism could hardly exist than the one which the Republican ['Blaine-led'] Party has suffered for many years." Baxter considered the state governor "a mere tool of Blaine's [ring, which] . . . for some years had its organization in every town in the state and through these organizations it ruled."[38]

According to Baxter, Blaine had, moreover, reduced Maine's Democratic Party to a "passel of lying, duplicitous knaves, effectively branded the 'Rum Party,'" because the Democratic press, the *Eastern Argus,* constantly denounced Maine's prohibition law as "unenforceable." Although as mayor of Portland he backed prohibition, Baxter too doubted the law's enforceability, and temperance ranters such as Rev. Matthew Hughes perpetually charged him with ignoring the illegal sales in Portland's hotels, drugstores, and rum shops, and excoriated Baxter's wine-imbibing Republican friends as "hypocrites."[39]

Portland Democrats like the satirist Benjamin Bunker loudly railed against the Maine Republican Party's manipulation of prohibition to benefit the Republican fold. By using revenues derived from fines to replenish Republican county treasuries, the ring "furnished bread and butter for a worthless pack of [Republican] officials." The temperance cause," wrote Bunker, "had fallen into the hands of a senseless, bigoted class, professional politicos who preach temperance from the pulpit and keep a private jug behind the bedroom door." Bunker in 1889 counted 134 places in Portland peddling "the vilest liquor that can be produced, and adding simultaneously to the Republican vote count and Republican coffers."[40]

Interestingly, Baxter assented wholeheartedly to Bunker's snide depiction of the Republican machine as "simply a well-regulated ring of politicians . . . whose appointments to office are made solely on account of political work, and not with regard to merit or efficiency."[41] Yankee reformer Baxter himself beheld corruption and inefficiency perpetuated by a spoils system that preserved mediocrity and incompetence in office, and militated against bringing to government and the commonweal the creative talent and expertise found in business.

In essence, Baxter, like fellow Portlander John Mead Gould, regarded urban politics as a righteous war pitting a well-bred and virtuous Yankee elite against the Republican "ring-controlled Democratic Wards" and the decadent rum shops. After one November election, Gould meandered past the Democratic political headquarters where "a gang of scum . . . settled around the *Argus* office this morning was a painful sight to look at. I didn't know there were as many good-for-nothings in the town."[42] Ring-rule, growled Baxter, kept his Republican political nemesis, George P. Wescott, president of the Portland and Rochester Railroad and Portland's mayor, 1873–1874, in power. In Baxter's words, Wescott typified the ring ilk, politicians "not working for the welfare of the city, but to gain a partisan advantage."[43]

Progressive reformers argued that to become modern, a complex, urban-industrial society demanded that the government assume greater responsibility for keeping order, correcting abuses, and enforcing morality. As the Mugwumps had done years earlier, reformers like Baxter pleaded that making government honest and efficient required the best men: competent, educated professionals or businessmen who transcended politics and venality. Once elected to office, public servants bore a public trust, the Progressive-minded Baxter believed. They should be "resolved to faithfully perform . . . [their] duties. . . . We [the elected]," he wrote, "are no longer members of opposing political parties, but public servants, having properly only the public welfare to serve."[44]

Mayor Baxter

Convinced that such an age of Yankee reform had dawned in Portland, Baxter tossed his hat into the political ring, running for mayor in 1893. Although a Republican in a Republican city and hailed by the *Evening Express* as "one of Portland's solid, progressive men [and] . . . identified with its best financial and industrial interests," Baxter faced a formidable opponent in the incumbent, Darius H. Ingraham, a liberal, Progressive Democrat who during his term, 1892–1893, cut taxes and ran a businesslike and strong administration. Ingraham championed the interests of the city's growing ethnic working class and represented a party which, despite Gould's and Baxter's contempt for it, periodically mustered enough voter support for victory.

Portland's ex-mayor (1873–1874) and Republican boss George P. Wescott, in fact, advised Baxter to take no chances in 1893, and he boldly if naively urged the candidate "to contribute money to influence Irish Catholic voters in [his] favor." His words shocked Baxter: "I had rather be defeated by such voters than win with them; besides I felt that there was also disposition on W[escott]'s part to lay me under obligation to him and, of course, the water company of which he is the boss." Angry at Baxter's refusal, Wescott retorted that the party needed Irish votes and had done nothing for the Irish to deserve them. He offered up the name of an Irishman for city marshal to enforce prohibition! The proposal rendered Baxter dumbfounded. "And the man is a Roman Catholic," exhorted Baxter. "I suppose an Irish Catholic marshal would have meant no interference with the rum shops, and disgrace me as mayor."[45]

On election day, March 6, 1893, Yankee Baxter anticipated "trouble in the Irish wards where rum and rapacity rule." He hardly expected the fraudulent vote count in Ward One and the announcement of his defeat. Suspecting that skulduggery had occurred, Ingraham very honorably declined the certification of election. A later investigation and trial produced Baxter's belated victory, and jail for Warren Harper, the Democratic election clerk charged with ballot tampering.[46]

Portland's new mayor brought to the city not only the reformer's zeal for an honest, efficient, ring-free government but also his Boston-honed, Frederick-Law-Olmsted-inspired vision of a park-adorned, "emerald-necklaced" Forest City. Olmsted himself had introduced Baxter to his necklace of parks interconnected with parkways that the famous landscape architect and author of New York's Central Park had designed to encircle Boston. But Baxter sought more than beauty alone for his reformed city. Using his business acumen and experience to make city government more efficient ranked high on his agenda. He was convinced that under the old regime, scoundrels like Wescott had ensconced incompetent ne'er-do-wells in key posts, especially in the Streets Department. Portland's "weak-mayor government," however, which he pledged to scrap through charter reform, gave him little power. The City Council had the authority to appoint department heads and to make budgetary and other key decisions. Since council members were elected by wards controlled by political bosses, Baxter saw city government steeped in corruption. A strong, honest mayor—the voice of the people—might circumvent some of that corruption; meanwhile, he could create expert-chaired commissions to bring such departments as Streets, Sewers, Fire, and Police under civil service rules. The city engineer, E. C. Jordan, lobbied hard for a Commission on Streets and Sewers, basing his case on his study of such commissions in Europe.[47]

Positive that economy and efficiency in government could be achieved only by separating the operations of government from politics, city councilman and shingle-style architect John Calvin Stevens in 1890 had recommended consolidating the offices of city engineer and street commissioner. Mayor Baxter successfully pursued Stevens's idea: he created a streamlined Street and Sewer Commission which forthwith built the Commercial Street sewer, installed new citywide curbing, surfaced city streets with asphalt, and widened Portland, Front, and Oak Streets.[48]

Baxter had long preached that Portland's future rested on its oceangoing commerce and aesthetic attributes, not industrialism. Moreover, he argued that luring Canadian investment—especially in the Grand Trunk Railroad and in the upgrading of the Grand Trunk's aging Portland infrastructure by building new, larger grain elevators—hinged on the deepening of the city's harbor to accommodate larger ships. Joined by the Board of Trade, Baxter lobbied Congress for a federal appropriation to have the Army Corps of Engineers in 1894 dredge a deeper harbor channel. Induced by the dredging, and by a sizable $175,000 city contribution-in-aid, the Grand Trunk in 1897 built the largest grain elevator on the East Coast of the United States: it had the capacity to store one million bushels of grain. A second giant elevator followed. "Portland Will Become a Great Grain Port," proclaimed the *Portland Press*. The giant, modern elevators that now dominated Portland's skyline handled five miles of grain cars. In the words of the general manager of the Grand Trunk Railroad, the elevators "made Portland . . . the real Atlantic terminus of the Grand Trunk, Montreal being a merely summer port open only for business four months of the year" (fig. 16).[49]

Baxter's own Spartan formal education aside, he, like all Yankee New Englanders and Progressive reformers, valued public education. In the city's public school classrooms—as at Fraternity House—Irish waifs, Jewish street peddlers, Italian and Polish youths alike absorbed not only the rudiments of math, English, and American history but also moral values and orderly behavior. Yet, pleaded Baxter, the present system of education was fitting Portland youth to enter business and the professions rather than practical, industrial careers. Manual education would solve that problem. Deeply committed to the idea, Baxter inaugurated the first manual training school in Portland and donated his mayor's salary to help support it. Blocked year after year from building a

16. Grand Trunk grain elevators. By 1890 two such giant grain elevators dominated the eastern end of Portland Commercial Street, where the Grand Trunk rail yards were located. Courtesy of Maine Historic Preservation Commission.

model manual training school by political opponents accusing him of extravagance, in 1901 he finally succeeded in getting a well-equipped training facility and in having manual education made an integral part of the Portland school system.[50] Likewise, Baxter fought for a school for the deaf, and for repairing and significantly modernizing the shabby sanitary condition of Portland schools, including the construction of a new high school.[51]

Reforming City Government

Baxter's struggle to remove the police and fire department from patronage politics and to carry out school, sanitary, and other urban reforms faced stiff political opposition from Republican politicians such as George Wescott and Charles Randall, and from what Baxter called the ring. Their opposition drew Baxter steadily toward his goal of radically restructuring city government by redrafting the city charter to transform Portland government from a weak-mayor, bicameral form into a strong-mayor system. Baxter decried the unsound and outdated charter and upbraided the city's ward system as "devised to enable dishonest politicians to thrive at the public expense." Speaking before Portland's exclusive Fraternity Club, Baxter charged that the corrupt ward system "obligated [those elected] to consider the claims of their own wards or districts . . . [rather than] those of the whole city"—a universal theme among Progressive reformers who assailed the fragmentation of ethnically rooted, ward-based, urban machine politics. A new charter for Portland would establish city government on "sound business principles."[52]

Citing for his support Charles Francis Adams, the Municipal League of Boston, and others who similarly excoriated the corruptibility and inefficiency of bicameral legislatures and weak-mayor governments, in the spring of 1896 Baxter assembled the Portland Charter Commission, chaired by John Calvin Stevens. That November, the commission published its proposed charter. Modeled on the Swiss system, it would abolish the common City Council and create a strong mayor who, like councilmen, would serve a two-year term. The empowered mayor would appoint the city marshal, the commissioner of the Public Works Department, and the fire chief. The charter also proposed reducing the size of the Board of Overseers of the Poor from fifteen to seven.[53]

Most of the press and public reaction to the charter, from ex-mayors Francis Fessenden and Charles J. Chapman and others, applauded the strong-mayor provision while expressing mixed opinions on the abolition of the common council. Portland's Catholic Church opposed the idea of a "city-wide, elected school committee."[54] City boss George P. Wescott (in Baxter's verbiage, "this slimy creature in Council"), as well as Wescott's cohorts Fagin and Isley, vehemently opposed the new charter and in early 1897 voted to carry it over to the next council. When Baxter lost the 1897 primary election, the reform charter initiative died.[55]

With charter reform dead, another issue on Baxter's progressive agenda loomed: the annexation of the Deering suburbs. Deering, which included the busy Morrill's and Woodford's Corners, had broken away from Westbrook in 1871. In Deering—as in Chicago's suburbanizing North Shore communities and in many nineteenth-century commuter suburbs elsewhere, connected to cities by rail lines—citizens coveted the lower taxes and better police, fire, and sanitation services found in an adjoining metropolis. Thus, a sizable body of Deering residents clambered aboard the Board of Trade's bandwagon arguing that an enlarged Portland would mean "more wharves, more stores, more manufacturing, more employment for wage earners, and more money for all."[56]

Baxter, who in the 1890s owned a real estate subdivision in Deering, with lots there for sale, labored assiduously for annexation. Deering residents, however, stood divided on the issue. Annexation had failed in 1890, and despite

Baxter's toils, it failed again in 1894—each time by a close vote. Deering officials knew that the public was divided but also realized that joined to Portland, they would have more monies to spend on needed improvements. Said one official, "We feel Portland's prosperity and depressions as quickly, if not more, than do the various wards and we ought to be under the same government to share the benefits that those residents have." After a third, razor-thin (753-to-717) vote, Maine's state legislature simply overrode the plebiscite and approved the Deering annexation on February 2, 1899, thus significantly expanding the size of what was now Greater Portland. Perhaps, too, the Maine legislature had one eye cocked to New York, which, through annexation in that same year, 1898, forged Manhattan, Brooklyn, Queens, the Bronx, and Staten Island into Greater New York.[57]

Baxter and the City Beautiful

While constantly hailed by Baxter and Board of Trade boosters as the "Beautiful City by the Sea," Portland still bore some telltale blemishes of nineteenth-century urban industrialization, scars denounced by municipal art and civic improvement organizations such as Portland's Civic Club. Indeed, just opposite the State Street entrance to beautiful Deering Oaks Park stood a high wooden fence, an eyesore plastered with faded and tattered advertising. Civic improvers regarded billboards as a particular bane of urban civilization. Nearby, on a narrow street, sat a cluster of unpainted wooden hovels. Many such tiny streets and courts remained unpaved, and dirt or gravel sidewalks were commonplace. And although by Pittsburgh or Providence standards, Portland boasted bright, smokeless skies, in 1896 the Back Cove's vile stench continued to offend the nostrils of resident and tourist alike. Reform mayors like Portland's Baxter sought to purge the city of all such uncomeliness. Baxter's frequent trips to Boston had familiarized him with how Olmsted and his Brookline firm had addressed both the stench from Boston's Back Bay fens and the unsightliness of the Boston Common as part of its public park system. Expanding Deering Oaks and the Eastern and Western Promenades and finally solving the pollution problem of the Back Cove topped his 1897 agenda.

Neither an engineer like William Goodwin nor an architect like Stevens, Baxter nevertheless shared the early planning profession's passion for applying forethought and reason to a systematic shaping of the urban environment. For Baxter, Boston represented a planning tour de force and a model for city building in Portland. Olmsted and Elliot had deftly woven together the Back Bay fens, sanitary drainage systems, city parks, and city roadways and waterways, linking them seamlessly to their work on the Boston Common, to produce the acclaimed "emerald necklace." In 1894, as mayor, Baxter visited Boston, where Mayor Nathan Matthews had showed him how intelligent park and sanitary planning not only benefited the health and comfort of the working masses but also increased the attractiveness of the city and the value of urban land. Park and sanitary planning led to an explosion of pricy residential development and soaring tax valuations.[58] By 1896 the park/residence synergy first indentified by development adjacent to New York's Central Park had become gospel. According to Portland's Park Commission, America's experience with parks confirmed that "civic decorations attract culture and refinement, wealth and plenty. Thousands of people establish their residence in such cities because of the added pleasure of life."[59] Baxter contended that Portland had equal if not greater possibilities for a "park system not only of great beauty, but one which, by the increase it will make in taxable property, will repay the cost of construction." He envisioned the "Breezy homes of Deering Woods" connected with Eastern and Western Promenades by arbored drives and carriageways or esplanades bordered with trees and shrubbery like those he admired in Boston. But to the north of Deering Woods, where Baxter could imagine a parkway encircling the Back Cove, he beheld "a sink of corruption," a "slimy and ill-odored waste . . . offensive to the nostril and eye [and] a menace to the health of the city."[60]

Just as Olmsted could envision Boston's foul Back Bay fens as parkland, so Baxter could imagine Portland's Back Cove sinkhole redeemed as a jewel in the city's emerald necklace, a future place of fine homes, and a key to making Portland New England's premier residential city and tourist Mecca. "Portland can never be a large manufacturing city," Baxter wrote in 1904, a point he had proclaimed earlier, in 1895, when he declared Portland to be "more beautifully situated for a residential city than any other on the Atlantic coast. . . . And [here he addressed the Board of Trade's periodic drumbeat for more manufactories] we should not desire [them]." Baxter then unwisely added the politically incorrect words that probably cost him another mayoral election in 1905: "What advantage can be derived from an ignorant foreign population which every manufacturing city attracts to it? The perils which such a population brings to a community are seen every day in the columns of our newspapers, which depict in lurid terms the anarchy, strife, and bloodshed which results from gathering together large numbers of ignorant men in towns where manufacturing enterprise predominates. No, we should not desire to make Portland a distinctly manufacturing city; indeed, we cannot. Its situation and surroundings forbid it. It must forever be a commercial and residential city, and this is the best kind of city. Its situation is unsurpassed for beauty and health and our aim should be directed especially to this end. Adorn our city with parks and statues and pleasant drives, so as to draw people here to reside."[61]

Even before his Boston trips, Baxter had taken steps to build upon Goodwin's once ambitious plans for expanding and linking Portland's park system. To capitalize on his city's beauty and on its destiny (in his mind) to be an ideal residential city, in 1894 he unveiled a series of projects aimed at acquiring additional land on the two promenades and in Deering Oaks Park, and "creating arbor ways and outlooks, such as landscape architects now so artistically fashion."[62] Backed by the Board of Trade, Baxter determined, moreover, to create a "park system of which any city of its size in the country may be proud."[63] Therefore, using economical means such as his personal and the public acquisition of small parcels, and a series of land exchanges and installment purchases, Baxter acquired the Larabee lot at the foot of High Street and other properties that extended Deering Park to the Portland and Rochester Railroad tracks and to Forest Avenue, thus enabling the city to demolish the ugly old industrial building (the Casco Tannery and the Pork Packing Company) that had long defaced a main corner of the fabled park. From the Preble, Anderson, and Boyd heirs Baxter had the city purchase three acres of land on the slopes of the Eastern Promenade, pushing Fort Allen Park with its spectacular ocean views northward and eastward to the edge of Casco Bay (fig. 17). If the city had not acquired this land, Baxter was sure cheap houses would have been built there, spoiling the views. Likewise, on the Western Promenade the city under Baxter secured ownership of land sloping from the crown of Bramhall Hill down toward St. John Street, which the city had hoped in vain to convert into a magnificent public park. In addition to these extensions of the promenades and Deering Oaks Park, Baxter oversaw considerable physical improvement to the park system, further beautifying the city. In 1894, architect Frederick Thompson designed and, with surplus lumber, the city built near the duck and skating pond a small (16 by 25 foot) but attractive stone Victorian-style waiting room with a fireplace to warm winter skaters. Over the fireplace were inscribed Longfellow's famous words: "A boy's will is the wind's will, and the thoughts of youth are long, long thoughts." A few years later, in 1902, Thompson designed impressive twenty-three-foot classical pillars for Deering Park's majestic State

17. Fort Allen Park on Eastern Promenade, ca. 1890. Note the schooners anchored offshore with Fort Gorges, Great Diamond, and Peaks Islands behind. Courtesy of Maine Historic Preservation Commission.

Street entrance. A stone bridge added additional charm to what Baxter and the city viewed as not only the "people's park" but a key tourist attraction.[64]

The Back Cove and the Olmsteds in Portland

No one questioned the stunning beauty of Portland's two promenades, or the idyllic, haunting quality of Deering Oaks. The Back Cove, however, the problematic missing gem in Goodwin's and Baxter's emerald necklace, had long been a noisome embarrassment for boosters who touted Portland as healthful. The stench insulted not only Portland but also the Town of Deering, which bordered the northern and eastern shores of the cove. Goodwin in 1884 had devised a sophisticated sewage system, yet it had failed to extinguish the foul odors. In 1890 Public Works undertook extensive filling and planting along the Back Cove shore, but the problem persisted: the putrid effluent of 20,000 residents of the city's Bayside and Munjoy Hill neighborhoods and of Back Cove industry (the tannery, slaughterhouse, Portland Stoneware, and the P&R) flushed into the tidal reentrant waters of the cove. A federal government–maintained channel kept commercial ships serving cove industry.

Soon after his 1893 inaugural, the progressive mayor Baxter had mobilized a sizable body of experts, including city and federal sanitary and hydrological engineers together with landscape architects, to study the problem. Simultaneously, he retained the esteemed New York City engineer Rudolph Herring to consult with Portland engineers Edward C. Jordan and George Fernald. Herring, Jordan, and Fernald produced a plan for an intercepting sewer to collect the vile waste which, once discharged at high tide, they hoped would be deposited beyond Tukey's Bridge and carried far out to sea.[65]

Accordingly, Baxter called upon the federal government to rebuild the Tukey's Bridge entrance to the Back Cove. Planning for such a sewer and drawbridge complex spawned the idea of using dikes to narrow the opening to the cove sufficiently that tide gates might be installed, blocking the ebb and flow of the sea water enough to keep the offensive, unsightly, and unhealthy mudflats submerged. The prospects of Tukey's Bridge and dikes as a solution to the ancient stench problem resurrected the old idea for constructing a carriageway or boulevard around the border of the Back Cove. In 1894, an enthusiastic Baxter had commissioned the Olmsted, Olmsted and Elliot firm of Brookline, Massachusetts, to prepare a report on the Back Cove as a sanitary project, one Baxter believed to be in part similar to the Boston fens. Although Frederick Law Olmsted Sr. in 1895 was already suffering from the illness that would soon permanently hospitalize him, his name and the firm's radiated authority in 1894. Olmsted's genius as displayed in New York's Central Park and at the 1893 Chicago World's Fair had bestowed national fame and credibility. Baxter dealt mainly with Olmsted's stepson, John C. Olmsted, whose final report on the assignment, "Landscape Architect's Report on the Improvement of Back Cove, 1895–1896," arrived on Baxter' desk on May 26, 1896.

Olmsted's report commenced by declaring the Back Cove potentially "ideally healthful." Next it explained the sewerage-created source of the problem and how the proposed interceptor sewers might remedy future pollution—but, he warned, without really addressing the immediate stench that foreclosed any practical residential or recreational use of the area. The firm's creative plan, which kept intact the ship canal, rail facilities, and other industrial uses, recommended construction of a long dam or dike to be located wholly north of the ship canal, which would therefore not require a costly lock as in the Herring proposal. Since the dam could be built from material dredged from the shoreline, Olmsted called the cost "trifling." He then presented in detail his design for a boulevard and parkland surrounding a sparkling, 336-acre saltwater pond.

He described a tree- and shrub-lined shore drive traversing impressive bluffs and inlets and featuring residential estates interspersed with public parks, playgrounds, and ball fields.[66]

Baxter and Edward C. Jordan, the city's chief engineer, embraced the Olmsted firm's plan not only as a public health measure but also—and especially—for how the Back Cove boulevard skirting the Deering shore promised new residential development that would boost the city's tax base. The Board of Trade and the city's Republican press joined in praising Olmsted's plan with emphasis on the improvements' role in promoting both real estate and tourism. Like Deering Oaks and the promenades, said the *Portland Advertiser,* the boulevard is "not for pleasure merely. [It] will be a profitable investment in making the city more healthful and increasing its attractiveness. Portland is growing in favor as a summer resort. Everything possible should be done with a view to attracting this class of [summer visitors] and making it pleasant for them." Baxter immediately began buying and assembling land for the boulevard and by February 1896 had deeds for and promises of willingness to convey property to the city. But opposition to the boulevard plan arose quickly, mainly over the huge dikes, which, argued the opponents, would cut the cove in half leaving an unflushed, stagnant "dead body of water" next to the channel.[67]

Thus, while Republican city boosters cheered, others protested. Coming at the end of one of America's worst economic depressions, when some working-class Portlanders still felt the sting of low wages and unemployment, Baxter's "City Beautiful" planning outraged many citizens. The Back Cove boulevard scheme—coupled with Baxter's talk of "pleasing drives" and parks on the exclusive Western Promenade, the beautification of his own Deering Street, and work currently (in 1896) under way to transform Portland Street through Deering Oaks into a tree-lined parkway with double trolley tracks—exposed the progressive mayor to charges from his Republican primary rival, Charles H. Randall, that an elitist Baxter was ignoring the plight of the laboring masses. In the mayoral primaries of February 1897, Randall narrowly defeated Baxter, not necessarily on the charge of elitism but mainly because in the words of the *Evening Express,* Baxter's bid for a fifth term challenged the Portland voters' "deeply rooted opposition to anything suggesting the possibility of an indefinite perpetuation of executive influence and power in the hands of an individual."[68]

Baxter's primary loss halted further action on the Back Cove boulevard scheme. Portland's emerald necklace would remain unassembled until 1903, when city residents reelected Baxter mayor of Portland for the fifth time. In the interim, Mayors Charles H. Randall (1897–1899), Frank Robinson (1899–1901), and Frederick Boothby (1901–1903), in the interest of keeping Portland the Gateway to Vacationland, pursued Baxter's park beautification agenda, the upgrading of city streets, and the building of the interceptor sewer to halt further contamination of the Back Cove. In fact, under Boothby, the commissioner of Public Works, George Fernald, brought John C. Olmsted back to Portland to consult on improvements to Deering Oaks, including sidewalks, new entrances, and the location of park shelters.[69]

In 1903, Baxter immediately resurrected the Olmsted plan, but with modifications: for political reasons he canceled the dike feature and, with a $1,000 appropriation from the City Council, resumed land purchases and broke ground for the 100-foot-wide, tree-lined Back Cove Boulevard. Baxter's City Beautiful agenda in 1904 transcended his earlier sanitary focus. He now viewed the Back Cove Boulevard comprehensively, not only as linked to his view of the residential city but, more important, as part of a grand park and recreation system. In 1904, with the right-of-way for the parkway around the cove secured, he summoned John C. Olmsted back to Portland and escorted Olmsted and Fernald on a tour of the city's various parks, where he presented his "view of connecting them so as to have a continuous drive through them by way of my proposed boulevard." On November 15, 1905, Fernald wrote Olmsted that Mayor Baxter wishes you "to make a general plan for the improvement of the Eastern Promenade covering the ground shown on the blueprint which I sent you; also a general plan for the improvement of the Western Promenade. . . . He also wishes you to define a scheme for connecting the Western Promenade with Deering Oaks, and a scheme connecting the two promenades. . . . He also wants some scheme for the improvement of the entrance to the Eastern Promenade at Washington Avenue."[70]

Olmsted's reports, which enclosed exquisite colored drawings of the Eastern and Western Promenades and of a General Plan for a Park System (showing a dikeless Back Cove), appeared in May and June of 1905. To promote the plan politically, and at his own expense, Baxter took his city councilmen and aldermen on a trip to Boston "to visit with the Olmsted firm and talk about the Park Plan which they are making from my design."[71] The Olmsted drawings graphically portrayed an emerald necklace. Equally exceptional about the plan (done "Under the Direction of James P. Baxter") was its attention to playgrounds. For example, the plan for the development of the Eastern Promenade proposed a baseball field on an unused right-of-way of the Grand Trunk Railroad. The Brookline firm sited another playground opposite Montreal and Walnut Streets "for boys too young for baseball." Just off Cutter Street on the promenade the Olmsteds planned a little children's playground with swings and space for games.[72]

Baxter's work with Fraternity House, his interest in the playground movement, and his zeal for an emerald necklace of parks all reflected his central place in the city's Progressive movement. Bureaucratic-minded businessmen like Baxter endeavored to bring nonpolitical corporate efficiency to city government and community betterment. The inclusion of playgrounds in Olmsted's 1905 plan injected an element of practicality and usefulness into an otherwise romantic Olmsted design. The stress on playgrounds reached out to the city's Irish, Italian, and Russian Jewish working-class population. The Deering Oaks ice-skating rink, opened in 1888 and represented the city's first attempt to provide space for public recreation. Boston had inaugurated a city playground movement in 1885, but it was not until 1902 that Portland formally established public recreation. That year Portland appropriated $500 and the Commission on Cemeteries and Public Grounds cleared space for the city's first public playground. Yet although Baxter's and Olmsted's 1905 plan for the Eastern Promenade highlighted playgrounds—as did the city's public baths, invariably located at playground sites—it was not until 1916 that Portland created a Recreation Commission and that playgrounds with swings, ball fields, pools, and tennis and basketball courts appeared in Bayside, the Eastern Promenade, and East Deering. A year later (1917), in conformity with the Olmsted Plan, the now completed Baxter Boulevard opened, featuring also a large playground complex in the Back Cove.[73]

Baxter's Progressivism and his enthusiasm for and tireless dedication to parks and playground planning notwithstanding, he failed to subdue or pacify his critics. Charges of elitism constantly dogged his efforts and only intensified as the Portland labor movement gained strength and socialist rhetoric grew shriller. His defeat in December 1905 doomed for a time both his Back Cove and his comprehensive park plans. It was a decade later in 1915, under Democratic Mayor William M. Ingraham, that work again commenced on the Back Cove Boulevard (to be renamed Baxter Boulevard), which opened for public use November 13, 1917. Baxter sat in the first vehicle to traverse the parkway. He died four years later, in 1921, by then already recognized as the "Father of the Portland Parks." The vision of Portland for which he had planted the seeds, of a beautiful, healthful city of homes and a place that beckoned to tourists, had born plentiful fruit.[74]

Vacationland in the Progressive Era

By 1895 Maine and Portland's vacation industry was taking definitive form. Every summer, visitors from Boston, New York, Philadelphia, and Canada flocked to the state, staying two weeks or a month or—beginning in the 1880s—even all summer. Visitors lived either in grand summer hotels, such as Prouts Neck's Checkley (fig. 18) and Portland's Falmouth, or in the huge number of more modest, cedar-shingled Victorian cottages that dotted the rugged coastline. After 1900, however, given, first, the advent of the automobile as a legitimate alternative mode of transportation and, second, the spreading practice of corporate paid annual vacations, Portland, increasingly viewed this tourist industry as an important if not vital sector of its economy.[75]

Summer cottages and hotels lined the shores of Cape Elizabeth and of Cushing, Peaks, and Chebeague Islands, but Portland with its rail facilities viewed itself as the hub of Maine tourism. As early as 1887, Mayor Charles J. Chapman in his annual address had exhorted Portlanders that "due encouragement should be given to such projects as will bring Portland and vicinity into prominence as a place of summer resort." He specified building "charming suburban drives, accessible points of interest, [and] added improvements of man and art." He called for suburbs "laid out systematically . . . with some regard for the laws of symmetry [and for] private enterprise [to] provide enlarged facilities for the entertainment of visitors and their convenient transportation to and from islands and seashores."[76]

Chapman provided the template followed by Baxter and Olmsted and by other Progressive-minded officials. Mayor Frederick Boothby, the Portland ticket agent for the Maine Central Railroad, needed no lectures from the Board of Trade about the importance of tourism and of public policy in encouraging the industry. Under Boothby (1901–1903) the city greatly widened Commercial Street at India Street to accommodate the increased carriage and automobile traffic in front of the Grand Trunk Station, and it converted a shabby cobblestone section of old Fore Street into Boothby Square, complete with a "City Beautiful" horse trough.[77]

To boost tourism further, Boothby pressed for more and more conventions to be held in Portland. In the summer and fall of 1902 a number of organiza-

18. The Checkley located on Prout's Neck, ca. 1890. Note the bicycles, very popular in the period. Prout's Neck, near Portland, boasted several popular summer hotels. Courtesy of Maine Historical Society.

tions met in the city, including the Knights of Gold, Eagles, Knights of Malta, Women's Christian Temperance Union, Maine Grange, and General Passenger Ticket Agents. Boothby turned Old Home Week in August 1902 (a week celebrating throughout New England the region's Puritan heritage, promoting revival of the colonial image nationally, and, most of all, boosting tourism) into an extravaganza with flags and bunting flying from every building on Congress Street. President Theodore Roosevelt gave a speech, visited the Longfellow House, and lunched at the Cumberland Club.[78]

Mayors Frederick Boothby, Adam Leighton (1908–1909), and Oakley C. Curtis (1911–1914), all like Baxter, avowedly Progressive mayors, viewed civic works—promenades, squares, boulevards, parks, and other city beautiful improvements—as enhancing Portland's attractiveness to tourists. A 1904 prophetic drawing envisioning Portland in 1910 captured graphically how its decision-makers saw the city's future. To begin, the map depicted Greater

Portland, encompassing "suburban Deering, Falmouth, Cape Elizabeth, and South Portland." Here were tree-lined boulevards, promenades, and planned garden suburbs with cul-de-sacs and curvilinear streets. In this vision, numerous Chicago-worthy skyscrapers anchored monumental downtown avenues. It was Baxter's Portland, a city rife with commerce but, despite the many periodic Board of Trade campaigns, without significant industry. On the map, Casco Bay teemed with yachts and other sailing vessels, as well as Cunard liners, commercial steamships, and ferries. It was Baxter's dream city, a beautiful Portland, a residential city where international commerce and tourism thrived harmoniously.

As earlier, the city and its Board of Trade tirelessly cultivated this view of Portland as the beautiful metropolis by the sea that, although proud of its pod of manufactories, had escaped the wages of urbanization. In the Board's promotional literature, places such as Gorham's Corners with its dark courts and rum shops, India street with its Italian work crews and Russian Jewish peddlers, and the noisome Portland Stoneware Works with its Armenian workforce all vanish from sight, bleached away by the sunlight glittering off the surf crashing over Portland Head. In reality, even though Progressive-era reforms, Fraternity House programs, new schools, and neighborhood playgrounds somewhat eased the rigors of tenement life for Portland's immigrant youth, housing and other social improvements for the inhabitants of Gotham's Corners, Munjoy Hill and Bayside failed to materialize. Overcrowded tenements remained fixtures, but places to be brushed out of the booster literature and avoided by strolling tourists.

Consistent with the city's would-be image, Board of Trade pamphlets also blotted out its industrialism. By 1904, Baxter, Boothby, and the Board of Trade had helped mold a consensus that while Greater Portland housed more than 660 manufactories producing locomotives, sleighs, boots and shoes, matches, furniture, and paper, the city's future lay not in its historically undercapitalized factories but in commerce and tourism. In fact, Portland's trade boomed in the early twentieth century, when the city remained the chief port for Canadian grain. In 1902–1903 it imported goods worth $7,250,150 (up 7 percent from 1895), while exporting grain, flour, corn, earthenware, and other goods valued at almost $48,000,000. Three great railroads, especially the Grand Trunk with its giant grain elevators, handled 2,500,000 bushels of wheat, and 2,500 head of cattle packed the pens at the new East Deering rail yards and stockyards.[79]

In 1914, however, the Board of Trade ominously warned the city's business and civic leaders about the wages of its dereliction: Portland must invest in its aging, neglected port. The Board believed "great things will be accomplished in the future for Portland as a seaport," but, it cautioned, there are "few busy seaports in the world that have not been made so through engineering and through the expenditure of money." With more and more, larger and larger ships plowing the seas, "there has been an awakening all over the world to the necessity of widening and deepening channel approaches and to the need of providing adequate docking facilities." Liverpool, explained the Board, had invested over $100,000,000 in its port within the past fifty years, and in the past twenty years Hamburg and Antwerp had spent over $50,000,000. "Philadelphia is committed to a development policy for ships of wider beam and deeper draft. Portland should be made ready for this era. For political reasons Canada diverted much business that by all rights and reason should come to us. Now is the time to start [transforming] Portland into one of the greatest and most important of our Atlantic ports."[80]

The Tourist City

In 1914, while Portland's civic leaders clearly rebuffed manufacturing and, calling the Forest City a "progressive and enterprising trade center," pleaded for capital improvements to strengthen its port, at the same time they just as strenuously regarded their city as "a healthful summer resort," the "Gateway to Maine." Summer visitors, they repeated, "come because of our beautiful city, our wonderful climate . . . and variety of amenities." Visitors, touted the tourist literature, compare Portland to the Mediterranean.[81]

Portland offered "unsurpassed attractiveness as a summer home to visitors who desire to combine the charms of a summer resort with the sylvan attractions of country and comfort found in a modern and progressive city." But the official literature now also emphasized Portland's progressiveness, the "orderly, efficient management" of its park system, the unobstructed view from the Eastern and Western Promenades, the tree-lined boulevards and esplanades.[82]

The city had used public monies to develop its parks and embellish its beauty on behalf of tourism. Businessmen likewise took steps to accommodate the increasing tide of summer guests and enhance the popularity of the city as a resort. With its Union and Grand Trunk stations, Portland proclaimed itself a "distribution point" not only for tourists passing through on their way to the White Mountains, Boothbay Harbor, Camden, and Bar Harbor but also, thanks to its superb trolley system, for the city's own sights: the Longfellow House, the Baxter Library, Fort Allen, the Portland Observatory, Deering Oaks, and the evolving civic center.[83]

City boosters also advertised Portland's regional attractions such as the Underwood and Riverside Casinos, as well as its cosmopolitan culture, its literary and museum sites, and its modern, luxurious Jefferson Playhouse and Keith Theater. And for those turn-of-the-century gay blades who took pleasure in bicycling, Portland offered a variety of routes, including the city's many attractive residential streets such as Baxter's Deering and John Calvin Stevens's Bowdoin Streets—places, in Edward Fassett's words, that featured conservative, beautiful, but unpretentious architecture. Neither did the city and its sparkling island refuges want for hotel space for the gay blade crowd. In addition to island attractions such as Cushing's Ottawa House (still a favorite with Canadians) and the nearby Checkley at Prouts Neck, fashionable downtown hotels such as the fairly new Park Hotel (1896) and the Lafayette (1903) continued to attract a large clientele of both tourists and business people.[84]

Shaping Portland's New Downtown

Historian Alison Isenberg argues that guided by the new science of marketing, a new female-oriented American downtown emerged in the early twentieth century. Portland was no exception. With the opening in 1903 of the luxury Lafayette Hotel (home of Baxter's political nemesis George Wescott), the Davis and Baxter Business Blocks, the ten-story, 162-room Fidelity Building, and the 1908 Woolworth Five and Ten on Congress Street, only doors from Porteous's and Mitchells and Braun's department stores, Portland had evolved a classic, linear, twentieth-century downtown, a safe zone of public and private space for the exercise of consumption and social discourse. The Congress Street space (the Board of Trade called it "dazzling") appealed strongly to women shoppers. Significantly, the new Fidelity Building and the Lafayette Hotel actually bestowed upon the city a modest, albeit modern, skyline which, though hardly rivaling Chicago, Boston, or even Buffalo, now appeared prominently in the city's promotional literature. In truth the ten-story Fidelity tower soared well above an otherwise very "human-scale" three-, four-, and five-story nineteenth-century cityscape.[85]

19. Proposed 1908 civic center. It was an unbuilt "City Beautiful" plan for Portland that appeared in the wake of the City Hall fire of that same year. Courtesy of Earl G. Shettleworth Jr.

A number of prominent banks and other edifices still stood on Exchange Street, including the First National (opposite Post Office Square) and the Portland Savings Bank and H. M. Payson and Company at 33 Exchange. But Middle Street had emerged as the city's Wall Street, home of Chapman National Bank, the Casco National Bank, and the United States Trust Company at Middle and Union Streets near the newly renovated Falmouth Hotel. Yet even though Exchange and Middle Streets retained panache, the heart of Portland's new woman-friendly downtown was clearly Congress Street west of the nascent baroque city beautiful civic center (fig. 19) and anchored in 1914 by the rebuilt City Hall, the First Parish Church, and the heroic statuary of Monument

Square. Here along Congress Street in addition to the new Fidelity Building, the stately brick Preble House Hotel, the Brown Business Block and the Benoits, Porteous, Mitchells and Braun, and Woolworth shopping district, stood revered monuments such as the Longfellow House, the Maine Historical Society, the Baxter Library, and the Masonic Temple.[86]

Model Ts in Monument Square

In the early twentieth century the automobile became a key to Portland's tourist economy but also posed a threat to the city's venerated tourist trade. Portlanders had initially viewed the automobile in 1899 as not very useful, not especially desirable, and not particularly safe. A year later, to celebrate the new century, Portland merchant F. O. Bailey opened a carriage store featuring the latest in new phaetons and sleighs. Just four years later, however, the horseless carriage had become increasingly a necessity. Automobile service stations sprang up on Congress Street and on Forrest Avenue. H. J. Willard and Company opened a garage and dealership in the Old Portland Street Railway car barn at the corner of Spring and Clark Streets. There, in 1904, H. J. Willard demonstrated and sold automobiles. He also repaired them and operated an automobile school to train mechanics and chauffeurs. By 1907, Willard was selling a line of Packards, Buicks, Peerlesses, Cadillacs, Wintons, and Elmores. That same year, Maine Motor Carriages repaired and sold cars at the corner of Free and South Streets; J. A. Dowling did the same on Forest Avenue; and the always enterprising Portland Company experimented—although not too successfully—with the design and construction of an automobile at its Fore Street works. Nearby, at 135 Commercial Street, entrepreneurs and marine engineers dabbled in motorboat development.[87]

Few ordinary Portlanders visited Willard's Spring Street showroom in 1907, when Wintons and Buicks cost well over $1,000, and automobile owners still toured, rather than commuted, in cars. Henry Ford and William C. Durant changed all that in 1908. Both realized the value of the automobile as a marketable consumer good with appeal to American individualism. Most important, the automobile freed Americans from the social and physical discomfort of the rude, clanging, jostling trolley. It also broadened residential choice, and opened up suburban settlement space beyond the confining limits of the trolley tracks. Ford, who had started producing affordable automobiles in 1903, introduced his $895 Model T in 1908, the same year that Durant founded General Motors.

After opening his Highland Park, Michigan, plant in 1916, Ford dropped the price of his cars to $345. Mass-produced Model Ts created the car culture and transformed travel and tourism. In 1910, only two years after Ford had debuted the Model T, Portland's Board of Trade observed that "one of the most fundamental necessities to a prosperous city is good highways" and lamented that "as a result Portland is today tabooed by hundreds, if not thousands, of automobile tourists, who, having heard of the charms of our city, and its delightful surrounding... have headed this way only to be discouraged and turn[ed] back... by almost impassable roads." A proprietor of the largest summer hotel in the White Mountains informed the Portland Board of Trade that "some 70 percent of those who registered at this house during the past season were automobilists and almost all . . . came and went by other routes than the natural one, through Portland."[88]

By the World War I years, Maine had improved the Kittery-to-Portland road, and Portland could claim once more to be the "gateway to the summer playgrounds of America." Though once impassable, Maine roads, assured the Chamber of Commerce, are "now easy to travel." Portland in 1915 acclaimed itself "a great automobile center... one of the most beautiful cities in the country, located within easy reach of ocean, lake, forest, and mountain with roads that average well with country roads of other parts of the United States . . . [and] with the finest hotels,... [a] Mecca of thousands of motorists from every part of America."[89]

Portland's Chamber of Commerce in 1910 had seemingly protested too much the city's evident indifference to its loss of hub status in an America swept up in the new car culture. It would be not the advent of the car but the extinction of Portland's historic Canadian grain commerce that ultimately shocked the city's economy. But that came later, after German U-boats in 1917 sank the British *Lusitania* and swept Portland with the nation into the War to End All Wars. Meanwhile, thanks to James Phinney Baxter, Portland's other Progressive mayors, and the age of reform, Yankee Portlanders entered the Great War convinced that their city was a more beautiful, more healthy, and better groomed place than ever, and that once the war had made the world safe for democracy, tourists again would come by rail, by steamship, and by automobile.

CHAPTER FIVE

The Sunrise Gateway in Depression and War

In 1915—still headquartered at 34 Exchange Street—the Portland Board of Trade changed its name to the Chamber of Commerce of Maine. Simultaneously, it unveiled a vigorous new campaign to rebrand Portland as "The Sunrise Gateway." The phrase captured the essence of the city which each morning officially welcomed the sun to America (and, thus, still boasted being the American port city closest to Europe). In addition, the chamber extolled Portland's role as the gateway to the splendors of vacationland Maine. "For half a century or more Portland had been the recognized capital of America's Summer Playground," blustered the Chamber of Commerce in May 1916, "and the city today is not one bit less charming than when the first summer tourist came within the gates."[1]

Like peacocks, Portland's Yankee business leader strutted proudly in 1916. From 1890 to 1920 the city's population, fattened by the annexation of Deering in 1898, swelled 90 percent, from 36,425 to well over 69,000. Canadian grain, arriving daily via the Grand Trunk Railroad, still poured into the two giant elevators dominating Portland's eastern waterfront (see fig. 16). Transatlantic steamships of the Allan, Dominion, Hamburg-American, Leyland, and Thompson lines plied the sea lanes between Portland and Liverpool, London, Glasgow, Bristol, Antwerp, and Hamburg. Brisk coastwise trade brought coal from Charleston to be bunkered by the Pocahontas Coal Company, pulp and china clay for Maine's growing paper and stoneware industries, and larger tanker loads of oil. During the summer months, tourists came aboard the Eastern Steamship Lines (sailing from Boston and New York), the Grand Trunk or the Boston and Maine or the Maine Central (hailing from Montreal, New York, Philadelphia, Cleveland, or Chicago), or now even the automobile, bound for the Boothbay Harbor, Camden, and Bar Harbor regions—and a number to Portland itself.[2]

Like much larger cities in 1916 and 1917, amid what historian Robert Fishman has called the heyday of the "Metropolitan Tradition," Portland had attained the stature of a metropolis, a core city lodged at the heart of a regional economy and centered on the "downtown." Portland bustled on the eve of World War I, the node of government, retail, and cultural institutions. Retail, mainly along Congress Street, flourished. The new City Hall, dedicated in August 1912 with its 6,000-pipe Kotszchmar organ, the largest in the United States, added even greater luster to Portland's reputation as a center of music, history, and theater as well as natural beauty.[3]

Downtown shoppers and theatergoers in 1917 shared a gnawing common anxiety, however: Portland was growing not only in size but in social and cultural complexity. Indeed, as Robert Fishman observed, each glittering American metropolis doubled as the capital of the world's poor because it served as both a place of work and a place of hope. Portland was hardly an exception. On the eve of World War I, Yankee Portlanders, sauntering along the city's narrow, peninsular streets increasingly encountered not only traditional Irish faces but a growing, polyglot mix of Italians, Russian Jews and Armenians, many of whom had fled the war in Europe which had begun August 10, 1914. And though President Woodrow Wilson promised American neutrality, dreaded involvement seemed imminent in 1917. Anxious Portlanders feared that American entry into the war augured extraordinary change for a Yankee culture built firmly on rockbound tradition.[4]

Portland and the War to End all Wars

Tied by their city's Canadian grain trade and transatlantic commerce to the Atlantic World, Portlanders heard the distant guns of August 10 loudly and had intently followed press reports of Verdun, the Somme, and the horrors of trench warfare. Even before the U.S. Congress declared war on April 6, 1917, Portland appointed a Committee of Public Safety, and Maine's National Guard enlisted troops. A huge recruiting tent arose in Monument Square, and when Congress ordered a draft in July 1917, Portland filled its entire quota with volunteers. Among 1,000 Portland doughboy casualties, 228 Forest City youth died in action in World War I.[5]

Wilson's war to save civilization stirred to life Portland's moribund shipbuilding industry. Washington believed that wooden schooners might be invulnerable to mines and submarines, and thus safely carry cargo to European allies. Portland Shipbuilding Company hired over 1,000 men to build a number of wooden schooners, which, unfortunately, did not prove as invincible as had been hoped.[6]

With its spacious harbor and proximity to Europe, Portland saw itself strategically placed as a key to American coastal defenses—therefore also vulnerable to attack. In early 1917, after memorials from the city's Chamber of Commerce, Washington ordered an official survey of Casco Bay with an eye to increasing the harbor's depth to accommodate large military ships. On August 8, 1917, as a war measure, Congress approved the Rivers and Harbors Act, which funded deepening the Portland channel to thirty-five feet, and at last provided a berthing space for deep-draft vessels.[7]

Portland endured the hardships of war. The many bond drives, the commodity rationing and scarcity, the daily news of Portlanders dying and injured at places such as the Argonne Forest and St. Mihiel made the war personal. Then suddenly, in 1918, with the German army at last in retreat, another enemy threatened—this time, Portland's claim to be the healthiest city: influenza struck, particularly the military-age young. The virulent flu spread rapidly from midwestern military encampments to Baltimore, Philadelphia, New York, and into Fort Devens in Massachusetts, where many local soldiers trained. From there it attacked Portland itself. On September 28, 1918, the city and Governor Carl E. Milliken banned all public gatherings, including school classes, funerals, and even church services. In October of that year, city physicians reported another 150 flu cases of what would ultimately be 2,499 cases in the city. For America's Sunrise Gateway, the healthiest city, the flu epidemic on top of war compounded the dilemma of a precipitous drop in summer tourism. Portland, confessed the city's health officer at the close of 1918, "is a most important gateway for tourist traffic. . . . We should leave nothing undone which would make them [tourists] secure against preventable communicable disease."[8]

But the war took an even deeper toll on Portland and the nation than the lives lost at Chateau-Thierry and to influenza. The Portland Liberty Bond drives, the nurtured fear of spies, the Espionage Acts, the encouraged public persecution of German Americans, George Creel's campaign for "One Hundred Percent Americanism," the 1917 Russian Revolution, and fear of anarchism at home all bequeathed a thick residue of disillusionment, paranoia, and finally xenophobia. In Portland the new temperament manifested itself in a generalized anxiety, a feeling mainly among the city's large Yankee class. After Armistice Day on November 11, 1918, Portland, their home, unfolded before them as a social and cultural landscape strangely unfamiliar and equally disturbing.

In truth it was an unveiling long in the making. Since the beginning of the new century, Portlanders such as John Mead Gould and J. P. Baxter had bemoaned the rise of giant, monopolistic corporations that rendered their city's smaller, locally owned and capitalized manufactories like the Portland Company less competitive. By 1919 the war-born growth in corporate scale and in new, streamlined technology had accelerated those trends, not only in the volume of industrial production, but also in the growth of corporate management, the increasing importance of mass consumption, mass marketing, and the role of the consumer. While Portland and its new Chamber of Commerce knew the consumer well, and as the Board of Trade had for years been marketing the "beautiful city" as a commodity, the city's more staid and demure, budget-conscious Yankee middle class had abjured the more brazen, glitzy marketing and the conspicuous-consumption patterns identified with larger cities.[9]

Likewise, respectable Yankee Portlanders such as Gould dreaded the steady immigration of Irish, Italian, and Russian Jewish immigrants into Gorham's Corners, Munjoy Hill, and Bayside. They abhorred the rise of commercialized entertainment, the spread of dance halls, nickelodeons, and movie houses that seemed to cheapen and debase the staid Puritan demeanor of the Gateway City and, moreover, increasingly brought working-class and middle-class youth into recreational contact. It was commercialized vice, Portland's sixteen brothels and numerous second-class hotels on Commercial, Franklin, and Congress Streets which especially alarmed Yankee Portland about the moral chaos of the metropolis and had triggered the creation in 1913 of a citizens' committee headed by an Episcopalian priest, Rev. Robert Codman. Although the committee, which included architect John Calvin Stevens, existed only from 1913 to 1914, it aroused fear about middle-class self-control, and about the corruptibility of the city's upstanding youth, now exposed to the loose, immigrant-contaminated commercial culture of the modern city. The war had only heightened those fears.[10]

Portland and the New Pluralism

World War I considerably slowed the tide of European immigration; nevertheless, by 1920, Portland possessed a visible immigrant population, still concentrated, but not ghettoized, in the city's three ethnic neighborhoods: Gorham's Corner, Bayside, and Munjoy Hill. Yet Portland remained essentially a Yankee city. Native-born whites made up 52 percent of Portland's 69,272 residents in 1920, very close to the 53 percent in 1910. European-born whites constituted 19 percent of the population, down only 1 percent from 1910; and of these, 19 percent were Irish-born, 9.6 percent were Italian, 1,103 or 8.3 percent were Russian-Jewish; 4,984 or 27 percent of the city's foreign-born were either French- or (mainly) English-speaking Canadians. While Portland's population rose just 6.2 percent between 1920 and 1940, from 69,272 to 73,643, because of the 1921 and 1924 national immigration-restriction legislation the basic ethnic composition of the city stayed unchanged (i.e., Yankee, Canadian, Irish, Italian, and Russian-Jewish with a sprinkling of Polish, Scandinavian, German, and African American).

Between 1910 and 1940, however, the foreign-born segment slipped from 21 percent to 13.4 percent, and the 47.5 percent of Portland's population either foreign-born or native-born of foreign-born or mixed parentage—especially second-generation Irish—were now somewhat scattered throughout most of the city's wards. That over the years the Irish had steadily gained political representation, if not some power, aroused concern among the city's Yankee class. In the 1920s Munjoy Hill and the large old Bayside neighborhood, home to the Gould family, included increasingly large populations of Irish, Italians, Russian Jews, and also Armenians. The Armenians had come to Portland in the 1890s, and many more came in 1921 after persecution by the Turks intensified during World War I.[11] Starkly in the shadow of Portland High School and City Hall, Bayside loomed as what the Chicago School of Sociology termed a zone of emergence. Boarding houses abounded; 77 percent of the residents rented. The 1924 reassessment found many of Bayside's homes overcrowded, and 87.9 percent of the population lived without a bath. Outside water closets were common.[12]

Portland's huddled, shabbily dressed immigrant class challenged the Longfellowian image of the city as a sparkling, healthy, seaside vacationland. True, in 1928 the City Council chairman Lester F. Wallace, would write that Portland was "peculiarly fortunate, not only by the gifts of nature, but also . . . [for]

those strangers from foreign lands who have come to live with us [and] are law abiding and home loving." They offer, Wallace continued, "no problem of the melting pot." Nevertheless, the Portland police still disproportionately arrested the Irish. Though 66 percent of those arrested in 1917 were "Americans," a significant 960, or 13 percent, were Irish. By 1927, Americans represented 73 percent of those arrested, the Irish a mere 7.5 percent. But in 1920, Irish, Italian, Canadian, Swedish, and just-plain-foreign families made up four-fifths of those assisted by the Overseers of the Poor, Americans just a fifth. Likewise, foreigners constituted the many families given safe, sanitary fresh milk and other services by Portland's Baby Hygiene and Child Welfare Association, which worked closely with the city's Board of Health nurses to improve immigrant hygiene practices.[13]

Indeed, immigrant health problems belied Portland's healthy-city image. The wartime draft discovered that hundreds of the city's immigrant youth were unfit for service, raising concerns that their families failed to get decent medical service. Portland's Board of Health nurses became vital for immigrant well-being after Bowdoin College closed its Portland Medical School in 1921. Bowdoin's action effectively terminated the school's Edward Mason Dispensary and Clinic, a facility that had been extensively used by the city's poor and working class.[14]

Fraternity House continued to serve the many Irish, Italian, and other immigrant youth and young adults who frequented the settlement house for recreation, classes in English, and vocational training. Of course, city playgrounds remained crucial in the 1920s for immigrant youth. Concern for playground space in one immigrant neighborhood prompted the city to secure from the Grand Trunk Railroad a five-year lease on some land on Fore Street at the foot of Munjoy Hill, "a congested part of the city where there are many small children, . . . for the most part being our foreign population."[15]

The City and Postwar Anxiety

Despite their only slightly declining demographic superiority, Yankee Protestants in the Forest City feared being culturally overwhelmed by their ethnic neighbors. Their once sacrosanct peninsular social space seemed violated by foreign-looking attire, foreign speech, and the foreign religions of Catholicism and Judaism. The melting pot seemed an alien intrusion upon the imagined pristine Yankee New England world of the Browns and the Baxters, the image purveyed in tourist literature. The apocalyptic events of 1919—strikes in the coal and steel industries, the Seattle general strike led by the International Workers of the World (IWW), the Boston police strike, the Red Scare and Attorney General J. Mitchell Palmer's raids and deportation of thousands of immigrants—only heightened Yankee anxiety. Even the passage of the Volstead Act, October 28, 1919, and the Eighteenth Amendment to the Constitution, ratified in January 1920, failed to assuage their fear of moral decline, especially after the subsequent dawn of flappers and speakeasies, along with the lax enforcement of Prohibition.[16]

In Portland, political fears fueled these cultural anxieties, even though the imminent statewide consolidation of the city's newspapers under the Gannett family promised to make the once-Democratic *Portland Evening Express* editorially Republican, thus firming a Republican media stranglehold. It was in part that nagging dread of ring-rule that rendered the city's Yankee class discomfited with a local ward system of government built, they suspected, on alliances with socially and morally impaired immigrant voters. In his seminal *The Ku Klux Klan in the City,* historian Kenneth Jackson observes that such entrenched anxieties about moral political and social decay and the growing influence of Catholic immigrants gave birth momentarily to a resurgent Ku Klux Klan (KKK) ensconced as much in American cities as in the small towns. Between 1923 and 1926 Portland became one place where the Maine Klavern established a foothold. Led by Grand Dragon F. Eugene Farnsworth, who touted "one hundred percent Americanism," the Klan fought as much *against* the Portland Catholic Diocese's effort to win local public aid for parochial education as *for* reform of the city's ward-based government. Farnsworth enlisted about 2,700 Portlanders in the Maine Klan and claimed over 50,000 white-robed supporters statewide. It is difficult to discern accurately the real size and depth of Klan support in Portland. Prolific diarist John Mead Gould never mentions the phenomenon, and the press never speculated. Certainly, the presence of the Klan undermined the city's claim to social harmony. Crosses burning in the shadow of surf-splashed shores and summer cottages discouraged the carefree tourist crowd.

The Klan's high point in Maine came in April 1923, when for $75,000 Farnsworth purchased the Rollins property on Forest Avenue, a large Gothic mansion on eight acres, for the Klan's state headquarters. There Farnsworth built a huge 4,000-seat auditorium housing also a banquet hall, temple, meeting rooms, offices, and a 100-car garage. Before the giant edifice burned to the ground on December 12, 1924, it hosted numerous ceremonial events, meetings, musical and other forms of entertainment. After the fire, with the national Klan embroiled in scandal and litigation, the Maine Klan languished. It sold its Rollins property for $60,000 in 1926, then disappeared.[17]

Although fleeting, the Klan's presence in Portland proved politically significant. During those Klan years the city restructured its government: the council-manager form it adopted in 1923 had originated historically in 1900 in Galveston, Texas, in the wake of a devastating flood. In the name of efficiency, Galveston in 1901 scrapped its mayor-council form of government for commission rule. In 1914, badgered by both floods and heavy debt, Dayton, Ohio, installed city-manager government, which quickly became a model for reform nationwide. Portland opted for a variant form: in 1923 it scuttled its century-old weak-mayor, bicameral legislative system for a five-person unicameral council elected by voters at large (not by ward): that council selected a chairman who performed a mostly ceremonial role as mayor; more important, it hired a professional administrator to manage the city's business. Voters selected the School Committee, but council members served as the Boards of Health, of Recreation and Parks, Police, and Fire, and the latter two were placed under civil service protection.

Rooted in Mayor Baxter's turn-of-the-century campaign for reform, governmental restructuring had simmered in Longfellow's town until 1918, when the Chamber of Commerce sponsored the Committee on Municipal Research, chaired by John Calvin Stevens and charged with investigating city government reform nationally. The committee's survey discovered a consensus favoring the city-manager system. Forthwith the chamber convened the Citizens Committee of One Hundred, which quickly drafted a reform charter calling for council-manager government. Submitted to the Portland electorate in September 1921, the charter, failed, but just barely. Two years later, with minor revisions—requiring the election of School Committee members at large rather than by ward, and the provision of "initiative and referendum as a check on Council power"—the reform charter was resubmitted to Portland voters.

Wielding the power of the press, Guy Gannett, owner of the *Portland Press Herald,* championed the new charter, writing editorially on June 11, 1923, that "the citizens of Portland are convinced that the handcuffs of mounting indebtedness and stagnation in public improvements cannot be shaken off until city government has been purged of partisanship and logrolling politics."[18]

Stated simply, the nonpartisan reform initiative, heavily backed by the city's Yankees, the Chamber of Commerce, and powerful Protestant clergy, promised to replace tinkering and corruption with economy and efficiency. The anticharter forces (which included the bulk of immigrant voters) that favored the existing ward-based city government had the backing of the *Evening Express*, the Catholic Church, and the city's established political class, including Mayor Carroll S. Chaplin. A key part of the anticharter campaign spotlighted the bedfellows of the Portland charter reform movement: the Ku Klux Klan. On September 7, 1923, the Maine KKK rallied its members behind the new charter in a demonstration staged in front of the Portland City Hall. Farnsworth told the crowd that efficient council-manager government would effectively purge city government of Jews and Catholics, and he further vowed to make "our enemies in the Catholic wards . . . vote honestly." Not surprisingly, the enemies of the charter tirelessly observed that the Committee of One Hundred, which had drafted the charter, counted one lonely Catholic and no Jews among its members. They charged that the Protestants and the Klan had plotted to seize control of city government. Despite the opposition, voters approved the charter, and city manager government became law.[19]

A Beautiful but Fragile Seaport

Underlying Yankee anxieties about Portland's moral muscularity, government inefficiency, and the durability of Yankee virtue lay a visceral concern for the sustainability of the city's historic maritime economy. Indeed, Portland's viability as America's Sunrise Gateway seemingly hinged—as John Poor had imagined it in 1846—on the continued salience of its port. In the early 1920s that long-threatened primacy faced extinction.

Earlier chapters have alluded to the tenuousness of the umbilical relationship to Montreal and Quebec which made Portland Canada's winter port. Since the late nineteenth century, Canadian nationalists had railed that—Portland's geographic advantage notwithstanding—steering their grain trade to the U.S. port discriminated against their native maritime ports: St. John, New Brunswick, and Halifax, Nova Scotia. That nationalist discourse intensified in 1919, when Ottawa poured Canadian resources into rebuilding those ports, dredging and developing both harbors and aiding in the construction of elaborate dry-dock facilities. Although World War I had interrupted this development, by 1923 superb port facilities existed in both places, and Ottawa proclaimed St. John a modern national port. Canada's commitment to St. John and Halifax coincided with the British-controlled Grand Trunk Railroad's financial collapse, which resulted in part from the wartime loss of European trade. Ottawa rescued the line by absorbing it into the state-owned Canadian National Railway (CNR), and the move impelled Canada to name St. John thenceforth the destination for the bulk of Canadian winter wheat. Ottawa also ordained that the low rates of the British Preferential Tariff would thereafter be granted only to cargoes landed at Canadian sea or river ports without transshipment. To overcome the geographical disadvantages of more remote Halifax and St. John and to enhance their desirability, Ottawa added a 10 percent discount on tariff rates for all cargo routed through those maritime ports. Those actions, executed in the name of Canadian nationalism, demolished John A. Poor's old economic argument for Portland supremacy as "Canada's Atlantic Port," a case the Forest City had constantly but quietly pressed, utilizing the method of "friendly approach."[20]

During the 1920s, the international steamships of the Allan, Dominion, and Thompson lines continued to stop at Portland to load cattle and grain but only after first discharging their Canadian-bound cargo at St. John and Halifax. Meanwhile, the total volume of Canadian grain business plunged in that decade and to a trickle by 1934. Ottawa trade policies victimized Portland, not the United States, for the ports of Boston and New York experienced only modest losses. Between 1919 and 1934 the volume of Canadian exports through Portland dropped from a 1,183,968 short tons to 21,120 short tons. By 1934, then, during the Great Depression, business activity at the eastern end of Commercial Street, in the shadow of the two looming, now ghostly, Canadian National Railway elevators, had vanished.[21]

All of Portland endured the loss, not least its Irish and Italian longshoremen, the city's teamsters, and the Portland Company. Harbor activity itself suffered. In 1924 the city's harbormaster had registered as Portland-based ships sixty-five steamers, twenty-four barges, and twenty-one schooners. Only three years later, in 1927 he registered only forty-one steamers, seven barges, and twelve schooners, a far cry from Longfellow's Casco Bay filled with billowing sails. Indeed, a November 1927 article in the *Portland Press Herald* titled "Captain Joseph York Skipper of Many Voyages" amounted to an epitaph for Longfellow's bygone city of sail. It told of the *Edward Lawrence*, "the last of the line of famous six stickers" (six-masted schooners) tied up in Portland Harbor since March 5, and doomed never to sail again.[22]

Canada's 1923 breech shattered the Chamber of Commerce's carefully nurtured image of Portland as the Gateway City. With confidence in the viability of the economic argument and the method of friendly approach, Portland for the most part had abjured industrialism and buffered its brisk Canadian winter trade with summer tourism. When earlier anxiety, in the 1910s, had forced the Board of Trade, almost phlegmatically, to rekindle interest in industry, the city added a ready-made-clothing factory on Commercial Street, a new paper box factory, and the Burnham and Morrill cannery on an abandoned shipbuilding site in East Deering on the east side of Tukey's Bridge, where Portland in 1917 opened its first industrial park.[23] But if the notion of industrialism had all but withered in the early part of the century, so, tragically, did the city's touted port facilities. Once regaled as commodious, by 1910, on the eve of the city's duel with St. John and Halifax, observers decried Portland's moldering piers, wharves, and warehouses as crowded and inadequate. Crowding forced cargo ships entering Casco Bay to anchor in the ship channel. Even the Grand Trunk Railroad's once-modern Galt Pier languished, unkempt, needing to be dredged, and unable to accommodate large ships. On the eve of World War I, Portland still lacked a modern municipal or public pier with deep-water berths and spacious warehousing facilities, a point stressed by the Board of Trade when in 1917 as a "war measure" it sought federal aid for harbor dredging. In concert, Maine's senatorial delegation added a clause to the dredging bill affirming that if approved, the state would fund "adequate berthing for deep draft ships."[24]

Exacerbating the city's port problems, Maine's railroads in the 1920s faced equally uncertain times. Besieged since the 1870s by state and federal regulations well-intentioned and often necessary but despised for the burden of debt and political chicanery they imposed on cities such as Portland, during the 1920s Maine railroads for the first time encountered real competition from trucks and the automobile. It was Maine's railroad system—the Grand Trunk (now part of the CNR), the Boston and Maine, and the Maine Central—that had converged on the city and, with its coast and international steamship service, made Portland the Sunrise Gateway. The yards, wharves, elevators, rail, and other massive infrastructure for handling freight and passengers dominated the cityscape. By 1928 the Portland Terminal Company controlled all the terminal property formerly owned by the Boston and Maine and the Maine Central. The company's rails, which laced Commercial Street, served the entire waterfront. Portland's Union Terminal and Grand Trunk Station, hives of activity during the summer months, stood simultaneously at the heart of Maine's tourism. Yet freight rates always discriminated against Portland in comparison with New York and Boston. In 1924, truck transportation posed a new and different challenge to the city, forcing the Boston and Maine to undertake a study of the issue. "Inroads of motor competition in the Boston and Maine Territory have been constantly growing," stated J. H. Hustis of the Boston and Maine, "and have reached the stage where the railroad must determine what its future attitude toward the competition will be. The question [is] . . . whether the railroad or motor truck can both serve the territory. . . . [E]ither one or the other must prevail." For anxious Portlanders, the Forest City's days as a railroad center were numbered.[25]

Portland Responds to Uncertainty

Despite omens portending disaster, feared pluralism, the loss of both Yankee Puritan hegemony and the Canadian grain trade, Portland in truth weathered the 1920s relatively unscathed, evidence again of the city's extraordinary resilience. Work on a state pier, mandated in 1917 by the federal legislation ordering the dredging of Portland Harbor to thirty-five feet, commenced in 1919. Voters that year approved a bond issue for construction of the Maine State Pier and warehouse. Portland business leaders, excited over the prospects of a modern public pier, predicted the dawn of new year-round port activity, including weekly steamship service to Liverpool, London, Scotland, and even French ports.[26] To make plans for the pier and the comprehensive development of the harbor, a new Maine law combined the towns of Portland and South Portland into a single Port Authority charged with the construction of the public piers and other public works and with the oversight and administration of all terminal facilities.

The 1,000-foot-long, 144-foot-wide Maine State Pier opened in 1923, the very same year that Ottawa slashed its Canadian grain trade with Portland (fig. 20). While the pier accommodated transatlantic vessels and housed facilities for processing arriving foreign immigrants, it was particularly designed to promote coastal and intercoastal trade. Prior to the Great Depression, the new pier, heralded as the "best ocean terminal on the Atlantic Coast under one roof," in tandem with a booming Maine paper industry, kept port activity lively. The volume of petroleum cargoes also rose steadily during the decade, compensating somewhat for a decline in coal tonnage shipped from the American South to the Pocahontas Fuel Company bunkers at the Long Wharf.[27]

20. The Maine State Pier with USS *Sicily* in berth, 1949. Courtesy of *Portland Press Herald* Still-Film Negative Collection, Portland Public Library Special Collections and Archives.

Canada's 1923 trade and tariff policies were restructured without completely severing Portland's commerce with Montreal. For example, during the 1920s, Canadian cattle shipped by rail to Portland were herded aboard White Star Dominion Line ships bound for Liverpool; moreover, during the decade Portland still annually exported 20,000 bushels of Canadian grain (down 75 percent from 1919 totals, however) to English ports.

Therefore, despite the precipitous decline in its historic winter grain business, Portland—armed with its new Maine State Pier and Maine paper-pulp-industry-generated commerce—preached optimism. Steamers, foreign and domestic, still arrived in Casco Bay. Oil tankers shared harbor space with Eastern Steamship vessels and the transatlantic fleet: the Anchor-Donaldson, Cunard, Leyland, Thomson, and White Star Dominion ships. In addition, intercontinental ships, the Argonaut-Ishman and Dollar Steamship lines, often crewed by Filipino sailors, arrived in Portland bearing freight brought from the West Coast through the Panama Canal. This flurry of maritime activity gave an otherwise fretful Yankee city hope that a "new spirit existed, that a new generation of progressive leaders" would move the city forward, that "we can change all this."[28] Undaunted, some Portlanders in the 1920s, exuding confidence in the city's possibilities, lobbied to make Portland a "free port": that is, one free of customs duties. Some even imagined Portland rivaling Hamburg and Rotterdam.[29]

Oil bunkering (or tank storage) emerged in the 1920s as a relatively new but extremely auspicious business for maritime Portland. In 1928 only the Mexican Petroleum Company's South Portland facility handled large tankers; smaller ships docked at the Standard Oil piers also located in South Portland. By 1929, oil had surpassed grain and coal as the most important commodity handled by the port. Though Portland retained only a diminishing portion of its grain business in the 1920s, a growing coastwise commerce kept its piers busy. Along with coal (both anthracite and bituminous), which remained a profitable commodity, pulpwood, china clay, and Texas Gulf sulfur—all used in the paper-making industry—surged in importance. China clay poured into the port in the 1920s, much of it from Fowey, England. The *Press Herald* in 1926 cheered news of three steamers chartered to bring china clay from Fowey to Portland, ranking that commodity "among the highest and important . . . for the city's commerce." Likewise, the city shipped—by sea, rail, and truck—paper manufactures, cannery goods, fish, lobsters, cotton bagging, rope, lumber, marine hardware, machinery, and other products including potato chips.[30]

Portland's Chamber of Commerce in the 1920s found optimism in recognizing not only a still-busy port but also a booming downtown, returning summer tourists, and evidence of a newly efficient, nonpartisan government. Although opposition from Portlanders favoring "a political form of city government" lingered, council-manager government—first under city managers Harry Brinkerhoff (1924–1928) and James Barlow (1928–1946)—produced a stable, conservative, and cost-effective administration. Enforcement of prohibition still proved vexing throughout the 1920s, and charges of lax liquor-law enforcement persisted. Nevertheless, in the words of the City Council chair in 1927, Portland government achieved "efficient, courteous, intelligent conduct of . . . city affairs." In 1929 Portland bonds sold readily and at a low interest rate. Revenues also rose, benefitting from a meticulously and vigorously prosecuted 1924 property revaluation. Undertaken in midwinter, the property reassessment, however, disclosed missing and inadequate plumbing, poor and missing wiring, and other serious shortcomings in the city's aging housing stock, and evidence that the war had accelerated overcrowding and dilapidation, especially in such places as Bayside and Munjoy Hill.[31]

Planning and Zoning Longfellow's City

Like the presence of the Ku Klux Klan, reports of housing problems blemished Longfellow's image of the beautiful city by the sea. Even before the 1924 reassessment disclosed slum conditions, the Fraternity House nurse and the Civic Club's Tenement House Committee had reported bad, unsanitary housing and signaled Portland's civic and political leaders that modern cities required a more systematic, comprehensive approach to urban problems.

Portland came to the city planning movement slowly. Nationally, urban planning had its roots in nineteenth-century sewer, water, carriage, and park planning endeavors. Portland's ambitious sewer, street, and park work under William A. Goodwin, and the city's Olmsted-designed 1896 Back Cove plan, as well as its 1905 Olmsted and Baxter Comprehensive Park Plan, connect Portland firmly to that history. Inspired by the 1893 Chicago Columbian Exhibition, evidence of formal city planning appeared in the early twentieth century. Professionalized city planning arrived later, the exact date marked by the first meeting in 1909 of the National Conference on City Planning in Washington, D.C., and the ascendancy of Frederick Law Olmsted Jr. as the spokesperson for the City Efficient, a theme Baxter had espoused as early as 1896. Much of pre-1909 city planning in America, like Daniel H. Burnham's Plan for Washington, D.C., had stressed baroque design, diagonal boulevards, neoclassical architecture, formally arranged mall-like settings. Unlike so many larger cities—Chicago, San Francisco, and Pittsburgh in the Progressive era—Portland did not create an official city planning body before World War II, or engage in any formal city planning. Nonetheless, influenced by the national trend, the Forest City had between 1906 and 1911 developed a formal assemblage of buildings in a parklike, baroque setting intended as a civic center.[32]

Lincoln Park was Portland's central square, an attractive place for afternoon and evening strolling graced in the center by an ornate Victorian fountain. Located on wide and fashionable Congress Street, Lincoln Park served as the city's common. Three large churches either faced the park or were close by: First Parish, Payson Memorial Methodist, and First Baptist. As the downtown area moved westward toward Monument, Congress, and Longfellow Squares, however, and as Franklin Street, adjoining the park, grew more and more congested with members of the city's ethnic working class, city officials seized the opportunity to shape the Lincoln Park area into a "civic center." In 1905, architects submitted plans for a new Cumberland County Courthouse at Federal and Pearl Streets on the southern border of the park. George Burnham's winning neoclassical *Ecole des Beaux-Arts* design proposed a grand, pillared and pilastered baroque pile that provided the essential monumentality to anchor a civic center. A local architect, the thirty-one-year-old Burnham, was related to George Burnham of Burnham and Morrill, the East Deering cannery famous for its baked beans. The Federal Courthouse, 1908–1911, another neoclassical tour de force, balanced Burnham's Beaux-Arts triumph.

North and just west of the park in 1906 stood Portland City Hall. Rebuilt by Francis H. Fassett after the 1866 fire, it bore Fassett's strong Queen Anne–style signature. Then, in 1908, fire again ravaged City Hall. As in 1866, the fire hardened the city's determination, this time to remake the Lincoln Park area as Portland's architectural masterpiece. A 1908 artistic rendering showed an enlarged Lincoln Park adorned as a Beaux-Arts court of honor with a newly rebuilt city hall stationed at the center Lincoln Park court and an assemblage of monumental civic palaces lining Congress and Federal Streets (see fig. 19). The heady vision never materialized in that grandiose form, but New York architects Carrere and Hastings, working with Portland's John Calvin Stevens, did design a new city hall in the spirit of Paris's Hotel de Ville. It boasted a civic auditorium which, thanks to Portland-born Philadelphia publisher Cyrus Curtis, housed a grand pipe organ dedicated to city organist Herman Kotzschmar. A mere glimpse at the 1914 Richard's Map of Portland revealed that though incomplete, the essential design elements of a civic center appear. Portland had added another exhibit to its arsenal of summer tourist attractions.[33]

Although Portland failed to join other cities in the rush toward professionalized city planning and balked at the cost of creating a planning department, it did in the 1920s acknowledge the need for planning to combat such growing city problems as traffic congestion, caused mainly by the incompatibility of narrow city streets and mounting automobile ownership. Parking also posed a problem; so did railroad and trolley tracks blocking the center of most of Portland's important arteries. To combat this congestion, the city—like so many others—experimented with one-hour parking and no-parking areas.

Portland's earlier informal planning had hardly ignored parks and playgrounds, which importantly served the city's immigrant class, and the city continued to address the issue of urban recreation. By 1926, Portland owned (or rented) eleven playgrounds and prided itself on having a well-used municipal bathing beach, located in the East End and replete with ninety-odd beachfront dressing rooms. After years of wrangling, in 1926 the city finally purchased for $5,000 the former tannery site facing the Back Cove and adjacent Forest Avenue and Deering Oaks. The tannery had been a profitable enterprise for years, but its industrial imprint and its foul stench belied the legendary sylvan tranquillity and tourist attraction of the area, and its purchase had been a Baxter priority.[34]

First and foremost, city civic leaders and other policymakers in the 1920s focused on the downtown, the heart of Longfellow's little metropolis by the sea. As much as the new Maine State Pier, the still-arriving Cunard and Thomson liners, and those daily cargoes of China clay, pulpwood, and oil pumped vitality into the city's weakening economic veins, it was also the intense building activity along Congress Street and the drumbeat of business there that kept Portlanders exuberant. Indeed, the very same years that Ottawa cast Portland adrift, the city enjoyed, according to the *Evening Express*, "a flurry of building activity such as Portland has not experienced since the days long before the war. . . . The majority [of new buildings] are substantial building blocks." Construction during the 1920s remade the physiognomy of the city, replacing its low-scale nineteenth-century cityscape around Monument Square—buildings such as the Preble House Hotel and Portland Theatre—with modern, high-rise architecture such as the Chapin Bank at the corner of Preble and Congress, which, according to the *Express*, "rivaled in splendor and importance the new million dollar City Hall with its magnificent auditorium" (see fig. 14). It topped by a story the equally splendid ten-story Fidelity Building, which stood close by the newly built Clapp Memorial Block, whose principal tenant was the powerful Cumberland County Power and Light.[35]

Mushrooming downtown automobile traffic—a problem compounded by the modern preference for high-rise office buildings—plus multiplying garages and service stations intensified the need to bring order to Portland's metropolitan form. Zoning or districting, pioneered in New York and elsewhere, seemingly solved the problem of preserving order and taxable values by, in the words of historian Constance Perin, putting "Everything in Its Place." In 1925, Portland's city manager, Henry Brinkerhoff introduced before the state legislature a Zoning Enabling Law. After the State Supreme Court in 1925—and before the U.S. Supreme Court in *Euclid v. Ohio*, 1926—found zoning constitutional, Portland City Council, on August 3, 1925, appointed a zoning commission, chaired by John Calvin Stevens, with Brinkerhoff as a member and with prominent Cambridge, Massachusetts, professional planner Arthur Comey as its consultant. Born in Kittery, Maine, Harvard-educated, a protégé of Frederick

Law Olmsted Jr., and a member of the World War I U.S. Housing Commission, Comey boasted considerable experience in zoning, having helped draft the ordinances for a number of cities, including Detroit and Milwaukee.

Portland's ordinance, submitted August 1, 1926, took aim directly at mixed land-use neighborhoods such as Bayside, Gorham's Corner, and Munjoy Hill, where houses and apartments sat crammed between workshops and warehouses, and where children played in streets where "factories, large and small . . . [gave] off smell and smoke." In the preface to the ordinance, Comey saw Portland rebuilt in the next fifty years. "Now is the time," he wrote, "to zone Portland, while the city is still able to prevent serious mistakes." In an age that continued to view oceans and rivers as highways for commerce, not sites for waterfront restaurants and hotels, Portland's 1926 ordinance directed commerce and heavy industry to the shores of the Presumpscot, along the banks of the Fore River, and to the city's waterfront, as well as the Deering rail yards. It concentrated tall buildings in the downtown and, for the city's large transient population, created an apartment house zone in suburban Woodfords and Morrills Corners. The ordinance listed Bayside as "B," for limited business, and designated the area of the Maine Medical Center as an "apartment zone." "The balance of the Mainland Section . . . ," wrote Comey, "[was] for general residence exclusive of apartments and three-family [read triple-decker] homes. . . . Thus, at one strike all intruding of isolated local stores [and garages] on quiet residential streets is stopped. . . . As the great tourist center and principal distribution point of Maine, Portland has an assured future to live up to."[36]

Tourist City in the Automobile Age

At least since the 1870s, Portland had capitalized on its beauty and on making tourism and its port commerce the twin pillars of its urban economy. Much of its planning and development over the years aimed at buttressing those supports, particularly tourism, and Comey pointedly acknowledged tourism in his zoning report. But while still marketing itself as "Longfellow's beautiful town that is seated by the sea, whose native air is pure and sweet," and accentuating its healthfulness, Portland in the 1920s promoted in addition its new metropolitan stature and cosmopolitan attractions. The city highlighted its theater life, and recitals on the Kotzschmar organ. The Boston and Maine Railroad's 1925 promotional booklet, *Along New England Shores,* extolled Portland not only as the birthplace of Longfellow but as a "prosperous and attractive metropolis of Maine." A 1927 Chamber of Commerce advertisement promoting automobile tourism pictured a sailboat and a waterfall but also a scene of bustling Monument Square with the gleaming, modern Fidelity Building centered in the background.

For tourists in the early 1920s, squeamish about violent cities, Portland publicity as in the past ignored the ongoing discontent of its longshoremen and stressed the city's "freedom from strikes with their attendant chaos." And while downplaying its industry, it now for the first time amplified its thirty-five-foot deep seaport, the eighth largest port in the United States, with steamship service to London, Liverpool, Hamburg, and Antwerp. Moreover, not only was Portland the gateway to Maine's summer fun and its health-bestowing air and waters; it was now also the gateway to winter sports: snowshoeing, skiing, skating, and tobogganing. "Winter sports," advised the Chamber of Commerce, "are an asset for the tired, worn, jaded city dweller who can in one week of bracing winter aid get more good [*sic*] than from a month of the best vacation of summer."

By 1921, Portland was boasting its accessibility by automobile as well as by rail and by sea. Significantly, the *Official Automobile Blue Book* and the *Automobile Green Book* (published by the Automobile Legal Association), guides for popular 1920s motor touring, commenced their descriptions of all automobile tours of both Maine and the White Mountains with Portland, a place where motorists could find good hotels, garages, and service stations, including the Portland Company, which now advertised the Portland Company Garage at 58 Fore Street with the slogan "Years of Experience in Repair Work: No Waiting." Portland hotels—the new Chase House, the Falmouth, the Congress Square, and the Lafayette—all announced that they were "homelike resorts for automobile and touring parties." Enhancing Portland's appeal to automobilists and conventioneers, in June 1926, Henry P. Rines opened at Congress Square the posh new twelve-story Eastland Hotel with its Egyptian-décor dining room. There were limits to Maine's auto-friendliness, however. Using mainly tarred macadam, the state had greatly improved the roads in and around Portland, but north of the city, around Bethel and Bretton Woods, the Blue Book told touring readers to expect the roads to be "mostly gravel."[37]

But the roads to Portland's Eastland Hotel were paved. Tourists and conventioneers crowded the lobbies of the Eastland and Falmouth and Lafayette Hotels in the summer of 1929. Ships berthed at the Maine State Pier; others offloaded China clay and bunkered coal at the Pocahontas dock, or pumped oil into Standard Oil tanks. Indeed, tourists and many Portlanders alike might readily have agreed in 1929 that the Forest City seemed to have safely overcome the catastrophic loss of its once cherished Canadian grain trade.

Portland and the Great Depression

On October 27, 1929, along with the rest of the nation, Portlanders had watched securities plunge 43 percent. By November, stocks had skidded downward 228 points, ending the Roaring Twenties. Wall Street's collapse marked the denouement of America's nineteenth- and early twentieth-century age of urban industrialization; likewise, it signaled a new federal-urban relationship whereby desperate city mayors, city managers, and other urban officials plaintively turned to Washington for assistance. It was a partnership actually foreshadowed by World War I and by some of Herbert Hoover's policies, first as secretary of commerce in the 1920s and then as president, 1928–1932. It lasted into the 1970s.[38]

During the Great Depression, American cities, especially those with large industrial economies such as Chicago, Philadelphia, Pittsburgh, Baltimore, Cleveland, and Detroit, suffered deeply. In Chicago, by 1932, 40 percent of the city's workforce looked for work. Philadelphia had more than 300,000 jobless in 1933. Sheriffs' writs dispossessed over 19,000 Philadelphia families. Soup kitchens sprang up throughout urban America, as did shantytowns bitterly called Hoovervilles. Portland endured none of this large-scale misery but hardly avoided the Great Depression, and despite its government-averse Old Guard Republican politics, in Portland, as in cities across America, the federal government there played a significant role in aiding the jobless poor.[39]

Hard times struck Portland later than in most cities. Its population had reached 70,810 in 1930, and its department-store- and Fidelity-Trust- and Chapman-Building-bedecked downtown sporting eighteen hotels, and eleven theaters, still prospered in that early Depression year, seemingly unfazed by the dark tumult of Wall Street and the agony of mortgage foreclosures, soup kitchens, and Hoovervilles. In 1930, Portland's new city manager, James E. Barlow called for expanding the city's waterfront "for commercial purposes" and recommended upgrading the city's East End bathing beach as a tourist attraction.[40]

As commerce and manufacturing nationwide crumbled during the years 1932–1933, however, Portland at last felt the impact. Manufacturing activity in the city's foundry, stoneware, and garment industries, all slipping in the 1920s, plummeted 58 percent between 1929 and 1933. During the same years industrial wages fell 51 percent. Commerce followed suit. Maine paper-mill production had dropped 50 percent by 1933, greatly reducing shipments to the city of china clay, pulpwood, and sulfur. Neither was Portland's fishing industry left unscathed. Both falling prices and foreign competition slashed earnings in half for the city's fishing fleet between 1929 and 1933. Tourism too, still profitable in 1930 and 1931, edged downward 20 percent in 1932. For the state, tourism decreased from an estimated $100 million industry in 1929 to under $85 million in 1934. In 1932, pummeled by truck and automobile competition as well as the Great Depression, Eastern Steamship Lines ceased operation of its once popular night-boat service between Boston and Portland. Steamship service between New York and Portland ended in 1941.[41]

Portland's economic woes battered both its financial institutions and its government. In 1933, three of the city's principal banks closed, including Casco Mercantile Trust and Fidelity Trust, whose Gothic Revival office tower at Congress and Preble had symbolized Portland's rise to modern metropolitan status in the 1920s. The bank crashes reflected waning business profits, reduced wages, joblessness, and also declining real estate values, all of which undermined the city's ability to deliver basic services. In 1929 Portland fixed the taxable assessed value of Portland property at $117,711,525 and collected slightly over $4 million in taxes. By 1933 the Great Depression had reduced the real estate valuation 20 percent to $95,356,000, and, in the face of rising relief costs, and despite a slight compensatory increase in the millage rate, tax collections as expected—slumped more than 9 percent, in part because of unpaid taxes.[42]

Chronic unemployment in Portland had begun in the mid-1920s with the city's longshoremen.[43] A sizable increase in the number of persons receiving outdoor relief in the Poor Department appeared in 1926. Between 1926 and 1930, presumably good years, the city's outdoor relief load (aid in one's home rather than in the poorhouse) rose 37 percent from 1,208 persons in 1926 to 1,651 in 1930. Outdoor relief costs jumped at the same time 89 percent, from $37,500 in 1926 to $71,000 in 1930 and then skyrocketed in the next four years. The number of persons aided by outdoor relief jumped 281 percent from 1,651 in 1930 to 5,857 in 1932; the price of relief in the form of coal, wood, clothing, and food spiraled upward in that same year to $271,387. In the spring of 1932, in addition to the 1,387 families aided with fish, fuel, and clothing and those aided at the poor farm, over 100 unaided jobless slept nightly on the Eastern Promenade. Headlines announced that the Poor Department had exceeded its

21. Portland bread line during the Great Depression of 1930s. Courtesy of *Portland Press Herald* Still-Film Negative Collection, Portland Public Library Special Collections and Archives.

budgeted appropriation by $100,000. Faced with crises in June 1932, Barlow and the City Council turned to work relief: they authorized 100 jobless men to be employed by the Public Works Department at two dollars daily. Many of these relief workers performed local road work, toiled in Deering Oaks Park, labored on Baxter Boulevard, or constructed paved walkways on the Eastern Promenade. Some built the Cutter Street parking lot adjoining the East End Municipal Beach (fig. 21).

One group found public employment constructing Portland's first, 123-acre, nine-hole golf course located on the Presumpscot River. Defended as both a tourist attraction and healthful recreation for working-class Portlanders, the professionally designed links, seeded with imported fescue, seemed a barely affordable luxury in the depths of 1932. The exotic New Zealand fescue became even more questionable when in June 1932, in accordance with strict fiscal retrenchment and the city's customary policy in dealing with economic depression, the council slashed the city manager's salary 21.5 percent, and all other municipal salaries 17 percent.[44]

Portland's Gorham's Corner Irish and Munjoy Hill Italians cheered as news blared over the radio on November 9, 1932, that Franklin Delano Roosevelt had been elected president of the United States. The new president promised the kind of bold, persistent experimentation historically repugnant to Portland's economically conservative Yankee elites. From the first, Portland's Yankee leadership and Republican press, convinced as they were of Hoover's greatness and the wisdom of his anti-Depression policies such as the Reconstruction Finance Corporation (which made loans to banks and railroads), had like Hoover predicted imminent recovery and prescribed balanced budgets. Portland groaned when after a decade in which not a single Maine Democrat had been elected to Congress, Maine in September 1932 elected a Democrat, Louis J. Brann, governor. They feared the vote foreshadowed Roosevelt's election In November.[45]

FDR took office in March. That same month, every Maine city but Bath voted Democratic in the 1933 mayoral elections. The *Portland Press Herald* chided the state when it re-elected Brann in 1934. The newspaper blamed the Democratic swing on the hard times and the voters' desperate hope for fiscal retrenchment. Once in office, FDR immediately declared a bank holiday and called for a repeal of Prohibition; but he also urged a balanced budget. Portland cheered the balanced budget but, as home to the Maine Law, gave only muted support to the president's request to repeal the Eighteenth Amendment. A supportive *Press Herald,* however, editorialized that the Volstead Act had failed: "The nullification of the act is everywhere evident and repeal of the Amendment [should] be voted at once."[46]

Portland, Relief, and Depression Politics

Democratic victories in Maine resulted more from candidate popularity (Brann) and from Republican squabbling than from the state's embrace of the New Deal. Soon the Maine Democrats themselves, the Brann faction and that of the U.S. Congressman from Rockland, Edward C. Moran Jr., split over loyalty to the New Deal and the national Democratic Party: Moran was intense; Brann, cool. The split slowed the progress of federal relief delivery in Portland and the rest of Maine, but so did Maine's repugnance to the whole idea of the dole. In 1933 and 1934 Roosevelt's Federal Emergency Relief administrator, Harry L. Hopkins, dispatched across America a team of investigators led by a hard-nosed, seasoned Associated Press reporter, Lorena Hickok, an intimate friend of Eleanor Roosevelt. Hopkins ordered Hickok and her team, which included Mainer Lincoln Colcord, "to go out around the country and look things over, . . . to talk with preachers . . . businessmen, workers, and the unemployed." Hickok in late September 1933 found herself in Maine, where she discovered "people who would almost rather starve than ask for help." Her lengthy report disclosed "a good deal of inadequacy [in relief] and some pretty bad administration . . . where relief agencies dispensed relief to deserving cases based on rigid nineteenth century standards of cleanliness, physical and moral. Portland, *really only a trading center* [original emphasis]," she wrote, "suffered terribly from bank failures . . . Bankers there feared to lend" and "the city was getting along only fairly well." As for the city's political posture, "their ideas," she wrote, "don't fit in with ours."[47]

Hickok understood Portland's mood in 1933. City manager Barlow, in concert with the Chamber of Commerce, complained about the National Recovery Act (NRA), which in addition to relaxing antitrust laws to boost business profits gave labor new rights versus capital. This meant for angry Portland businessmen that the NRA allowed hated collective bargaining, lowered workers' hours, and raised wages. Barlow complained that the NRA "virtually eliminated competitive bidding on some commodities, thereby increasing prices . . . [and] operating expenses." Indeed, the city's Republican press viewed the New Deal with its NRA, TVA, CCC, FERA, and AAA as a gigantic poker game, gambling the taxpayer's money on questionable bets—among them Roosevelt's proposed Passamaquoddy and Grand Coulee Dams.[48]

Efficiency-obsessed Barlow may have blanched at the cost, but for Portland in 1933 and 1934, with its surging jobless caseloads, federal relief assistance loomed in importance. It impacted not only the city's jobless but the city's crumbling roads, parks, and other urban infrastructure. Federal relief also helped transform the city's welfare services. Years ago, historian Roy Lubove showed that the Federal Emergency Relief Administration (FERA) imposed professional, modern social-casework, standards upon historically politically operated city welfare agencies. To receive federal dollars, states like Maine were compelled by FERA to create professional state agencies such as the Maine Emergency Relief Administration (MERA), which then imposed modern social-casework standards on local bodies such as the Portland Poor Department. MERA's Social Service Division carefully ascertained a budgetary deficiency for each Maine relief family.[49]

Federal intervention in Portland relief began formally in 1933 with the Civilian Conservation Corps (CCC) operated in Maine under the Maine Forest Service. During the 1930s, CCC youth engaged in a host of conservation projects in the Maine woods and paid their relief families $25 monthly. From 1933 to 1935, MERA under John A. McDonough and his 500-person staff provided a comprehensive and impressive range of relief assistance. Portland was one of MERA's sixteen Maine districts where federal grants supplied commodities and other help for the jobless. Through MERA's Work Division, the agency employed able-bodied men and women for jobs on roads, city playgrounds, sewers, and school maintenance, and on sewing projects, mainly making mattresses. During the harsh winter of 1933–1934, under MERA, the federal Civil Works Administration (CWA) in Portland, in the wake of the city's earlier work relief projects, worked on the East End Beach and the Eastern Promenade, building wading pools in city playgrounds, and grading and paving city streets. The CWA shut down in April 1934, but work relief continued.[50]

In 1935 Congress passed the Social Security Act, giving Washington—through Old Age Pensions, Aid to Families of Children, and other forms of disability compensation—care of the state's physically impaired, aged, and blind citizens and dependent children. For those able to work, Washington created the Works Progress Administration (WPA), headed again by Harry Hopkins and, like FERA, decentralized. After an interminable delay caused by Congressman Moran and Governor Brann's feud over WPA patronage, Hopkins finally appointed Bowdoin political scientist Albert Abrahamson (whom Brann regarded as a young idealist) to direct the Maine WPA. Abrahamson, a registered Republican but otherwise scrupulously non-political, proved diligent but discomfited by the burden of the responsibility, and he returned to blissful Bowdoin in July 1937. John Fitzgerald, an assistant to Abrahamson, replaced him.[51]

Setting aside Barlow's complaints about the burden of the city's 25 percent sponsor's share of WPA project costs (for nonrelief labor and for materials), and ignoring Portland's phlegmatic response to the WPA largess (Portland voted against Roosevelt in the 1936 election), the federal agency proved vital to the city, not only to its jobless but also for its streets, parks, cultural life, and the future of tourism. Statewide, between 1935 and 1942, the WPA employed over 14,000 of the state's jobless, more than 30 percent of whom came from cities such as Lewiston, Augusta, Bangor, and Portland—though in fact, Portland workers made up only 9 percent of Maine's WPA workforce.

Much of Portland's WPA work, as in other cities, simply upgraded or maintained the city's streets, parks, sewers and other infrastructure, kept services intact and Longfellow's beautiful city beautiful. On any day in 1937, the WPA put to work an average of 740 jobless Portlanders, men and women, down from 1,100 in 1936. Statewide street- and roadwork employed almost 40 percent of Maine's jobless. In Portland the WPA, like CWA and FERA before it, continued the street and park projects begun by Barlow in 1932. Thanks to the 1935 bond issue, Portland in 1936 undertook a $157,300 comprehensive street improvement project that included the construction of Maine's first traffic circle at St. John and Danforth Streets. Elsewhere on the peninsula and in Deering and Westbrook, WPA workers graded and paved public thoroughfares, removed streetcar tracks on Woodford Street, and labored on the municipal golf course, on playgrounds, and in Deering Park. Others constructed retaining walls on the Western Promenade, laid a major sewer along Baxter Boulevard, rebuilt both the Danforth and Fore Street sewers, built a new sewer on Washington Avenue, and endeavored to beautify the often still unsightly Back Cove. WPA workers also finished the South Portland Airport, constructing not only runways but also an administration building. In 1937, Portland had purchased the privately owned Stroudwater Airport and now used WPA labor to transform it into the city's municipal airport. By 1938 the airport operated for both mail and passenger service.[52]

While men toiled on labor-intensive street, sewer, park, and airport projects, Portland's jobless women found work in WPA sewing rooms, making mattresses, sheeting, shirts, nightgowns, quilts, and layettes, all for distribution to the poor. Housed in the unused Brackett Street School and in the old Cumberland Street Post Office, the sewing rooms employed between 132 and 150 persons who in 1939, in addition to bedding, produced over 312,000 garments for the needy. WPA white-collar projects employed Portlanders to compile an inventory of the city's historical records and all of the city's movable property; a WPA bookbinding project repaired all the worn textbooks used in the city schools; unemployed teachers boosted adult literacy in Portland by teaching reading and writing in WPA classrooms. Elsewhere, jobless workers provided hot lunches to school children, and in 1938 a WPA Housekeeper Project provided temporary help for WPA families struck by illness or other emergencies. Portland benefited as well from the WPA's celebrated Writers', Art, and Music projects. Among the writers' projects was the acclaimed *Maine Guide* (1937), part of the WPA *State Guide* series. WPA artists painted murals for two Portland hospitals—including a magnificent one in the Portland Children's Hospital—and for both the South Portland and Portland post offices. In 1939 the Portland WPA orchestra performed thirty-two concerts before audiences estimated at 15,290 persons.[53]

Most significantly for this book, many WPA projects—especially those in the parks, to improve the Back Cove, for a building on St. John Street to house the Portland Publicity Bureau, and for the purchase and restoration of the historic 1807 Portland Observatory—promoted tourism, as did the *Maine Guide.* The Great Depression underscored the importance of tourism, given the negative impact of the economic decline on the city's maritime industry. Portland waterfront business during the decade faced not only sagging commerce but also truck competition and increased union demands. Except for some continued interest in developing the port's oil trade, the waterfront languished during the 1930s. The number of longshoremen and other maritime workers dropped over 32 percent, from 3,976 to 2,678. Because the State Pier was relatively new, and the other piers privately owned and ineligible for federal works projects, neither the jobs-producing Public Works Administration (PWA) nor the Civil Work Administration (CWA) nor the WPA steered funds toward waterfront improvements or maintenance. Port damage from the horrendous 1938 hurricane was left unrepaired, and with sagging revenues, the city failed to address a worsening harbor pollution problem.[54]

More encouraging, Maine tourism, sluggish in the early 1930s, had inched upward by 1936, thanks to a boost in state publicity spending. During the Great Depression teachers, ministers, and others from Philadelphia, Boston, and elsewhere, their wages slashed, found the beautiful and historic coast of Maine with its inexpensive lodging, cheap seafood dinners, and cool, healthful air an affordable as well as relaxing vacation. The Maine Publicity Bureau blanketed the East with its brochure *Maine Invites You.* Responding to the decade's embrace of history and historic preservation, New England's regional identity with the romanticized, imagined Puritan past captured in Robert Frost's poetry, the popularity of *Yankee* magazine, and Kenneth Robert's historical novels, the bureau cast Maine's appeal in eighteenth-century discourse. "Know Ye all People that Ye Maine Hosts," stated the brochure, "have banded themselves together in a most solemn covenant . . . to assure all wayfarers a cordial welcome to YE STATE OF MAINE . . . and to provide only ye best accommodation and entertainment at all places conducted by YE MAINE HOSTS." The bureau proclaimed Portland the "beautiful vacation city on Casco Bay," featuring excellent hotels and comfortable tourist homes, splendid restaurants, concerts on the Kotzschmar organ, theaters, museums, and "motor rides of endless variety." "No finer summer headquarters can be found," boasted the Chamber of Commerce in 1941, "than right here in the City of Portland."[55]

Portland Goes to War

Hitler's rise to power in 1930s Germany, Mussolini's accession in Italy, and Japan's invasion of Manchuria all found space in the Portland press without apparently affecting the city's life—at least until 1939. That year the German Reich invaded Poland. Having long feared an inevitable conflict with the European dictators, FDR ordered a mobilization for defense. An avid sailor, friend of the navy, and familiar with Maine and Portland from summers at Campobello Island, Roosevelt knew well the strategic importance of Casco Bay. When in 1939 the Fifth Infantry, garrisoned since 1924 at the harbor's defense forts, left Portland for duty in the Panama Canal Zone, it was promptly replaced by an antiaircraft regiment. To further defend the harbor, Washington in 1940 activated the 240th Coastal Artillery Regiment of the Maine National Guard, which was shortly joined by the Eighth Coastal Artillery Regiment. Then, in the spring of 1941 the United States Navy made Portland the headquarters of the Atlantic destroyer fleet assigned to escort merchant convoys across the U-boat-infested Atlantic. Portland became a key part of the so-called Bridge of Ships that helped Britain and Russia survive the bleak years of 1941 and 1942.[56]

Washington's decision to shelter the destroyer fleet in Casco Bay had enormous significance for Portland. If federal WPA spending impacted the city positively, defense and war spending transformed it. Maine and Portland prided themselves on their long, patriotic history of military service. War memorials abounded; the one at Monument Square was in the heart of the city. Though the city had balked at spending federal money for relief, it welcomed Washington's aid for defense. Portland became a proud martial metropolis, a military town with both the benefits and liabilities of such a place.

To service the Atlantic destroyer fleet, Washington built a huge refueling station on Maine's Long Island (then part of Portland) and facilities there to train sailors for the operation. In addition to modernizing the city's existing gun batteries, Washington enhanced Portland's defenses by adding one 16-inch and three 6-inch batteries, as well as observation towers and submarine mine facilities, making Portland one of the most heavily defended harbors in the country. The federal government spent over $130,000,000 on Portland defenses in 1940 and over $500,000,000 the next year, boosting city employment and incomes.[57]

The war accelerated private spending as well. Since the early twentieth century, Portland had steadily elevated its stature as an oil port. Fearing in mid-1941 that its many oil storage tanks were vulnerable to attack, Standard Oil of New Jersey announced construction of a 236-mile pipeline for the safe transport of petroleum to its subsidiary in Montreal. It was completed November 14, 1941. Standard Oil had built the pipeline for the very same reason Poor had built his rail line in the 1840s: Portland offered the shortest route to Montreal. A year earlier, in December 1940, Bath Iron Works shipbuilding had joined with Todd Ship to create the Todd-Bath Shipbuilding Corporation. The firm won a British contract for thirty cargo (Liberty) ships, and the two firms eventually merged to form the New England Shipbuilding Company. NES became Portland's primary wartime employer, supporting a workforce of over 30,000 persons, including more than 3,700 women.[58] Located at the Cushing Point site in South Portland, its facility was greatly expanded under orders from the U.S. Maritime Commission, which ordered the emergency wartime construction of vast shipyards on both the east and the west side of Cushing Point (fig. 22).

What was at first called defense mobilization but after December 7, 1941, war production brought thousands of military personnel and migrant workers flocking to Portland, all seeking shelter in a city whose aging housing stock had already been deemed inadequate. War, therefore, forced Portland's Yankee leadership into an unprecedented conversation about how a renowned tourist city could adapt its housing, recreational, and other services to the needs of a mass, working-class population.

Between 1941 and 1943 Portland's population of 73,634 (up 4 percent from 1930) spiraled upward an estimated 17 percent. South Portland, the actual home of the giant Todd-Bath Iron Shipbuilding Corporation (the New England Shipbuilding yards), rose even more. Studies by the Federal Office of Production Management's Division of Housing coordinator and the Federal Housing Administration charted Portland's growing housing crisis, which by Pearl Harbor Day was considered acute. Todd-Bath, joined by the Southworth Machine Works, Maine Shipbuilding, and Standard Oil, all reported in 1941 a demand for well over 4,000 outside laborers, and thus an urgent need for additional housing. Thousands of army, navy, and coast guard personnel and their families swelled the population seeking living space. A significant part of this in-migrant population consisted of single persons. The Chamber of Commerce, which operated Portland's federally prescribed Homes Registry Office, hired off-duty policemen and architects to cruise the city, spotting vacant housing. As in other cities, municipal and business officials insisted that the existing

22. World War II Liberty Ship SS *Nordica* under construction by the New England Ship Company, South Portland. Courtesy of Maine Historical Society.

stock could be expanded to accommodate the new demand; tenements and other private properties (even summer cottages) could be subdivided and converted into additional units. Washington disputed those findings, contending that most of the identified vacant units were either substandard or unsuitable for year-round residence. Further, in 1937 the WPA had reported 17 percent of the city's housing to be without private tubs or showers and 13 percent in need of major repairs.[59]

Under the Lanham Act of 1940, and to the chagrin of the Portland Chamber of Commerce, Washington ordered in February 1942 that the Federal Public Housing Authority of the Federal Works Agency build 550 units of permanent public housing in the Portland area. The 250-unit Redbank project arose near the municipal airport in South Portland; the 200-unit Sagamore Village just off Brighton Avenue; and Broadview Park also in South Portland. John Howard Stevens and John Calvin Stevens II designed Redbank with its modest, wood-framed, Colonial Revival–style units as a planned New England community. In the mode of the 1890s British Garden City and World War I Emergency Fleet Corporation developments (designed as complete communities of affordable housing), Redbank featured curvilinear streets, a school, a community center, and open play space complete with spray pool. The wartime Sagamore and Broadview Park housing had less distinguished architectural lineage.

That housing stock did not appreciably lessen Portland's shelter problem, which was mainly, and inadequately, addressed by the conversion, stretching, and subdividing of existing old, large, single-family, two-family, and multifamily residences into even more units. In many respects, the inadequate response to the housing crisis of World War II aggravated an affordable housing problem that has lingered into the twenty-first century.

The war and Portland's booming growth from in-migrant labor and naval personnel also spawned social problems. The Forest City hardly stood alone in 1941 and 1942. Margaret Chase Smith became Maine's new senator in 1940 when her husband, Senator Clyde Smith, unexpectedly died in office. In 1943, as a member of the Naval Affairs Subcommittee, Smith toured a number of cities congested by wartime activity. After Norfolk, San Diego, and Newport, Rhode Island, her committee arrived in Portland, now teeming with bell-bottomed sailors and Rosie the Riveters. Not surprisingly, her committee's report on Portland described housing conditions for navy personnel as "inadequate," "so acute . . . that naval personnel were warned not to bring their families until they had found suitable accommodations." The report also castigated the city's recreational opportunities for military personnel. It found that theaters were "poorly ventilated and that very little reputable commercial dancing was to be found here the past winter." Moreover, civilian hospitals in this war-boomed community were overtaxed."

The situation alarmed many Portlanders. The Social Protection Committee of the city's Council of Social Agencies studied the city's wartime social dynamics and labeled one important part of it the Girl Problem. The presence of thousands of sailors and unattached shipyard workers attracted single women, many of whom were just teenagers. Although Portland had long feared its lure for women of the night, the committee deemed the size of the World War II problem unprecedented—and now the element of once-forbidden beer was added to the social equation. To measure the Girl Problem, the Social Protection Committee conducted a very unscientific study of the city's many hotels, dance halls, beer parlors, juke joints, and restaurants, inquiring whether or not they were "frequented by unaccompanied girls and women meeting servicemen," and questioning their standards of operation. The committee concluded that regulatory controls were needed, plus policing and, especially licensing.[60]

The city's new Planning Board, created in 1942—which included City Manager Barlow and the Cambridge planning and zoning consultant Arthur Comey—saw the Girl Problem stemming as much from wartime crowding as from the lack of wholesome alternatives for the courting ritual. The Planning Board's 1943 Long Range Recreation Plan for Portland prepared by the National Recreation Association, declared that "the impact of the war has greatly increased the population of the city and has dramatized the lack of opportunity for wholesome recreation." The plan called for significantly increasing the number of playgrounds, as well as opportunities for indoor recreation.[61]

Portland weathered the war years, but as in other cities, wartime demands had mobilized every resource of the city, human and material, toward the singular purpose of victory. Its Longfellowian image of the beautiful city by the sea was put in storage; all other urban needs languished. Although wages rose and the pall of economic depression lifted, the city with its aging nineteenth-century housing stock and its automobile unfriendly, now touristless, downtown withered. Indeed, by the end of World War II, Portland appeared a crowded, bleak place, bereft of the allure that had made it the Gateway to Vacationland.

CHAPTER SIX

Postwar Portland, 1943–1965

Maine's Portland-born state historian Earle G. Shettleworth Jr. tells the story of a Portland merchant who in the 1950s sold books from a small, shabby Victorian storefront on Exchange Street. Nearby sat a clump of three or four moldering, half-vacant Italianate piles, their sills rotting and cornices sagging. Once stately, the buildings veritably begged to be rehabilitated. Interested in rescuing Portland's post-1866 fire architectural heritage, the old bookseller visited a prominent Portland realtor. "Oh," said the realtor, "you can have the whole bunch for $3,000 or $4,000 apiece, but why would you want them?"

After 1945, brutal social and economic changes already visible in the 1930s severely undermined Portland's once carefully cultivated image as Longfellow's beautiful city by the sea. Suburbanization, deindustrialization, globalization, and modernism devastated its role as a Gateway to Vacationland and undermined the tourism industry that since the 1870s had buttressed the its weak industrial and fragile maritime commercial economy. Portland ultimately responded to this evisceration of its historic gateway role by emulating Pittsburgh, Baltimore, Boston, New Haven, and the rest of urban America plagued by declining economies, blighted housing, and eroding, obsolete downtowns. It turned to urban renewal.

Nationwide, postwar urban revitalization used federal dollars to promote investment in aging urban infrastructure. But in Portland, as in places such as Boston and Philadelphia, renewal forced cities to choose the commercial value of glassy, streamlined modernism over the patina and ambience of the urban past. Renewal compelled the Forest City to weigh its Longfellow, Gould, and Baxter legacy of tree-lined, Greek Revival, Colonial Revival, and Shingle-style streetscapes against sleek, wide thoroughfares and gleaming, glass-fronted office towers conjured up in postwar, modernist planners' imaginations and put on display in General Motors' famous Futurama Exhibit at Robert Moses's 1939 New York World's Fair. Indeed, renewal put Portland's "city by the sea" character firmly on the line, since as a tourist destination the Forest City had long marketed its quaint, historical cachet.[1]

That cachet, however, harked back to the city's remembered Yankee maritime past, not necessarily the past of the Irish, Italian, or Russian-Jewish residents of Gorham's Corner or Munjoy Hill. After World War II, many of the Yankee residents abandoned the aging, begrimed city for the Cape Elizabeth, Falmouth, and Cumberland suburbs, leaving a new generation of non-Yankee decision-makers to wrestle with Longfellow's legacy. The outcome of that conversation would not become clear until the late 1960s.

Postwar Portland

Historian Jon Teaford finds that most American cities, battered in the 1930s by the Great Depression, with the help of the federal Works Progress Administration and the Public Works Administration, had by 1940 retreated from the economic abyss. Wartime military spending on fortifications, naval contracts, and the salaries of military personnel had likewise fattened Portland's revenues and the economy of the city as a whole. Wartime businesses along Congress Street—Rines', Woolworth's, Kresge's, Benoit's, Porteous, Mitchell and Braun's—prospered.[2]

But, while wartime Congress Street thrived, the crush of military personnel and shipyard workers (as chapter 5 explained) taxed the city's already strained resources. Despite the Lanham Act, giving birth to the Sagamore Village and Redbank housing, many shipyard workers crowded into tiny apartments in subdivided triple-deckers. Others commuted in rickety vehicles from as far away as Wiscasset. Still others lived in their cars, parked off the road. By the end of the war, experts in the city's infant planning department, like many other Portlanders, viewed the city's crowded, dilapidated housing, together with the its overburdened sewers, clogged streets, and inadequate recreation facilities as part of an impending urban crisis.

In 1944 as many as 90,000 people jammed the city's streets and alleys and byways. Portland boosters prayed that many of these skilled shipyard workers and servicemen stationed at Fort William, some originally from Canada, West Virginia, Florida, Texas, and elsewhere, would stay, and many did. But too many who had moved elsewhere—especially college-educated Mainers, after working in Connecticut, California, New York, and Chicago—never returned. Still, unlike Boston, Cleveland, and Pittsburgh, which lost population in the 1930s Portland had actually grown by 4.5 percent during the Depression decade. And although it failed to reach 80,000 in 1950, the city did boost its population by 5.4 percent to peak at 77,634 that decennial year. Then, like almost every old northeastern and midwestern city in America, Portland lost population in the 1950s: it dropped an alarming 6.5 percent to 72,566 in 1960, although South Portland next door rose 4.4 percent.

The 1960 census revealed that, as noted, it was the Yankee class that had left for the suburbs, making Portlanders of immigrant stock more than 30 percent of the city's population. Irish Americans, Italian Americans, and Canadian Americans constituted the bulk of the ethnic population, with smaller numbers of Scandinavian, Russian, Armenian, and German Americans. The city's miniscule population of 371 African Americans in 1960 remained exceptional in urban America.[3]

But Portland offered postwar veterans and their families little more than healthy Maine air and a Maine quality of life. The city's wartime industrial boom vanished quickly, almost overnight, and with it the fleeting diurnal rhythms of industrialism so strange to Longfellow's city. New England Shipbuilding, which at its peak in December 1944 employed more than 30,000 people, and during the war built 236 Liberty ships, shut down its massive West Yard in February 1945. Within a year its equally massive East Yard ceased operation and NES's Bath Iron Works partner had retreated to its historic roots in Bath, Maine.

Almost all of Portland's modest industrialism had been mobilized during the war. The Portland Company, for example, built steam turbines for ships and cast 30,000-pound propellers for the Todd-Bath Liberty ships. After the war it won contracts to produce reactor shells for New England atomic power plants, while still manufacturing elevators, boilers, pulp digesters, and washing equipment for the paper industry. In 1956 the company, still firmly situated at its old 1846 facility on Fore Street, was sold to New York–based United Industries. The ancient firm struggled through the 1970s, and in 1982 the property was sold to a local entrepreneur, Phineas Sprague.[4]

After the war, Portland retained its historic diversity of small manufactories: chewing gum plants, canneries, shoemakers, and producers of clothing, stoneware, metal stoves, and marine hardware, but neither the number of Portlanders employed in manufacturing nor the value added of Portland's manufactured goods ever matched Lewiston's or, for that matter, that of any other manufacturing city in New England. Moreover, throughout the 1950s and into the 1960s, only 12.2 to 17.4 percent of the city's workforce engaged in manufacturing. In 1957, Greater Portland, embracing the city and South Portland as well as Westbrook, Gorham, Cumberland, Gray and Freeport, counted only nineteen firms—including the Burnham and Morrill Cannery, S. D. Warren Paper, Sebago Shoes, and the Portland Company—which employed more than 150 workers. Soon, with deindustrialization, many small manufactories such as the Thomas Laughlin Marine Hardware Company would be acquired by larger national firms like American Hoist and Derrick, and then ultimately liquidated.[5]

Seeking to recapture Portland's wartime-fueled industrial energy and ebullience—and starved for land useful for industrial development—the city in 1946 established industrial zones, one along Marginal Way and the Back Cove, historically the city's second hub of industrial activity behind the port itself and the Fore River. Fully aware of the significance of the approaching Maine Turnpike,and of land contiguous to the highway for industrial sites with plentiful parking and easy truck access, the city spotlighted Deering's Riverton area and the Warren Street corridor for industrial development. But, as was true during the age of James Phinney Baxter, the industrial dream proved chimerical. Some industrial growth occurred, especially in the suburbs, but only barely materialized within the city itself. By 1949, Portland's postwar business leadership preached the importance not only of luring industry but also of reinvigorating commerce and reviving tourism. In 1950, the region's brightest new prospect seemingly lay in the world of shipping and commerce; it was petroleum.[6]

When New England Shipbuilding shut down its South Portland yards between 1945 and 1946, it bequeathed to the region a giant industrial complex consisting of the federally financed West and East Yards. The West Yard, estimated to have cost over $6,000,000, included 140 acres of land and a million square feet of floor space in fourteen huge buildings housing overhead cranes and served by eight miles of railroad sidings. To manage and develop this regional asset, in 1945 the State of Maine chartered the Greater Portland Public Development Commission (GPPDC), which by 1948 had redesigned the West Yard site and tenanted there a fish cannery, a lobster-processing business, and a lumber mill.

Soon, GPPDC had gained possession of the East Yard as well, which through sales of land to the Pocahontas Terminal Company and the Portland Pipe Line Company made the site the region's biggest postwar enterprise: that is, the transshipment of oil to Canadian refineries via the pipeline to Quebec built in 1941 by America's Standard Oil Company. In 1946, Standard Oil sold that pipeline to British American Oil, Imperial Oil, McColl-Frontenac Oil, and Shell Oil—a Canadian conglomerate. That same year, the conglomerate constructed a concrete pier in South Portland, and three years later an eight-tank oil storage farm adjoining an existing eight-tank facility. Soon afterward, the company completed a new eighteen-inch pipeline to Quebec, laid beside the original twelve-incher (fig. 23).[7]

South Portland reaped the benefit of the new Portland-Canadian crude oil nexus, but the old port languished. Some sections of old wharf infrastructure fared better than others. The Maine paper industry's ongoing demand for such bulk products as china clay, casein (from Australia and New Zealand, a protein from milk used as adhesive in fine paper), tapioca (a paper binder), and titanium dioxide kept commerce alive at the wharves of the Portland Terminal Company, subsidiary of the Maine Central Railroad. Its wharves, streamlined efficiently to unload and store china clay, sat underneath and in the shadow of the Million Dollar Bridge, completed in 1916, which connected South Portland to the city. Likewise the 200,000-square-foot Maine State Pier at the foot of Franklin Street accommodated a mix of commerce, ferry service, and administrative offices, including that of the Maine Port Authority, founded in 1923. But most of the remaining uncomely piers in the city's once flourishing Commercial Street waterfront complex steadily deteriorated. Some serviced the city's groundfish and shellfish fishing fleets; a few handled scrap metal; but other piers simply rotted.

A 1935 study of the Port of Portland had reported that these aging wharves "possessed little to no accommodations for the economical handling of cargo and with but little depth of water alongside them. Many of the wharves," continued the report, "are now used not for waterfront business, but rather for

23. South Portland tank field. Beginning in the late 1920s, petroleum shipments via pipeline from Portland to Montreal replaced grain as the centerpiece of Portland's maritime economy. Courtesy of *Portland Press Herald* Still-Film Negative Collection, Portland Public Library Special Collections and Archives.

storage and commercial operations of various types." That remained unchanged after the war.[8] A 1948 *Portland Evening Express* editorial, ignoring positive news about the nascent oil boom in South Portland, focused instead on the lull along old Commercial Street. Portland, wrote the *Express,* "is still one of the seaboard's finest harbors. But it does so little business nowadays! Wharves that might be jammed with shipping lie idle too much of the time. Portland literally has to fight for what little share of the nation's seaboard trade it does get. But, evidently, Portland is not fighting hard enough."[9]

Yet in 1948 a parade of tankers was delivering crude oil to South Portland docks—a lively commerce that meant little for the old piers along the Commercial Street corridor, however. Statistics for 1947–1965 highlighted the problem. Indeed, after World War II the Greater Portland–based commerce in the pipeline delivery of Canadian-bound crude oil, and in the New England regional distribution of imported refined petroleum—both centered in South Portland—skyrocketed. By 1965 this commerce in tonnage terms made Greater Portland the second major oil port in America. Crude oil exports, just over 4 million tons in 1950 jumped to about 10.5 million in 1955, before soaring to over 12 million in 1965 and 23 million five years later. Imported refined petroleum for the New England market rose from 305,000 tons in 1950 up to almost 2 million tons in 1965. By comparison, commerce in the once thriving paper and paper pulp sector appeared modest and grew (or not) even more modestly: Portland handled 84,000 tons of paper pulp in 1950 but only 25,000 tons in 1965. China clay, tapioca, and casein amounted to 35,000 tons in 1950 and 74,000 in 1955 but declined to only 37,000 tons in 1965.[10] Similarly, with the postwar popularity of clean oil and gas home heating, the port's once brisk coal commerce declined drastically from 1950 to 1970.

From Munjoy Hill, where Longfellow once viewed the city in the mid-nineteenth century, Portland in 1963 offered a much different panorama. Instead of gazing out at the breathtaking spectacle of sleek clipper ships and down-easters, their sails billowing, the modern observer beheld a brace of 700- or 800-foot supertankers with 102-foot beams. Several lay at Portland Pipeline's 1,975-foot South Portland pier. Tugs maneuvered another giant tanker into the company's Front Street Terminal in South Portland, and smaller 400- to 500-foot tankers lay at anchor in Casco Bay, awaiting berthing at the California Oil pier, or piers owned by Getty Oil, Mobile, Texaco, Amoco, and Chevron. Portland, once the great international grain port, had become an oil port visited in 1963 by 388 vessels, which unloaded in that one year alone 93.6 million barrels of crude oil.[11]

In 1965, however, on the eve of large-scale urban renewal, little stirred on hoary Commercial Street. Since 1945, the grand, 100-foot-wide doorstep of the once picturesque old port had grown seedier and seedier. Once the teeming, clanging, boisterous heart of Portland's brisk wholesaling business, the broad, rail-littered thoroughfare lay eerily silent in 1965. At its eastern end loomed the remaining 1,500,000 bushel Grand Trunk Railway grain elevator and, adjoining it, the massive Grand Trunk wharves serviced by a huge conveyor belt which jutted out into the Fore River. Five-years later in 1970 the giant conveyor belt burned in a spectacular fire that astoundingly spared the elevator—which, alas, two years later was demolished. In 1965 only the U.S. Commodity Corporation utilized the elevator and conveyor belt to store barley, wheat, and oats shipped from western and Maine farms. After Congress approved the Tariff Act of 1930 allowing the United States to seize cargos of grain after ten months of storage, all shipments of Canadian grain had ceased. Only the

Canadian National Railway and its Grand Trunk infrastructure remained as a vestige of Portland's glorious Canada-linked past.[12]

Portland's Aging Postwar Downtown

Sluggish port activity along Commercial Street and the migration of commerce, industry, and middle-class families to the more spacious and modern planned housing subdivisions in Deering, Falmouth, Yarmouth, Cumberland, and South Portland threatened the viability of Portland's traditional downtown, including the Congress Street shopping hub, the Middle Street hotels and banks, and old Exchange Street's professional offices, quirky bookstores, and paper jobbers. This heart of the city—the 1866 burn area, the city's hotel region centered on Middle, Congress, and Monument Square—had been inextricably part of Portland's historic vacationland.

It had declined slowly, not suddenly. During the 1940s, with the city's population still rising and its trolley-riding and downtown-shopping habits intact, center city's Porteous Mitchell and Braun department store and its Woolworth's, Benoits, and Filene's, as well as its Exchange Street lawyers and booksellers, maintained their solid, traditional customer base. Little neighborhood businesses flourished—like Earle Shettleworth Sr.'s Munjoy Department Store, whose plentiful stock of thread and yarn catered to the area's many Italian women and their proclivity for making their own clothes.[13]

Most Portlanders in 1948 still assumed, along with Chicago School geographers, that urban form was fixed. World War II seemingly vindicated the metropolitan tradition of a core city where men worked and women shopped, surrounded by rings of class- (and race-) segregated residential neighborhoods connected to the downtown by trolley and train lines. After World War II the automobile, cheap government mortgages, and the lure of spacious lawns and modern one-floor or split-level homes shattered this preconception about urban form. After 1950 in Portland, and across urban America, the grip of the downtown steadily weakened.[14]

Until the 1970s, the heyday of mall building nationally, and the opening of the Maine Mall (near Portland's Jetport and the Maine Turnpike exit in South Portland), Greater Portland had abjured the large regional malls, sanctuaries for shopping, such as Seattle's open-air Northgate (1950), Northland (1954) near Detroit, or Southdale (1956) in Minneapolis's Edina suburb. Beginning in the mid-1950s, Portland developers opened smaller strip shopping centers such as suburban South Portland's Mill Creek, inaugurated with a ribbon-cutting ceremony on June 20, 1955. Housewife-friendly Mill Creek featured a typical array of stores and small shops anchored by a Shaw's Super Market. Among the stores was a branch of the Maine Savings Bank, a laundromat, a beauty shop, a shoe store, a state liquor store, and a children's wear shop. Mill Creek also boasted a department store (a branch of Portland's Owen Moore and Company), and most significantly, parking for 300 to 350 cars.[15]

With tract housing sprouting north of Portland in the Deering section, Northgate at Allen's Corners in North Deering opened two years later, in 1957, again with a Shaw's Super Market, a branch bank, a Wellwood's Five and Ten, and a shoe store. A 1959 "Map of Portland: Shoppers Guide" now oriented the viewer not to the peninsula and Congress Street but to suburban Woodfords, Deering, and to South Portland. Conspicuously absent from the list of map advertisers was Benoits and Porteous, Mitchell and Braun. Only the Casco Arcade, an "all under one roof indoor shopping center," and the Columbia Hotel represented the historic downtown. The other advertisers like Mill Creek's Bowl-a-rama and Woodford's Toyland promoted suburban shopping.[16]

The trend intensified. In the early 1960s developers cut the ribbon for several new stripmalls including the Falmouth Shopping Center on Route 88 just off the proposed Interstate 295 expressway; Westgate off Forest Avenue; and the Portland Shopping Plaza (built on the site of the demolished Union Station). With plentiful parking, an air of efficient modernity, and locations convenient to the Maine Turnpike and other major suburban thoroughfares, these second-tier strip malls helped siphon traffic away from Portland's once glamorous, now struggling downtown.[17]

The Bane of Blighted Neighborhoods

According to 1950s retail studies, the middle-class women shoppers who increasingly eschewed downtown stores dreaded not only central city traffic congestion but also the swath of slums encircling the old center-city shopping districts. In Philadelphia and Baltimore, these were neighborhoods of seedy two- and three-story brick row and hidden-alley housing, crowded in 1950 with newly arrived African Americans from Virginia and the Carolinas. In Boston, Providence, and Worcester, downtown neighborhoods featured aging Second French Empire and Italianate triple-deckers often squeezed incongruously on awkwardly configured lots. Interspersed throughout these ethnic and often racially segregated neighborhoods were tiny food stores, corner taprooms, warehouses, icehouses and junkyards, garages, small machine shops, and other modest businesses. They clearly bore the patina of antiquity in an upbeat postwar age that—in architectural design, in appliances and in transportation modes—embraced sleek, streamlined modernity and cursed the old and obsolescent.[18]

Portland's aging downtown neighborhoods, Bayside, Munjoy Hill, Gorham's Corner, and Bayside, have been well introduced. By 1944, many of the city's large second- and third-generation Irish had already vacated Gorham's Corner, and some of the neighborhood's dilapidated tenements in the shadow of Fraternity House had been replaced by ice cream factories, garages, cold storage, plumbing supply and furniture and other warehouses. The Great Depression and the World War II crush of in-migrant labor had greatly overtaxed most the housing stock of Bayside and Munjoy Hill, the neighborhoods through which in the 1950s suburbanites from Deering, Falmouth, Cumberland, and Yarmouth regularly passed on their commute to and from downtown.[19]

Portland had been awakened to the squalor of the Bayside slum before 1950: the 1924 reassessment and the 1940 census had revealed unsafe, dilapidated tenements with absent or unsanitary plumbing. In 1943 the city's fledgling planning department, led by Cambridge consultant Arthur Comey, in concert with the Portland Health Department, undertook a housing survey of the neighborhood which produced a report, "Does Bayside Need Rebuilding: A Study of Housing Conditions in a Problem Area of Portland, Maine." The Planning Board had retained Allan Twitchell of the American Public Health Association (APHA) (famous for his scientific numerical rating system of bad housing) to survey Bayside, the area already highlighted in the 1940 census for its overcrowding. Twitchell confined his investigation to the Bayside area bounded by Cumberland Street to the south, Lancaster Street and Somerset on the north, and west and east by Elm Street and Anderson. Twitchell found nothing charming or romantic about the tree-lined streets and Queen Anne, French Empire, or Colonial Revival piles bordering Chestnut, Pearl, and Mayo Streets. He focused scornfully on the neighborhood's deficiencies and lack of modernity. His study revealed that over half the dwellings had one or more substandard conditions such as no central heating, cold water only, windowless rooms, and dangerous physical deterioration. Such conditions, stressed the APHA, "are ordinarily linked with infant mortality, tuberculosis, juvenile

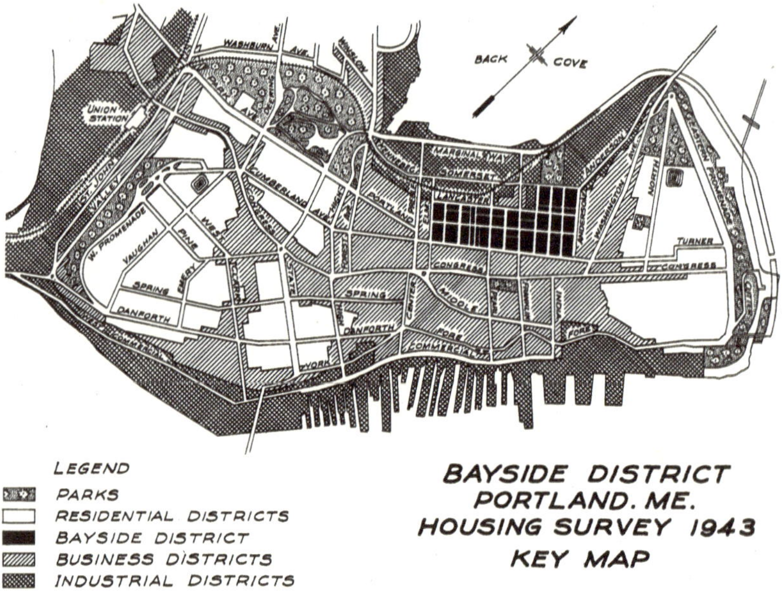

24. Allan A. Twitchell's 1944 American Public Health Association map of Portland documenting that Portland needed to be "rebuilt." Courtesy of Portland Department of City Planning Library.

delinquency, adult crime, and high government cost." The report, which divided the neighborhood into four sectors, branded Bayside's housing substandard overall. Although Twitchell found that none of the four sectors "fell into the extreme slum classification," he concluded that "much of the housing in the Bayside District is fundamentally so obsolescent that it cannot be modernized without improvement so expensive or structurally so difficult as to make them [*sic*] economically impractical" (fig. 24).

Interestingly, what Bayside's critics in the 1940s labeled obsolescent, later in the 1960s and 1970s social critics and architect-planners found to be to safe, delightful, communal living environments. The neighborhood's streets were narrow and its dwellings stood on narrow lots, close to the streets. The community was dotted with little groceries and other first-floor storefronts, which in the 1940s was considered evidence of overcrowding and poor planning.

Bayside's notoriety had only intensified by 1945. Police records that year indicated that the neighborhood housed the heaviest concentration of Portland's criminals and welfare cases. A horrendous 1947 tenement fire compounded the ignominy, confirming for city officials the fire threat of unkempt slums and the fiscal as well as the social costs of slums. Just in time for the Christmas season of 1948, the *Portland Evening Express* ran a front-page exposé of the beleaguered place which mobilized public indignation and unleashed a full-fledged anti-slum crusade in Longfellow's beautiful city. The *Express* series focused on Bayside. The newspaper exposé, beginning December 6, 1948, and continuing until just before Christmas, fleshed out Twitchell's 1943 report with lurid photographs and extensive quotations from municipal court judges, the county attorney, Health Department personnel, and both landlords and tenants. Unlike Twitchell, who tempered his rhetoric by observing that some Bayside housing was actually good and that Bayside was remarkably free of noisy and noisome industry, the *Express* reviled the whole neighborhood as "squalid and shocking," its housing "unfit for swine . . . [and] a breeding ground for juvenile delinquency." In one loathsome hovel huddled nine children and six adults. Two hall toilets, located in an unheated, scabrous cubicle and overflowing with filth, accommodated six wretched families. In another pest hole reporters discovered a baby, its legs covered with maggot eggs. Elsewhere, children played on "rat infested lots; a waterless third-floor flat sheltered four children and their parents. Floor boards oozed with sewage, and maggots abounded. Without running water, threatened by fraying electrical wire, crumbling plaster, and exposed lathing, tenants desperate for shelter survived at the mercy of unscrupulous landlords.[20] At $12 to $15 monthly, rent-controlled units left little incentive for owners to make repairs. "If they [tenants] don't like it," said one landlord, "they can leave." Still, argued the *Evening Express,* tenants in America should never be forced to live like animals; such deplorable conditions victimized tenants, threatened the public safely, fomented communism, and begged for remediation. Charles Dickens and Jacob Riis could not have painted London's Bethnal Green or Bermondsey or New York's Hell's Kitchen more graphically and despairingly than the *Express* portrayed Bayside.[21]

Any similar investigation of Munjoy Hill, the neighborhood contiguous to Bayside, might have found similar conditions. Working-class families living there in the 1940s, often first- and second-generation Italians, Russian-Jews, Scandinavians, and Armenian Americans, crowded into a mélange of Victorian triple-deckers (many built in the 1880s and 1890s) and nineteenth-century Victorian two- and three-story double and single houses, many, especially along Congress Street, recklessly subdivided during the war into multifamily living quarters and many with deficient plumbing and electric wiring. At the foot of Munjoy Hill, close to the downtown, the waterfront, and the original

1630s George Cleeve settlement, sat an area bounded by Middle Street to the north, Fore on the south, and Pearl and India west and east, with Vine, Deer and Chatham Streets in between. In 1955 it was an old, mixed-use neighborhood of derelict, rotting, clapboard and brick houses, of wholesale leather dealers, plumbing supply firms, little ethnic groceries, automobile garages, and other small shops. It also included Longfellow's birthplace, the three-story brick Wordsworth-Longfellow house on Hancock Street, a popular tourist attraction.[22]

Portland tourist guides had long listed Longfellow's birthplace as a destination, together with Monument Square, City Hall, the Portland Observatory, and the Eastern and Western Promenades. With its steamship service from New York and Boston, its daily trains from Philadelphia, New York, and Boston, its extensive trolley and interurban rail connections, Portland had historically functioned, through wars and depressions, as a "gateway to vacationland." But, just as Congress Street's appeal to shoppers dimmed after the war, Portland's fabled attractiveness to tourists as a place of delight, a health spa, and trove of literary, art, and maritime history likewise faded in the 1950s, fueling well-founded fears for the city's future. Portland's newspapers in the middle and late 1940s still spoke of tourism, but the war with its gas rationing and suspension of private automobile production had severely hobbled the industry. The "Maine" advertising supplement included in the July 4, 1946, *Evening Express* mentioned only one Portland hotel, the Graymore. Titled "Its [Portland's] Hotel Industry," the advertisement features a black and white photograph of the Graymore apparently taken on a gray, overcast day. The ground is wet; a solitary automobile stands parked outside the hotel. It is a film noir image, lacking only Humphrey Bogart leaning against the 1941 Plymouth. A somber accompanying image of the hotel's vacant cocktail lounge begs the presence of Peter Lorre and Lauren Bacall at the bar.[23]

With Ford and General Motors in full production by 1949 building newly designed modern cars, tourism returned in the 1950s, but Maine tourist publicity no longer highlighted Portland as a favored destination. In the 1930s the automobile Green Guides ceased carrying full-page ads for the city and contained not even one mention of a Portland hotel. By contrast, a full-page ad appeared for the Boothbay Harbor region and its Newagen and Sprucewold Inns. Postwar transportation trends as much as anything doomed the city and its once-touted gateway status. Boston and New York to Portland steamship service had been permanently discontinued by 1944. The Maine Central, Boston and

Maine, and Canadian National Railroads slogged through the Great Depression only to surge with wartime business; but after the war, rising automobile use cut deeply into rail ridership. Between 1948 and 1954, passenger revenues of the Boston and Maine plummeted. To compensate, the line raised fares and cut the number of trains serving Portland. When that failed, it continued to cut service, and in 1960, together with Maine Central, terminated all rail passenger service to Maine. The Canadian National operated passenger trains for a few more years and then shut down. Maine's glorious rail age was over. In 1961, with hundreds of strategically placed dynamite charges, the railroads demolished their magnificent Union Railroad Station on St. John Street.[24]

Air service replaced rail. In 1946, Congress enacted the Federal Airport Aid Act providing cities like Portland with matching grants for the construction of local airfields. Between 1946 and 1957, airline passenger ridership rose nationwide from 13 million annually to 53 million. Airports eclipsed train stations as transportation centers, a tragedy for downtowns but a boon to suburbia. Portland seized the opportunity to upgrade its South Portland Airport, especially since Northeast Airlines had introduced scheduled daily service to Portland in 1946.[25]

Automobile use, sprightly in the 1920s and 1930s, also boomed in the 1950s, bringing hope of revitalized tourism. Car travel, too, changed. In the 1940s, Maine-bound drivers, albeit very few in number, followed U.S. Route 1, the historic Boston Post Road, northward through town after town, traffic light after light, from Portsmouth, New Hampshire, across the Piscataquis River into Kittery, past York and Old Orchard Beach, thence to Portland. All along the way, gas stations, garages, gift shops, guest houses, tourist cabins, and motor courts welcomed vacationers. But the romance of Route 1 ended abruptly after the war. Impressed by the progress of the Pennsylvania Turnpike, built by the New Deal Public Works Administration, Maine in 1946 floated a $20 million bond issue, and in 1947 unveiled the first forty-four miles of the four-lane Maine Turnpike, an alternative to Route 1, from Kittery to Portland.

As the Bureau of Public Roads and the new (1944) Federal Highway Administration ordered, however, the superhighway did not enter Portland but was aligned to the west, forcing motorists to access the city and the downtown on a fairly long stretch of stop-and-go traffic down Congress Street. To funnel turnpike traffic closer into the downtown, as early as 1953 the planning department had proposed an expressway, clearly delineated on a 1954 planning map. Federal funding for high-cost urban expressways spiraled upward with passage in 1956 of the Interstate Highway Act, which created the National Highway Trust Fund. Despite the boost to highway building, federal approval and funding for Portland's I-295 expressway did not arrive until 1965, and this beltway section from the turnpike through South Portland, cutting through Deering Oaks Park, skirting the edge of the Back Cove, and finally reconnecting to the turnpike in Falmouth, would not be completed until November 1974. A new era had arrived. Tourists in their cars could now easily enter Portland, either through South Portland, the Forest Avenue Exit, or, in the 1970s, on the new Franklin Arterial. But that is another story, one that involves the history of urban renewal in Portland.[26]

Blight and Postwar City Planning in Longfellow's City

Portland's socially and politically conservative Yankee class in late 1948 responded viscerally to the *Evening Express*'s aforementioned expose of Bayside's overcrowded tenements, overflowing toilets, rats, and fly larvae. They cringed, too, at pronouncements and speculation about historic Portland's demise as a hub of commerce and tourism. But even before the shock of Pearl Harbor, the city's civic, professional, and business elites had cringed at the mounting evidence of Portland's decaying residential, commercial, and industrial infrastructure. The rising tide of in-migrant defense workers had suddenly awakened Portlanders to the city's housing crisis and to its haphazard, muddled land-use patterns. A chagrined Forest City at last fully embraced professional urban planning.

In 1941, prodded by the *Evening Express* and *Press Herald,* a broad-based Citizens Planning Committee (CPC) had formed, chaired by Albert Tardiff and comprising thirty-seven labor leaders; representatives of the city's Irish longshoremen; fifty-five civic-minded women, chaired by Mrs. Gladys S. Chapman; and eighty-six businessmen and civic leaders (medical and professional), chaired by Neal W. Allen. Among the businessmen and other civic leaders were Henri Benoit and Louis Porteous.[27] Portland's CPC sought to modernize a perceived obsolescent urbanism, but not without paying homage to the city's reputed beauty. In the long run, however, reconciling beauty and practicality proved harder than had been imagined. The CPC hailed planning for "its emphasis on the usefulness of artistic practicality over the mere quaintness of laissez-faire indirection," and it viewed the creation of a five-member planning board, advocated by the committee, as a "non-political way to reconcile business interests and those devoted to an orderly and beautiful development of our city." Mrs. William E. Wing, committee member and honorary president of the Longfellow Garden Club, revealingly described herself as "one of the many homeowners who have decided that we wish to see put in action . . . a city planning board which will base its plan upon a full consideration of the past, present and future of historic Portland . . . [a city that] can ill afford to lose its reputation as a city of homes, the City Beautiful seated by the sea." The CPC triumphed when Portland in 1942 voted to create a five-man City Planning Board (CPB) appointed by City Council. The board oversaw a three-person planning department that retained the Cambridge-based Olmsted protégé Arthur Comey as its consultant. A year later the council created the Portland Housing Authority (PHA).[28]

During World War II, the CPB responded to the federal National Resources Planning Board's urging that the city plan for expected postwar unemployment by preparing a long list of city public works projects, including the rebuilding of blighted urban neighborhoods. Immediately, the board crafted a Portland Master Plan, defined as a single static document but as a process, a set of documents or templates for guiding future urban growth. Early documents included plans or statements regarding recreation, schools, land use, sewers, and major streets. By 1945 and V-J Day, Portland planners had already identified Marginal Way and Warren Streets as industrial corridors and, with state and federal highway fund assistance, aligned the future 295 expressway between the Back Cove and the proposed Marginal Way industrial zone. The CPB also launched an ambitious and costly agenda of sewer upgrading, track removal, park and playground improvements, and street upgrading that involved trying to relieve the city's frustrating traffic and parking problems.[29]

Beginning in 1943, however, it was blighted housing that most preoccupied the young planning body. The theme reverberated from the pages of the Planning Board's September 1946 report, "Urban Redevelopment for Portland." "Portland has failed to realize its environmental possibility," stated the report. "In a city such as Portland with a superb natural location, in an area [such as Bayside] with wonderful view sites, one finds the oldest and poorest housing." With the exception of Bramhall Hill and such streets as Chadwick, Vaughn, and Thomas in the West End and the Eastern Promenade on Munjoy Hill, the report rated housing in the rest of the peninsula as "poor" to "very poor." The front-page image of the study, an aerial photograph of the Portland peninsula east to west from well aloft in the Portland Observatory, captured graphically the dense nineteenth-century settlement pattern, the mishmash of streets overbuilt with triple- and quadruple-deckers, and with brick and graying clapboard double houses.

The report blared out a shrill and concise message about the costs of urban decay without any allusion to aesthetic concerns. "Decaying sections like Bayside," exhorted Comey, "are not only unhealthful, but are breeding grounds of juvenile delinquency, tuberculosis, and high welfare caseloads." Comey stressed the social cost of bad housing and deliberately contrasted Portland's new outlying suburbs with the declining, "once stable residential sections" such as Bayside, where "many of the houses were built too close together" and many of the old three- or four-decker types had stairways that were poorly located and hence were a dangerous hazard in case of fire. Not only did Bayside breed crime, delinquency, and dependency (1945 police records indicated that, as earlier noted, it housed the heaviest concentration of both criminals and welfare cases), but such areas "return far less in tax revenue than they cost to maintain."

He admitted that the high cost of land, the "cost of acquiring and removing outmoded buildings, . . . the difficulty of acquiring large enough tracts of land, now in diverse ownership," and the "displacement of the present population" represented serious obstacles. To overcome those obstacles, Comey drafted three model pieces of legislation. One was an "Act for Urban Redevelopment." A second provided for the creation of a city land authority with power to declare areas blighted and use tax funds and federal and state grants-in-aid to acquire condemned land and completely replan a blighted district. To house those uprooted by redevelopment, the third piece of legislation proposed a mutual housing trust, enabling Portland's ill-housed renter class to own equity shares in a mutual housing corporation, just as Amalgamated Clothing Workers did in New York City's Amalgamated Homes, built in 1926.[30] Alluding to the recent war, Comey asked, "Will those who sent their sons out to fight a war on foreign shores approach the achievement of a better and more spacious way of living at home, as fearlessly as their sons did abroad? The bombed and impoverished cities of England are building anew along freer and more spacious lines, while we, with the wealth of a free nation whose shores were not touched in the devastation, timidly falter about rebuilding outworn sections lest we lose an increment of value." A modernist houser at heart, Comey urged Portland to rebuild places like Bayside with modern Bauhaus-style housing developments similar to Philadelphia's Public Works Administration–financed Carl Mackley Homes, built in the1930s for the American Federation of Full-Fashioned Hosiery Workers.

Not surprisingly, staunchly antiunion and anti–public housing Portlanders balked at Comey's seemingly radical request.[31]

After the war, a suburban, rather than urban, aesthetic prevailed. American magazines like *Life* and *Better Homes and Gardens* juxtaposed grim images of moldering slum housing in dark, narrow streets with blithe photographs of grassy, picket-fenced suburban homes. Such images fed environmentalist arguments linking the wartime and postwar rash of zoot-suited juvenile delinquency and teenage gang membership to America's congested slums. Thus, postwar suburbanization itself justified rebuilding Bayside. Bayside threatened the economic viability of Portland's adjoining downtown, a place that civic leaders and businessmen imagined as locked in a life-and-death struggle with emergent suburbia.[32]

Despite some 1930s-era Art Deco and Art Moderne storefronts, downtown Congress Street itself, with its graying 1927 grand hotel, its old brick and stone five- and six-story business blocks, and increasingly uncomely Monument Square, looked forlorn. City planners, city retailers, city realtors, as well as West End homeowners dreaded the allure of suburban strip malls and feared for the viability of the city's historic commercial core.[33]

The *Portland Evening Express*'s December 1948 series on Bayside's slums, with its wrenching images of besmeared children in tattered clothing, touched Portland hearts, graphically articulated the city's worst fears, and added enormous impetus to Comey's call for urban redevelopment. Together, the series and the 1946 redevelopment report had mobilized a full-fledged discourse in Portland about slums, Bayside, the downtown, and how the city should attack the problem. Portland was not alone. Many other cities, among them New York, Chicago, Philadelphia, Pittsburgh, and Baltimore, were also plotting strategies to attack urban decay.[34]

As the urban conversation about Portland blight and the city's future intensified, Washington fueled the discussion with talk of pending legislation to enable cities to solve one of the greatest problems facing urban rebuilders: how to underwrite the astronomical costs of purchasing inner-city slums, clearing the properties, and preparing them for modern residential or commercial development. Redevelopment legislation had been introduced in Congress in 1945 and became part of President Harry S. Truman's Fair Deal. By 1949 the Wagner-Ellender-Taft housing and slum-clearance legislation had attracted a host of diverse supporters from modern housing reformers (called housers) such as Catherine Bauer Wurster to labor, bankers, downtown businessmen, lawyers, and other professionals who saw the legislation as an opportunity to purge slums and redesign and "rehouse" the central city in a modern fashion competitive with suburbia. The Housing Act of 1949 established as a national goal a "decent home and a suitable living environment for every American family." It also aimed to clear and rebuild downtown slums, and under Title I the law authorized a first-year appropriation of $1 billion in federal grants and loans to enable local redevelopment authorities to purchase, clear, and prepare urban land for redevelopment. To the joy of housers (and the bane of private realtors, homebuilders, and anti-Communists like Wisconsin Senator Joseph McCarthy), Title II of the law revived the New Deal's dormant public housing program by scheduling construction of 810,000 units over six years. For those Portlanders who imagined a modern city by the sea arising from the mélange of narrow streets, old warehouses, crusty storefronts, and scabrous Victorian piles which was postwar Portland, the Housing Act of 1949 elevated expectations.[35]

While Congress added the finishing touches to the 1949 legislation, Governor Frederick Payne in Augusta prepared a state slum clearance law that summoned Maine cities to create housing authorities and provide low-cost public housing. In 1947, after extensive debate and long delay, and with tireless prodding from Senator Margaret Chase Smith, Portland's City Council at last agreed to assume ownership of Sagamore Heights, the Lanham Act defense housing project built in 1941. Portland's conservative establishment, which included City Council, had resisted the Sagamore deal and was equally wary of Payne's bill and Washington's housing legislation, especially the Title II provision for new public housing. With politically charged rhetoric building in America about an Iron Curtain across Europe and an impending Red Menace, Portland's home builders decried the socialistic, New Deal features of the proposed Maine redevelopment law, which they saw as paving the way to serfdom. They deemed slum clearance and public housing unnecessary in Portland.

Much of the city's old housing and slum neighborhoods like Bayside, argued the home builders, could be conserved through rehabilitation and enforcement of the city's housing and building codes. To underscore their arguments, and fend off public housing, in January 1949 the Maine Home Builders' Association invited to Portland an outside expert from Baltimore, Maryland, a city then famous for its housing conservation program as conducted in the red-brick, row-house neighborhood of Waverly. In fact, the earnestness of housing conservation in Edgar Allen Poe's city earned the conservation approach its name: Baltimore Plan.

The expert, Robert Bready, chair of the National Home Builders Association's Slum Clearance Committee, hailed from Baltimore and had helped author the Baltimore Plan, which opposed massive clearances, and asserted that most old buildings could be saved. Rather than clearance and new construction, the plan promoted intensive code enforcement plus cooperative agreements among local banks and property owners to rehabilitate housing and clean up and revitalize slum neighborhoods. Molded by mall developer James Rouse, the plan would influence the 1954 Housing Act.

Together with Arthur T. Row and N. Norton Maxfield of the CPB, City Manager Lyman S. Moore, Carroll Beck of the Maine Home Builders' Association, and Albert Hobbs of the Housing Authority, Bready—unfazed by Maine's January cold—was escorted through the city's Bayside slum. On Wilmot Street the group halted to inspect a decrepit, two-family dwelling with bulging walls and a crumbling foundation. Following the tour the delegation reassembled for dinner and Bready's speech at the Falmouth Hotel. There Bready declared Portland's slums "as bad as anywhere else." He confessed that "these areas are disease and rat ridden" and that "there is not much there for tenants to take care of." But he also declared much of the city's old housing stock, with its typically big rooms and location on wide, tree-lined streets, to be salvageable, and, predictably, he cautioned Portland against hasty demolition. Instead, he called for municipal trash collection and a more efficient system of handling tenant complaints. "Give tenants decent housing," pleaded Bready, "and that will take care of it."[36]

Not fully satisfied with Bready's verdict, Portland's realtor and home builder alliance, which believed slum clearance would lead down a primrose path to socialistic public housing, invited Detroit's Rodney Lockwood for a second expert tour of Bayside. Lockwood obligingly told the home builders that he "didn't see any substandard housing." That startling testimony only hardened the pro–slum clearance cohort's determination. Hurriedly, the Citizens' Housing Committee, a body formed by the CPB to investigate housing conditions, unveiled its own survey, disclosing that 19,800 (or 23 percent) of Portland's 84,000 citizens lived in substandard housing. Admittedly, "slums do not always look like slums, and there are many examples of good housekeeping in buildings which should never be occupied," stated the committee, but the "rusty, unsanitary toilets, the missing plaster, dank basements, and repeated sewer stoppages, evidence slums."[37]

Portland's ordinarily conservative *Portland Press Herald*, together with the *Evening Express,* urged the city "to surrender its antipathy for government activism. If there are those who prefer our slums to the 'injustices and 'inconveniences' of public slum clearance programs, let them say so. Let them stack their arguments against those of the people who see our slums as a growing emergency which demands government aid and intervention."[38]

Portland's Planning Board fully acknowledged the usefulness of Bready's Baltimore Plan, but as only one weapon against the slum. Accordingly, the board presented a broad strategy for combatting blight, which recommended first strengthening the city's minimum standard housing code, then enforcing the city's zoning and building codes, and conserving/rehabilitating existing sound housing. Finally, in defiance of city home builders and realtors, it proposed what it admittedly called the radical idea of demolishing and redeveloping the most blighted areas and recommended public housing for those displaced Portland families unable to pay even the lowest rents for standard private shelter. Currently, confessed the CPB, redevelopment was stymied because "there is no place for displaced families to live because of the housing shortage."[39]

Although the absence of low-rent public housing posed an obstacle to any plans for full-scale clearance and the relocation of uprooted families, redevelopment enjoyed momentum in Portland, where businessmen and civic leaders relished the opportunity to use federal dollars to clear slums and modernize the downtown area. Maine passed a State [Redevelopment] Enabling Act in 1951, but, consistent with the state's anti–New Deal spirit, it barred the reuse of condemned land for public housing. One year later, in 1952, Portland created a Slum Clearance and Redevelopment Authority of Portland (SCRAP) whose acronym, oddly, raised few eyebrows.

Working closely with the Planning Board, which served as the official city planning agency for all proposed slum clearance and redevelopment projects, SCRAP promptly identified for redevelopment four major survey areas totaling 272 acres. For immediate attention, it selected two of these: the 22-acre eastern half of Bayside (named Bayside Park), and the 6.3-acre Vine-Deer-Chatham site located at the foot of Munjoy Hill, adjoining the city waterfront. At the Vine-Deering-Chatham site, commerce and industry had invaded an old residential neighborhood, and redevelopment plans there involved mainly demolishing 119 dwelling units and developing instead a light industrial zone, thus helping to reinvigorate the city's sagging postwar economy.[40]

Two other renewal sites, a small downtown one and the old Munjoy Hill area adjacent to Bayside, completed SCRAP's agenda. In 1952, however, the process halted. The Housing and Home Finance Administration's (HHFA) Division of Slum Clearance and Urban Redevelopment (DSCUR) barred Portland from proceeding until the constitutionality of Maine's redevelopment legislation had been tested in the courts. For the challenge, SCRAP chose the smaller and better-positioned Vine-Deer-Chatham site with its mottle of commercial, industrial, and residential property. A favorable State Supreme Court decision on the constitutionality of urban renewal did not come until the fall of 1954, and an appeal of that decision stalled further action until 1956.[41]

During the four years that Portland lawyers defended Maine's redevelopment law, Portlanders executed the Baltimore Plan, or neighborhood conservation, approach: the city instituted strict enforcement of its housing code and zoning ordinance, plus a clean-up, fix-up, paint-up program. Led by its Health Department, Portland in 1954 launched a block-by-block housing survey, backed by code enforcement and an ambitious program of housing rehabilitation, which endeavored to combat blight and restore beauty. Essentially, the city encouraged owners to rehabilitate their property beyond the minimum standards set forth in the housing code.[42]

Notwithstanding widespread praise for the housing preservation program, even the city's Health Department expressed doubts about its ultimate success. The department estimated that a thoroughgoing block-by-block survey would take over ten years, during which time cancerous blight threatened to overwhelm more and more of the city.[43]

Slum clearance proponents bemoaned the sluggish pace of Portland's block-by-block housing rehabilitation agenda. In 1954 the influential pastor of the large Woodfords Congregational Church, the Reverend Doctor Frederick H. Thompson, delivered a scathing Sunday sermon attacking the squalor of Portland's slums and accusing City Council of underfunding the vital task of clearance.[44]

Meanwhile, President Dwight D. Eisenhower, like Portland's business and civic officialdom in the 1950s, embraced the Baltimore Plan. In 1953 he established an Advisory Commission on Government Housing Policies and Programs, chaired by Baltimore's celebrated mall developer James Rouse. The Rouse committee report informed much of the 1954 Housing Act, which substituted the word "renewal" for "redevelopment." Like Portland's program, the 1954 act favored housing rehabilitation and blight prevention. It also, however, gave the pro-growth clique of city officials and downtown business developers much greater latitude by elevating commercial over residential development, the latter the focus of the earlier 1949 Wagner-Ellender-Taft legislation.[45]

In 1954 the Maine Supreme Court upheld slum clearance and renewal, declaring it legal to take land and then use it for private development, because destroying slums served the greater public good of bettering public health, morals, and public safety. Now unencumbered, the Vine-Deer-Chatham renewal site, located at the heart of the old waterfront district, breathed new life. Not for long. Lawyers for a number of the sixty-four families, twenty-eight individuals, and twenty-seven small businesses resident there (many of them Italian, Russian-Jewish, and Armenian owned) filed one suit after another. Some opponents charged the city with socialism and Soviet-style tyranny. Others—like Popkin Zakarian, owner of a doomed-site business—opposed any publicly funded redevelopment, protesting that urban renewal at Vine-Deer-Chatham and Bayside revealed rich bankers, lawyers, and public officials squandering taxpayer dollars to reduce perfectly good business and residential property into an ugly heap of rubble.[46]

Nevertheless, in late 1955 City Council voted to proceed with renewal at Vine-Deer-Chatham. Fifty-nine buildings fell to city bulldozers, creating a wide swath of rubble in the once historic and densely developed area of the city. As engineers straightened serpentine Fore Street, Vine and Deer and Chatham Streets disappeared. In place of the scraggly wholesale houses, hovels, and (yes) Longfellow's birthplace, arose the modern headquarters of Jordan's Meats, Casco Printing, a state liquor store and vehicle registry office, a parking lot, and land reserved for the future widening of Franklin Street.[47]

The Bayside Park renewal actually conformed closely to the 1954 legislation. Portland planners cleared a very limited portion of that twenty-two-acre project area, selectively demolishing 507 dwelling units of what the Portland Planning Board called the worst housing. In SCRAP's words, the project sought to "stabilize the area so that new housing investment could occur." The next year, in a letter forwarded to Housing and Home Finance administrator Albert Cole regarding Portland's "Workable Plan" for renewal (mandated by the 1954 Housing Act), John Orr, the city manager, stated that the city was "confident that the redevelopment program for the City of Portland is the most advanced of any city in New England, and compares favorably with the programs of the largest cities."[48]

As Twitchell had in 1943, and Breading in 1949, Portland's planning board in 1953–1954 conceded that despite evidence of shabbiness, big-city blight hardly enshrouded Bayside. "There is no area where there are not perfectly good houses next to 'real wrecks,'" admitted Portland Planning Director Roger L. Creighton. Rather than massive clearance, therefore, SCRAP instead espoused spot clearance, the extirpation of pockets of excrescence. Nevertheless, Creighton could still excoriate Bayside as "notorious for complete [social] breakdown," and the city's planning models built in order to graphically display Portland's renewal scheme showed Bayside stripped of its density. In the planners' minds, here festered the dark, albeit once beautiful, cityscape of old Portland with its alleys and dank dooryards. Now planners branded Bayside unsafe, a mean, unhealthy place bereft of safe play areas; an obsolete place to be transformed into an airy, modern Elysium. Portland's 1957 "Bayside Report" clearly echoed the language of the 1949 and 1954 housing acts. Submitted to HHFA for approval of the sixty-one-acre Bayside Park project, the report focused on the neighborhood's narrow, crooked, unsafe streets and its deficient recreational space, concluding that Bayside did not "provide the environment necessary for reasonable living conditions."[49]

Unlike the Vine-Deering-Chatham site, little opposition to the Bayside renewal plans erupted. Since part of the city's 1955 "Workable Program" mandated citizen participation in planning, SCRAP requested the Council of Social Agencies to form a citizens' committee representative of Bayside.[50] But the federal requirement that cities contribute half the total cost of site purchase and preparation stalled action on the Bayside project until the 1960s.

SCRAP renewal maps in 1955 displayed two other proposed projects: a small downtown commercial clearance site and the much larger Munjoy South, a massive 79.4-acre residential renewal project involving 1,265 families. An area rife with triple-deckers, but also exquisite Italianate, Second French Empire, and Gothic Renaissance gems, it covered all of the eastern peninsula south of Congress Street from Mountfort Street to the Eastern Promenade overlooking Casco Bay. Like Bayside, Munjoy South combined housing rehabilitation with block-scale demolition. Housing and Home Finance chief Robert Weaver approved the project in 1962. The Portland Renewal Authority (PRA—a more sensitive name replacing SCRAP) regarded the bulk of Munjoy South's housing as substandard, and selected for demolition an 11-acre swath of 116 buildings off Congress and Mountfort, stretching to Fore Street. A private developer contracted with the PRA to rebuild the section with modern, moderate-income townhouses. Advertised in 1967 as "MUNJOY SOUTH: Overlooking Picturesque Portland Harbor," the complex purported to feature New England architecture and to be "imaginative and unique in design." A smaller, 2.9-acre Munjoy North clearance project followed in 1966.[51]

Together, Bayside, Vine-Deer-Chatham, and Munjoy South by 1965 had destroyed over 530 buildings, most residential, and displaced well over 500 families. In the process it greatly intensified the city's postwar housing shortage. In 1950, despite the existence of the Portland Housing Authority, politically anti–New Deal Portland had no low-rent, publicly owned housing. As early as 1947 Washington had offered the city's housing-starved citizens the Lanham Act–built project Sagamore Heights, on the condition that the City Council assume responsibility for its streets, sewers, and other infrastructure. Portland's American Legion and other veterans' groups joined the League of Women Voters (LWV) and the Portland Citizens Housing Committee (CHC) in cheering the offer. Realtors and city home builders opposed it, thus triggering the debate over creeping socialism that infused the anti–urban redevelopment rhetoric of early 1949, when the governor and state legislature introduced redevelopment legislation permitting municipalities to create housing authorities and enabled the use of federal funds to build and manage public housing. Although the CHC balked at considering public housing the sole solution to the problem, labor, the LWV, Child and Family Services, the YMCA, and other liberal groups again supported the legislation. "If public housing were found the logical solution," stated the Housing Committee, "the legislation would give Portland the means of going ahead." But Portland City Council in 1949 squelched any further debate by voting to reject all public housing.[52]

In 1953, however, City Council finally approved the necessary cooperative agreement with the federal Public Housing Administration, and the Portland Housing Authority (PHA) acquired its first public housing project, Sagamore Heights. Portland would not vote to approve new public housing, though, until 1961, and the city would not build its first units of public housing (Bayside Park, later Kennedy Park) until 1963. Kennedy Park opened in 1965, and the adjoining 24-unit Bayside Terrace opened a year later. In 1967, for seniors and disabled persons, the PHA unveiled its first and only Corbusian "tower in the sky," the 16-story, 200-unit Franklin Towers, the tallest building in Maine.

(The Corbusian vision of "towers in the sky" was named for the Swiss-born modernist Le Corbusier, who as a member of the Congrès Internationaux d'Architecture Moderne (CIAM) espoused the use of architecture and urban design to purge the detritus of the industrial past. His architecture and the ideas of the German Bauhaus school, popular at Harvard, flourished in cities such as Philadelphia but not in culturally conservative Portland.)[53]

With over 530 families displaced by renewal and only 270 units of public housing—and the relocation services of Portland's Child and Family Society notwithstanding—the city's efforts to rehouse displaced families sputtered in the early 1960s. By the mid-1960s, Portland, like the nation, was slowly retreating from large-scale neighborhood slum clearance. Simultaneously, urban progrowth coalitions nationwide—their ranks, as in Portland, comprising largely urban politicos, civic leaders, business and professional luminaries, and federal officialdom—pressed for a more downtown-focused rebuilding agenda.

Yet not everyone thrilled at the modernist vision of purified cities sporting wide avenues of shimmering glass towers. New York architectural critic Jane Jacobs in her *Death and Life of Great American Cities* assailed the wholesale destruction of the urban fabric and its replacement with what she called sterile, antihuman modernist architecture. Jacobs's broadside echoed earlier criticisms by the esteemed houser Catherine Bauer Wurster, and it launched a chorus of attacks on renewal by Marc Fried, Martin Anderson, Herbert Gans, and others.[54] In Portland, a group of citizens awoke to the enormous threat that renewal posed. But this new awareness that untamed renewal endangered both the social and the historic fabric of the Forest City failed to temper concern for Portland's downtown, where, since 1929, neither banks, businessmen, nor any other investor had erected a single new office building.[55]

At the end of Great Depression and World War II, Portland appeared an aging, exhausted, and yes, unkempt place. Faced with the prospect of rampant suburbanization, with deindustrialization, dying railroad service, the further decline of the city's port commerce and of tourism, and housing deemed largely substandard, Portland beheld a grim future. In 1943, egged on by labor, club women, civic and business elite, and the federal government, the city turned to planning and pronounced the need for slum clearance. By 1948 Portland had spotlighted first Bayside and then a seedy waterfront industrial and residential area located around India Street and the old Grand Trunk Railroad terminal, the historic neighborhood where Longfellow had been born. But, as Jane Jacobs, Martin Anderson, and Marc Fried disclosed in the early 1960s, the bulldozers and wrecking balls cleared away more than dilapidated buildings; they eviscerated communities, memories, and the sense of place captured in John Mead Gould's diary entries about walks down Pearl Street on snowy mornings in 1900.

Portland's civic, business, and political leadership fully realized in 1965, that in the face of decades of weak investment in the city's port, housing, and other infrastructure, Longfellow's city bore but the faintest relationship to either the poet's musings or Gould's jottings. Although the Chamber of Commerce still campaigned for conventions, urged greater tourist promotion, sought to make the waterfront tourist friendly with marinas and restaurants, and exulted that Portland was now accessible by both automobile and air service, too much contrary evidence belied its attractiveness and desirability as a tourist destination. In 1946, Portland boasted fourteen hotels, including the splendid Falmouth, the St. Regis, and the Congress Square. Twenty years later none of those three were among the mere seven hotels serving wayfarers to the city. Although Porteous, Mitchell and Braun, W. T. Grant, Woolworth's, Rines Brothers, and Owen Moore still clung to their Congress Street moorings, most department stores featured suburban branches. And downtown after-shopping cuisine, with the exception of the Eastland and Charley's on Monument Square, consisted mainly of banal grills, cafes, and lunch spots.[56]

In 1965, Portland was still waiting for the final verdict on urban renewal. The Planning Board and Renewal Authority exuded confidence, but the visual evidence that year proved disturbing. Viewers beheld vast, scarred urban wastelands. Gould's Bayside and the historic Vine-Deer-Chatham area adjoining Newbury Street remained rubble strewn moonscapes. And, where Longfellow was born—nothing!

The final decision about renewal came in the late 1960s and early 1970s, on the heels of a significant change in the city's political leadership; as a consequence of Portland's selection by the new federal Department of Housing and Urban Development to be a Model City; and with a deepening popular conviction that in its history and its historic Longfellow legacy lay the building blocks for the city's redemption.

CHAPTER SEVEN

The Gateway Reborn, 1965–1985

The currents of radical change that unraveled American culture in the 1960s transformed Portland politics and society, giving voice to Irish, Italian, and Armenian constituents rarely heard in the city's Yankee past. Yet the sinews of Portland's past as a city with a rich maritime history, a city that honored its Longfellow legacy of ocean-splashed beauty, and a city long wedded to both commerce and tourism, ultimately held tight. Indeed, in a post-industrial era, it grew stronger.

Most Portlanders would have found such a prospect unimaginable in the early 1960s. The new decade did begin hopefully, as a new young president with his beautiful family brought Camelot to the Potomac. But Camelot faded quickly. In 1963 Lee Harvey Oswald assassinated President John F. Kennedy. President Lyndon Johnson escalated a conflict in Southeast Asia into a socially and politically costly war in Vietnam. At home, Martin Luther King's civil rights movement mushroomed into the Black Revolution; student protest burgeoned into the Summer of Love and the Berkeley free-speech riots. The decade ended with Patti Hearst and the Symbionese Liberation Army.[1]

Staid Yankee Portland likewise experienced the tumult of the 1960s. Albeit small, its African American community (estimated at forty families in 1965) was centered mainly just off St. John Street near the newly demolished Union Station. In 1964 Portland blacks formed a branch of the National Association for the Advancement of Colored People (NAACP) and elected Gerald E.

Talbot its first president. Though focused mainly on both subtle and overt housing and employment discrimination in the city, the Portland NAACP marched in force down Congress Street protesting violence in Mississippi in 1965 and the murder of Martin Luther King in 1968. The activist organization helped win a Maine Fair Housing Law in 1965 and human rights legislation in 1971.[2]

Meanwhile, the city's youth in the 1960s did not keep their hair short or their bras on. According to Portland historian Bonnie Blythe, the city's hippies congregated at the Good Day Market, a natural-foods cooperative; and Vietnam veteran Raymond Luc Lavasseur, turned long-haired revolutionary, ran the Red Star Bookstore. With other Portlanders Lavasseur formed the radical United Freedom Front; however, his revolutionary career ended in prison for the bombings of U.S. corporations.[3]

New Leaders for a New Age

The broad social and political currents of the 1960s formed the backdrop for a new age in Portland politics. The postwar middle-class exodus, the coming of age of Portland's non-Yankee (though white) minorities, and the unraveling of the deferential tradition loosened the historic Yankee grip on the city's political culture in the 1960s and created a new social and political fermentation: a restiveness, impatience, and disposition to resist the lure of the city's Longfellow past, to abjure satisfaction with the status quo, and to engineer change. A fresh crop of leaders ascended Portland's political stage, people eager to work closely with local pro-growth entrepreneurs and Washington bureaucrats alike. City Council in the early 1960s lost its Yankee Republican homogeneity. It now included not only the Armenian American grocer Ralph Amergian but also Amergian's friend from his youth on Munjoy Hill, the Irish bricklayer's son and fellow Democrat Harold Loring. In his 1959 council race, Loring had boldly challenged the Yankee establishment.

Loring was not alone. In 1962 a young Portland-born Italian/Armenian American, and a graduate of both the University of Maine and the University of Pennsylvania's Fels Institute of Government, John Menario took an internship in the Portland city manager's office, headed at the time by another Fels grad, Graham Watt. Menario later became the city's first finance director and, in 1967, city manager. He was a central figure in Portland's 1970s renaissance.[4]

If the second-generation Irish and Italian Americans aspired to change Portland, so did its business leaders, bent as they were on modernizing the old-fashioned city of narrow streets and Victorian brick business houses. Business leaders like Porteous, Benoit, Casco Bank's Halsey Smith, and Canal Bank's Widgery Thomas aspired to transform the Congress–Middle Street corridor into a modern, sparkling, and inviting downtown. Interstate 295 approached Portland in 1965, and the prospect of the four-lane circumferential highway's arrival stirred visions of sleek looping interchanges giving access to multilane arterials that would speed traffic into the heart of the city. Likewise, the dazzling vision of a Portland served by both an international airport and streamlined superhighways rather than railroads rekindled the memory of Portland as the Gateway City. It intensified the hope that modern highways would lure shoppers and tourists again to the city.

James H. Burke, chair of the Portland Redevelopment Authority in 1965, fervently espoused this vision. An analyst in the Post Office, Burke, with PRA member, slum foe, and fiery pastor of the Woodford Congregational Church, Frederick H. Thompson, along with Loring, Amergian, Menario, and Porteous, ushered in Portland's new era of downtown renaissance.[5]

Between 1965 and 1985 this coalition of politicos and civic and business leaders, armed with federal aid—including the Model Cities program, and Richard Nixon's urban development block grants—undertook to renew or rehabilitate much of the Portland peninsula. While industry remained mainly in places such as the Riverside and Warren Avenue industrial corridors, and while the city in the 1980s voted to keep the Commercial Street wharves and piers a working waterfront rather than a festival marketplace in emulation of cities like Baltimore and Boston, Portland in the 1970s and 1980s increasingly transformed itself from a commercial economy into a city delivering modern financial, real estate, insurance, legal, medical, educational, and other services. Most important for the theme of this book, in this period Burke, Menario, Loring, and Porteous forged a partnership with a new organization, Greater Portland Landmarks, whose membership possessed mainly old Yankee credentials. Together they resurrected another city industry deeply rooted in the city's past: tourism.

Burke vividly captured the spirit of a new age of renewal in a somewhat florid introduction to the Portland Redevelopment Authority's 1965 annual report. "The climate of municipal improvement through federally aided programs," he opined, "has never been so favorable." He agreed with renewal critics Jane Jacobs and Martin Anderson that "the days when massive . . .[urban renewal] was furnished by the bulldozer is rapidly coming to a close. . . . The ugly wounds on the urban landscape are being healed and . . . new and exciting forms of steel and stone are rearing their triumphant heads against the sky." Burke feared that Vietnam might threaten President Johnson's Great Society; nevertheless, he hoped that the promise of renewal would overcome "the forces of hesitance" currently "suffocating our downtown business life." He spoke of the forthcoming "General Neighborhood Renewal Plan being drafted by the city's new planning consultant, the nationally famous Victor Gruen, who, Burke announced, would try "to instill a little imagination into lazy local dollars. Our consultants," he added, are also "showing the City of Portland the consequences of not going with Downtown Revitalization."[6]

In the downtown, Burke argued, large numbers of people did not have to be relocated, he wrote, "the city authorities . . . do not have much choice in the matter. . . . If they do not intervene, *downtown will fall like an outgrown lobster shell to the bottom of the sea* [emphasis added]. However, if it does intervene, . . . [there] is a good chance . . . of coming up with a shining new set of ratables. . . . The development of the downtown can become an opportunity to start a new life—an opportunity for social fragments [rich and poor, Yankee, and immigrant] to be brought together in things we create together. A revitalized downtown could be an attainment in which we all share, and in sharing create friendships, which are the basis of the good life."[7]

Victor Gruen and the Gruen Plan for Portland

Burke's report cited the General Neighborhood Renewal Plan, the federally mandated planning study under way by the city's consulting firm, Victor Gruen Associates. In 1964 the Chamber of Commerce joined with the City of Portland to hire both the internationally known, Viennese-born architect-planner Gruen and Spencer Hurtt Associates to consult with the Portland Planning Board (PPB) on a scheme for the renewal of the downtown area. A modernist, Gruen bore the imprint of architects such as Camillo Sitte and Le Corbusier. But he also admired the organic nature of the medieval town and thus pronounced 1950s suburbia too atomized. In fact, Gruen designed the regional mall as an antidote. His designs recentered suburban life by bringing socially disconnected people together in a commercial universe where they could share a common social, cultural, and recreational experience while shopping. Gruen's celebrated Southland Mall outside Minneapolis, Northgate near Seattle, and Northland near Detroit pioneered the concept. But Gruen eventually publically denounced the baneful effect of mall-induced sprawl on America's downtowns. His remedy? Remake downtowns as malls.

Gruen's 1964 book *The Heart of Our Cities* viewed the historic downtown—that is, the medieval city—as the "cradle of civic virtue." The automobile had disfigured cities he wrote, not only with traffic congestion and sprawl but also with billboards and junkyards; it produced a lifeless "anti-city," a place whose once pulsating but now sclerotic heart beat feebly. Why not, therefore, remake the downtown into a pedestrian-friendly, culturally edifying, socially and recreationally exciting place—in effect, into a mall? Using multistory garages, walkways, outdoor cafes, fountains, statuary, and kiosks, all well-landscaped in a European-like plaza, Gruen attempted to replicate the rooted community of the medieval city. He ringed his automobile-friendly, mall-oriented downtowns with a beltway marked, like the medieval city, with a portal or gateway—in this case, of with multistory garages.[8]

For example, in Lancaster, Pennsylvania, a city similar in size to Portland, Gruen in 1966 transformed its heart, the 100 block of North Queen Street, into a huge, modernistic, concrete shopping and entertainment complex void of traffic and anchored by two department stores, plus a hotel, movie theaters, and a variety of shops. He arranged all this commerce about a landscaped public piazza (Lancaster Square) with tree plantings, gardens, park benches, and artwork. Here Lancastrians could walk, talk, shop, and engage in reinvigorated public discourse. That Gruen's Fort Worth mall never materialized, or that Lancaster's North Queen Street failed left Gruen's fame as a planning maestro undiminished.[9]

Portland in late 1965 eagerly anticipated Gruen's report, due in early 1966. City bankers and businessmen, described as "poised to invest in the future of Portland," hoped it would be "ambitious and dramatic." But not too dramatic: "For those who cherish Portland's heritage as a beautiful city by the sea," presciently editorialized the *Evening Express,* "it will be a time for more than marveling. All those who have a taste for the best in art, in building, in design for city living will have a special responsibility to see that the ideals of beauty and of grace are not sacrificed to commercial or other practical considerations."[10]

Portland planners in 1965 defined the downtown as the area of the peninsula bounded by Cumberland Street on the north, Fore Street on the south, Pearl Street to the east, and State Street on the west. Gruen's September 1966 report, "Downtown Portland, Maine: General Neighborhood Renewal Plan," fit the architect-planner's standard model for diagnosing urban ills. Portland, stated

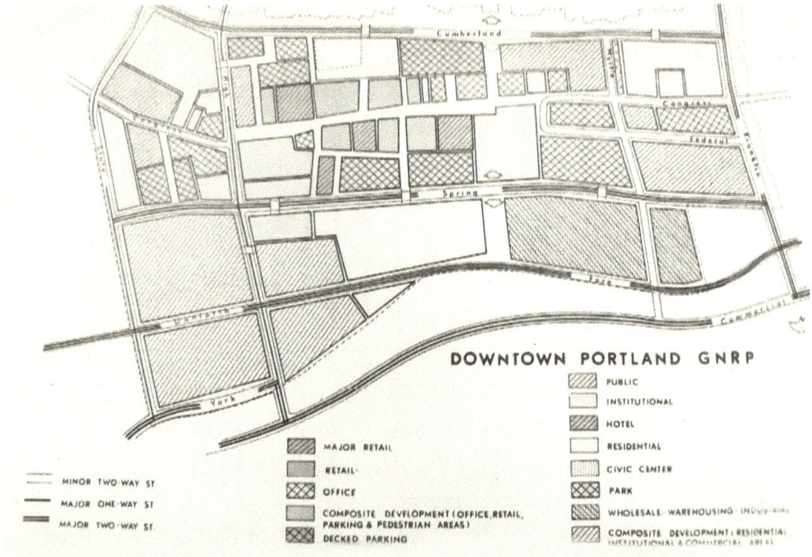

25. Victor Gruen's General Neighborhood Renewal Plan for Portland. The map shows not only the ring highway with parking around the downtown but also the proposed four-lane express highway on Commercial Street. Courtesy of Portland Department of City Planning Library.

the report, suffered from three main problems: bad housing, bad streets, and bad parking. The 1960 census had found 28.8 percent of its downtown housing stock to be substandard. The city endured horrid traffic circulation patterns; Gruen deemed its streets inefficient, narrow, and discontinuous. And on-street parking made it inhospitable to modern automobility. Thus, Gruen's plan for Portland, like his plans for Lancaster, Fort Worth, and Fresno, bore signature features: a pedestrian mall, peripheral garage parking, and a ring highway. By eliminating dingy rooming houses, single-room occupancy hotels, and other scabrous downtown housing; building a ring road and devising a traffic circulation system bordered by strategically located parking garages; adding a million square feet of retail and office space, 280 new hotel units, 316,000 square feet of state, local, and federal office space; and identifying a traffic-free pedestrian zone, Gruen would remake Portland's shabby downtown into the scintillating, pulsating heart of the city (fig. 25).

To make Portland a regional center of civic, cultural, and recreational life, Gruen proposed a civic center complex with concert hall, theaters, art galleries,

26. Franklin Arterial under construction. Courtesy of *Portland Press Herald* Still-Film Collection, Portland Public Library Special Collections and Archives.

and convention space. For critical downtown access, Franklin Street—a narrow, densely populated, tree-lined residential street bisecting the Bayside neighborhood—would be widened into a divided four-lane central artery looping off the interchange of proposed I-295, and thus, as long envisioned, connecting Portland directly to the Maine Turnpike (fig. 26). In the future, Gruen recommended converting the Forest City's spacious oceanfront and pier-lined Commercial Street into a highway, speeding turnpike traffic directly into the heart of the city.[11]

In Gruen's defense, he recognized Portland's heritage of eighteenth- and nineteenth-century architecture as an asset, especially the historic character of Congress Street, the so-called spine of the peninsula. Congress Street boasted the revered preserved home of Henry Wadsworth Longfellow, as well as Congress and Monument Squares; historic districts located just off the Congress Street such as Park Street; and High, Danforth, State, and Spring Streets. As in Fort Worth, Gruen proposed converting Congress Street between Pearl and High, the heart of Portland's downtown and the site of its principal banks and the Benoit and Porteous department stores, into a pedestrian mall.[12]

Gruen's plan left an enduring imprint on the city. In fact, at first using both city and state—not federal—funds, Portland acted immediately to widen Franklin Street into a divided, four-lane central artery providing unobstructed access into the downtown, and to turn a widened Spring Street into part of Gruen's downtown loop, replete with the Spring Street parking garage. In 1967, Portland applied for a multimillion dollar grant to undertake the Downtown Two project (the Congress Street banking and retail center, another part of Gruen's plan), which in 1969 ultimately became the Maine-Way project. Significantly, it neatly dovetailed with the 1967 Model Cities program, an undertaking meant to make Portland's renaissance as much about enhancing the city's deteriorating social environment as about restoring and beautifying its physical appearance. Model Cities also underscored Portland's historical legacy and accentuated the importance of preserving that historical fabric in any revitalization scheme.[13]

Edmund Muskie and Model Cities

Portland's Model Cities program owed an enormous debt to Maine's Senator Edmund Muskie. Born in Rumford, Maine, educated at Bates College and Cornell Law School, a World War II veteran who practiced law in Waterville, Muskie was elected a state legislator in 1946, governor in 1954, and a United States senator in 1958. Lyndon Baines Johnson initially relegated Muskie to the Subcommittee on Intergovernmental Relations and the Banking and Currency Committee, but Muskie deftly used his effectiveness on these committees to chart a highly successful senatorial career. Known for his work on water- and air-quality issues, Democrat Muskie, like Maine's Republican Senator Margaret Chase Smith, took an equally keen interest in poverty, housing, and urban redevelopment issues. In 1966, President Johnson wisely tapped Muskie to manage his new Model Cities program, originally called Demonstration Cities. The legislation as it was drafted and presented to Congress initially called for a mere handful of cities to participate, but as his reward for shepherding the bill, Muskie had Johnson's word that Portland would be one of those cities, its size notwithstanding.[14]

Demonstration Cities faced hurdles. Many in Congress questioned the title itself and believed, as Alabama's John Sparkman did, that the word "demonstration" conjured up ugly, frightening images of young, long-haired radicals and fiery urban riots. Southerners also objected to language barring segregation in any low-cost housing built in Demonstration City neighborhoods. Muskie used Post Office Department money to have some of the key architects of the legislation, including Joseph Califano, Larry O'Brien, and Milton Semer, flown aboard a Beechcraft plane to Kennebunk Beach, Maine, where he owned a summer home. Muskie's wife, Jane, served a steaming lobster stew, and in the wake of the feast the final form of the legislation appeared.[15]

Jane Muskie's lobster stew altered the legislation little from the original form drafted by the Robert Wood committee, however. To placate Sparkman, Muskie and his colleagues substituted the words "afford maximum opportunity of choice of housing accommodations" for the more liberal language proscribing segregation. Although the official title of the legislation remained intact, the group adopted Model Cities as the popular name for a program which, rather than spotlighting 66 large cities (with 20 having populations under 200,000), ultimately encompassed 150 cities and towns, some the size of Winooski, Vermont. Most significantly, Muskie also insisted that the legislation emphasize novel and imaginative housing and renewal programs and (crucial for Portland, a city poised for potentially large-scale renewal amid a rich architectural heritage) that surveys of historic resources and efforts at historic preservation accompany any proposal for slum clearance or housing rehabilitation. With passage of the National Historic Preservation Act of 1966, and the creation of the National Register of Historic Places, the Maine senator ardently supported historic preservation. Muskie's action assured that Model Cities funds would be used, typically with matching private funds, to prepare feasibility studies for rehabilitating rundown but National Register-eligible inner-city buildings for residential use.[16]

Finally, Muskie added a crucial second step and, thus, a second year to the application process. Cities would first request monies from a $12 million fund to underwrite an initial program planning stage. Those cities favored with planning funds would apply for supplemental monies for the all-important five-year action phase.[17]

Portland: A Model City

The civic, political, and business leadership in Portland, once a staunchly fiscally conservative Republican city that fiercely resisted federal programs such as public housing, in the 1960s rallied behind Model Cities. In 1967 there was a more progressive, activist City Council led by people such as Harold Loring, corporate counsel at a large city law firm: Bernard Shur, Sawyer & Nelson. Loring, Shur, and new city manager John Menario all showered expressions of gratitude upon both Maine senators, Muskie and Smith, for their efforts assuring that Portland was "on the approved list for the Model Cities program and [we] have real hope that this program will provide meaningful solutions for some of our serious problems."[18]

On November 11, 1967, the Department of Housing and Urban Development (HUD) administrator Robert Weaver announced that Portland had been selected for a planning grant of $1,834,000 to develop its Model Cities program. Ultimately, the city received $7,594,429 in Model Cities monies; however, combined with targeted funds from the Federal Housing Administration, the Office of Economic Opportunity, Health, Education and Welfare, and federal law enforcement, Portland's Model Cities largesse amounted to almost $31,500,000. Unlike the city's Office of Economic Opportunity agency (Portland Regional Opportunity Program, or PROP), where local citizens not only participated in policy decision-making but also had control over the disposition of federal funds flowing into the agency, Model Cities monies in Portland came directly to City Council, which selected a director, Robert Hawkins, who reported to John Menario. Closely supervised by council chair Loring and Model Cities administrator Hawkins, and under the watchful eye of Muskie and his aide, Don Nicoll, and mindful of HUD's admonition that all proposals must demonstrate "ongoing maximum citizen participation," Portland launched its Model Cities planning process. HUD made very clear that while "the success of [Model Cities] demand[ed] an effective citizen role in decision-making . . . ultimate authority and responsibility for the program is necessarily vested in elected officials."[19]

Model Cities represented a revolutionary new and, its creators hoped, more effective form of federalism. In Model Cities the federal government stripped away the burdensome layers of red tape that had frustrated urban renewal progress in the 1950s and shepherded recalcitrant, overly bureaucratic federal agencies such as OEO (Office of Economic Opportunity), HEW (Health, Education and Welfare), and HUD behind a concerted solution to urban problems.[20] The Forest City's chosen Model Neighborhood was called Portland West, an area that included, in the words of the city's application, "virtually the entire western end of the [Falmouth] peninsula, plus an area of considerable blight adjacent to it immediately north of the central business district." Portland West embraced as well a crucial segment of the city's waterfront, plus rich, early

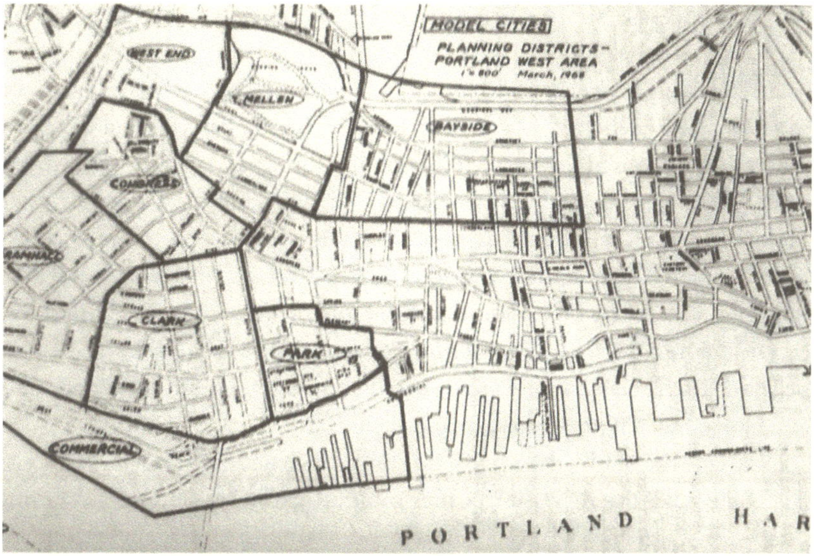

27. Map of Portland West, the Model City. Found in Portland Model Cities Application, Muskie Archives, Bates College.

nineteenth-century Federal and Greek Revival–style architecture, along with the city's Frederick Law Olmsted–designed Western Promenade (fig. 27).[21]

City Council designated the Portland West Advisory Committee (PWAC) as the local Model Cities agency. Most of the real citizen participation, however, took place in the seven, thirty-person task forces empowered to hold hearings, accumulate evidence, deliberate, and formulate first "statements of condition" and then prepare "recommended solutions" and proposed budgets for what were identified as Portland West's key problems: housing, health, education, employment, economic development, recreation, crime and juvenile delinquency, and, finally, social services.[22]

Although Portland Model Cities literature insisted that the program was "a 'people program' intended to improve the life which may be lived by the people in Portland West," and, moreover, although most of the task forces wrestled with jobs, poverty, health care, and other social issues, and although Model Cities publications muted the role of "slum clearance," in truth the city assigned a very high priority to Portland West's physical revitalization.[23] Indeed, a successful 1967 request for a planning grant stated explicitly that "the City primarily sought to improve the quality of housing" of Portland West, provide relocation services, improve public facilities, and "restore neighborhood attractiveness."[24]

All these goals were considered vital to a renewed downtown, a downtown literally surrounded by Portland West. Muskie's Senate Banking and Currency Committee exercised legislative responsibility for urban renewal, and Muskie in the early 1960s fretted that with urban renewal growing day by day more unpopular—attacked from the right and the left—without prompt action Maine might fail to benefit from the needed largesse. Muskie believed that Portland stood poised for both waterfront and downtown renewal. An advocate of a more comprehensive, coordinated approach to urban renewal, Muskie believed that Model Cities was the potential instrument for a more effective and integrated, but also more humane renewal.[25]

Not coincidentally, then, Howard Heller, executive director of the Portland Renewal Authority, shortly after submitting the Model Cities Planning Grant, forwarded to HUD a Survey and Planning Grant application for Downtown Two, a project to be funded under HUD's General Neighborhood Renewal Plan (GNRP) program. Asked in its GNRP application to specify how the Downtown Two project "meets [HUD's] national goals and urban renewal priorities," Heller pointed to Portland's federally unassisted Franklin Arterial project, its active housing rehabilitation and housing code enforcement programs, its federally assisted elderly and 221 (d) 3 assisted (low- and moderate-income multifamily) housing, as well as the city's recent application for a Model Cities grant. Portland, he wrote, is emphasizing an increase in "the supply of low and moderate income housing. . . . *Many of these units will be included in the Model Cities Program which has been designed for an area close to downtown. This will become an area of restored and new housing for all income groups, with the largest concentration in the low income and moderate income ranges. The appropriateness of these programs has been predicated on the assumption that downtown would be renewed and new employment opportunities would be created in this area* [emphasis added]."[26] But Downtown Two mainly involved "environmental upgrading" in an effort to keep in town such large, established city business houses as the A. H. Benoits and the Porteous, Mitchell and Braun department stores, the Casco Bay and Canal Banks, and the Union Mutual Insurance Company. Since HUD favored activities such as the expansion of housing supply for low and moderate income families and the creation of new employment opportunities, it initially gave Portland's Downtown Two project a low rating.

Consequently, Portland endeavored to dovetail its Downtown Two and Model Cities programs. The Gruen plan had projected that by providing downtown access and modern parking facilities for Sears and Roebuck, Benoits, Porteous, Woolworth's, Grant's, and the city's banking offices, the renewal potentially added 300 new jobs in the downtown. Model Cities provided the vocational training, new and rehabilitated housing, and an enhanced quality of life for this workforce. Portland, in fact, had specifically tailored its renewal to meet the national goal of conservation and housing expansion, contending that the downtown would become a district of job opportunity, and Portland West a Mecca for good housing. Applications for Model Cities and GNRP grants, therefore, were developed jointly and complementarily.[27] Heller, in an explanatory letter to HUD's Renewal Assistance administrator Charles Horan, minced no words in urging approval of the city's Downtown Two application. Hundreds of jobs, he argued, hinged on Portland's not losing employers like Union Mutual, Benoits, and Canal Bank, and "I would like to point out that our Model Cities Program, which encompasses the area immediately adjacent to the downtown, has been designed to supplement downtown renewal. Without downtown renewal, it seems doubtful that the adjacent Model Cities neighborhood can be revitalized."[28]

Rebuilding neighborhoods and revitalizing the downtown formed the central themes of Portland's Model Cities agenda. Unlike Poor's and Baxter's visionary tableaus of the past, the Portland Redevelopment Authority and Portland West plans employed a nonsentimental, nonromantic, efficiency-driven approach to the withering of the city's social and physical fabric. Portland's new generation of progressive, well-educated leaders sought systematic, bureaucratic solutions to urban problems. They meant not only to spruce up and modernize the city but also to address the untended social, educational, health-care and job-training needs of the city's working-class population. Early on, beauty, the legacy of Longfellow's city by the sea, only rarely entered the consciousness or the lexicon of the PRA or Portland West planners. But that aesthetic dimension ultimately appeared, sparked by the realization that in Portland's historic image and fabric lay the city's economic future, one that the whole city: its Yankees, Irish, Italian, Armenian, French Canadian, African American, and Hispanic alike might share.

Portland's path from Model Cities and downtown renewal to historic preservation and Old Port revival gradually unfolded in the 1970s and 1980s. Downtown Two helped launch the process. In the fall of 1967, the presidents of almost every major downtown firm beseeched HUD to fund Downtown Two in conjunction with Model Cities.[29] Arthur Benoit, whose store stood prominently on Monument Square, "couldn't remember when there was quite as much team work within the community on any project as there is with regards to this. . . . There was never a more clear case of urgency for anything than that facing Portland for the next three years. We just cannot hope to survive in the classic sense of the city unless we receive the Renewal Funds."

As Portland's task forces held hearings, carried out research, and compiled data to define Portland West's employment, housing, education, health, crime, and recreation problems, and sculpted a Model Cities program, the City Council and planning department increasingly focused on identifying the crucial nexus between urban renewal and human renewal. Meeting with city business leaders, Muskie reiterated the new social emphasis of HUD. "The agency would look especially favorably," he told them, "at Portland's [downtown] urban renewal program as it related to the 'people problem' of the Model Cities."[30]

Muskie's words resonated with the planners. By 1969, Portland had moved from the planning stage into the First-Year Action phase, and clearly the city now saw the various segments of Model Cities—housing, job training, health services, policing, and historic preservation—tightly linked to the future of the downtown. Indeed, by 1972, when Downtown Two, now called the Maine Way project, was well under way, the annual report of the Portland Renewal Authority wove the two HUD programs together seamlessly. Clearing blight and rehousing Portland West benefited the downtown.[31]

To declare Portland West—that tangle of old tree-lined streets and alleys abutting the downtown—blighted seemed to stretch the definition of that word. Eight neighborhoods, or planning districts, were involved: the West End, Bramhall, Mellen, Bayside West, Congress, Clark, Park, and Commercial. They included the magnificent Colonial Revival mansions overlooking the Fore River on the Western Promenade, the exquisite collection of John Calvin Stevens Shingle-style architecture on Bowdoin Street, and even attractive Queen Anne triple-deckers in the Parkside district. Other neighborhoods in the Model Cities district contained similar rich collections of early Federal and ornate Victorian treasures.[32]

No doubt, many parts of Bayside and the West End harbored what postwar planners viewed as cancerous, tumescent lesions: seedy rooming houses, crowded, unkempt triple-deckers, and ramshackle hovels. They were not the large, dense slums of Philadelphia, Chicago, or Detroit, red-lined in the 1930s by the Federal Housing Administration, and doomed in the 1950s and 1960s; such ghettos never existed in the Forest City. Instead Portland proscribed what was deemed obsolescent, overcrowded, and unsightly, that segment of the residential stock housing the city's poor. The 1960 census had branded 2,700 dwelling units in the city "deteriorated" and stressed that Portland still suffered from a severe shortage of decent affordable housing. But the poor housing, like Portland West's failing schools (16.3 percent of the residents had less than an eighth-grade education), dearth of recreational facilities, and meager mental health care were all symptomatic of the real problem: low income. "Poverty," argued Hawkins and the other authors of the action plan, was "the real specter which forever haunt[ed] the Portland West community. . . . Forty-one percent of its children suffered from hard-core poverty." Hopelessness and defeatism accompanied poverty. Here lived an older, somewhat transient, undereducated, underserved population needing to be reintegrated into the social and economic orbit of Portland's urban life by rebuilding the social and physical fabric of a Model City.[33]

In truth, urban renewal, code enforcement activities, and the Franklin Arterial project had severely rent the urban fabric, undermining Portland's housing stock. Renewal unmercifully attacked the city's old tenements and rooming houses, focusing particularly on its triple-deckers, long condemned as fire and social menaces, the antitheses of the American Dream. Nineteenth-century reformers and 1960s renewers alike ignored the potential social role of inexpensive tenement shelters as incubators of upward mobility, or, as James Borchert noted in *Alley Life in Washington D.C.* as a nurturer of folk, ethnic, and racial cohesiveness and survival. Instead they ruthlessly removed such dwellings. During the mid-1960s, SCRAP demolished 245 housing units in the Bayside Park area and 289 units in Bayside West (the Chestnut and Stone Streets area); 462 units fell in the adjoining Munjoy Hill renewal site. Between 1961 and 1972 urban renewal and other government activities cost Portland over 2,800 housing units (against the addition of just 539 new units, including public housing). Many such demolitions occurred in Bayside (1,148, to be exact) and Munjoy Hill, neighborhoods called home by Portland's small but cohesive Italian and Armenian communities. Code enforcement and renewal activities also expunged triple-deckers, apartments, boardinghouses, and other so-called deteriorated housing in the neighborhoods of the West End, and many were highly affordable units. [34] Maine's paucity of publicly owned and subsidized housing hardly absorbed that loss.[35]

Portland's social-welfare renaissance neared on December 13, 1968, when on behalf of Portland West and the seven task forces, Robert Hawkins for the City of Portland submitted a $2 million application to HUD for funds to execute the city's First Year Action Program for the year 1969. A large segment of the bulky document spotlighted chronic neighborhood joblessness, poor health, educational failures, and shabby or nonexistent social services. According to the application, alcoholism, crime, and juvenile delinquency ravaged the tree-lined, Victorian clapboard-sided streetscapes. To remedy these problems, Model Cities would flood Portland West with new programs, including an experimental elementary school, vocational education, adult education, Head Start, a model police unit, and a halfway house for alcoholics. Many of these activities were conventional Johnson-era, War on Poverty programming. Some were boldly innovative: for example, a $200,000 income-maintenance experiment wherein the money would be used as child allotments—an idea swiftly rejected by city councilors. But a number of other programs—such as Pharos House to combat criminal recidivism, a neighborhood class in classical music appreciation, a drugstore cooperative, and COMBAT (Consumers in Maine Bringing Action Together)—despite the radical tinge of the last and business disapprobation, won council approval.[36]

Keyed as it was to the city's broader urban strategy of general downtown renewal, physical development—purging the unseemly refuse of the past—naturally ranked high as Portland's Model Cities goal. The city aspired to restore Bramhall, Mellen, Park, and the other five neighborhoods of Portland West to their nineteenth-century respectability. In fact, one of those neighborhoods, the Western Promenade, crowned by an Olmsted-designed park that offered a distant vista of Mount Washington, had long housed the city's economic elite. To adequately serve Portland's projected, newly expanded downtown workforce, these neighborhoods had to feature not only clean, safe streets but also good schools and, most of all, plentiful affordable housing. Studies conducted jointly by the city's Housing Inspection Department, the Housing Task Force, and Portland Landmarks had also identified structures "historically, aesthetically, or architecturally worthy of preservation." Those less distinguished were deemed "eligible for federal renewal, rehabilitation, redevelopment and code enforcement" action. Many in Bayside and Munjoy Hill rated demolition.[37]

The 1968 Action Plan summoned Portland West to become "a balanced [innovative] mixture of uses, [residential] structure types, and open space" in order to meet "the highest standard of urban design that preserves the classic character and charm of our present city." The attention to the "charm of the present city" made Model Cities a key part of downtown renewal and of a larger, more nebulous concern for urban beautification in general.[38]

Rather than replicating Portland's existing subsidized housing designs from places such as Munjoy Hill, Model Cities stressed housing experimentation. Since 1937, federal housing administrators had always encouraged innovation in design and supply, hoping to employ technology to solve the problem of delivering affordable mass housing. During 1968, Portland's Housing Task Force enthusiastically seized upon the idea of an experimental housing program, and, according to city manager Menario, "indicated a deep desire that [the city] standards be high quality housing designed with relevance for inner-city housing and middle-income residents."[39]

The Chamber of Commerce perceived experimental housing as an ideal re-use for the aging and abandoned piers moldering from disuse on Portland's western waterfront. City officials had quite creatively included this waterfront infrastructure as part of the Portland West neighborhood. Model Cities administrator Hawkins extolled the Westinghouse Corporation's proposals for space age, modular housing designs, especially one for "air rights housing": units built on stilts, which seemed ideally adaptable for unused city piers. Portland included the idea in its 1968 Model Cities application for supplemental funds; but while air rights housing never advanced beyond the fantasy stage, the city did feature an architectural rendition of the design on the cover of its 1975 "Model Cities Final Report."[40]

More realistic was the Chamber of Commerce's sponsorship of Portland Housing Opportunities, Inc., a nonprofit, limited-dividend corporation formed to build innovatively designed and affordable rental and homeownership housing. Much of this would be infill housing, located on space freed by Title I slum clearance activity. Housing Opportunities, Inc., functioned as a site developer to work with local, state, and federal agencies to navigate the code restrictions and other parts of the permitting process and to expedite the construction of HUD Section 235 subsidized homeownership housing, and HUD Section 236 assisted rental housing. Using 236, Housing Opportunities proposed construction of 105 high-rise units for low- and moderate-income families. At Dermot Court, by employing an experimental modular design and construction techniques, Housing Opportunities erected sixteen 235-type ownership units which, notwithstanding their architectural dissimilarity to the surrounding Victorian homes, provided good housing.[41]

Muskie exuded enthusiasm for Portland's Housing Opportunities, Inc., as an experimental housing program. Nevertheless, Portland's "Final Report on Model Cities" deemed the innovative program a failure. Although it did build Dermot Court, Housing Opportunities' plans for a much-needed 105-unit, eleven-story high-rise never left the architect's drawing board, and the nonprofit housing firm permanently shut its doors on June 30, 1973.[42]

Still, Housing Opportunities had stimulated interest in Section 236 subsidized housing, and in the face of a national housing slowdown, caused in part by rising interest rates, 170 units of 236 housing, as well as units of turnkey and leased public housing, arose in Portland West—mainly as infill units. That was, however, barely half of what the PWAC demanded. The Nixon administration's moratorium on all federally funded housing and renewal programs also affected rehabilitation, the most successful Model Cities housing program in Portland West. Thanks in large part to the MICAH housing program (a play on the biblical Micah and the acronym for Metropolitan Council on Affordable Housing), Model Cities blanketed Portland West with rehabilitation loans, effectively making rehabilitation the chief vehicle for better housing in the district and, in effect, preserving Portland's nineteenth-century housing stock and making the neighborhood a still-fashionable address.

Over the five-year life of Model Cities funding, 1969 to 1973, MICAH received $672,000 in grants, $550,000 of which went directly to low- and moderate-income homeowners and generated over $1.25 million in rehabilitation activity. MICAH closely coordinated its work with city housing inspectors, and intensified city code enforcement in the Portland West neighborhood. Grants funded by both Model Cities and Federal Housing Administration (FHA) enabled owners of substandard, nineteenth-century housing to correct major interior and exterior code violations. A vital part of MICAH's work involved the purchasing, rehabilitating, selling, and renting of deteriorated residential structures often originally held by absentee owners. That highly profitable venture made MICAH a self-sufficient, nonprofit corporation that in addition to its rehabilitation work assisted many individuals to own homes. Renters, too, were aided: in 1973, MICAH controlled 106 units of rehabilitated rental homes in the Danforth Street neighborhood. In 1973, however, Washington impounded rehabilitation monies—which was later ruled illegal—crippling both MICAH's work) and other Model Cities celebrated housing conservation work in Longfellow Square.[43]

Portland West's disappointing experimental housing record aside, Model Cities accomplished much in housing rehabilitation, in historic preservation, in neighborhood beautification, and in bettering neighborhood education (by building the innovative Reiche Community School, for example, which stressed unique organization, technology, and other experimental teaching methods). It also built a highly praised model police station and halfway houses, and underwrote successful youth opportunity programs and day care centers.[44]

Anno Mirabilis

After 1968, to Muskie's dismay, President Nixon slowly phased out Model Cities, extinguishing it in 1974. But with I-295 pushing toward Tukey's Bridge in the early 1970s; Gruen's Spring Street and Franklin arterials, as well as the Spring Street Parking Garage, under way in 1969; Portland West easing some of the city's worst social and housing problems; and Maine Way, Portland's downtown tour de force, launched in 1971, long-absent urban investment capital suddenly reappeared. Indeed, as envisioned, Gruen's plan, together with Model Cities and Maine Way, transformed Portland's Congress Street and downtown from a nineteenth- and early twentieth-century hub of shopping, hotels, banking, and commerce into the nerve center of a modern service-oriented city.

A glimpse at Portland's economy in 1970 reveals a trend already under way. The population had declined from its peak of almost 78,000 in 1950 to 72,566 in 1960 to 65,116 in 1970. The decline provoked a series of studies. A 1969 Regional Planning Commission–sponsored "Economic Review of Greater Portland" found that from 1960 to 1969 while jobs in fishing and machine and textile manufactures shrank, employment in finance and service industries grew by 20,000. Few Portland manufactories (American Hoist and Derrick for one, Burnham and Morrill canning for another) employed over 200 persons; the vast majority of manufacturing industries employed fewer than 100. Finance, insurance, and real estate firms in 1970 employed 1,922 persons; personal and professional services, 6,276; and public administration, close to 1,400. Those firms located as much outside the city, in spacious campuses near the turnpike, as they did in the downtown.[45]

Greater Portland Chamber of Commerce discourse reflected this statistical portrait of the city's economy. In 1970 the chamber spoke of Portland's two "dominant shopping areas. One is downtown continually upgrading with new fronts, new buildings and new sub-areas. The other is the Maine Mall regional shopping center in South Portland now scheduled to open in the spring of 1971." With the 10-story, modern glass Casco Bank tower rising in 1970 at the Elm Street end of Monument Square: and the three-story, 200,000-square-foot Union Mutual Insurance center under way on outer Congress near the turnpike; and New England Telephone breaking ground for a new thirty-eight-acre campus nearby, Portland's future as a regional center of finance, insurance, and real estate services seemed sealed. Accordingly, its gritty waterfront seemed incongruous.[46]

A year earlier, in 1969, the Chamber of Commerce had commissioned the revealing "Port of Portland, Maine, Development Plan," a report done by the Urban Design Group of Newport, Rhode Island. UDG urged Portland to first clear the harbor of oil spillage and raw sewage pollution. It also proposed transforming the city's historic Commercial Street pier complex from fishing, processing, warehousing, and other working uses into a mixed-use residential and recreational area that would attract tourists. The design featured motels, marinas, a city aquarium, and a naval or marine-resources research center—not to mention the popular "air rights housing" design from the original Model Cities plan. (UDG did identify space for a container storage facility at the eastern end of Commercial Street on the site of the old Grand Trunk grain piers.)[47]

Meanwhile, PRA renamed the Downtown Two Project Maine Way, and work on Portland's renaissance forged boldly ahead. In June 1971, ground was broken for Maine Way, a plan built upon Gruen's earlier projected downtown renewal plans for Spring Street and the Franklin Arterial, plus parking, the Casco Bank, and a Holiday Inn. Confined to a narrow but crucial downtown corridor between Spring and Congress Streets and Oak and Market Streets (just east of Exchange), Maine Way combined demolition of aging (and obsolete) commercial buildings and the renovation and rehabilitation of existing historic structures. Its goal was to boost the urban economy by strengthening the attraction and irresistibility of the downtown core. Gruen-like, Maine Way prescribed pedestrian walkways, open spaces, skyways, plazas, courts, and arcades, all tastefully landscaped with trees, ground cover, and other plantings.

Portland's renaissance burst into full bloom in the year 1972, the *anno mirabilis*. That year the Forest City alone saw over $42,000,000 invested in new construction, including sixty new corporate and industrial buildings among them the Holiday Inn, the Casco National Bank, the Maine Savings Bank, the Canal Plaza Buildings, and a new parking garage. The Herriot Company in

1972 produced drawings for an estimated $15 million in Maine Way development in the Federal, Temple, and Middle Streets area. Elsewhere in Portland, the University of Maine Law School arose on Bedford Avenue in Deering, and HUD monies subsidized housing for seniors and low-income families at Bayside Terrace, Washington Square, and Harbor Terrace. In early 1973 the Union Mutual Life Insurance Company unveiled architectural drawings for two high-rise, luxury condominium towers on the Eastern Promenade overlooking Casco Bay[48]

In the same way that the Urban Design Group's waterfront study invoked the tourism value of history, Maine Way triggered a reassessment of the commercial significance of the city's historical legacy. While replete with pro-growth awareness of the dangers of obsolescence and overtures to the imperative of modernization, both Gruen's 1964 plan and the 1971 Maine Way had also acknowledged the role of historic preservation. Portland, as this book emphasizes, had long traded not only on its beauty but also on its history as home to Longfellow, Preble, Chamberlain, and Czar Reed and the architectural heritage of Alexander Parris, John Kimball, Fassett, and John Calvin Stevens. In the 1960s the siren call of progress and the appeal of jet-age modernism had threatened that legacy. The destruction of Portland's chateauesque Union Station in 1961 accentuated the danger. John Bundy Brown's Falmouth Hotel on Middle Street fell in 1963, and in 1965 renewal toppled architect Alfred B. Mullett's stunning Greek Revival–Old Post Office at Middle and Exchange Streets. The Grand Trunk Railroad Terminal succumbed a year later.[49]

A Modern Portland Conjures Its Past

Those losses of architecture and history would be mourned. Mrs. Kenneth Sills, widow of a president of Bowdoin College and a genteel Portland dowager, had transformed the parlor of her stately John Calvin Stevens residence at 134 Vaughn Street into a salon, where on a crisp fall afternoon "Yankee women from established families" (to quote historian Joseph Conforti) and a few men, including a young outsider, gathered to consider timely issues. In 1961 the issue was the demolition of Union Station and the need to preserve the city's imperiled history. Sills, who had hosted Portland College Club gatherings at her house, now in 1962 founded the Sills Committee, among whose members were the famed maritime historian and Portlander Robert Greenhalgh Albion, Mrs. Loyall Sewall, Mrs. Charles Dodge, Mrs. Neal Allen, and John Pancoast, president of the Portland Art Society, as well as architect John Calvin Stevens II and Portland High School history teacher Elizabeth Ring, accompanied by her best student, fifteen-year-old Earle Shettleworth. At first the Sills Committee sounded the alarm, engaging mainly in public education, sponsoring slide lectures, and historical awareness (fig. 28).[50]

On July 31, 1964, with Stevens as president, and young Shettleworth as assistant secretary-treasurer, the group incorporated as Greater Portland Landmarks (GPL), dedicated to "preserving and maintaining land, buildings, monuments, and other structures of an historical or educational nature in the Greater Portland area." Largely a coterie of two or three dozen West End, Cape Elizabeth, and Falmouth elites, it was not dissimilar to the original makeup of William Sumner Appleton's Society for the Preservation of New England Antiquities (which today is called Historic New England) and preservation advocacy in Pittsburgh, Providence, and other cities. By 1966, however, the year of the Historic Preservation Act, Landmarks had broadened into a dues-paying membership of 325, which by 1970 had climbed to almost 500.[51]

Rooted in the nineteenth-century preservation endeavors of Ann Pamela Cunningham at Mount Vernon, of Appleton at Paul Revere's house in Boston, and of Rev. W. A. R. Goodwin and John D. Rockefeller at Williamsburg, Virginia, historic preservation came of age in the 1930s with historic zoning at Charleston, South Carolina, in 1931, and the national Historic American Building Survey and Historic Sites Acts of 1933 and 1935. Congress chartered the National Historic Trust in 1949, and in 1966 the Preservation Act created the National Register of Historic Places, which allowed state preservation offices to establish standards or guidelines for listing sites, structures, and districts deemed part of the nation's or a state's or a locality's heritage. In 1976, federal legislation propelled the movement by providing tax incentives for preservation action.[52]

With Greater Portland Landmarks at the helm, but not without struggle or setbacks, Portland, like Providence, made preservation a vital part of the planning process. GPL's incorporation coincided with Model Cities. The young organization collaborated closely with the city in framing its Model Cities application, and from Model Cities it got funding to hire Urban Design Group, which produced two reports. The first established a city survey methodology, the second, a model historic preservation survey of the Clark and Park districts, an area encompassing almost the entire West End from High Street to Bramhall Hill. The document likewise set forth Portland's goal: "Mak[ing] preservation of our heritage a dynamic part of community planning and development."[53]

28. Portrait of Earle Shettleworth Jr. and Elizabeth Ring, two original members of the Sills Committee. Shettleworth had been a student of history teacher Ring's at Portland High School. Courtesy of Greater Portland Landmarks.

While UDG toiled on its report, GPL pursued other avenues. Using member donations, it undertook preservation work, restoring the Daniel How and the William Ingraham house, both in the Park and Spring Street area. In 1969, Landmarks hired Pamela Plumb to be its first executive director. But it was Gruen's plan for turning Spring Street into one part of the express highway system encircling the downtown, plus the Portland Redevelopment Authority's Maine Way plans, that plunged GPL into the thick of the battle to save Portland's architectural past. From the beginning, city planners had involved GPL in Maine Way. Paul Stevens served as a consultant on Maine Way, and the PRA invited GPL to survey the Congress, Spring, Oak, and Market Street area and to meet with members of the city redevelopment authority. The process persuaded GPL that the city considered the organization's point of view, and was emphasizing rehabilitation of existing downtown buildings, and "the restoration of Exchange Street, and the importance of new development that blends with nineteenth-century commercial architecture." Indeed, the city's Maine Way plan, submitted to HUD in June 1971, specifically mentioned that one goal of the project would be "undertaking renovations in areas of architectural and historical significance," and linking the Old Port with the "new downtown."[54]

But the duo of Maine Way and the thrusting of the Spring Street Arterial into the exquisite old-brick commercial core proved devastating to the city's historic fabric. In 1972, PRA demolished Francis Fassett's 1867 Keazar Building. GPL in September 1973 fought for but failed to save the Chilton Block. The Spring Street trajectory carried the expressway to Portland's architectural sanctum sanctorum, Spring and High Streets.

The new Holiday Inn proposed for the widened Spring Street endangered an entire historic streetscape. Near the location stood the Clapp Mansion, the McLellan Mansions, the Victoria Mansion, the Park Street rows, the William Moulton Ingraham House—and, on High Street, the Safford House, the current home of Greater Portland Landmarks. Moreover, the fourteen-story, glassy, modern Holiday Inn required the demolition of Gothic House, in addition to posing height issues, and being architecturally unsympathetic to the neighborhood. GPL lost the design battle with Holiday Inn but counted itself victorious when the hotel corporation agreed to move the Gothic House to a site that Landmarks owned farther west on Spring Street.

Moreover, in 1969 on behalf of GPL, Pamela Plumb and Paul Stevens persuaded the Redevelopment Authority to surrender its plans for continuing Spring Street as a six-lane highway to State Street. Simultaneously, the authority conceded that "Portland HAS a history and architectural environment and that should be considered in the planning process and has been admitted in Council Chambers and proclaimed throughout the state." GPL's case was strengthened even more in 1969 when the National Register of Historic Places accepted Spring Street as a National Historic District. At the same time GPL worked with the National Park Service to make the Old Port part of a Portland Waterfront Historic District.[55]

If preserving Gothic House and winning national historic status for Spring Street counted as victories in those trying years for fledgling Landmarks, then publication in December 1972 of *Portland,* a beautifully crafted photographic volume celebrating the city's architectural legacy, marked a triumph. It not only stamped the organization with legitimacy but at a critical time served effectively to educate the city about the high cost of bulldozer-style redevelopment. GPL introduced the book at a well-publicized Casco Bank reception and very quickly sold out the first 5,000-copy printing.[56]

In 1972, GPL purchased the Nutter House at Pleasant and Maple Streets with money raised from the sale of the Guptil Building and the Howe House, and thus inaugurated its revolving fund. Year by year the organization focused greater effort on growing its revolving fund. It invited Arthur Zeigler of the Pittsburgh History and Landmarks Foundation to speak in 1978 about his experience using a revolving fund to revitalize the Steel City's North and South Side neighborhoods. That same year, having considerably boosted its revolving fund through a sizable challenge grant from the National Endowment of the Arts, and also with grants from the Department of Housing and Urban Development and the National Trust for Historic Preservation, GPL purchased the seedy Upper H. H. Hay Block at Congress Square and proceeded to restore the exterior of the flatiron building built in 1826 by Charles Q. Clapp. Ultimately, the $200,000 project formed part of a larger city undertaking to restore the once-elegant Congress Square.[57]

After 1976, GPL blended its revolving fund monies with tax incentives from the Bicentennial Historic Preservation Tax Act legislation to aggressively restore Portland to the beautiful city that had once beckoned tourists with its parks, tree-lined streets, and exceptional architecture. Tax credits (limited to commercial and rental properties) underwrote the rebuilding and preservation of numerous Portland office and retail properties, as well as commercial residential developments including the Brooks Block, the John D. Carroll Block, the Richardson Wharf project on Commercial Street, the Masonic Temple on

Congress Street, the Congress Square Hotel, the Thomas and Widgery and Deering Blocks on Exchange Street, and the James Merrill House on Spring Street—all of which were among the sixty-three projects undertaken between 1976 and 1986.[58]

Old Port Exchange

The projects on Exchange Street and Commercial underscore Portland Landmarks' and the Old Port Association's effort to halt what in 1965 seemed like the almost inevitable advance of Vine-Deer-Chatham-type renewal cutting a swath of rubble and ruin from India Street to Exchange, between Newberry Street and Commercial. In 1968 the Portland Redevelopment Authority informed Frank Akers, president of a brass castings firm, that his offices on Spring Street would be demolished to make way for the new modern artery. Akers relocated his business to the corner of Fore Street and Exchange, only to be told that the brick Victorian commercial building he had just purchased would itself soon be bulldozed away. Enamored by the building's old Victorian charm and by the potential of its Old Port location, Akers fought back with the support of Greater Portland Landmarks. In 1968 Old Port streets such as Exchange, Fore, and Middle, in addition to the old book shops, wholesale businesses and lofts housed an assemblage of artists, lawyers, and young architects drawn by the cheap rents. Akers had visited Denver's Larimer Square (which opened in 1964) and recognized the power of that city's restored nineteenth-century warehouse district, cloaked with nostalgia, to attract tourists. San Francisco's similar Ghirardelli Square thrived in the 1960s. Later in the 1970s, James Rouse would restore and open Boston's Faneuil Hall Marketplace. GPL's 1968 UDG preservation planning report had made the link between preservation and tourism explicit: "Historic sites and structures," stated the report, "are not just curiosities to be prized by the specialist, but resources that can enrich the environment . . . and contribute to a unique experience for visitors to the city."[59]

In 1968, Akers founded the Old Port Exchange Association, and by 1972, GPL enthusiastically supported urban development funding for this "unique and very special urban heritage district." Indeed, GPL gave its very first annual preservation award in 1974 to Richard Berman, president of Old Port Exchange, and it worked closely with merchants in 1975, seeking bank approval for restoration ventures in the Old Port district. Several years later, plentiful evidence of progress abounded in the once shabby port commercial area. In 1978,

29. Exchange Street, the heart of Portland's "Old Port." These brick buildings all date from the late 1860s and early 1870s, built in the wake of the July Fourth fire of 1866. Photograph by Barbara Bauman.

GPL sponsored a summer walking tour called "Upstairs and Down in the Old Port Exchange," which showed off the quaint new shops, restaurants, studio apartments, and other signs of rejuvenation in an area steeped in nostalgia.[60]

Most of this early rebirth of Longfellow's city transpired along Exchange and Fore Streets, where preservation-minded entrepreneurs converted old warehouses and loft space into fashionable law and professional offices, small banks, and chic apartments. But, proclaimed GPL, "the story of the Old Port Exchange is by no means complete." Wharf Street, it said, awaited transformation and "Commercial Street offered tantalizing possibilities." By the mid-1980s, using Tax Act and revolving fund monies, that metamorphosis did happen. Hundreds of thousands of investment dollars poured into the Old Port Exchange area for the restoration of the Brooks, Moulton, and John D. Carroll Blocks on Commercial Street; the Deering, Centennial, and Fessenden Blocks on Exchange; and the Tukesbury and Clapp Blocks on Fore. By 1990 the rich panoply of delightful shops and dining places in the Old Port had helped make Portland once again a tourist destination, and tourism a vital cog in the city's modern, service-oriented economy (fig. 29).[61]

Whither the Portland Waterfront?

The restoration of historic Commercial Street, however, and the conversion of the Thomas, Brooks, Moulton, and Carroll Blocks from old stone and brick wholesale houses into gift shops, restaurants, interior design and kitchenware emporiums failed to end the debate about the future of Portland's waterfront. Although the Maine Way and Old Port Exchange projects revitalized downtown commerce, helped define Portland's new service economy, and energized a once sluggish tourism, such development ignored the waterfront, which continued to languish in 1972. Only the decision by Sweden's Lion Ferry Company to select Portland over Gloucester, Massachusetts, for the terminus of ferry service between Nova Scotia and the United States lifted commercial prospects there, if only slightly. Basically, little more than foreign crude oil cargoes for South Portland's Canadian pipeline sustained port activity. Wood pulp barely trickled into the port, especially after Scott Paper Company, which owned Canadian timberlands, acquired the S. D. Warren Paper Company. In 1970, cheap Georgian clay replaced china clay from Fowey, England. By 1976, Portland generated only 42,000 tons of general cargo: stoves, sardines, and seaweed incoming; potatoes and wood pulp, loaded in bales and rolls, outgoing.[62]

Even the memorable symbols of Portland's storied commercial past had disappeared. On July 28, 1970, a spectacular fire with flames leaping 100 feet into the sky engulfed the eastern waterfront, destroying the massive Grand Trunk Railway's grain piers but miraculously sparing the landmark grain storage tower still guarding the eastern end of Commercial Street. Only a few thousand bushels of Commodity Credit Corporation surplus grain remained in the elevator. Following the fire, and after GPL had documented the elevator for the Historic American Engineering Record, the structure was demolished in 1973. The builders of the Samoset Inn in Rockland, Maine, used the giant main beams of the grain elevator in constructing the hotel.[63]

Throughout the 1970s, the city debated the port's future. The 1969 Urban Design Group's port study had proposed marinas, hotels, experimental housing, and a container-loading facility. Other plans also stressed the tourist and recreational potential of waterfront space, especially for motels and an aquarium to be located near the new International Ferry Terminal. Meanwhile, pier facilities steadily deteriorated. A 1977 *Evening Express* article called the problems immense; it branded 36 percent of the waterfront buildings "dilapidated" and eleven of the thirty-four piers "substandard." It found long-derelict and untended pilings rotting. Fishermen who worked on the wharves constantly sidestepped gaping holes in the decking. More problematic, after years of complaints, raw sewage still poured into the harbor and, together with floating debris, made the once sparkling waters of the Fore River little better than a putrid cesspool.[64]

Concern for the port's multiple problems produced funding in 1973 for a "Comprehensive Waterfront Improvement Plan" to be overseen jointly by the City Planning Department and Greater Portland Landmarks. Monies for the plan came from the National Endowment for the Arts (NEA) through a nationwide, thirty-seven-community program called "City Edges." (On the eve of 1976, NEA's City Edges was designated a national bicentennial activity.) Significantly, in 1974, thanks to GPL, the National Park Service listed Portland's "Waterfront Historic District" on the National Register of Historic Places. The district embraced Center Street to Pearl and included within those boundaries all or parts of Exchange, Market, Commercial, and Middle Streets to Federal.

When it was fully completed in 1975, the Comprehensive Waterfront Improvement Plan proposed instituting regulatory controls over the Waterfront Historic District, and residential, retail, and commercial "mixed-use" of the city's larger waterfront. "City Edges" covered not only the designated Historic District but the waterfront from Fort Green Park on the Eastern Promenade to Veteran's Bridge on the western edge. In addition to "Marine Related Industries," and "Mixed Transportation," the plan also called for space for pier residences, a new city-owned fish pier, a loading dock for container ships, slips for recreational boating, a waterfront park, museums, and other recreational uses.[65]

Pamela Plumb, once executive director of Landmarks and in 1975 a member of City Council, endorsed the "City Edges" plan, but planning director Donald Megathin, together with the fishing interests and many other Portlanders, championed instead the idea of a traditional "working waterfront" that would bar all noncommercial uses. They cited contemptuously Old Mystic, Connecticut, once a working waterfront now transformed into a maritime museum. Megathin advocated upgrading the waterfront and creating a modern fish pier, where fishermen could land their catch and process, freeze, store, and sell it at auction. He also called for dredging the harbor and for improved city sewers and sewage treatment.[66]

These two visions—the festive waterfront for hotels, housing and recreation versus the unadorned, authentic working waterfront—clashed in the 1980s. In the years 1982–1983 both the American City Corporation and the city itself unveiled waterfront plans building on "City Edges" with proposals to develop the city's piers with condominium complexes, shipbuilding, history-of-commercial fishing museums, an aquarium, and other tourist attractions. Opponents of a "tourist-friendly waterfront" met in 1982 at Boone's (waterfront) Restaurant, where they organized a Waterfront Preservation Association. By 1986 a variety of positions on the waterfront issue had evolved.[67]

For many, covering Chandlers Wharf with condominiums in the 1980s had already shattered the quaint, even enchanting, image of Portland's waterfront. Many insisted that the city's historic finger piers should remain unaltered as the home of small, independent fishermen and the ice, warehousing, cordage, and chandlery businesses that supported them. Others argued that everything should be allowed there as long as it contributed to the city's tax base. A number favored a balance of fishing, industrial, residential, and recreational uses.[68]

Another body of thought shared by Jeffrey Monroe, a Portlander who in 1986 served as senior deck training officer and director of educational programs at the State University of New York Maritime Academy, believed that despite major changes in the technology of port operations, the waterfront and its infrastructure for barges, freight, tankers, fish landings, and processing and support industries remained vital to the city's economy. He noted that containerization had greatly altered the dynamics of port operations and dreaded the waning of wood pulp and Canadian oil shipments through Portland. Monroe also feared that the city's plans for a competing $4 million public cargo pier might discourage private investment in the piers. He applauded Merrill Industries' willingness to invest in a private cargo facility but supported the city's plan for a new fish pier. Portland, he argued, "will never be a great seaport with great industrial complexes occupying every square inch of our waterfront, [but] an active maritime industry can be an important contributor to the revenues which keep the area sound."[69]

The great waterfront debate culminated in a March 1987 referendum pressed by the Waterfront Preservation Association, which asked Portlanders to approve an ordinance allowing only "marine-related" development on the waterfront. Voters overwhelmingly approved the referendum, 2 to 1. In 1993 the ban on nonmarine uses of the waterfront was made law by City Council. With but a few exceptions, the "working waterfront" concept guided Portland waterfront development into the twenty-first century.[70]

In many American cities, post–World War II urban renewal ravaged old neighborhoods (like Bayside and Munjoy Hill), uprooted ethnic communities, and with the destruction of landmarks like Longfellow's birthplace, the Falmouth Hotel, and the Old Post Office destroyed crucial nodes of historic memory. But, this "creative destruction" aside, much of Portland's urban fabric had survived and formed a vital part of the new service-oriented economy that emerged in the early 1970s. Indeed, by the 1980s some Portlanders felt that tourism and the Old Port had carried the city too far from its roots as an authentic city. In fact, the 1987 referendum expressed Portland's revulsion at the prospective Disneyfying of the Portland waterfront and the desire for that authenticity much more than it was a vote against the new service city and tourism. In many respects the working waterfront was perfectly consistent with Portland's past *and* present tourist appeal. After all, Portland's waterfront—even at the turn of the century—reeked of grittiness and saltiness. Tourists and Portlanders strolling there, like John Mead Gould, could hear the stream of wheat rushing into the hold of European-bound steamers. They heard the deafening clang of coupling and uncoupling railway cars and the screeching of wheels, and inhaled the nostril-offending stench from bait barrels. These sounds and smells, and the sights of unpainted warehouses, patched decking, listing piers, shouting draymen, and drunken sailors had given the waterfront its unique and unforgettable ambience. In the 1970s it made the working waterfront, together with the Old Port shops, taverns, and restaurants, an integral part of a deliberately cultivated nostalgic experience.

Even after the city removed the rails from Commercial Street and the last vestige of Portland's hallowed role as Canada's winter grain port had vanished, a visitor standing at the foot of Pearl Street and Commercial could—with very little imagination—conjure the sounds and the sights of the nineteenth-century era when Gould prowled the waterfront hoping to salvage the endangered souls of wayward seafarers. Similarly, because the work of Model Cities, Greater Portland Landmarks, and the city itself had spared much of the urban fabric of the West End and Munjoy Hill, and because Longfellow's Deering Woods still whispered and the Western and Eastern Promenades lured lovers, Portlanders and tourists alike could fathom what had long ago inspired the poet to apprize the city as such a special place, and what special ingredients made it the Gateway to Vacationland.

CONCLUSION

Service City, Tourist City, Modern Portland

By 1987, Portland had redefined itself as a modern service-oriented city, one whose now exquisitely preserved residential and commercial architecture, complete with a working waterfront, had restored the city to its nineteenth- and early twentieth-century stature as a tourist destination. If it was no longer a gateway city in the nineteenth-century sense—a conduit for Canadian wheat and a hub of railroad transportation and coastal and international steamship commerce—it remained a gateway for cruise ships and for tourists intrigued by its reputation for hospitality and excellent restaurants. Indeed, tourists visiting the city by the sea in 2011 could choose from eighteen hotels (within city limits), including the 1927 Eastland, but also the Portland Regency (once the Portland Armory), the Holiday Inn on Spring Street, and the new Marriott Residence Inn on Fore Street, located opposite the ancient brick machine shops of the Portland Company—now a reception facility.

The preserved Old Port with its thick historic Victorian veneer harked back to an age of tall ships. Its rich assemblage of Queen Anne, Second French Empire, and Italianate commercial facades in the twenty-first-century house an array of boutiques and quaint waterfront restaurants, bars, and taverns, many—like Three-Dollar Dewey's and Gritty McDuff's—bearing the patina of a bygone, pre–Neal Dow era when rum and cheap beer flowed freely on the raucous waterfront. Portland's Old Port, its numerous other historic districts, its charming and carefully preserved West End and Munjoy Hill neighborhoods with their promenades and spectacular Fore River and Casco Bay views intact, contributed to elevating the small city to the realm of America's Most Livable Cities, a goal—though not a designation then available—once devoutly sought by James Phinney Baxter as early as the 1890s.[1]

In effect, Portland's 1960–1970 renaissance produced a postindustrial city that Baxter and John Mead Gould might have cheered. In time, prodded by organizations such as Greater Portland Landmarks, the city's leaders successfully blended Portland's assets of natural beauty, rich maritime history, and Longfellow's dreams of youth with a mixture of financial, management, educational, library, museum, health care, and other services.

Despite this success, welcomed by the city's pro-growth cohort and its historic preservation camp alike, Portland in the late twentieth century and early twenty-first faced persistent problems, some, like decent affordable housing, traceable to World War II. Population growth remained unstable. Portland's population, which had failed to reach an expected high of 80,000 in 1950, dropped to 72,566 in 1960, down again to just over 65,000 in 1970, then further to 61,572 in 1980. It rose to 64,358 in 1990, however, only to slip back slightly to 64,249 in 2000. On the eve of the 2010 census it hovered at around 62,500. While Portland's population in 2008 remained overwhelmingly of North and South European descent, it had also in the 1990s added diversity with approximately 2 percent of the population black (including a number of newly arrived immigrants from Somalia) and Hispanic.[2]

Finally, the Portland waterfront in the early twenty-first century remained, as always, contested urban space. The 1987 moratorium forbidding all nonmarine waterfront development resulted in the building of a city-owned fish pier with a fish exchange and auction house. The expansion of protected American fishing grounds to the 200-mile limit proved a boon to New England fisheries, as was evident in 1994, when 350 vessels landed their catch at the bustling pier. The fish pier itself became a popular summer tourist attraction. The city-owned International Marine Terminal adjoining the Million Dollar (later Casco Bay) Bridge had long berthed the *Scotia Prince* Yarmouth-to-Portland Ferry but also served cargo ships carrying wood pulp. On the eastern end of the Commercial Street waterfront, using state and city bond issues, Bath Iron Works (BIW) in the 1980s moored a giant floating dry dock for the repair of large naval ships. Nearby, an occasional large cruise ship tied up to the now aging Maine State Pier, where a whale mural adorned the western wall.[3]

The remainder of the 1.5-mile, fifty-acre working waterfront zone however, (the pre-1987 DiMillo's Floating Restaurant at the foot of Long Wharf and the condo-covered Chandlers Wharf excepted), including the Customs House,

Widgery, Chandlers, and Union wharves, begged for major improvements. A 2000 Waterfront Task Force report, one of twenty such reports issued between 1982 and the millennium year, put the price tag for such major repairs at $1.8 million and stated, furthermore, that "the public sector must do more to help marine-related business and the rest of the working waterfront survive and prosper." A *Press Herald* editorial accompanying the report pleaded for a better consensus on plans for using tax-increment financing for waterfront improvements, and applauded proposals for a Gulf of Maine Aquarium and new cruise ship piers as compatible with traditional waterfront uses.[4]

Nine years later on the former site of the old Grand Trunk wharves and the BIW dry dock, sat the new glittering, modern Ocean Gateway Terminal, meant to be home to the Portland to Bar Harbor to Yarmouth, Nova Scotia, ferry, before Canada in 2010 ended its subsidy and Bay Ferries Ltd. terminated the service. The facility brought needed parking and efficiency to the Portland waterfront, however, as well as enhancing the city's ability to handle cruise ships. On the waterfront's western end stood the new Gulf of Maine Research Center. But all was still not well. Nothing moved at Portland's empty International Marine Terminal. Shipments of wood pulp had ceased in June 2008. Elsewhere, stricter federal rules on the number of fishing days for haddock and other ground fish stalled activity at the fish pier and fish exchange. An impressive 350 vessels had landed over 30 million pounds of fish at the Portland Fish Exchange in 1994, and although considerably down, Portland's fishing fleet had still landed 17 million pounds at the city's seafood auction in 2006. In 2008, however, a mere 70 boats docked at the fish exchange. Even more stringent government fishing rules went into effect in 2009, and that year Portland's dwindling fishing fleet landed a paltry 6.3 million pounds of fish at the city-owned fish exchange.[5]

Oil tonnage, the mainstay of the port since World War II, also dropped in 2008, albeit slightly, from 168 million tons in 2007 to 149 million in 2008. Significantly, tonnage fell because Canadian-mined shale oil reduced demand for foreign crude oil. Portland now hoped for a reversal of oil flow on the Portland to Montreal pipe lines of Canadian oil moving to American refineries.[6]

At the end of the first decade of the twenty-first century, being a mature service-oriented city and the financial and information capital of Maine, Portland—as it had in the nineteenth century—looked even more eagerly toward increased tourism, especially the growing business of serving the mega-cruise ships making scheduled stops in Portland Harbor. With its attractive parks, promenades, historic homes, and views intact, plus the legacies of Fassett, Stevens, Baxter, and the city builders of the past, Portland could see itself as another Miami, Rio, Nice, or Barcelona—a New England cruise ship destination, a veritable tourist ship capital. In 2007 almost 49,000 passengers disembarked at the Maine Pier and by foot, jitney, or bus, left to shop at the Old Port, visit Longfellow's home on Congress (adjoining the Maine Historical Society), or eat at any of the city's host of celebrated restaurants. Unfortunately, once completed, the Ocean Gateway Terminal proved too small for giant cruise ships such as the Carnival liners. Portland in 2009 hoped to use federal stimulus dollars to build a mega-berth adjoining Ocean Gateway but failed in its bid.[7]

Sadly, one of Portland's twenty-first-century plans—to remodel the deteriorating Maine State Pier into a cruise ship terminal, hotel, and office complex—foundered when the developer, Ocean Properties, withdrew its offer in January 2009. Nevertheless, capitalizing on its beauty, charm and nostalgia, Portland clung tenaciously to its cruise-ship-capital vision, and pressure grew in 2010 for the city to soften its waterfront zoning to permit more nonmarine, tourist-friendly uses for aging piers still in desperate need of improvement. In fact, marine uses—especially fishing, bait shops, and chandleries—were generating steadily diminished revenues, and parking now consumed about 30,000 square feet of space. With no rebound in fishing predicted, and with revenues too slim to care adequately for the aging waterfront structures, pier owners demanded looser zoning regulations to allow more nonmarine uses such as offices, restaurants, and hotels, a move still vigorously opposed by city fishing interests. City Council had already altered waterfront zoning to allow nonmarine businesses on the upper floors of city wharf buildings, and by 2010, seeking the beauty and charm of waterfront space, fifty such businesses had moved there, including the offices of Pierce Atwood, northern New England's largest law firm. Helped by a $2.6 million tax break to assist with $12 million in necessary renovations, Pierce-Atwood moved into the 150-year old Cumberland Cold Storage facility on Merrills Wharf not far from Gorham's Corner. The structure lacked plumbing, and its windows had been mortared over. Before the Civil War, the five-story brick building had stored rum and molasses. Under City Council's December 2010 zoning-change proposal—still vigorously opposed by fishing interests but pressed by pier owners—almost half of the ground floor space in wharf buildings could be used for nonmarine purposes such as offices, shops, and restaurants. Condominiums, however, remained banned.[8]

While the city balanced rival visions for waterfront usage, in Bayside, once the focus of Portland's postwar redevelopment planning and demolition, new moderate-income housing arose in the 1980s and 1990s. Even more auspicious, moreover, an upscale Whole Foods emporium anchored one end of a Somerset Street commercial thoroughfare in Bayside, and an equally chic Trader Joe's market opened nearby on Marginal Way, which now unfolded as an avenue of apartments, banks, offices, and stores just off the I-295 expressway.[9]

Tempered by historic preservation, therefore, which reminded Portland about the economic value of its Longfellow legacy, the Forest City entered the twenty-first century optimistically, even though its historic waterfront still struggled. Maine Way and the rejuvenation of the Old Port had breathed fresh life into Portland's downtown, transforming it into a pedestrian-friendly, attractive, service center—no matter that the battle with the suburban Maine Mall had proved unremitting. Amid a national economic downturn in 1990, Congress Street's eighty-four-year old Porteous, Mitchell and Braun department store locked its doors. But even though its departure saddened many and heightened fears for the ultimate survival of the downtown, Congress Street, remained vital. That same year, a Wednesday farmers' market was reestablished in Monument Square, site of the city's original haymarket, where farmers had brought produce. Not far from Monument Square on Cumberland Street, Elizabeth Noyce—the divorced wife of Intel Communications founder Robert Noyce and the creator of the Libra Foundation—funded the creation of an indoor farmers' market, a venture that unfortunately failed.

Noyce also invested in real estate on Congress Street, where she enticed L. L. Bean to open an outlet store, which has since closed. Still, with the presence of the Maine Historical Society, the Maine College of Art, the architecturally stunning Portland Art Museum, the Children's Museum, plus a host of chic coffee shops and restaurants, Congress Street survived as an integral part of a blossoming Arts and Culture District—which, with Baxter's old Fassett-designed library building, the historic H. H. Hay Building, Eastland Hotel, and many other architectural landmarks, inspired the Portland Planning Department and Greater Portland Landmarks to add Congress Street to the city's collage of historic districts, which included the Old Port, the West End, Deering Street, and the tiny How House District.[10]

Portland in the early twenty-first century, with its City Hall, its courthouses, federal buildings, downtown cultural district, famed Old Port, sprawling Maine Medical Center dominating the skyline of the Western Promenade, its colleges and universities (University of Southern Maine, University of New England, Andover College, Southern Maine Community College, and Maine College of Art), its Portland Stage Company, its world-class symphony orchestra led in 2010 by Robert Moody, make the city (like Boston, Providence, Philadelphia, Pittsburgh, and San Francisco) a modern finance, real estate, and service-driven urban economy. Not only is it a regional cultural and service center, but as it has been since the nineteenth century, Portland is the finance capital of Maine. Interestingly enough, for that urban restructuring to take place, Portland had to stray very little from the path laid out for it in the 1890s by Mayor James Phinney Baxter, who saw beauty and livability as Portland's principal assets and envisioned for it an urban future built on commerce and tourism. Although the city, with the nation, had over time endured the hardships of depressions and war, and though Portland's "road to renaissance" seemed "rough" at times, and contentious waterfront issues dating back to the 1890s if not earlier still remained, could they miraculously return to their beloved city, clearly Henry Wadsworth Longfellow, John Poor, John Bundy Brown, and even John Mead Gould would smile fondly at their "beautiful city by the sea."

Notes

Introduction

1. See Dana A. Souza, "Park Management and Administration," in Theo H. B. M. Holtwyik and Earl G. Shettleworth Jr., eds., *Bold Vision: The Development of the Parks of Portland, Maine* (Portland: Greater Portland Landmarks, 1999), 136–37; Earl G. Shettleworth Jr., interview by author, July 12, 2010.
2. See Richard Florida, *The Rise of the Creative Class* (New York: Basic Books, 2003). On "locavore" restaurants, see "36 Hours: Portland, Me.," *New York Times*, August 22, 2010, Travel section. Maine sponsors a "Locally Grown" program and a "Locavore Network": www.locavorenetwork.com.
3. Matthew Klingle, *Emerald City: The Environmental History of Seattle* (New Haven: Yale University Press, 2007), 9.
4. William Willis, *History of Portland, 1632–1864* (Portland: Bailey and Noyes, 1865; repr., Portland: New Hampshire Printing and Maine Historical Society, 1992).
5. John T. Hull, ed., *Handbook of Portland* (Portland: Southworth Publishing, 1888); Edward Elwell, *Portland and Vicinity, 1876*, repr. ed. (Portland: Portland Landmarks, 1975).
6. Joseph A. Conforti, ed., *Creating Portland: History and Place in Northern New England* (Hanover, N.H.: University Press of New England, 2005).
7. Robert H. Babcock, "The Rise and Fall of Portland's Waterfront," *Maine Historical Quarterly* 22, no. 2 (Fall 1982): 63–99.
8. Longfellow's 1877 poem "My Lost Youth" contains ten verses; however, five of them, which serve as the epigraph to this book, are most important for their romantic portrayal of Portland, a portrayal that became so deeply etched on the city's consciousness that I refer to it as the "Longfellow legacy."

CHAPTER ONE
From Beleaguered Outpost to Booming Port City, 1632–1860

1. Samuel Longfellow, ed., *Life of Henry Wadsworth Longfellow: With Extracts from His Journals and Correspondence*, vol. 1 (Boston: Ticknor, 1886), 9; James Phinney Baxter, "The Story of Portland," *New England Magazine*, November 1895, James Phinney Baxter Papers, Baxter Memorial Library, Gorham, Maine (hereafter cited as Baxter

Papers). On premier harbors, see Robert Greenhalgh Albion, *The Rise of New York Port, 1815–1860* (New York: Scribner's, 1970), 23.

2. See Albert F. Barnes, ed., *Greater Portland 350: A Commemorative Edition* (Portland: Gannett Books, 1984); William Willis, *History of Portland, 1632–1864* (Portland: Bailey and Noyes, 1865; repr., Portland: New Hampshire Publishing and Maine Historical Society, 1992), 49–275; on the early history of Machigonne (Falmouth, then Portland), see Emerson W. Baker's excellent contribution, "Formerly Machegonne, Dartmouth, York, Stogummor, Casco, Falmouth: Portland as a Contested Frontier in the Seventeenth Century," in Joseph A. Conforti, ed., *Creating Portland: History and Place in Northern New England* (Hanover, N.H.: University Press of New England, 2005), 1–16.
3. See Willis, *History of Portland;* and Barnes, *Greater Portland 350.*
4. John T. Hull, ed., *1786–1886 Centennial Celebration: An Account of the Municipal Celebration of the One Hundredth Anniversary of the Incorporation of the Town of Portland* (Portland: Owen, Strout, 1886), 89; Willis, *History of Portland,* 440–68; Barnes, *Greater Portland 350,* 20–21.
5. On Portsmouth, see Richard M. Candee, *Building Portsmouth: The Neighborhoods and Architecture of New Hampshire's Oldest City* (Portsmouth: Portsmouth Advocates, 1992), 1–5.
6. Sam Bass Warner, *The Private City: Philadelphia in Three Periods of Its Growth* (Philadelphia: University of Pennsylvania Press, 1968); Willis, *History of Portland,* 442–43; Barnes, *Greater Portland 350,* 32.
7. Willis, *History of Portland,* 465; Barnes, *Greater Portland 350,* 22.
8. Willis, *History of Portland,* 465. On the preindustrial city, see Gideon Sjoberg, *The Preindustrial City: Past and Present* (New York: Free Press, 1960); Warner, *The Private City,* 3–49; Gary B. Nash, *The Urban Crucible: Social Change, Political Consciousness, and the Origins of the American Revolution* (Cambridge: Harvard University Press, 1979), 3–26.
9. Charles P. M. Outwin, "Thriving and Elegant Town: Eighteenth-Century Portland as a Commercial Center," in Conforti, *Creating Portland,* 35. On cosmopolitan Philadelphia, see Carl Bridenbaugh, *Cities in the Wilderness: The First Century of Urban Life in America, 1625–1742* (New York: Knopf, 1938).
10. James S. Leamon, "Falmouth, the American Revolution, and the Price of Moderation," in Conforti, *Creating Portland,* 45–58; Charles P. M. Outwin, in "Thriving and Elegant, Flourishing and Populous: Falmouth in Casco Bay, 1765–1775" (Ph.D diss., University of Maine, 2009), 220–25, contends that Mowatt was less motivated by vengeance than by zeal to do his duty.
11. On Presbyterianism in Maine, see Calvin Montague Clark, *History of the Congregational Church in Maine, 1600–1826* (Portland: Congregational Church Conference of Maine, 1935); also Willis, *History of Portland,* 382–85 and 438–41; Hull, *1786–1886 Centennial Celebration.* On Mowatt's capture and revenge, see Leamon, "Falmouth, The American Revolution," in Conforti, *Creating Portland,* 57–61; also Edward Elwell, *Portland and Vicinity 1876,* repr. ed. (Portland: Greater Portland Landmarks, 1975).
12. William David Barry, *A Vignetted History of Portland Business, 1632–1982* (Boston: Newcomen Society, 1982); Longfellow, *Life of Henry Wadsworth Longfellow.* Carl Bridenbaugh uses the term "pearls" to describe early Atlantic Coast cities in his *Cities in the Wilderness, 1625–1742* (New York: Knopf, 1938).

13. Willis, *History of Portland,* 555; John T. Hull, ed., *Handbook of Portland, Old Orchard, Cape Elizabeth, and Casco Bay* (Portland: Southworth Publishing, 1888), 12–17; Barnes, *Greater Portland 350,* 37; William David Barry, photocopy of handwritten "Analysis of Petition to Incorporate Portland," in possession of author; *Biographical Sketches of Leading Citizens of Cumberland County* (Boston: Biographical Review Publishing, 1896); on Whig politics, see Sean Wilentz, *The Rise of American Democracy: Jefferson to Lincoln* (New York: Norton, 2005), 402–546; and Charles G. Sellers, *Market Revolution: Jacksonian America, 1815–1846* (New York: Oxford University Press, 1991), 348–63.
14. Willis, *History of Portland,* 560. On relationship of Portland merchants with hinterland, see Joyce Butler, "Family and Community Life in Maine, 1783–1861," in Richard W. Judd, Edwin A. Churchill, and Joel W. Eastman, eds., *Maine: The Pine Tree State from Prehistory to the Present* (Orono: University of Maine Press, 1995), 217–40.
15. Willis, *History of Portland,* 562–77; William Goold, "Old Business and Businessmen of Portland," in Edward Elwell, *Successful Business Houses of Portland* (Portland: W. S. Jones, 1875); Barry, *A Vignetted History of Portland Business.* On Portland and West Indies, see David Carey Jr., "Comunidad Escondida: Latin American Influences in Nineteenth and Twentieth Century Portland," in Conforti, *Creating Portland,* 90–118.
16. Earle G. Shettleworth Jr. and William David Barry, *Mr. Goodhue Remembers: Scenes from the Mid-Nineteenth Century* (Augusta: Maine Historic Preservation Commission, 1981); Goold, "Old Businesses and Businessmen of Portland."
17. Willis, *History of Portland,* 576.
18. Joyce Butler, "Family and Community Life in Maine, 1783–1861," in Judd et al., *Maine,* 222–23; Barnes, *Greater Portland 350,* 37. See also Arthur Gerrer, "Lower State Street Neighborhood Development," n.d., manuscript report of survey, Greater Portland Landmarks, Portland, Maine, held at Maine Historical Society Library, Portland (hereafter cited as MHSL); Willis, *History of Portland,* 550–53; Greater Portland Landmarks, *Portland* (1986; repr., Portland: Greater Portland Landmarks, 1999); Shettleworth and Barry, *Mr. Goodhue Remembers.* On Ingraham, see Elwell, *Portland and Vicinity, 1876.*
19. Willis, *History of Portland,* 575; Baxter, "Story of Portland," 360. On Maine Statehood, see Judd et al., *Maine.*
20. Longfellow, *Life of Henry Wadsworth Longfellow,* 2–15 and 88–89.
21. David Schuyler, *The New Urban Landscape: The Redefinition of City Form in Nineteenth-Century America* (Baltimore: Johns Hopkins University Press, 1986). On clipper ships, see William Hutchinson Rowe, *The Maritime History of Maine: Three Centuries of Shipbuilding and Seafaring* (1948; repr., Gardiner, Maine: Tilbury House Press, 1989); Robert Greenhalgh Albion, Benjamin Labaree, and William A. Baker, *New England and the Sea* (Mystic, Conn.: Mystic Seaport Museum, 1970). For the urban threshold reference, see Stuart M. Blumin, *The Urban Threshold: Growth and Change in a Nineteenth-Century American Community* (Chicago: University of Chicago Press, 1976).
22. For Portland's population increase, 1800–1850, see decennial cenus reports, U.S. Bureau of the Census, *United States Census of Population, 1800–1850* (Washington, D.C.: Bureau of the Census, GPO, 1800–1850). The U.S. Census was not actually published on the decennial year; for example, the Seventh Census of the United States,

1850, was published by the GPO in 1853. For a pioneering demographic analysis of antebellum urban mobility, see Blumin, *Urban Threshold,* 224.

23. For my sources of data on Portland occupations for the years 1840–1850, see *Portland Directory and Reference Book* (Portland: B. Thurston, 1840 to 1850 inclusive) (hereafter cited as *Portland Director*); and Portland Tax Book for 1849, both found in Special Collection Archives, Portland Room, Portland Public Library (hereafter cited as PRSC).

24. John Cullem, "A Map of Portland and the Latest Improvements, 1836," and Portland Tax Book for 1849, both in PRSC; Everts and Peck, *History of Cumberland County with Illustrations and with Biographical Sketches of Prominent Men and Businesses* (Philadelphia: Everts and Peck, 1880).

25. On Exchange Building and City Hall, see Greater Portland Landmarks, *Portland,* 80–81 and 124–25.

26. See Joseph A. Conforti's excellent *Imagining New England: Explorations of Regional Identity from the Pilgrims to the Mid-Twentieth Century* (Chapel Hill: University of North Carolina Press, 2001), 123–202.

27. On politics in the New Republic, see Willentz, *Rise of American Democracy,* 243–518; Philip Ethington, *The Public City: The Political Construction of Urban Life in San Francisco, 1850–1900* (Berkeley: University of California Press, 1994), 1–38; Richard P. McCormick, *The Second American Party System: Party Formation in the Jacksonian Era* (New York: Norton, 1973).

28. On the canal, see "Cumberland and Oxford Canal: Origin and Organization," pamphlet at MHSL; Barnes, *Greater Portland 350,* 56; Joel W. Eastman, "Transportation Systems in Maine, 1820–1880," in Judd et al., *Maine,* 310–14; Edward E. Chase, *Maine Railroads: A History of the Development of the Maine Railroad System* (Portland: A. J. Huston, 1926).

29. Lawrence C. Allin, "Ships and Shipbuilding in the Period of Ascension," in Judd et al., *Maine,* 297; William Hutchinson Rowe, *Shipbuilding Days in Casco Bay, 1727–1890; Being Footnotes to the Maritime History of Maine* (Yarmouth, Maine, 1929), 58–79; Shettleworth and Barry, *Mr. Goodhue Remembers,* 7–9. For ship production 1845–1848, see *Portland Directory,* 1850.

30. See Marcus Rediker, *The Slave Ship: A Human History* (New York: Penguin, 2007), 72.

31. Wayne M. O'Leary and Lawrence C. Allin, "Maine's Maritime Trades in the Period of Ascendancy," in Judd et al., *Maine,* 289–96; see also "Portland Past and Present," in *Portland Board of Trade Journal* (hereafter cited as *PTJ*) 5 (April 1893): 360.

32. On Brown, see Willis, *History of Portland; Portland Directory,* 1850, 208; correspondence and other documents in the John B. Brown and Sons Records, Baker Library, Harvard University (hereafter cited as J. B. Brown Records).

33. Barry, *Vignetted History,* 12–13; letter from Phillip Clifford presenting papers to Baker Library, in J. B. Brown Records; Stuart Blumin, *The Emergence of the Middle Class: Social Experience in the American City, 1760–1900* (Cambridge: Cambridge University Press, 1989); Robert H. Babcock, "The Decline of Artisan Republicanism in Portland, Maine, 1825–1850," *New England Quarterly* 63 (March 1990): 3–34.

34. See John Neal, *Portland Illustrated* (Portland: W. S. Jones, 1974), 12.

35. Ibid., 14.

36. "Fore Street," n.d., part of a larger survey of Portland area historic resources undertaken by Greater Portland Landmarks, found in Greater Portland Landmarks Library,

Portland, Maine; Baxter, "Story of Portland," 362–65; J. D. McClatchy, ed., *Henry Wadsworth Longfellow: Poems and Other Works* (New York: Library of America, 2000); *Portland Directory,* 1841; *Portland Directory,* 1850.

37. Augustus F. Moulton, *Portland by the Sea: An Historical Treatise* (Augusta: Katahdin Publishing, 1926), 203; Schuyler, *New Urban Landscape,* 62–65; Theodore H. B. M. Holtwijk and Earle G. Shettlworth Jr., eds., *Bold Vision: The Development of the Parks of Portland, Maine* (Portland: Greater Portland Landmarks, 1990), 1–15.

38. Holtwyik and Shettleworth, *Bold Vision;* Earle G. Shettleworth Jr., "Creating and Preserving Portland's Urban Landscape, 1885–1925," in Conforti, *Creating Portland,* 252.

39. See Paul Boyer, *Urban Masses and Moral Order, 1820–1920* (Cambridge: Harvard University Press, 1992); Thomas Bender, *Toward an Urban Vision: Ideas and Institutions in Nineteenth-Century America* (Lexington: University of Kentucky Press,), 118–21; on culture, see Elwell, *Portland and Vicinity 1876;* Willis, *History of Portland;* see address of Mr. W. E. Gould, in Hull, *1786–1886 Centennial Celebration,* 194–98; see "*The Constitution of the Portland Provident Association with a Short Historical Sketch,*" in Provident Association Papers, Coll. 725, MHSL.

40. Babcock, "Decline of Artisan Republicanism"; Robert H. Babcock, "An Old Mercantile Center in Transition," in Judd et al., *Maine,* 455–56; Sean Wilentz, *Chants Democratic: New York City and the Rise of the American Working Class, 1788–1850* (New York: Oxford University Press, 1984). Francis Couvares uses the term "Craftsmen Empire" in *The Remaking of Pittsburgh: Class and Culture in an Industrializing City, 1877–1919* (Albany: State University of New York Press, 1984).

41. Shettleworth and Barry, *Mr. Goodhue Remembers,* 10; Hull, *1786–1886 Centennial Celebration,* 84–85; H. H. Price and Gerald Talbot, *Maine's Visible Black History: The First Chronicle of Its People* (Gardiner, Me.: Tilbury House, 2006), 42–43.

42. The historian John Bodnar contends that the main stream of the Irish exodus caused by the Great Hunger emanated from the "dynamic" Irish counties of Connaught and Leinster, not from more ravaged rural western counties such as Tipperary. See John Bodnar, *The Transplanted: A History of Immigrants in Urban America* (Bloomington: Indiana University Press, 1985), 5–6; Matthew Jude Barker, "The Irish Community and Irish Organizations in Nineteenth-Century Portland, Maine," in Michael C. Connolly, ed., *They Change Their Sky: The Irish in Maine* (Orono: University of Maine Press, 2004), 141–43.

43. Barker, "Irish Community," 143; Hull, *1786–1886 Centennial Celebration,* 88; James H. Mundy, *Hard Times, Hard Men: Maine and the Irish, 1830–1860* (Scarborough, Maine: Harp, 1990), 7–20.

44. Barker, "Irish Community," 143; Maine Laws, Chapter 167, March 29, 1853, State Archives, Augusta.

45. On Dow and his crusade against demon rum, resulting in the Maine Law, see Neal Dow, *The Reminiscences of Neal Dow: Recollections of Eighty Years* (Portland: Evening Press Publishing, 1898), 221–358; on the Irish and the "cratur," see Mundy, *Hard Times, Hard Men,* 18–21; Barker, "Irish Community," 164–65.

46. Barker, "Irish Community," 166–68; Hull, *1786–1886 Centennial Celebration,* 132–37. On anti-Irish nativism in other cities, see Sam Bass Warner Jr., "Riots and the Restoration of Public Order," chap. 7 in *The Private City: Philadelphia in Three Periods of Its Growth,* 2nd ed. (1968; Philadelphia: University of Pennsylvania Press, 1987),

125–57; and Oscar Handlin, *Boston Immigrants, 1790–1880* (Cambridge: Belknap Press of Harvard University Press, 1991), 178–206.

47. Edward C. Kirkland, *Men, Cities, and Transportation: A Story of New England History, 1820–1900* (Cambridge: Harvard University Press, 1948), 194–221; Chase, *Maine Railroads,* 2–12; Joel Eastman and Paul E. Rivard, "Transportation and Manufacturing," in Judd et al., *Maine,* 315; Robert H. Babcock, "The Rise and Fall of Portland's Waterfront, 1850–1920," *Maine Historical Quarterly* 22, no. 2 (Fall 1982): 60–65; Robert H. Babcock, "Economic Development in Portland and St. Johns, New Brunswick during the Age of Iron and Steam, 1850–1914," *American Review of Canadian Studies* 9 (Spring 1979): 3–37.

48. Kirkland, *Men, Cities, and Transportation,* 207. Although Poor argued that the railroad would bring manufacturing to Maine, he correctly saw industry locating in places like Lewistown and Skowhegan, not in Portland. He had studied Maine's water resources and identified places with water power as industrial sites. Portland lacked such water resources. See Babcock, "Economic Development in Portland and St. Johns."

49. Kirkland, *Men, Cities, and Transportation,* 204–5.

50. On Poor and his trip, see Chase, *Maine Railroads,* 14; Eastman and Rivard, "Transportation and Manufacturing," 316–17; Moulton, *Portland by the Sea,* 200; Kirkland, *Men, Cities, and Transportation,* 210–12.

51. Babcock, "Rise and Fall of Portland's Waterfront," 60–61; Chase, *Maine Railroads,* 16.

52. Moulton, *Portland by the Sea,* 201; Chase, *Maine Railroads,* 30–45.

53. Chase, *Maine Railroads,* 6–27; Eastman and Rivard, "Transportation and Manufacturing," 316–17.

54. Babcock, "Economic Development in Portland and St. Johns," 3–37.

55. Moulton, *Portland by the Sea,* 202; Willis, *History of Portland;* Babcock, "Economic Development in Portland and St. Johns." On landmaking in other cities, see Matthew Klingle, *Emerald City: An Environmental History of Seattle* (New Haven: Yale University Press, 2007), 86–115; and Nancy S. Seasholes, *Gaining Ground: A History of Landmaking in Boston* (Cambridge: MIT Press, 2003).

56. Kirkland, *Men, Cities, and Transportation,* 214; G. F. Shepley, Canal Bank, to William Pitt Fessenden, May 26, 1858, reel 1, Fessenden Papers, Library of Congress, Washington, D.C.

57. David H. Fletcher, *The Portland Company, 1846–1982* (Charleston, S.C.: Arcadia, 2002); Walter MacDougall, "The Portland Company: Wood-burning Locomotives to Atomic Reactors," in *Downeast Magazine* 10, no. 6 (March 1964); Portland Company Records, Coll. 242, MHSL; Board of Directors Minutes of the Portland Company, November 11, 1846–July 24, 1860, in Portland Company Director's Records, 1846–1902, Coll. 242 A, 1990, vol. 30, MHSL.

58. On early tourism, the discovery of the scenic White Mountains, and Portland's rail connection, see Dona Brown, *Inventing New England: Regional Tourism in the Nineteenth Century* (Washington, D.C.: Smithsonian Institution Press, 1995), 41–74. Brown's solid and insightful study of tourism as an industry, scenery as a commodity, and the tourist as consumer focuses mainly on rural tourism, not the attractions of cities such as Portland.

59. See Catherine Cocks, *Doing the Town: The Rise of Urban Tourism in the United States, 1850–1915* (Berkeley: University of California Press, 2001), 41–52.

60. See Richard R. Wescott, "Economic, Social and Government Aspects of Development of Maine's Vacation Industry" (master's thesis, University of Maine, Orono, 1961), 2.

CHAPTER TWO

Civil War, the Great Fire, and Reshaping Portland's Urban Image

1. John A. Garraty, *The New Commonwealth, 1877–1890* (New York: Harper, 1968). On robber barons, see Matthew Josephson, *The Robber Barons: The Great American Capitalists, 1861–1901* (New York: Harcourt, Brace and World, 1962); John Frazier Wall, *Andrew Carnegie* (Pittsburgh: University of Pittsburgh Press, 1989).
2. Jude Barker, "Irish Organizations and the Irish Community," in Michael C. Connolly, ed., *They Change Their Sky: The Irish in Maine* (Orono: University of Maine, 2004), 152–56; Dow speech in John T. Hull, ed., *1786–1886 Centennial Celebration: An Account of the Municipal Celebration of the One Hundredth Anniversary of the Incorporation of the Town of Portland, July 4th, 5th, and 6th, 1886* (Portland: Owen, Strout, 1886), 179–85; James H. Mundy, *Hard Times, Hard Men: Maine and the Irish, 1830–1860* (Scarborough, Maine: Harp, 1990).
3. Samuel Longfellow, ed., *The Life of Henry Wadsworth Longfellow*, vol. 1 (Boston: Ticknor, 1886).
4. Committee on Investigation, *Report of the Committee on Investigation of the Riot in the City of Portland* (Portland: Benjamin D. Beck, City Printer, 1855). Also on Rum Riot, see "Old Market Square: The Rum Riot 55 Years Ago and Another Incident," *Eastern Argus*, June 4, 1910.
5. On the advent of the Civil War, see Avery Craven, *The Coming of the Civil War* (Chicago: University of Chicago Press, 1967); J. G. Randall and David Donald, *The Civil War and Reconstruction*, 2nd ed. (Boston: D. C. Heath, 1961); on Portland and Maine, see Louis Clinton Hatch, ed., *Maine: A History: A Facsimile of the 1919 Edition* (Somersworth: New Hampshire Publishing, 1974), 288–91; on antislavery, and abolitionism in Portland, see "The Reverend Dr. Dalton's Address," in Hull, *Centennial Celebration*, 187–93.
6. On Woolheads and Wildcats and the origin of Maine's Republican Party, see Hatch, *Maine;* and Mark O. Hatfield, "Hannibal Hamlin," in *Vice Presidents of the United States, 1789–1993* (Washington, D.C.: GPO, 1997).
7. William E. Gienapp, *The Origins of the Republican Party, 1852–1856* (New York: Oxford University Press, 1987); Richard W. Judd, Edward A. Churchill, and Joel A. Eastman, eds., *Maine: The Pine Tree State from Prehistory to the Present* (Orono: University of Maine Press, 1995); also Charles Jellison, *Fessenden of Maine, Civil War Senator* (Syracuse, N.Y.: Syracuse University Press, 1962).
8. "Beecher's Bibles" were, in fact, rifles; on the Portland Company and Civil War, see Portland Company Records, File 242A, Directors Minutes, vol. 30, December 4, 1860, December 13, 1860, June 7, 1862, April 3, 1866, April 11, 1874, MHSL; Walther MacDougall, "The Portland Company," *Downeast Magazine* 4, no. 6 (1964): 50.
9. Robert H. Babcock, "Economic Development in Portland, Maine, and St. Johns, in the Age of Iron and Steam," *American Review of Canadian Studies* 9 (Spring 1979): 30–37.

10. Everts and Peck, *History of Cumberland Co., Maine, with Illustrations and Biographical Sketches* (Philadelphia: Everts and Peck, 1880), 18.
11. Few histories or sources refer to the impact of the Maine Law on Portland's economy. For one that does, see "Portland's West India Trade," *Board of Trade Journal* (hereafter cited as *BTJ*) 6 (June 1893): 38. See also correspondence and other documents in the J. B. Brown Records; and Charles S. Fobes, "Changes in the Commerce of Portland for Half a Century," *BTJ* 16 (January 1904): 314–16.
12. On bounties and war costs, see Address of Mayor A. E. Stevens in *Auditors Annual Report of the Receipts and Expenditures of the City of Portland for the Fiscal Year 1867–1868, with the Mayor's Address* (Portland: David Tucker, 1868) (hereafter cited as *AAR*). This publication continued during the late nineteenth and early twentiteh centuries, variously published by David Tucker, William Marks, B. Thurston, Ford and Rich, and the Daily Press Printers.
13. See John Mead Gould Diaries, August 3, 1867, September 19, 1867, August 6 and 19, 1873, Coll. 1033, vol. 9, MHSL. The John Mead Gould Diaries (hereafter cited as Gould Diaries) contain daily entries about Portland politics and culture. They run from 1859 to Gould's death in 1929 and are bound in volumes of about six years' duration. On the monument, see Earle G. Shettleworth Jr., "Creating and Preserving Portland's Urban Landscape, 1885–1925," in Joseph A. Conforti, ed., *Creating Portland: History and Place in Northern New England* (Hanover, N.H.: University Press of New England, 2005), 218–47; and Gould Diaries, vol. 10, October 28, 1873.
14. See Edward Elwell, *Portland and Vicinity 1876,* repr. ed. (Portland: Greater Portland Portland Landmarks, 1975), 20.
15. See *AAR,* 1867–1868, appendix, 92–93.
16. Prentice Loring, "Portland, Past and Present," *BTJ* 5 (April 1893): 360; Ida M. Tarbel, *The History of the Standard Oil Company* (New York: Norton, 1966); Philip Scranton, *Figured Tapestry: Production, Markets, and Power in Philadelphia Textiles, 1855–1941* (Cambridge: Cambridge University Press, 2002); Jackson Lears, *Fables of Abundance: A Cultural History of Advertising in America* (New York: Basic Books, 1994). See also David R. Goldfield and Blaine A. Brownell, *Urban America: A History,* 2nd ed. (Boston: Houghton Mifflin, 1990); Thomas Cochrane and William Miller, *The Age of Enterprise: A Social History of Industrial America* (New York: Macmillan, 1942); Alan Trachtenburg, *The Incorporation of Modern America: Culture and Society in the Gilded Age* (New York: Hill and Wang, 1982).
17. Wayne M. O'Leary, Lawrence C. Allin, James B. Vickery, and Richard Judd, "Traditional Industries in the Age of Monopoly, 1865–1930," in Judd et al., *Maine,* 391–403, and Nathan Lipfert, Richard Judd, and Richard R. Wescott, "New Industries in an Age of Adjustment, 1865–1930," in Judd et al., *Maine,* 421–31. See also Charles S. Fobes, "Changes in the Commerce of Portland for Half a Century," *BTJ* 16 (January 1904): 314–16.
18. On cities and product branding, see Goldfield and Brownell, *Urban America,* 94–95; on Pittsburgh and industrialism, see Francis G. Couvares, *The Remaking of Pittsburgh: Class and Culture in an Industrializing City, 1877–1919* (Albany: SUNY Press, 1984); on Portland's failure to compete, see Fobes, "Changes in the Commerce of Portland," 314.
19. Philip Scranton, *Endless Novelty: Specialty Production and American Industrialization, 1865–1925* (Princeton: Princeton University Press, 1997).

20. The *BTJ* regularly featured profiles of Portland firms and industries, usually profiling one in each monthly issue; see, for example, "Thomas Laughlin Company," *BTJ* 16 (January 1904): 304–5.
21. Portland Company Records, Coll. 242, Directors Minutes, August 3, 1866; John Neal, *Account of the Great Conflagration in Portland, July 4, 5, 1866, and a New Business Guide* (Portland: Starbird and Twitchell, 1866), MHSL. See also Everts and Peck, *History of Cumberland Co., Maine, with Illustrations and Biographical Sketches of Its Prominent Men and Pioneers* (Philadelphia: Everts & Peck, 1880); and James P. Baxter, "The Story of Portland," *New England Magazine* 19, no. 3 (November 1895): 365.
22. "Appeal from Portlanders," December 13, 1867, Fessenden Papers, reel 4, Library of Congress, Washington, D.C.
23. Address of Mayor A. E. Stevens, *AAR,* 1865–1867, 8.
24. Shettleworth, "Creating and Preserving Portland's Urban Landscape"; see also Elwell, *Portland and Vicinity 1876,* 2–4.
25. On the hotel, see *Eastern Argus,* June 29, 1868, 2; see also Elwell, *Portland and Vicinity 1876,* 64; and "Falmouth Hotel Opens with Fanfare," in Albert F. Barnes, ed., *Greater Portland 350: A Commemorative Edition* (Portland: Gannett Books, 1984), 106.
26. See *AAR,* 1866–1867, 7–15; *AAR,* 1867–1868, 14–19; Elwell, *Portland and Vicinity 1876,* 48–67; Everts and Peck, *History of Cumberland County, 1880;* Augustus F. Moulton, *Portland by the Sea: An Historical Treatise* (Augusta, Maine: Katahdin, 1926), 222–25.
27. David Schuyler, *The New Urban Landscape: The Redefinition of City Form in Nineteenth-Century America* (Baltimore: Johns Hopkins University Press, 1986), 59–76; Charles E. Rosenberg, *The Cholera Years: The United States in 1832, 1849, and 1866,* rev. ed. (Chicago: University of Chicago Press, 1987); Nelson Manfred Blake, *Water for the Cities: A History of the Urban Water Supply Problem in the United States* (Syracuse, N.Y.: Syracuse University Press, 1956). See also Martin V. Melosi, *The Sanitary City: Urban Infrastructure in America from Colonial Times to the Present* (Baltimore: Johns Hopkins University Press, 2000).
28. On suburbanization, see Kenneth T. Jackson, *Crabgrass Frontier: The Suburbanization of the United States* (New York: Oxford University Press, 1985), and Robert Fishman, *Bourgeois Utopias: The Rise and Fall of Suburbia* (New York: Basic Books, 1987); on Portland trolley system, see Edwin "Bill" Roberts, *Remember the Portland, Maine, Trolleys* (Portland: Robertson Books, 1982); Barnes, *Greater Portland 350,* 80–81.
29. Address of Mayor Moses M. Butler, *AAR,* 1877–1878, 14; Jon Teaford, *The Unheralded Triumph: City Government in America, 1870–1900* (Baltimore: Johns Hopkins University Press, 1984), 17; John F. Bauman and Edward K. Muller, *Before Renaissance: Planning in Pittsburgh, 1889–1943* (Pittsburgh: University of Pittsburgh Press, 2006).
30. See Report of Street Commissioners, *AAR,* 1866–1880; see, in particular, *AAR,* 1871–1872, Address of Mayor Benjamin Kingsbury, 9, and appendix: Report of the Civil Engineer and Report of the Street Commissioners, 71–87.
31. See Maine Laws, February 1866, chap. 159, 125. On New York crowding, see Roy Lubove, *The Progressives and the Slums: Tenement House Reform in New York City, 1890–1917* (1962; repr., Westport, Conn.: Greenwood Press, 1974); Robert H. Bremner, *From the Depths: The Discovery of Poverty in the United States* (1962; repr., New Brunswick, N.J.: Transaction, 1992).
32. Address of Mayor William Lebaron Putnam, *AAR,* 1869–1870, 8; "Great Fire Decides Sebago Question," in Barnes, *Greater Portland 350;* Moulton, *Portland by the Sea,* 223.

33. Address of Mayor George P. Wescott, *AAR,* 1872–1873, 10.
34. "An Ordinance Entitled 'An Ordinance Additional to the Revised Ordinance of 1868 Relating to Health,'" in appendix, *AAR,* 1878–1879, 68–69.
35. Address of Mayor Frances Fessenden, *AAR,* 1876, 12.
36. Address of Mayor Moses M. Butler, *AAR,* 1877–1878, 18.
37. Ibid., 21; see also Jon C. Teaford, *The Unheralded Triumph: City Government in America, 1870–1900* (Baltimore: Johns Hopkins University Press, 1984); on sewers, see Stanley Schultz and Clay McShane, "To Engineer the Metropolis: Sewer, Sanitation, and City Planning in Late-Nineteenth-Century America," *Journal of American History* 65 (1978): 389–411.
38. William A. Goodwin, Chief Engineer's Report, *AAR,* 1878–1879, 183.
39. Address of Mayor Moses Butler, *AAR,* 1876–1877, 32; Teaford, *Unheralded Triumph.*
40. Address of Mayor Jacob McLellan, *AAR,* 1866–1867, 13; see also mayoral addresses of A. E. Stevens and William Lebaron Putnam in *AAR,* 1867–1868, 17, and *AAR,* 1869–1870, 20; A. W. Smith, "Portland's Parks and Promenades," *BTJ* 19 (January 1907): 455; Shettleworth, "Creating and Preserving Portland's Urban Landscape."
41. John F. Bauman, "Before the Bungalow: The Three-Decker as Affordable Housing in Portland, Maine," Presidential Address delivered at Annual Meeting of the Society for City and Regional Planning History, St. Louis, Mo., 2003.
42. John Neal, *Portland Illustrated* (1874), 82–83, in MHSL. Neal gives a detailed and personal account of the evolution of Brown's holding on Bramhall Hill; information can also be extrapolated from J. B. Brown Records; for footprint of estate and its location, see William A. Goodwin, City Engineer of City of Portland, *Portland Revaluation Map, 1882,* found in PRSC.
43. U.S. Bureau of the Census, *The Tenth Census: 1880, Population* (Washington, D.C.: GPO, 1882); and Goodwin, *Portland Revaluation Map*, 1882.
44. Elwell, *Portland and Vicinity 1876,* 68–69; Report of City Engineer, *AAR,* 1877–1878; Report of City Engineer, *AAR,* 1878–1879; Address of Mayor Moses Butler, *AAR,* 1877–1878; Shettleworth, "Creating and Preserving Portland's Urban Landscape."
45. Gould Diaries, vol. 10, February 29, 1872.
46. Ibid., "Review of [the year] 1876."
47. Neal, *Portland Illustrated,* 149, which quoted the *Eastern Argus* that "the Panic, which causes such a crash in New York and other large business centers hardly made a ripple here." Neal goes on to say that "all departments may not be doing equally well." Evidence from Gould and the *AAR* do not substantiate Neal's sanguine assessment.
48. Gould Diaries, vol. 10, June 24, 1872.
49. Ibid., "Review of Month," May 1875; see also entries for September 28, 1873, and February 9, 1875.
50. Address of Mayor Frances Fessenden, *AAR,* 1875–1876, 9.
51. Gould Diaries, vol. 10, March 29, 1877.
52. Address of Mayor Moses Butler, *AAR,* 1876–1877, 20–21.
53. Ibid., 1877–1878. On the Greenback issue, see Robert P. Sharkey, *Money, Class, and Party: An Economic Study of Civil War and Reconstruction* (Baltimore: John Hopkins University Press, 1959), 83–131; and Unger, *The Greenback Era;* see also Chase, *History of the Development of the Maine Railroad System,* 46–53.
54. Address of Mayor George Walker, *AAR,* 1878–1879; see Elwell, *Portland and Vicinity 1876,* 28–30.

55. See *Portland Directory,* 1877, 268–69. Until 1890 the Portland City Directory was called the *Portland Directory and Reference Book.* Because of its publisher it was referred to simply as the Thurston Directory. After 1890 it became the *Directory of Portland and Vicinity,* and after 1905 *The Directory of Portland.* It was published by B. Thurston, Brown and Thurston, Thurston Printing, and, after 1901, by the Portland Directory Company. On Gould's Sunday morning work, see Gould Diaries, vol. 10, January 14, 1875.
56. Address of Mayor Benjamin Kingsbury Jr., *AAR,* 1871–1872, 6.
57. Edward Elwell, *Successful Business Houses of Portland* (Portland: W. S. Jones, 1875), 4–15. On Curtis Gum and Thomas Laughlin Company, see "World Leaders in Their Time," *BTJ* 16 (January 1904): 304–5; and William David Barry, *A Vignetted History of Portland Business, 1632–1982* (Portland: Newcomen Society), 13–14.
58. Wall, *Andrew Carnegie;* Cochrane and Miller, *Age of Enterprise.*
59. On Brown, see Records of the John B. Brown Co., Ledger of J. B. Brown, Co., vol. BA 1, Accounts, July 1865–1871 (includes sugar accounts, molasses, gold investments, and some real estate), in J. B. Brown Records; see also Ledger of J. B. Brown Company, vol. BA 2. Although John B. Brown died in 1881, the J. B. Brown and Sons firm lasted until December 1893, when it simply closed its books and disappeared.
60. See Baxter Papers; "James Phinney Baxter," in *Biographical Review of Leading Citizens of Cumberland County, Maine* (Boston: Biographical Review, 1896), 37.
61. Elwell, *Portland and Vicinity 1876,* 20.
62. Baxter, "Story of Portland," 365–66.
63. On the story of Deering Farm, Deering Oaks, and the origin of the Parkside neighborhood, see Bauman, "Before the Bungalow." See also Address of Mayor William Senter, *AAR,* 1879–1880, 13–14; A. W. Smith, "Portland's Parks and Promenades," *BTJ* 19 (January 1907): 455.
64. Report of Mayor William Senter, *AAR,* 1880–1881, 3–11.
65. Gould Diaries, vol. 11, January 9, 1881.

CHAPTER THREE
James Phinney Baxter's City, 1882–1896

1. "Doing Better Now," *BTJ* 1 (October 1888): 182.
2. Robert H. Babcock, Yves Frenette, Charles A. Scontras, and Eileen Egan, "Work and Workers in the Industrial Age, 1865–1930," in Richard W. Judd, Edwin A. Churchill, and Joel W. Eastman, eds., *Maine: The Pine Tree State from Prehistory to the Present* (Orono: University of Maine Press, 1995); U.S. Bureau of the Census, *The Tenth Census: 1880, Population* (Washington, D.C.: GPO, 1882).
3. See *BTJ* 6 (June 1893): 40.
4. See *Portland Directory,* 1885; also advertisements in *BTJ* 3 (May 1890).
5. For business listings, see *Leading Businesses of Portland and Vicinity* (Boston: Mercantile Publishing, 1887). See also Maine State Industrial Bureau, *Maine Industries, 1884* (Augusta, 1884), 30–37; Edward H. Elwell, *The Successful Business Houses of Portland* (Portland: W. S. Jones, 1875); John T. Hull, ed., *Hand-book of Portland, Old Orchard, Cape Elizabeth, and Casco Bay* (Portland: Southworth Publishing, 1888), 132–39; and "Portland in a Nutshell," *BTJ* 4 (June 1891): 59.

6. On New England industrialism in the nineteenth century, see Edward Chase Kirkland, *Industry Comes of Age: Business, Labor and Public Policy, 1860–1897* (New York: Holt, Rinehart and Winston, 1961); and Tamara Haraven and Randolph Langerbach, *Amoskeag: Life and Work in an American Factory City* (New York: Pantheon, 1978).
7. Address of Mayor John W. Deering, in *AAR,* 11.
8. "Portland's Possibilities Are Great," *BTJ* 2 (March 1890): 327. See also Robert H. Babcock, "Economic Development in Portland and St. John, N.B., during the Age of Steam and Iron, 1850–1914," *American Review of Canadian Studies* 9 (Spring 1979): 30–37.
9. Edward E. Chase, *Maine Railroads: A History of the Development of the Maine Railroad System* (Portland: A. J. Huston, 1926), 59–81; Babcock, "Economic Development in Portland and St. John," 30–37; John Neal, *Portland Illustrated* (Portland: W. S. Jones, 1874), 90; Louis Clinton Hatch, ed., *Maine: A History: A Facsimile of the 1919 Edition* (Somersworth: New Hampshire Publishing, 1974), 708.
10. See *Eastern Argus,* April 1, 1868.
11. Ibid., April 3, 1868,
12. Hatch, *Maine,* 712; Babcock, "Economic Development in Portland and St. John"; Chase, *Maine Railroads,* 88. On P&O receivership, see *Portland Sunday Times,* February 20, 1881; see also Address of Mayor Charles J. Chapman, *AAR,* 1886–1887, 20.
13. Address of Mayor Charles J. Chapman, *AAR,* 1885–1886, 22–23.
14. Chase, *Maine Railroads,* 89–94.
15. See William A. Goodwin, City Engineer of City of Portland, *Portland Revaluation Map, 1882,* pl. 19; and Hull, *Hand-Book of Portland, Old Orchard, Cape Elizabeth and Casco Bay,* 162.
16. *BTJ* 2 (August 1889): 101.
17. *BTJ* 1 (May 1888): 17.
18. Address of Mayor Charles J. Chapman, *AAR,* 1887–1888, 12–13; Hull, *Hand-Book of Portland, Old Orchard, Cape Elizabeth, and Casco Bay,* 27; Bill Roberts, *Remember the Portland, Maine, Trolleys* (Portland: Robertson Books, 1982).
19. Babcock, "Economic Development in Portland and St. John," 30–37.
20. Gould Diaries, vol. 13, September 3, 1895.
21. For fleet data, see *Portland Directory,* 1871, 267–72; *Portland Directory,* 1881, 327–31; *Portland Directory,* 1881, 899–901. The same information can be found in *Auditors Annual Reports.*
22. "The New Year: How Stands Portland?" *BTJ* 4 (January 1892): 262; Robert H. Babcock, "The Rise and Fall of Portland's Waterfront," *Maine Historical Society Quarterly* 22, no. 2 (Fall 1982): 63–99. On wharves, see Walker Lithograph and Publishing Company, *Map of City of Portland and Vicinity* (Boston: Walker Lithograph and Publishing Company, 1919) (hereafter Walker *Map of Portland, 1910*), found in PRSC.
23. Babcock, "Rise and Fall of Portland's Waterfront," 72–74.
24. James P. Baxter, "Portland: Maine's Commercial Center," *BTJ* 16 (January 1904): 284–85; Michael Coleman Connolly, "The Irish Longshoremen of Portland, Maine, 1880–1923" (Ph.D. diss., Boston College, 1988), 53 100–103; *Portland Directory,* 1890.
25. See Connolly, "Irish Longshoremen of Portland," 77–78; "City Hall Matters," *Eastern Argus,* February 8, 1896; Babcock, "Rise and Fall of Portland Waterfront," 71, 82; *Portland Directory,* 1900, 926.
26. *BTJ* 5 (1892), 330; Gould Diaries, vol. 13, December 21, 1891.

27. For data on Portland industrialism, 1880–1890, see U.S. Bureau of the Census, *Report of Manufactures of the United States, 1880, General Statistics* (Washington, D.C.: GPO, 1883); U.S. Bureau of the Census, *Report of Manufacturing Industries in the United States at the 11th Census, 1890, Part II, Statistics* (Washington, D.C.: GPO, 1895); Bureau of Industries, Labor Statistics for the State of Maine, *Twenty-fourth Annual Report of the Bureau, 1910* (Augusta: Kennebec Journal, 1910), 79–89.
28. On the Portland Company, see David H. Fletcher, *Images of the Portland Company, 1846–1982* (Charleston, S.C.: Arcadia, 2002), found in Portland Company Records, MHSL; see advertisements for Milliken Company and Thomas Laughlin in *BTJ* 5 (July 1892): 89; on Portland Company expansion, see *Eastern Argus*, May 1890; on new pulp business, see "Maine Boom," *BTJ* 2 (May 1890): 6.
29. "Manufactures for Portland," *BTJ* 4 (October 1891): 167.
30. "The New Year: How Stands Portland," *BTJ* 4 (January 1892): 262.
31. See Gould Diaries, vol. 13, January 1, 1890. Gould began each year of his diary with a biographical entry. He noted on January 1, 1890, that he did not have a hired girl, that Annie, his daughter, expected to return to Mt. Holyoke for the spring term, that he was a member of the board of trustees of the Seamen's Bethel [Congregational] Church at 183 Fore Street, (also called Bethel Church for Seamen), and that he was "unable by reason of nervous prostration and writers' cramp or rheumatism, in right arm, to do the 101 things that in former years have made life busy and full."
32. *Tenth Census: Population;* U.S. Bureau of the Census, *Report of Population of the United States at 11th Census, 1890: Part 1* (Washington, D.C.: GPO, 1895); Babcock, "Economic Development in Portland and St. Johns." On servant staff, see James Phinney Baxter Journals, Baxter Memorial Library, Gorham, Maine (hereafter cited as Baxter Journals).
33. John Bodnar, *The Transplanted: A History of Immigrants in Urban America* (Bloomington: Indiana University Press, 1985).
34. Michael C. Connolly, "Nationalism among Early Twentieth-Century Irish Longshoremen in Portland, Maine," in Michael C. Connolly, ed., *They Change Their Sky: The Irish in Maine* (Orono: University of Maine Press, 2004), 280–82; Connolly, "Irish Longshoremen of Portland," 96; on Armenians, see Anthony P. Mezoian, *The Armenian People of Portland* (Durham: University of New Hampshire Department of Media Services, 1985). Portland had a small Jewish population in 1866 which grew slowly in the 1870s. In 1874, when the Jewish community was described as small yet vigorous, the city emerged as the seat of Maine's B'nai B'rith Lodge, drawing members from Bangor, Lewiston, and Waterville. See Benjamin Band, *Portland Jewry: Its Growth and Development* (Portland: Jewish Historical Society, 1955), 8–10; see also "Ethnic Groups Prosper," in Albert F. Barnes, ed., *Greater Portland 350: A Commemorative Edition* (Portland: Gannett Books, 1984), 112.
35. Connolly, "Nationalism," 280. On organizations, see also *Portland Directory*, 1881, 373, for description of Irish American Relief Association.
36. Connolly, "Nationalism," 279; also Connolly, "Irish Longshoremen of Portland," 37.
37. Bureau of Industrial and Labor Statistics for State of Maine, *Fourteenth Annual Report, 1900* (Augusta: Kennebec Journal Press, 1900); Bureau of Industrial and Labor Statistics for State of Maine, *Twenty-Fourth Annual Report, 1910* (Augusta: Kennebec Journal, 1910), 79–89.

38. Bureau of Industrial and Labor Statistics, *Twenty-Fourth Annual Report, 1910,* 79–89.
39. Gould Diaries, vol. 13, May 24, 1895; Bureau of Industrial and Labor Statistics for the State of Maine, *Fourteenth Annual Report,* 1900.
40. H. H. Price and Gerald E. Talbot, eds., *Maine's Visible Black History: The First Chronicle of its People* (Gardiner, Maine: Tilbury Press, 2006), 22. On Italians, see Bureau of the Census, *Report of Population . . . 11th Census, 1890;* and Charles A. Scontras, *Organized Labor and Labor Politics in Maine: Twentieth-Century Origins, 1880–1890* (Orono: University of Maine Press, 1966), 64.
41. Gould Diaries, vol. 10, May 19, 1872. See Matthew Jude Barker, "Irish Organizations and Irish Community," in Connolly, *They Change Their Sky,* 171–72; also Connolly, "Irish Longshoremen of Portland," 147.
42. U.S. Bureau of the Census, *U.S. Census Tract Data, Portland, 1880* (Washington, D.C.: GPO, 1880); Goodwin, *Portland Revalutation Map,* 1882; *Portland Directory,* 1880–1890; Barker, "Irish Organizations and Irish Community," 172.
43. Hull, *Handbook of Portland, Old Orchard, Cape Elizabeth, and Casco Bay,* 164, describes Munjoy Hill as "covered with houses, the comfortable homes of our business and industrial classes"; see also Goodwin, Portland Revaluation Map, 1882, sheet 20; and *Portland Directory,* 1883 and 1884.
44. On Portland Jews, see Band, *Portland Jewry;* "Ethnic Groups Prosper in Area," in Barnes, *Greater Portland 350,* 112–13; Hull, *Hand-Book of Portland, Old Orchard, Cape Elizabeth, and Casco Bay,* 161; Bureau of the Census, *Report of Population of U.S. at 11th Census, 1890 Part 1 (1895);* Babcock," Economic Development in Portland, Maine and Saint John," 30–37.
45. Barnes, *Greater Portland 350,* 113; Scontras, *Organized Labor in Maine,* 64.
46. John F. Bauman, "A Saga of Renewal in a Maine City: Exploring the Fate of Portland's Bayside District," *Journal of Planning History* 56, no. 4 (November 2006): 333–36; *Sanborn 1886 Insurance Map of Portland* (New York: Sanborn Map and Publishing Company 1886); and *Sanborn 1896 Insurance Map of Portland* (New York: Sanborn Map and Publishing Company, 1896), both found in Osher Map Library, University of Southern Maine, Portland.
47. Mezoian, *Armenian People of Portland,* 1–10.
48. See John F. Bauman, "Before the Bungalow: The Three-Decker as Affordable Housing in Portland, Maine," Presidential Address delivered at Annual Meeting of Society for City and Regional Planning History, St. Louis, Mo., 2003; see Oscar Handlin, *Boston's Immigrants: 1790–1880* (Boston: Atheneum, 1969), 88–123; on Chicago, see Thomas Philpott, *The Slum and the Ghetto: Neighborhood Deterioration and Middle-Class Reform, Chicago 1880–1930* (Chicago: University of Chicago Press, 1978).
49. See Catherine Cocks, *Doing the Town: The Rise of Urban Tourism in the United States, 1850–1915* (Berkeley: University of California Press, 2001), 145–50. Note that in 1892 the Board of Trade called summer travel in Maine and Portland a "highly lucrative industry . . . amply appreciated by our thrifty citizens who profit from it extensively." See "Outings Season of 1892," *BTJ* 5 (September 1892): 134.
50. Jackson Lears, *No Place of Grace: Antimodernism and the Transformation of American Culture, 1880–1920* (New York: Pantheon, 1981); Peter Schmidt, *Back to Nature: The Arcadian Myth in Urban America* (New York: Oxford University Press, 1969).
51. *BTJ* 3 (May 1890); "Maine Central Railroad," *BTJ* 5 (1892).
52. Neal, *Portland Illustrated,* 6.

53. "The City of Portland," *BTJ* (August 1888): 45.
54. "As Others See Us," *BTJ* 2 (October 1889): 185.
55. On Back Cove and healthfulness, see Address of Mayor William Senter, *AAR,* 1880–1881, 16; Report of City Engineer, *AAR,* 1885–1886, 120; also Address of Mayor Charles J. Chapman, *AAR,* 1886–1887, 23.
56. "Portland, Maine," *BTJ* 3 (August 1890): 109.
57. "Stop at Portland, the Most Beautiful Pleasure Resort on the Coast," *BTJ* 3 (May 1890): 13.
58. "Portland for Health," *BTJ* 6 (August 1893): 107.
59. "Maine Seashore," *BTJ* 4 (May 1891): 8.
60. Earle G. Shettleworth Jr., "Creating and Preserving Portland's Urban Landscape, 1885–1925," in Joseph A. Conforti, ed., *Creating Portland: History and Place in Northern New England* (Durham: University of New Hampshire Press, 2005), 247–95.
61. Richard R. Wescott, "Economic, Social, and Government Aspects of Development of Maine's Vacation Industry" (master's thesis, University of Maine, Orono, 1961), 33–34, 50–55. On Cushing Island, see also "Portland's Changing Resorts," *BTJ* 2 (1889): 50.
62. See "Beautiful Portland," *BTJ* 5 (August 1892): 102.
63. "More Hotels Wanted Here," *BTJ* 10 (1897): 137; Cocks, *Doing the Town.* See also Daniel J. Boorstin, *The Americans: The National Experience* (New York: Vintage Books, 1965), 135–47.
64. On Portland and Portland region hotels, see ads in *BTJ* 9 (May 1896): 21; *BTJ* 15 (March 1902): 348; *BTJ* 17 (June 1904): 96. On Glen House, see *BTJ* 3 (May 1890): 40.
65. Address of Mayor Charles J. Chapman, *AAR,* 1885–1886, 25.
66. *AAR,* 1884–1885, Ordinances, 151. On the City Beautiful movement and the dawn of city planning, see William H. Wilson, *The City Beautiful Movement* (Baltimore: Johns Hopkins University Press, 1989); Jon A. Peterson, *The Birth of City Planning in the United States, 1840–1917* (Baltimore: Johns Hopkins University Press, 2003); and John F. Bauman and Edward K. Muller, *Before Renaissance: Urban Planning in Pittsburgh, 1889–1943* (Pittsburgh: University of Pittsburgh Press, 2006).
67. "Dr. A. W. Smith, Secretary of Portland Park Commission," *BTJ* 9 (May 1896): 7.
68. Neal, *Portland Illustrated,* 187; Address of Mayor Charles J. Chapman, *AAR,* 1886–1887, 15–16; Annual Report of the Commission of Parks, Cemeteries, and Public Grounds, *AAR,* 1887–1888; Annual Report of the Commission of Parks, Cemeteries, and Public Grounds, *AAR,* 1889–1895.
69. Gould Diaries, vol. 12, January 19, 1886, and April 2–April 8, 1886; Address of Mayor John Deering, *AAR,* 1884–1885, 14.
70. Gould Diaries, vol. 12, January 19, 1886; "A Proposed Use of Old City Hall," *Eastern Argus,* June 11, 1910; Shettleworth, "Creating and Preserving Portland's Urban Landscape."
71. "Historic Tablets," *BTJ* 9 (May 1896): 9.
72. "Fair Portland," *Portland Telegram* (c. 1895), found in Baxter Scrapbooks, MHSL (hereafter cited as Baxter Scrapbooks), which contain news clippings registering almost every mention of Baxter in the city press. The clipping files also contain a copy of almost everything he wrote that was published in the city newspapers, especially the Republican *Portland Press.* This article is very likely his. Most of the clippings, but not all, reference Baxter's political life. Unfortunately, many do not contain dates, and in too many cases the newspaper names are missing and must be deciphered from the context.

73. Shettleworth, "Creating and Preserving Portland's Urban Landscape"; see also *Richards Standard Atlas of City of Portland* (Springfield, Mass.: Richards Map Company, 1914), found in PRSC (hereafter cited as Richards Map, 1914).
74. "Arch of Welcome," *BTJ* 9 (May 1896): 8.
75. "Riverton-on-the-Presumpscot," *BTJ* 9 (May 1896): 15.

CHAPTER FOUR
City Growth, City Problems, City Beautiful, 1893–1915

1. On New England Yankees and the reform impulse, see Arthur Mann, *Yankee Reformers in the Urban Age: Social Reform in Boston, 1880–1900* (Cambridge: Belknap Press of Harvard University Press, 1954); on late nineteenth- and early twentieth-century reform and the rise of Progressivism, see Robert H. Wiebe, *The Search for Order, 1877–1920* (1967; repr., Westport, Conn.: Greenwood Press, 1980); on reformers and efficiency in government, see Martin J. Schiesl, *The Politics of Efficiency: Municipal Administration and Reform in America, 1800–1920* (Berkeley: University of California, 1977); on Social Gospel, see Henry F. May, *Protestant Churches and Industrial America* (New York: Octagon Books, 1963). Note, too, the classic short treatment of the subject, Samuel P. Hays, *The Response to Industrialism, 1885–1914*, 2nd ed. (1957; Chicago: University of Chicago Press, 1995).
2. On Fort Hill, see Oscar Handlin, *Boston's Immigrants, 1790–1880: A Study in Acculturation*, rev. and enl. ed., 50th anniversary ed. (Cambridge: Belknap Press of Harvard University Press, 1991), 88–124. On Philadelphia, see John F. Bauman, "Disinfecting the Industrial City: The Philadelphia Housing Commission and Scientific Efficiency, 1909–1916," in Michael Ebner and Eugene Tobin, eds., *The Age of Urban Reform: New Perspectives on the Progressive Era* (Port Washington, N.Y.: Kennikat Press, 1977), 125–28; also John Sutherland, "Housing the Poor in the City of Homes," in Allen Davis and Mark Haller, eds., *The Peoples of Philadelphia: A History of Ethnic Groups and Lower-Class Life, 1790–1940* (Philadelphia: Temple University, 1973), 175–96.
3. On Bayside, see John F. Bauman, "The Saga of Renewal in a Maine City: Exploring the Fate of Portland's Bayside District," *Journal of Planning History* 5, no. 4 (November 2006): 329–55; *Sanborn Insurance Map of Portland, Maine, 1928, Volume 1* (New York: Sanborn Map and Publishing, 1928), Osher Map Library, University of Southern Maine, Portland. On Portland's ethnic groups, see U.S. Bureau of the Census, *Fourteenth Census of the United States: Census Tract Data 1910* (Washington, D.C.: GPO, 1910); Richards Map, 1914; City of Portland, 1924 Reassessment of the City of Portland, Card Data, in City of Portland Planning Department, Portland.
4. Address of Mayor George Walker, *AAR*, 1878–1879.
5. Annual Report of the Board of Health: *AAR*, 1887–1888, 119; *AAR*, 1892–1893, 244; and *AAR*, 1896–1897, 274.
6. "Mac," "District Nursing: What It Means," *BTJ* 18 (September 1905): 274–75.
7. On the "unsuitability" of the workhouse, see "The City Poor," *Eastern Argus*, November 30, 1894. On Poor Department and poor farm, see Address of Mayor Moses M. Butler,

AAR, 1877–1878, 26–28; Report of Overseers of the Poor: *AAR,* 1880–1881, 147; *AAR,* 1885–1886, 138–39; and *AAR,* 1895–1896, 162–63. On the subject of tramps, see Report of Overseers of the Poor, *AAR,* 1879–1880, 247, which suggested, "We may take courage that the genus tramp will soon be known only to history."

8. Jacob Riis, *How the Other Half Lives: Studies among the Tenements of New York* (New York: Bedford Books of St. Martin's Press, 1996); "Was It Murder?" *Eastern Argus,* June 12, 1900.
9. For crime statistics see Report of the City Marshal, *AAR,* 1876–1877.
10. Michael Coleman Connolly, "The Irish Longshoremen of Portland, Maine, 1880–1890" (Ph.D. diss., Boston College, 1988), 59–60. On race and ethnicity and urban crime, see Roger Lane, *Roots of Violence in Black Philadelphia* (Cambridge: Harvard University Press, 1986); also Eric H. Monkkonen, *Murder in New York City* (Berkeley: University of California Press, 2001); Report of the City Marshall, *AAR,* 1876–1897.
11. On the events of 1877 nationally, see Nell Irvin Painter, *Standing at Armageddon: The United States, 1877–1919* (New York: Norton, 1987). See also "Epidemic of Violence," *Eastern Argus,* July 25, 1877; and on 1894, see "Our Visiting Tourists," *BTJ* 7 (August 1894): 104.
12. "Labor Trouble Here," *BTJ* 10 (October 1897): 166.
13. Charles A. Scontras, *Organized Labor and Labor Politics in Maine: Twentieth-Century Origins, 1880–1890* (Orono: University of Maine Press, 1966), 158–59; Bureau of Industrial Labor Statistics for State of Maine, *Fourth Annual Report of the Bureau, 1890* (Augusta: Burleigh-Flynt Printers, 1891), 158–59; "Labor Agitation," *Eastern Argus,* May 5, 1890; "Central Labor Union," *Eastern Argus,* May 17, 1890; "Strike Failed," *Eastern Argus,* June 5, 1900.
14. If Portland business in the 1880s and 1890s failed to thrive, it did not impair the city's building industry. Mayor Charles Chapman in 1888 reported, "While we regret the continued suspension of some manufacturing businesses occasioned by the centralization of business in great Trusts, . . . yet we can congratulate ourselves that trade, in general has been remunerative, [and] . . . the era of building inaugurated several years since, has continued in marked degrees. . . . The more noticeable of these, in our business area, are the commodious Whitney Block, the outgrowth of the city's action relative to City Hall; the Jose Block commanding special attention from its unique appearance; the Oxford building unexcelled for its office convenience." See Address of Mayor Charles Chapman, *AAR,* 1888–1889.
15. On Portland's being "situated as to have hardly felt the agitation which has prevailed [elsewhere]," see Address of Mayor James Phinney Baxter, *AAR,* 1894–1895, 1.
16. See Baxter Journals, May 1, 1898; Robert H. Babcock, "The Rise and Fall of Portland's Waterfront, 1850–1920," *Maine Historical Society Quarterly* 22, no. 2 (Fall 1982): 76–77.
17. Scontras, *Organized Labor,* 13–14.
18. Charles A. Scontras, *The Socialist Alternative: Utopian Experiments and the Socialist Party in Maine, 1895–1914* (Orono: Bureau of Labor Education, 1985), 91–102; Robert H. Babcock, Yves Frenette, Charles A. Scontras, and Eileen Egan, "Work and Workers in the Industrial Age, 1865–1930," in Richard W. Judd, Edwin A. Churchill, and Joel W. Eastman, eds., *Maine: The Pine Tree State from Prehistory to the Present* (Orono: University of Maine Press, 1995), 474–75; Connolly, "Irish Longshoremen," 105–6.

19. "Our Labor Problems," *Eastern Argus,* May 12, 1890, 3. On Yankee anxieties, see Mann, *Yankee Reformers.*
20. Gould Diaries, vol. 13, March 7, 1893, 418.
21. See Gould Diaries, passim; "The Poor People," *Eastern Argus,* June 9, 1900.
22. Wiebe, *Search for Order,* 111–63; "Portland YMCA Is Fifteen Years Old," *BTJ* 16 (December 1903): 232.
23. Roy Lubove, *The Professional Altruist: The Emergence of Social Work as a Career, 1880–1930* (Cambridge: Harvard University Press, 1965); Richard Hofstadter, *The Age of Reform: From Bryan to F.D.R.* (New York: Knopf, 1955).
24. For a history of Fraternity House, see *Second Annual Reception, Drill and Ball of the Fraternity Primary Cadets at City Hall,* April 18, 1887 (Portland: Chris L. Wellander, 1887), found in Portland Fraternity Club Records, 1870–1923, Coll. 345, MHSL (hereafter cited as PFCR). See also "Its Working Capacity Outgrown Portland Fraternity House Property May Be Sold," *Portland Sunday Telegram,* December 2, 1917; "Over a Thousand People Regularly Attend Fraternity House Activities," *Sunday Press Herald,* March 24, 1935; "An Institution That Stands for Educational, Social and Ethnical Culture in Portland," *Portland Sunday Times,* December 10, 1905.
25. "Home for Friendless Boys," *BTJ* 18 (June 1905): 66–67; William David Barry, *The History of Sweetser Children's Home: A Century and a Half of Service to Maine's Children* (Portland: Anthoensen Press, 1988), 54. For list of charitable societies, see *Portland Directory,* 1888, and Portland Associated Charities, *A Manual of the Benevolent Organizations, Charitable Societies, Relief Associations, and Public Charities of the City of Portland* (Portland: Associated Charities, 1904), MHSL.
26. Baxter Journals, vol. 4, January 3, 1884.
27. On urban Protestant churches, see May, *Protestant Churches and Industrial America.* Biographical material on Perkins can be found in John Carroll Perkins, Records of First Parish Church of Portland, Coll. 1917, MHSL; also "Edward Everett Halle: Mr. Perkins Eloquent Tribute to Him," news clipping, Records of First Parish Church of Portland, Coll. 1917, MHSL (hereafter cited as FPCR). On High Street Church, see "Agency History," and "Men of High Street Church Parish," both in box 1, Papers of High Street Congregational Church, Coll. 1890, MHSL; on State Street, see State Street Congregational Church, *The Golden Candlesticks: 150 Years of Faith and Service, 1852–2002* (Portland: State Street Congregational Church, 2002), Pamphlet 3277, MHSL.
28. See "What Christian Citizenship Is," news clipping, December 17, 1904, FPCR; also, "The Liberal Ministers," January 2, 1905, news clipping, FPCR.
29. Allen F. Davis, *Spearheads for Reform: The Social Settlements and the Progressive Movement, 1890–1914* (New York: Oxford University Press, 1967); Lubove, *Professional Altruist; Constitution, By-Laws and Report of the Board of Directors of the Portland Fraternity,* 1890 (Portland: Stephen Berry Printers, 1891), found in Coll. 345, box 3, of Portland Fraternity Records (hereafter PFR), found in MHSL; see Portland Fraternity Annual Reports (hereafter PFAR), 1893–1894, 1896–1897, and 1901–1902, all in PFR. See also "Meeting of Executive Committee," January 9, 1906, PFR; "Report of Resident Head Worker," 1912–1913, PFR; "An Institution That Stands for Educational, Social and Ethical Culture in Portland," *Portland Sunday Times,* December 10, 1905.
30. On Bliss, see Description of Coll. 345 in PFR; on Emily, see Baxter Journals, vol. 3, April 6, 1899, April 8, 1899, December 15, 1899; also Neil Rolde, *The Baxters of Maine: Downeast Visionary* (Portland: Tilbury House, 1997).

31. See Report of Overseers of the Poor, *AAR,* 1908; Portland Associated Charities, *Manual of the Benevolent Organizations.*
32. See Report of Resident Head Worker, Portland Fraternity, May 20, 1907, and "Meeting of Executive Committee [of Portland Fraternity]," January 9, 1906, both in PFR; On Civic Club and civic improvement, see Scontras, *Organized Labor,* 65; also "Clean Towns: They Attract Home-seekers and Grow Very Rapidly," *BTJ* 16 (July 1903): 78.
33. Typed letter dated "Portland, Maine, May 20, 1907," PFR.
34. On the Center Street site of Fraternity House, see Richards Map, 1914; and 1924 Assessment of Portland, Maine, Portland Assessor's Office, Portland City Hall, Portland.
35. Elsie Nutt, "Report of Resident Head Worker, 1912–1913," PFR.
36. See Baxter Journals, vol. 3, March 27, 1890; Rolde, *Baxters of Maine.* On why Baxter was rejected for military service in the Civil War, see James P. Baxter, "Biographical Sketch," Journal No. 2 (March 12, 1885–November 6, 1886), dictated (1986) by Franklin Talbot, p. 23, found in MHSL.
37. See James Phinney Baxter, "The Story of Portland, *New England Magazine,* November 1895, found in Baxter Papers.
38. James Phinney Baxter, *History of a Ring: By One of the Governor's Wards* (Portland: J. P. Baxter, 1877), 1–13, in Baxter Journals, vol. 3, March 12, 1889, Baxter Papers.
39. *Evening Express,* January 25, 1894, Baxter Scrapbooks.
40. Benjamin Bunker, *Bunker's Text Book of Political Deviltry: A Record of Maine's Small Bore Politicians and Political Bosses* (Waterville, Maine: Kennebeck Democrat Office, 1889), 63–64. On liquor issue, see also *Eastern Argus,* June 9, 1900.
41. Bunker, *Bunker's Text Book,* 52.
42. Gould Diaries, November 8, 1876. See also John T. Hull, ed., *Handbook of Portland, Old Orchard, Cape Elizabeth, and Casco Bay* (Portland: Southworth Publishing, 1888), 17.
43. Baxter Journals, vol. 4, May 10, 1893.
44. Address of Mayor James Phinney Baxter, *AAR,* 1892–1893, 9–10; "How Portland Has Improved," *BTJ* 9 (December 1896): 230. See also Robert H. Wiebe, *Businessmen and Reform: A Study of the Progressive Movement* (Cambridge: Harvard University Press, 1962), 2–3.
45. Baxter Journals, vol. 4, March 4, 1893.
46. Ibid.; Gould Diaries, vol. 13, March 10, 1893; *Evening Express,* March 5–17, 1893; *Evening Argus,* March 5–17, 1893.
47. For the role of city engineers in promoting efficiency in nineteenth-century city government, see Jon C. Teaford, *The Unheralded Triumph: City Government in America, 1870–1900* (Baltimore: Johns Hopkins University Press, 1984); "A Proposed Commission for Streets and Sewers Department," *Evening Express,* February 7, 1893, and *Portland Press,* February 26, 1897, both in Baxter Scrapbooks. For the classic case against corrupt city government, see Lincoln Steffens, *The Shame of the Cities* (Mineola, N.Y.: Dover Publications, 2004); see also William L. Riordan, *Plunkitt of Tammany Hall: A Series of Very Plain Talks on Very Practical Politics* (New York: Signet Classics, 1995).
48. Baxter Journals, vol. 4, April 7, 1894; "Municipal Reform: What Mayor Baxter Had to Say about Commission on Street Work," *Portland Press,* December 31, 1895; Baxter Scrapbooks; "Portland Street Boulevard," *Board of Trade Journal* 9 (September 1896): 137. Democratic opposition stalled Baxter's plans to bring police and fire departments

under civil service jurisdiction. See Baxter Journals, vol. 4, April 7, 1894, and Address of Mayor James Phinney Baxter, *AAR,* 1892–1893, 14.

49. "Mr. Hays' Welcome Visit," *Portland Press,* July 17, 1893, Baxter Scrapbooks; "Portland Harbor Improvements, Past and Future," *Board of Trade Journal* 9 (January 1897): 269.
50. See Baxter Journals, vol. 5, November 8, 1901; Address of Mayor James Phinney Baxter, *AAR,* 1892–1893, 11–12.
51. See Address of Mayor James Phinney Baxter, *AAR,* 1895–1896, 11.
52. See news clipping on charter reform from *Eastern Argus,* December 23, 1896, Baxter Scrapbooks. The literature on nineteenth- and early twentieth-century urban reform politics is extensive, beginning with Steffens's classic *Shame of the Cities;* see also J. T. Salter's edited work *The American Politician* (1938; repr., Westport, Conn.: Greenwood Press, 1975); and Lloyd Wendt and Herman Kogan, *Bosses in Lusty Chicago: The Story of Bathhouse John and Hinky Dink* (Bloomington: Indiana University Press, 1971). For a more modern interpretation of urban politics, see Philip J. Ethington, *The Public City: The Political Construction of Urban Life in San Francisco, 1850–1900* (Berkeley: University of California Press, 1994). On Portland and Baxter's call for reform, see James Phinney Baxter, "Address to Fraternity Club on a New Charter for Portland," Baxter Journals, vol. 5 (November 26, 1896).
53. On the new charter, see James Phinney Baxter, "Address before the Women's Council," *Portland Press,* November 26, 1896, Baxter Scrapbooks; see also Address of Mayor James Phinney Baxter, *AAR,* 1895–1896, 30–33. For a draft of the charter, see "New City Charter," *Portland Press,* December 22, 1896, Baxter Scrapbooks.
54. On opinions, see "The City Charter: Some Views Expressed by Our City in Regard to It," *Portland Press,* December 22, 1896, Baxter Scrapbooks.
55. See Baxter Journals, vol. 5, December 28, 1896, January 12, 1897, and February 1, 1987.
56. Caitlyn Horose, "The B&M Baked Bean Factory in Portland, Maine: A Case for Historic Preservation" (seminar paper, Muskie School of Public Service, University of Southern Maine, Portland, 2007).
57. Deering official, in "Deering Annex," *Portland Press Herald,* December 1, 1897; see also "Greater Portland," special section of *Portland Evening Express,* July 3, 1896; "Deering's Status as City Short Lived," in Albert F. Barnes, ed., *Greater Portland 350: A Commemorative Edition* (Portland: Gannett Books, 1984), 124; "Annexation of Deering: The Movement Is Now Underway," *Portland Evening Express,* December 30, 1894, Baxter Scrapbooks; Baxter Journals, vol. 4, December 13, 1894, vol. 5, March 8, 1898; real estate flyer, "Home Seekers and Investors," Baxter Papers.
58. See "The Boulevard Project," *Portland Press,* February 4, 1897, Baxter Scrapbooks; see also Deborah Tracey Kichels, "James Phinney Baxter and the Portland Park System," in Theodore H. B. M. Holtwyk and Earle G. Shettleworth Jr., eds., *Bold Vision: The Development of the Parks of Portland, Maine* (Kennebunk: Greater Portland Landmarks, 1999), 113.
59. See newpaper clipping on parks, *Portland Press,* c. March 1896, in Baxter Scrapbooks.
60. James Phinney Baxter, "Something about Public Parks," *BTJ* 16 (January 1904): 341.
61. Ibid., 342.
62. Ibid., 363.
63. See "Portland's Beautiful Parks," *BTJ* 6 (January 1894): 272.
64. On Baxter and the Portland Parks, see James Phinney Baxter, *The Story of Portland: Reprinted from the New England Magazine, November, 1895* (Portland: J. P. Baxter,

1895), 366, in Baxter Papers; Kichels, "Baxter and the Park System," 109–19; see also Report on Cemeteries and Public Grounds, *AAR,* 1894–1895, 290; Report of Park Commission, *AAR,* 1894–1895, 341–47. On Deering Oaks, see Herbert Adams, "Deering Oaks," in Holtwyk and Shettleworth, *Bold Vision,* 74–93.

65. Kichels, "Baxter and the Park System." See "Back Cove," *Eastern Argus,* May 24, 1890, and "The Back Bay Problem: Mr. Herring Speaks of Its General Features," *Portland Press,* October 9, 1894, Baxter Scrapbooks; Address of Mayor James Phinney Baxter, *AAR,* 1894–1895, 9–11.
66. Olmsted, Olmsted and Elliot, "City of Portland: Landscape Architects Report on the Improvement of Back Cove, 1895–1896," Olmsted Associates Papers, Library of Congress (hereafter cited as OAP); Eleanor G. Ames, "Back Cove and Baxter Boulevard," in Holtwyk and Shettleworth, *Bold Vision,* 94–106. On Frederick Law Olmsted and the Chicago World's Fair, see Jon A. Peterson, *The Birth of City Planning in the United States, 1840–1917* (Baltimore: Johns Hopkins University Press, 2003), 62–66.
67. "The Boulevard Plan," *Portland Advertiser,* n.d., 1897; "Mr. Edward C. Jordan's Letter to the *Portland Press,*" *Portland Press,* c. June 6, 1896; and on dead body of water, see "Injury to Harbor," *Portland Press,* June 6, 1896, all in Baxter Scrapbooks.
68. For the reason Baxter lost, see "The Mayoralty," *Portland Evening Express,* February 16, 1897; Address of Mayor James Phinney Baxter, *AAR,* 1896–1897, 419; Kichels, "Baxter and the Park System," 114–15.
69. On John C. Olmsted's return to Portland, see "J. C. Olmsted, Report on Portland, Maine: Deering Oaks," March 1, 1902, Job 1862, OAP; Kichels, "Baxter and the Park System," 114–15.
70. See George Fernald to Olmsted Brothers, November 15, 1905, Job 1860, OAP.
71. Baxter Journals, vol. 6, June 16, 1905.
72. John C. Olmsted to Baxter, May 28, 1905, Job 1860, OAP.
73. On the playground and recreation issue, see report on public baths *AAR,* 1908, and *AAR,* 1909; Report of Recreation Commission, *AAR,* 1916–1917; see also Joel Eastman, "Public Recreation and Sports," and Dana A. Souza, "Parks Administration and Management," in Holtwyk and Shettleworth, *Bold Vision,* 120–26, 135–52.
74. Ames, "Back Cove," 99. On Baxter's dedication to parks, see also "Civic Betterment," *BTJ* 18 (January 1906): 498–501.
75. Richard R. Wescott, "Economic, Social, and Governmental Aspects of Maine's Vacation Industry, 1850–1920" (master's thesis, University of Maine, Orono, 1961).
76. Address of Mayor Charles Chapman, *AAR,* 1882–1883, 25.
77. On Boothby Square, see Address of Mayor Frederick Boothby, *AAR,* 1901, 13; on Boothby, see "Object Lesson in Civic Improvement," *BTJ* 20 (October 1907): 228. See also "Portland," *BTJ* 15 (April 1902): 373.
78. Address of Mayor Frederick Boothby, *AAR,* 1903; "Home Week Celebration," *BTJ* 13 (August 1900). On Home Week and its link to tourism, see Dona Brown, *Inventing New England: Regional Tourism in the Nineteenth Century* (Washington, D.C.: Smithsonian Institution Press, 1997).
79. "Portland: Maine's Commercial Center: An Important Sea Port and an Ideal Summer Resort," *BTJ* 16 (January 1904): 283–86.
80. "Portland as a Seaport," *BTJ* 27 (1914–1915): 103–7.
81. See "Portland: Maine's Commercial Center"; Edward A. Noyes, "Portland's Progress and Prosperity," *BTJ* 19 (January 1907): 451–59.

82. "Gateway to the Summer Playground of the East," *Chamber of Commerce Journal of Maine* 27 (April 1915): 448. The *Board of Trade Journal* (*BTJ*) in 1915 changed its name to *Chamber of Commerce Journal of Maine* (hereafter cited as *CCJ*) in recognition that the Board of Trade had become the Chamber of Commerce of the state. The *Board of Trade Journal* published into 1917 and then ceased after the war. The publication's changed title indicated that Portland now clearly viewed itself as the financial and business capital of Maine.
83. "Portland, Maine," *BTJ* 20 (June 1907): 57–65.
84. On local sites and hotels, see "Portland, Maine," *BTJ* 11 (August 1898): 103–7; "Handsome and Cleanest," *BTJ* 12 (August 1899): 105; Frederic Boothby, "Portland as a Summer Resort," *BTJ* 16 (January 1904): 290–91; "Portland, Maine," *BTJ* 13 (August 1900): 107; "Portland, Maine," *BTJ* 20 (June 1907): 63–65.
85. On "gendered downtown," see Alison Isenberg, *Downtown America: A History of the Place and the People Who Made It* (Chicago: University of Chicago Press, 2004), 13–41; "Gateway to the Summer Playground of the East," *CCJ* 4 (April 27, 1915): 447. On Woolworths, see *BTJ* 21 (1908–1909): 413; see also Richards Map, 1914.
86. Richards Map, 1914. On the Fidelity Building, see *BTJ* 22 (February 1910): 539, and "Gateway to the Summer Playground of Maine," *BTJ* 27 (April 1915): 447–56.
87. "A Maine Automobile Company," *BTJ* 19 (February 1907): 576; see also numerous ads for automobiles in the *Portland Press*, the *Eastern Argus*, the *Portland Sunday Telegram*, and the *Portland Evening Express*. A Pierce Arrow sold in 1907 for $4,000, too expensive for all but a Baxter.
88. On the automobile and its impact on Portland, see "Good Roads," *BTJ* 22 (January 1910): 428. By 1915 the roads had improved: see "Portland: the Metropolis of Maine," *CCJ* 28 (July 1915): 95–105; see also ads in *BTJ* 22 (January 1907). On the culture of the automobile, see James J. Flink, *The Car Culture* (Cambridge: MIT Press, 1975), and Clay McShane, *Down the Asphalt Path: The Automobile and the American City* (New York: Columbia University Press, 1994).
89. "Portland: The Metropolis of Maine."

CHAPTER FIVE
The Sunrise Gateway in Depression and War

1. "Portland Maine, America's Sunrise Gateway," *CCJ* 29 (May 1916): 59–63.
2. "Portland: Maine's Commercial Center: An Important Sea Port and an Ideal Summer Resort," *BTJ* 16 (January 1904): 283; "Portland as a Seaport," *BTJ* 27 (July 1914): 103–7.
3. See City of Portland, *Sixty-Sixth Annual Report, Fiscal Year 1924* (Portland: Marks Printing House, 1925), 219. In 1923 the title of the City of Portland's annual report changed from the *Auditors Annual Report* (cited as *AAR*) to the *Portland Annual Report* (cited as *PAR*).
4. See Robert Fishman, "The Metropolitan Tradition in American Planning," in Robert Fishman, ed., *The American Planning Tradition: Culture and Policy* (Washington, D.C.: Woodrow Wilson Center Press, 2000), 67–73. On the coming of World War I, see John Milton Cooper Jr., *Pivotal Decades: The United States, 1900–1920* (New York: Norton, 1990).

5. "Maine's Part in World War I," *Portland Sun Telegraph and Sunday Press Herald,* January 14 and 31, 1934; "Portland Supports War to End Wars," in Albert F. Barnes, ed., *Greater Portland Celebration 350: A Commemorative Edition* (Portland: Gannett Books, 1984), 135–36; "War or Cowardly Submission," *Portland Evening Express,* April 4, 1917.
6. "No Limit to Ships Maine Builders May Construct," *Evening Express,* April 17, 1917.
7. "Portland, Maine: The Nearest American Port to Europe," *CCJ* 29 (March 1917): 295; "Board of Engineers for Rivers and Harbors, War Department, in cooperation with the Bureau of Operations, U.S. Shipping Board," in *The Port of Portland, Maine* (Washington, D.C.: GPO, 1928), 1, 2; "Urge Ingraham to Aid in Securing Funds to Dredge Portland Harbor," *Portland Evening Express,* April 4, 1917.
8. "German Defenses Crumble," *Evening Express,* October 2, 1918; on influenza, see City Physician's Report, *AAR,* 1918; see also "Portland Doctors Report 150 New Influenza Cases," *Portland Evening Express,* October 1, 1918; "Another 150 Cases," *Portland Evening Express,* October 3, 1918; "Report Death Rate of Influenza Here Is Remarkably Low," *Portland Evening Express,* October 5, 1918.
9. On these trends elsewhere in America, see Jackson Lears, *Fables of Abundance: A Cultural History of Advertising in America* (New York: Basic Books, 1994); Lizabeth Cohen, *Making a New Deal: Industrial Workers in Chicago, 1919–1939,* 2nd ed. (New York: Cambridge University Press, 2008).
10. See Howard M. Solomon, "Combating the Social Evil: Masculinity and Moral Reform in Portland 1912–1914," *Maine History* 43, no. 3 (January 2008): 139–56.
11. Anthon P. Mezoian, *The Armenian People of Portland, Maine* (Durham, N.H.: Department of Media Services, 1985); U.S. Bureau of the Census, *Thirteenth Census of the United States, Volume 4: Population* (Washington, D.C.: GPO, 1910), 818; U.S. Bureau of the Census, *Fourteenth Census of the U.S., Volume III: Population* (Washington, D.C.: GPO, 1920); U.S. Bureau of the Census, *Fifteenth Census of the United States, Volume III, Part I: Population* (Washington, D.C.: GPO, 1930). See also John F. Bauman, "A Saga of Renewal in a Maine City: Exploring the Fate of Portland's Bayside," *Journal of Planning History* 5, no. 4 (November 2006): 329–55.
12. Bauman, "Saga of Renewal," 333–36.
13. See Commissioner of Police Report, *AAR,* 1918, 337–39; Commissioner of Police Report, *PAR,* 1923, 118; see also Report of Board of Health, *AAR,* 1920.
14. Report of Board of Health, *AAR,* 1920, 455.
15. On Fore Street playground, see *AAR,* 1918, 412; on Fraternity House, see "Parties Held at Fraternity House," *Portland Press Herald,* November 1, 1924.
16. On 1919, see Robert K. Murray, *Red Scare: A Study in National Hysteria, 1919–1920* (New York: McGraw-Hill, 1955); on prohibition, see Lynn Dumenil, *The Modern Temper: American Culture and Society in the 1920s* (New York: Hill and Wang, 1995), 202–3, 232; on the cultural anxieties of the postwar period and 1920s, see John Higham, *Strangers in the Land: Patterns of American Nativism, 1860–1925* (New York: Atheneum, 1972); and William E. Leuchtenburg, *The Perils of Prosperity, 1914–1932,* 2nd ed. (Chicago: University of Chicago Press, 1993).
17. See Kenneth T. Jackson, *The Ku Klux Klan in the City, 1925–1930* (New York: Oxford University Press, 1967), 182–83; "Will Start Alteration to New Klan Headquarters at Rollins Estate," *Portland Evening Express,* May 25, 1924; "Klan Property on Forest Avenue Sold," *Portland Evening Express,* June 10, 1926; Joel W. Eastman,

"From Declining Seaport to Liberty City: Portland during Depression and War," in Joseph Conforti, ed., *Creating Portland: History and Place in Northern New England* (Hanover, N.H.: University Press of New England, 2005), 274–75.

18. Edward F. Dow and Orren C. Hormell, "City Manager Government in Portland, Maine," University of Maine Studies, second series, no. 52, *The Maine Bulletin* 43, no. 4 (November 1940): 23.
19. "Klan Plays Part in Local Change," in Barnes, *Greater Portland 350,* 146–47; Dow and Hormel, "City Manager Government," 1–9, 21–25.
20. Robert H. Babcock, "The Rise and Fall of Portland's Waterfront," *Maine Historical Society Quarterly* 22, no. 2 (Fall 1982): 90–91; "Portland Loses Role as Canadian Port," in Barnes, *Greater Portland 350,* 148.
21. Robert G. Albion, "The Two Ports of Portland," *Ships and the Sea* 4 (Fall 1954): 49; War Department, *Port of Portland,* 41. On tonnage losses, see Dow and Hormell, "City Manager Government," 9.
22. Harbor Master's Report, *PAR,* 1927; "Captain Joseph York Skipper of Many Voyages Eager to Put to Sea Again," *Portland Press Herald,* November 11, 1924. For impact on Irish longshoremen, see Michael C. Connolly, "The Irish Longshoremen of Portland, Maine, 1880–1923" (Ph.D. diss., Boston College, 1988), 221–23.
23. Babcock, "Rise and Fall of Portland's Waterfront," 91. On Burnham and Morrill, see Caitlyn Horose, "The B&M Baked Bean Factory in Portland, Maine: A Case for Historic Preservation" (seminar paper, Muskie School of Public Service, University of Southern Maine, Portland, 2007).
24. War Department, *Port of Portland,* 39–40; Babcock, "Rise and Fall of Portland's Waterfront," 91–92.
25. Works Progress Administration, Federal Writers' Project, *Portland City Guide: American Guide Series* (Portland: Forest City Printing, 1940); War Department, *Port of Portland,* 69, 83; Richard H. Condin, Joel W. Eastman, and Lawrence C. Allin, "Maine in Depression and War, 1929–1945," in Richard W. Judd, Edwin A. Churchill, and Joel W. Eastman, eds., *Maine: The Pine Tree State from Prehistory to the Present* (Orono: University of Maine Press, 1995), 510.
26. "State Pier Will Bring Business Says Steamship Head," *Portland Evening Express,* August 2, 1919.
27. War Department, *Port of Portland,* 40–41, 104–5. On the "best ocean terminal," see Chamber of Commerce, "Portland," in *Portland Directory,* 1925; see also Albion, "Two Ports of Portland," 22, 44–50; Eastman, "From Declining Seaport to Liberty City," 276; also on Maine State Pier, see Dow and Hormell, "City Manager Government," 10.
28. See reference to Cyrus Curtis's speech in *Portland Press Herald,* March 7, 1925.
29. "Say Portland Has Wonderful Future," *Portland Evening Express,* May 3, 1923.
30. "Foreign Steamers Due Here with Wood Pulp Cargo," *Portland Press Herald,* June 14, 1926; "Record Cargo of China Clay," *Portland Evening Express,* May 11, 1926, 5. See also War Department, *Port of Portland,* 89–91.
31. Report of City Manager Harry Brinkerhoff, *PAR,* 1927: 13; see also City of Portland, 1924 Reassessment of the City of Portland, Card Data, found in City of Portland Planning Department, Portland. On housing conditions in Bayside in 1920s, see Gould Diaries, vol. 17, May 4, 1923, and October 10, 1925. On lax enforcement of liquor laws, see "Volstead Act: 16 Cases as Mockery," *Portland Evening Express,* June

10, 1926; "Clean Up the Police Force," *Portland Press Herald,* November 5, 1924. On prohibition as an issue in 1920, see Richard H. Condon, Joel W. Eastman, and Lawrence C. Allin, "Depression and War, 1929–1945," in Judd et al., *Maine,* 512–13. On the war's impact on housing, see "Portland Home-Builders Association," *CCJ* 1 (June 1920).

32. On Portland and interest in the City Beautiful movement, see Robert H. Babcock and Yves Frenette, "Workers and Community Control," in Judd et al., *Maine,* 461; Jon A. Peterson, *Birth of City Planning in the United States, 1840–1917* (Baltimore: Johns Hopkins University Press, 2003), 98–103; William H. Wilson, *The City Beautiful Movement* (Baltimore: Johns Hopkins University Press, 1989). For the case of Pittsburgh, see John F. Bauman and Edward K. Muller, *Before Renaissance: City Planning in Pittsburgh, 1889–1943* (Pittsburgh: University of Pittsburgh Press, 2006), 51–101.

33. Greater Portland Landmarks, *Portland* (1986; repr., Portland: Greater Portland Landmarks, 1999); Richards Map, 1914; see also Walker Map, 1910, which shows not only the Emerald Necklace and the views from the two promenades, but also the build-up of tenements along Franklin Street. On Lincoln Park and the Civic Center, see Earl W. Shettleworth Jr., "Lincoln Park," in Holtwiijk and Shettleworth, *Bold Vision,* 70–71; A. W. Smith, Secretary of Parks Commission, "Portland's Parks and Promenades," *BTJ* 19 (January 1907): 455–56; and "A Portland Architect's Plan," *Portland Sunday Telegraph,* January 1, 1905, 1.

34. On dressing rooms at East End Beach, see "Park Commission Report," *PAR,* 1926; on city parks and the tannery purchase, see "Park Commission Report," *PAR,* 1924, 1925, and 1926.

35. On downtown in the 1920s, see "Many Fine Buildings," *Portland Evening Express,* November 6, 1923; for other images of growing Portland in the 1920s, see the Photo Archives of the *Portland Press Herald,* now held by the Portland Public Library.

36. Portland Zoning Commission, "Proposed Zoning Ordinance for the City of Portland, Maine, August 1, 1926," in Papers of Arthur C. Comey, Frances Loeb Library: Special Collections, Harvard University Graduate School of Design (hereafter cited as Comey Papers); John F. Bauman, "Saga of Renewal in a Maine City: Exploring the Fate of Portland's Bayside District," *Journal of Planning History* 5, no. 4 (November 2006); "Legislature May Grant to Cities Police Authority," *Portland Press Herald,* March 4, 1925.

37. See General Passenger Department of the Boston and Maine Railroad, *Along New England Shores* (Boston: Boston and Maine, 1925), MHSL; Augustus Moulton, *Portland by the Sea: An Historical Treatise* (Augusta: Katahdin, 1926); *Tower Directory of the City of Portland, 1922; Tower Directory of the City of Portland, 1925* (hereafter *Tower Directory); Official Automobile Blue Book,* vol. 2: *New England, Eastern Canada, and Maritime Provinces* (New York: Automobile Blue Book Company, 1919, 1921, 1923); and Automobile Legal Association, *Automobile Green Book, Volume 1: 1925: Official Guide Book of ALA: New England States, Canada, Trunk Lines West and South* (Boston: Scarborough Motor Guide Company, 1925), all found at Osher Map Library, University of Southern Maine, Portland. On Eastland, see "Eastland Opens," in Barnes, *Greater Portland 350,* 150. For the Chamber of Commerce's automobile tourism ad, see Automobile Legal Association, *Automobile Green Book,* vol. 3 (Boston: Scarborough Motor Guide Company, 1927).

38. Mark I. Gelfand, *A Nation of Cities: The Federal Government and Urban America, 1933–1965* (New York: Oxford University Press, 1975), 37.
39. Robert S. McElvaine, *The Great Depression: America, 1929–1941* (New York: Times Books, 1993); John F. Bauman and Thomas C. Coode, *In the Eye of the Great Depression: New Deal Reporters and the Agony of the American People* (Dekalb: Northern Illinois University Press, 1988); Bauman and Muller, *Before Renaissance,* 194–227.
40. Condon et al., "Depression and War," 45; Barlow's Report, *PAR,* 1930, 20; see also Chamber of Commerce, "History of Portland," in *Tower Directory, 1932,* 10.
41. Dow and Hormell, *City Manager Government,* 10–11, 16–17; Lawrence G. Lashbrook, "Work Relief in Maine: The Administration and Programs of the WPA" (Ph.D. diss., University of Maine, Orono, 1977), 36–38. On end of night-boat service, see Albion, "Two Ports of Portland," 50.
42. On banks, see Dow and Hormell, "City Manager Government," 11; on declining real estate valuations, see Chair of City Council, Reports, *PAR,* 1927, 1929, 1930, 1931, 1932, esp. Report of Arthur E. Craig, Chair of City Council, in *PAR, 1933,* 14–17.
43. Connolly, "Irish Longshoremen of Portland, Maine," 233.
44. See Report of Overseers of Poor, in *PAR,* 1932, 202–3, and *PAR,* 1933, 180–81. On work relief, see Report of Overseers of Poor, *PAR,* 1934, 14–15. See also "Poor List to be Hired at $2 Day," *Portland Press Herald,* June 2, 1932; "Poor Department Will Exceed Appropriation by $75,000 to $100,000," *Portland Press Herald,* July 8, 1932; "Barlow and Horton Discuss Employment of Portland Poor," *Portland Press Herald,* June 24, 1932. On municipal golf course, see *PAR,* 1931, 256–57; on salary cuts, see "City Manager's Salary Cut 21.5 Percent," *Portland Press Herald,* June 14, 1932.
45. See Lashbrook, "Work Relief in Maine," 61–62, 119; "Exit a Great President," *Portland Press Herald,* March 8, 1933; Federal Writers' Project, *Maine Guide* (Portland, 1937), 46–47.
46. "President Orders Banks Closed 4 Days," *Portland Press Herald,* March 6, 1933; "Danger in Delay," *Portland Press Herald,* April 1, 1933.
47. Richard Lowitt and Maurine Beasley, eds., *One Third of a Nation: Lorena Hickock Reports on the Great Depression* (Urbana: University of Illinois Press, 1981), 42–43; see also Bauman and Coode, *In The Eye of the Great Depression.* On the relationship between Lorena Hickok and Eleanor Roosevelt, see Blanche Wiesen Cook, *Eleanor Roosevelt,* vol. 1: *1884–1933* (New York: Penguin Books, 1993), which focuses on the intimacy of their correspondence and on the fact that after FDR's death, Hickock lived in a cottage on the Hyde Park grounds.
48. See cartoon titled "Some of the Boys Are Just Getting Started," in *Portland Press Herald,* July 1, 1936.
49. Roy Lubove, *The Professional Altruist: The Emergence of Social Work as a Career, 1880–1930* (New York: Atheneum, 1971); Lashbrook, "Work Relief in Maine," 63–71.
50. See "Municipal Activities for 1936," *PAR,* 1936, 82–83; Reports of Recreation and Parks Commissions, *PAR,* 1934, 210–11; Condon et al., "Depression and War," 516–17; "Works Progress Activities, 1934–1935," Emergency Relief Administration, State Files, Maine, record group (RG) 69, in National Archives and Records Administration (NARA); Hildreth G. Hawes, ed., *Review of the ERA in Maine* (Augusta: Maine Emergency Relief Administration, December 31, 1934), Maine State Archives, Augusta.

51. On Hopkins, see Searle Charles, *Minister of Relief: Harry Hopkins and the Great Depression* (Westport, Conn; Greenwood Press, 1974); Hawes, *Review of the ERA in Maine;* Lashbrook, "Work Relief in Maine," 126–39; Joel W. Eastman, "From Declining Seaport to Liberty City," Judd et al., *Maine,* 277–78.
52. "Municipal Activities for 1936," *PAR,* 1936, 92–93; "WPA Projects Benefit Region," in Barnes, *Greater Portland 350,* 160–61; "$7,000,000 Bond Issue Proposed," *Portland Press Herald,* January 5, 1939, 1; "Western Promenade Retaining Wall Nears Completion with WPA Crew," *Portland Press Herald,* February 1, 1938, 10; "Barlow to Make Formal Request That WPA Resume Airport Work," *Portland Press Herald,* August 6, 1937. On the airport, see Eastman, "From Declining Seaport to Liberty City," 280.
53. On WPA white-collar projects, see Lashbrook, "Work Relief in Maine," 200–236, and "WPA Rolls in Maine Now 6,100," *Portland Press Herald,* January 6, 1938. On sewing projects, "Municipal Activities for 1937," *PAR,* 1937, 45; Agnes P. Mantor, Director of Women's Activities, to Mrs. Ellen Woodward, Assistant Administrator, WPA, December 17, 1935, WPA State Series, Maine 661, RG 69, NARA; and see R. C. Branion, Field Representative, to Harry Hopkins, April 6, 1936 (reporting on the sewing project in Portland, Maine), in WPA State Series, Maine 661, RG 69, NARA; Bruce McClure, Director of Professional and Service Projects, to Miss Rose Selter, Director of Professional Projects, 143 High St., November 20, 1935, in WPA State Series, Maine 651.37, RG 69, NARA.
54. Grace H. Cho, "Saving the Waterfront, Saving a Way of Life: The Battle over Portland's Waterfront, 1850–1992" (honors paper for Department of History, Bowdoin College, 2005). On unions, see "Richardson Dana Company Official Threatens to Abandon Warehouse Here," *Portland Press Herald,* August 7, 1937.
55. On Puritan image, see Joseph A. Conforti, *Imagining New England: Explorations of Regional Identity from the Pilgrims to the Mid-Twentieth Century* (Chapel Hill: University of North Carolina Press, 2001), 253–309; Condon et al., "Depression and War," 523; "Advertising the State," *Portland Press Herald,* July 6, 1936; and Portland Chamber of Commerce, *Maine Invites You* (1943), MHSL.
56. "Nation Unaware of Vital Part Casco Bay Played in Winning War, Says Capital Paper," *Portland Press Herald,* January 6, 1947.
57. See Roger W. Lotchin, ed., *The Martial Metropolis: U.S. Cities in War and Peace* (New York: Praeger, 1984); Eastman, "From Declining Seaport to Liberty City," 280–81.
58. "War Brings About Birth of Pipeline," in Barnes, *Greater Portland 350;* Condon et al., "Depression and War," 524.
59. Federal Housing Administration, Division of Research and Statistics, Memorandum Report: Current Housing Situation, Portland, Maine, March 10, 1941, FHA, Portland, box 13, entry 34, RG 207, NARA; Theodore Veenstra, Office of Production Management, to Samuel Dennis, Division of Defense Housing, August 14, 1941, and Howard Strong to Robert Drier, September 22, 1941, both in box 13, Records of HHFA, Records of Defense Housing Coordination, RG 207, NARA.
60. Social Protection Committee of Portland Council of Social Agencies, "Social Protection Problems of Greater Portland, Maine, Defense Area: Prepared for the Office of Civilian Defense" (Portland, 1942), mimeograph, Hawthorne-Longfellow Library, Bowdoin College, Brunswick, Maine.

61. National Recreation Association, "Long Range Recreation Plan for City of Portland, Maine: Prepared for the Park Commission and City of Portland Planning Board" (January 1943), in Comey Papers; City Planning Board, *Annual Report of the City Planning Board, 1942,* Portland Planning Department Library, Portland; City Planning Board, "The Fourth 'R' Recreation: A Master Plan for Parks and Recreation" (1943), mimeograph. On Comey, see Bauman, "Saga of Renewal," 338–39.

CHAPTER SIX
Postwar Portland, 1943–1965

1. Christopher Klemek, *The Transatlantic Collapse of Urban Renewal: Postwar Urbanism from New York to Berlin* (Chicago: University of Chicago Press, 2011), calls the complex of forces led by modernism the Urban Renewal Order. On Futurama, see Mel Scott, *American City Planning since 1890* (Berkeley: University of California Press, 1969), 360–63.
2. Jon C. Teaford, *The Rough Road to Renaissance: Urban Revitalization in America, 1940–1985* (Baltimore: Johns Hopkins University Press, 1990), 29; Bernard J. Frieden and Lynne B. Sagalyn, *Downtown, Inc.: How America Rebuilds Cities* (Cambridge: MIT Press, 1992), 20–35; Alison Isenberg, *Downtown America: A History of the Place and the People Who Made It* (Chicago: University of Chicago Press, 2004), 161–62.
3. U.S. Bureau of the Census, *Census of Population and Housing* for the years 1930, 1940, 1950, 1960 (Washington, D.C.: GPO); see Greater Portland Chamber of Commerce and Portland City Planning Board, *Portland, Maine, Economic Region: Population and Housing Data, 1960* (Portland: Chamber of Commerce, 1960), City Planning Department Library, Portland (hereafter cited as PDL). See also "State Gained Citizens in War, Lost Veterans to Other Areas," *Portland Evening Express,* June 1, 1950; "Maine Is Expected to Show Jump to 900,000 or More," *Portland Evening Express,* June 5, 1950.
4. See advertisement in *Portland Evening Express,* July 15, 1946; also a brochure, *The Portland Company,* in PRSC; David H. Fletcher, *Images of America: The Portland Company, 1846–1982* (Charleston, S.C.: Arcadia, 2002); "110-Year-Old Portland Company Sold to New York Firm," *Portland Press Herald,* January 6, 1956.
5. See Economic Development Department, City of Portland, "Economic Development in Portland, Maine: A Report to the City Manager," mimeograph, c. 1965, PDL; "Economic Review and Analysis of Greater Portland Region: A Report to Greater Portland Regional Planning Commission" (Public Affairs Research Center, 1969), Hawthorne-Longfellow Library, Bowdoin College, Brunswick, Maine (hereafter cited as HLL). See also Greater Portland Area Development Council, "Industrial Location Facts and Community Information," mimeograph, 1957, PDL.
6. See "Master Plan Studies: Land Use for Industrial, Commercial, Residential, and Public Development," mimeograph, March 6, 1957, PDL; "Chamber of Commerce Urges General City Promotion Program," *Portland Press Herald,* January 12, 1949; "City of Portland Emerges from Wartime Boom in Sound Condition," *Portland Press Herald* and *Evening Express,* July 4, 1946; "The City of Industrial Opportunity," special supplement, *Evening Express,* July 4, 1946.

7. See Martha S. Henry, "A Brief History of the Greater Portland Public Development Commission," mimeograph, Spring 1983, found in HLL).
8. See "Report of the Portland Port Committee Appointed by Governor Louis J. Brann to Study Conditions Affecting the Port of Portland, Maine," 1935, Portland Public Library (hereafter cited as Brann Committee Report). The study retained consulting engineers Fay, Spofford, and Thorndike.
9. "Fight to Get Ships," *Portland Evening Express,* June 7, 1948.
10. Maine Department of Transportation and Maine State Planning Office, "Feasibility Study of Development of Cargo Handling at Maine Ports," mimeograph, January 1978, PDL. Maine's booming turn-of-the-century paper industry considerably boosted commerce at the Port of Portland. China clay arose as an important product in port commerce in the 1920s. After World War II, Canadian competition cut into the newsprint business, but demand continued after 1946 for fine specialty paper. By 1950, New England still supplied 19.4 percent of the nation's paper, much of it produced in Maine. See Lloyd C. Irland, "Papermaking in Maine: Economic Trends from 1894 to 2000," *Maine History* 45, no. 1 (December 2009): 53–65.
11. See Maine Port Authority, *State of Maine Ports, 1965–1966* (Augusta: Maine Port Authority, 1966); and Greater Portland Chamber of Commerce, *Port of Portland, Maine* (Portland, Chamber of Commerce, n.d. [c. 1980]), HLL.
12. Brann Committee Report, 1935; photograph of Commercial Street in 1940, Library of Congress; images of Commercial Street, c. 1965, in *Portland Press Herald* Still-Film Negative Collection, PRSC.
13. See ads for Portland department stores in *Portland Evening Express,* May 2, 1945; on Munjoy Department Store, see Earle Shettleworth Jr., interview by author, Portland, January 12, 2010; for images of Portland department stores and stores on Middle and Exchange, see special (advertising) supplement in *Portland Press Herald* and *Evening Express,* July 4, 1946.
14. See Robert M. Fogelson, *Downtown: Its Rise and Fall, 1880–1950* (New Haven: Yale University Press, 2001); 317–18; see also Teaford, *Rough Road to Renaissance,* 129; Isenberg, *Downtown America;* and Robert Fishman, "The Metropolitan Tradition in American Planning," in Robert Fishman, ed., *The American Planning Tradition: Culture and Policy* (Washington, D.C.: Woodrow Wilson Center, 2000), 65–81.
15. "Mill Creek Shopping Center to Be Opened Wednesday," *Portland Sunday Telegram,* June 19, 1955, 9; Fogelson, *Downtown,* 380–89.
16. On Northgate, see "New Shopping Center to Open Wednesday," *Portland Sunday Telegram,* July 7, 1957; and *Map of Portland: A Shopping Guide,* 1959, PRSC.
17. Images of West Gate and the Falmouth Shopping Center and Forest Avenue Plaza can be found in *Portland Press Herald* Still-Film Negative Collection, PRSC.
18. John F. Bauman, *Public Housing, Race, and Renewal: Urban Planning in Philadelphia, 1920–1974* (Philadelphia: Temple University Press, 1987); Mary Ellen Hayward, *Baltimore's Alley Housing: Homes for Working People since the 1780s* (Baltimore: Johns Hopkins University Press, 2008). On modernism, see John F. Bauman and David Schuyler, "Urban Politics and the Vision of the Modern City: Philadelphia and Lancaster after World War II," *Pennsylvania Magazine of History and Biography* 132 (October 2008): 377–403.

19. On postwar Gorham's Corner, see *Sanborn Insurance Map of Portland, Maine, 1954, Volume 1* (New York: Sanborn Map Company, 1954); also Shettleworth interview. On Bayside, see John F. Bauman, "A Saga of Renewal in a Maine City: Exploring the Fate of Portland's Bayside District," *Journal of Planning History* 5, no. 4 (November 2006): 329–54.
20. For the series on Bayside housing, see *Portland Evening Express,* December 6, 1948–December 12, 1948, news clippings file, PDL.
21. On people in Bayside "living like animals," see *Portland Evening Express,* December 6–12, 1948; on communism and the postwar housing issue, see Joshua Olsen, *Better Places, Better Lives: A Biography of James Rouse* (Washington, D.C.: Urban Land Institute Press, 2003).
22. See Portland City Planning Board, *Urban Redevelopment for Portland,* September 1946, PDL; Portland Renewal Authority, *Portland Renewal: A Decade of Planning and Progress, 1951–1961* (Portland: Urban Renewal Authority, 1961), PRSC; also Shettleworth interview.
23. "Resorts Look Forward to Record This Year," *Portland Evening Express,* July 2, 1946; see also *Evening Express,* June 8–June 21, 1948. On Graymore Hotel, see "Its Hotel Industry," in "Maine" special supplement, *Portland Evening Express,* July 4, 1946.
24. See *Automobile Green Guide for 1933–1934,* Osher Map Library, University of Southern Maine, Portland, Maine; on railroads, see Teaford, *Rough Road to Renaissance,* 93; Report of "George F. Glacy, Vice President of Accounting, Boston and Maine Railroad, to Mr. Hunter Holding, Vice President of Equitable Life Assurance Society, New York, March 4, 1959, regarding Boston and Maine Progress and Accomplishments, 1955–1958," PRSC; on the trolley and interurbans, see "Electric Railroad Edition," *Exciter Magazine* (of Central Maine Power), n.d., PRSC.
25. "Northeast Airlines Offers Improved Summer Schedule," *Portland Evening Express,* July 2, 1946; Teaford, *Rough Road to Renaissance,* 94, 99; City of Portland, *Financial Report for the Year Ending December 31, 1947,* PRSC.
26. Note that the Maine Turnpike opened ahead of schedule: see "Kittery-to-Portland Toll Superhighway to Be Completed for Tourists in 1948," in "Maine" special supplement, *Portland Evening Express,* July 1946; Maine Turnpike Historic Overview, www.bostonroads.com/roads/me-turnpike; "Planning Board Issues Proposals for Expressway," *Portland Evening Express,* June 3, 1949; "Portland Sparkles with New Look of Superhighways and Overpasses," *Portland Press Herald,* October 16, 1954; Tracy B. Augur to R. L. Steiner, December 17, 1956, on "Uses of Urban Planning Assistance Program as an Aid to the Planning of Federal Aid Highways in Urban Areas," box 295, General Subject File, 1949–1960, Urban Renewal Papers, RG 207, NARA; and for reference to 1953 proposal, see Neal W. Allen, Chair of Planning Board, to City Council, January 22, 1954, letter transferring report to Council, in City of Portland, Annual Report of City Planning Board, 1953 (Portland, 1954), PDL.
27. On Citizens' Committee on Planning, see "Defense Demand for Housing Emphasizes Need for Planning," *Portland Evening Express,* November 29, 1941; full-page spread in *Portland Press Herald,* c. November 1941, news clippings file, PDL.
28. For Wing quote, see "55 Women Are Appointed to Citizens Planning Committee," *Portland Press Herald,* November 26, 1941; and "2 Local Leaders Join Citizens Planning Committee," *Portland Press Herald,* November 27, 1941; also "30 Labor

Leaders Named to City Committee on Planning," *Portland Press Herald,* November 25, 1941.

29. City of Portland, Annual Report of City Planning Board, 1943 (1944), and City of Portland, Annual Report of City Planning Board, 1945 (1946), both mimeographs, PRSC. On Comey, see biographical materials, "Box Comey, VF," Comey Papers; on Master Plan reports, see City Planning Board, "Master Plan Studies, Land Use Policy Statements and Land Allocation for Industry, Commerce, Residence, and Public Developments," March 1957, PDL.
30. Arthur Comey, "Summary of Urban Redevelopment, Portland, Maine, September 1946," typescript, Comey Papers.
31. On public housing, see Gail Radford's excellent *Modern Housing for America: Policy Struggles in the New Deal Era* (Chicago: University of Chicago Press, 1996); on Portland, see City Planning Board, "Urban Redevelopment for Portland," 1946, Comey Papers.
32. Elaine Tyler May, *Homeward Bound: American Families in the Cold War Era* (New York: Basic Books, 1988). On postwar Americans' image of suburban housing, see Lizabeth Cohen, *A Consumers' Republic: The Politics of Mass Consumption in Postwar America* (New York: Knopf, 2003), 112–23.
33. See Peter Marcuse, "Housing Policy and the Myth of the Benevolent State," in Rachael Bratt, Chester Hartman, and Ann Meyerson, eds., *Critical Perspectives on Housing* (Philadelphia: Temple University Press, 1986), 255. See also Isenberg, *Downtown America,* 174–93; and Fogelson, *Downtown.*
34. See *Portland Evening Express* series, December 6–12, 1948. On communism and the postwar housing issue, see Olsen, *Better Places, Better Lives.*
35. The literature on pre- and postwar housing and redevelopment is extensive. Much of it focuses on the racial aspects of urban housing and slum clearance, an issue not present in Portland. See Arnold Hirsch, *Making the Second Ghetto: Race and Housing in Chicago, 1940–1960* (Cambridge: Cambridge University Press, 1983); Bauman, *Public Housing, Race, and Renewal,* 94–97; Robert O. Self, *American Babylon: Race and the Struggle for Postwar Oakland* (Princeton: Princeton University Press, 2003); and Thomas J. Sugrue, *The Origins of the Urban Crisis: Race and Inequality in Postwar Detroit* (Princeton: Princeton University Press, 1996). See also Roger Biles, "Public Housing and the Postwar Urban Renaissance, 1949–1973," in John F. Bauman, Roger Biles, and Kristin Szylvian, eds., *From Tenements to the Taylor Homes: In Search of an Urban Housing Policy in Twentieth-Century America* (University Park: Penn State University Press, 2000), 143–63; for an excellent treatment of a city closer in size to Portland, see David Schuyler, *A City Transformed: Redevelopment, Race, and Suburbanization in Lancaster, Pennsylvania, 1940–1980* (University Park: Penn State University Press, 2002).
36. "Housing Expert Says City Could End Slums," *Portland Evening Express,* January 11, 1949, PDL.
37. *Portland Press Herald,* April 8, April 13, and June 23, 1949, news clipping file, PDL.
38. "Facing the Fact of Slums," *Portland Press Herald,* June 24, 1949, PDL.
39. *Portland Press Herald,* January 22, 1949, PDL.
40. See Roger I. Creighton, "Rethinking Urban Redevelopment—The Viewpoint of a Small City," *Journal of American Institute of Planners* 19 (Winter 1953): 95–100; and Slum Clearance and Redevelopment Authority (SCRAP), *Annual Report,* 1953, PDL.

41. For a chronology of Portland renewal history, see Bauman, "Saga of Renewal in a Maine City," 329–54; SCRAP, *Annual Report,* 1953, PDL; and *Portland Renewal Authority Annual Report, 1965* (Portland 1965), MHSL. On DSCUR request for court decision, see Portland City Planning Board to City Council, January 22, 1954, submitting *1953 Annual Report of Portland City Planning Board,* PDL.
42. Roger I. Creighton, Planning Director, to City Council, December 11, 1953, submitting *1953 Annual Report of Planning Board,* PDL.
43. *Portland Press Herald,* August 5, 1954. On Portland's "Conservation Program," see City Planning Board (Roger I. Creighton, Planning Director) to City Council, December 11, 1952, PDL. Providence, Rhode Island, was especially impressed with Portland's housing preservation program: see Donald Graham, Executive Director of Providence Redevelopment Agency, to Mayor Walter Reynolds of Providence, September 22, 1953, discussing "Minimum Standard Housing Code Enforcement in Portland, Maine: 1952," Reynolds Papers, Providence College Library Special Collections, Providence.
44. "Pastor's Criticism Bares Controversy," *Portland Evening Express,* January 28, 1954.
45. John Orr, Portland City Manager, to HHFA Administrator Albert Cole, April 14, 1955, forwarding "Workable Program," PDL; for pro-growth coalition, see John H. Mollenkopf, *The Contested City* (Princeton, N.J.: Princeton University Press, 1983).
46. See Clinton Wallace of 31–41 Elm Street to Edmund Muskie, March 21, 1961, box 530–5, Edmund Muskie Senate Papers (hereafter cited as MSP), Edmund Muskie Archives, Bates College, Lewiston, Maine (hereafter cited as MA); "Supreme Court Makes New Law, Upholds City's Redevelopment Act," *Portland Press Herald,* September 4, 1954; "Vine-Deer-Chatham: SCRA Plans Study On Wrecking," *Portland Press Herald,* August, 26, 1955; "Slum Panel Lists Steps to Improve Area," *Portland Press Herald,* September, 12, 1955. On Popkins Zakarian, see "City Council Defers Action on Redevelopment Project," *Portland Press Herald,* September 20, 1955.
47. See Portland Renewal Authority, *Portland Renewal: A Decade of Planning and Progress, 1951–1961,* 1962, PRSC.
48. Orr to Cole, April 14, 1955, forwarding "Workable Program."
49. Slum Clearance and Redevelopment Authority and City Planning Board, "Preliminary Report: Bayside Park Urban Renewal Project ME. R-1, Portland, Maine," March 1957, PDL; see also Charles Horan, Regional Director of Urban Renewal, Region I, to William Gelbach, Director of Administrative Branch, HHFA, August 15, 1961, submitting "Physical Progress Quarterly Report," RG 207, box 730, Urban Renewal Administration, Subject File 1961–1965, NARA. See Portland Renewal Authority, *Portland Renewal Authority Annual Report 1965,* PRSC; Portland Renewal Authority brochure, *Munjoy South,* c. 1970, PRSC.
50. See *Evening Express,* November 18, 1955. On 1954 Act, see Planning Department Head Roland Tyler to City Council, submitting Portland City Planning Board *Annual Report, 1954,* February 28, 1955, PDL.
51. See *Portland Renewal Authority Annual Report 1965,* PRSC; "Munjoy South" advertisement, *Portland Sun-Telegram,* June 11, 1967.
52. On the transfer of Sagamore Village Lanham Act housing project to the Portland Housing Authority, see "Excerpt from Report to the City Council on Disposal of Sagamore Village," by Francis Jensen, April 5, 1948, in General Records of HHFA, File 340, ME, box 11, RG 207, NARA; "New Portland Housing Act Has Good Chance

to Pass," *Portland Press Herald,* March 3, 1949; "Local Citizens' Panel Backs Public Housing Enabling Act," *Portland Press Herald,* March 24, 1949.

53. Portland Housing Authority, *Fiftieth Anniversary Report,* 1993, PDL. See correspondence between Milton Semer and Edmund Muskie (April 25, 1962), Robert C. Weaver and Donald Nicoll (March 13, 1962), and Milton Semer and Donald Nicholl (March 8, 1962), in Records of Public Housing Administration, Congressional Correspondence file 1942–1962, box 62, RG 196, NARA. On CIAM, the Bauhaus, and modernism, see Jill Pearlman, *Inventing American Modernism: Joseph Hudnut, Walter Gropius, and the Bauhaus Legacy at Harvard* (Charlottesville: University Press of Virginia, 2007); and Bauman and Schuyler, "Urban Politics and the Vision of the Modern City."
54. On retreat from renewal, See Klemek, *Translatlantic Collapse,* 79–129. On Fried, Bauer, Jacobs, and the opposition to renewal, see Jane Jacobs, *The Death and Life of Great American Cities* (New York: Vintage Books, 1961); Martin Anderson, *The Federal Bulldozer* (New York: McGraw-Hill, 1964). On Bauer, see H. Peter Oberlander and Eva Newbrun, *Houser: The Life and Work of Catherine Bauer* (Vancouver: UBC Press, 1999); and Biles, "Public Housing and the Postwar Urban Renaissance," 152–54.
55. Interview by author with Joseph Gray—until 2010, city manager of Portland Maine—in his City Hall office, May 30, 2006.
56. For changing downtown scene, see Portland Directories for years 1946–1965. On tourism, see "Task Force to Assemble Waterfront Renewal Plan," *Portland Press Herald,* April 7, 1961; Maine Port Authority, *State of Maine Ports, 1965–66* (Portland: Portland Port Authority, 1966), HLL; "C of C Urges General City Promotion," *Portland Press Herald,* January 12, 1949.

CHAPTER SEVEN
The Gateway Reborn, 1965–1985

1. Allen J. Matusow, *The Unraveling of America: A History of Liberalism in the 1960s* (New York: Harper and Row, 1984).
2. On the plight of urban blacks in a northern city with a significantly larger African American population than Portland's (the whole state of Maine had only 3,100 blacks in 1983), see Thomas J. Sugrue, *The Origins of the Urban Crisis: Race and Inequality in Postwar Detroit* (Princeton: Princeton University Press, 1996). A housing survey done by the Portland NAACP in 1965 described the black housing problem in the city as serious. For the best treatment of Portland's black experience, see H. H. Price and Gerald E. Talbot, *Maine's Visible Black History: The First Chronicle of Its People* (Gardiner, Maine: Tilbury House, 2006).
3. Bonnie Blythe, correspondence with author, February 4, 2010.
4. John Edward Menario, interview by Andrea L'Hommedieu, February, 19, 2002, Muskie Oral History Project, interview no. 329, Bates College, Lewiston, Maine (hereafter cited as MOH interviews); interview by author with Joseph Gray, until 2010 City Manager of the City of Portland, in his City Hall office, May 30, 2006; "Portland Enters an Active Period," in Albert F. Barnes, ed., *Greater Portland 350: A Commemorative Edition* (Portland: Gannett Books, 1984), 206.

5. Interview by author with Joseph Gray in his City Hall office, April 14, 2004; MOH interview no. 329; "Who Makes Portland Run?" *Portland Evening Express,* October 9, 1978; "Harold Loring Civic Leader: Obituary," in *Portland Evening Express,* February 11, 1985; "Man Who Criticized Slums Named to Renewal Board," *Portland Evening Express,* January 8, 1963; "Slum Area Residents' Welfare His First Concern, Says Burke," *Portland Evening Express,* January 7, 1961.
6. Portland Planning Department, Victor Gruen Associates, and Spencer Hurtt Associates, "Downtown Portland Maine: General Neighborhood Renewal Plan" (1966). The Gruen Plan appeared in printed form in Victor Gruen and Larry Smith Co. *Pattern for Progress: General Neighborhood Renewal Plan, Portland Maine* (Portland: City of Portland, January 9, 1967), found in PDL (hereafter cited as Gruen Plan); Portland Renewal Authority, *Portland Renewal Authority Annual Report 1965* (Portland, 1965), MHSL.
7. Portland Renewal Authority, *Annual Report, 1965,* MHSL.
8. Victor Gruen, *The Heart of Our Cities: The Urban Crisis: Diagnosis and Cure* (New York: Simon and Schuster, 1964).
9. David Schuyler, *A City Transformed: Redevelopment, Race, and Suburbanization in Lancaster, Pennsylvania, 1940–1980* (University Park: Penn State University Press, 2002), 93–99.
10. "The Future of Portland," *Evening Express,* December 14, 1965; "The Year of Decision," *Evening Express,* December 16, 1965; "Gruen Report on City's Downtown Should Bring Quick Go-Ahead Plan," *Portland Press Herald,* February 3, 1966. Likewise, Lancaster eagerly awaited a similar Gruen plan: see Schuyler, *A City Transformed,* 90–91.
11. On Gruen, see M. Jeffrey Hardwick, *Mall Maker: Victor Gruen, Architect of an American Dream* (Philadelphia: University of Pennsylvania Press, 2004). See also Gruen Plan; and City of Portland, Press Release, "Statement of Charles Allen," September 30, 1966, PDL.
12. Gruen Plan; see also Gruen, *The Heart of Our Cities.*
13. Gruen Plan; author interview with City Manager Joseph Gray, May 30, 2006; Portland Redevelopment Authority (PRA), "Long History of Renewal and Creative Planning," mimeograph, c. 1967, MSP, box 1107, folder 7, MA; Portland Economic Development Department, "Economic Development in Portland, Maine," 1965, PDL; Statement of Charles W. Allen, "Regarding Portland's Downtown Renewal Plans, PDL.
14. On Edmund Muskie and Model Cities in Portland, see John F. Bauman, "Model Cities, Housing, and Renewal Policy in Portland, Maine," *Maine History* 45 (December 2010): 233–59; David Nevin, *Muskie of Maine* (New York: Random House, 1972), 98–114; also on Muskie's role, see Walter Phillips to Muskie, August 2, 1968, MSP, box 620, folder 6, MA; Charles Allen to Muskie, November 21, 1967, thanking Muskie "for all you have done to assist City of Portland in its relationship with the Federal Government," MSP, box 763, folder 6, MA; and Barnett I. Shur to Muskie, May 15, 1967, MSP, box 763, folder 6, MA.
15. Muskie's aide Don Nicoll witnessed the event: see Don Nicoll, interview by Andrea L'Hommedieu, May 3, 2003, MOH interview no. 435.
16. Ibid. See also Bernard J. Frieden and Marshakll Kaplan, *The Politics of Neglect: Urban Aid from Model Cities to Revenue Sharing* (Cambridge: MIT Press, 1975), 58.
17. On Portland's application for a Model Cities planning grant, see Robert Weaver to Muskie, May 11, 1967, and June 1, 1967, MSP, box 763, folder 7, MA.
18. See Robert C. Weaver to Margaret Chase Smith, November 16, 1967; Edward Allen to Margaret Chase Smith, August 2, 1967; and John E. Menario to Margaret Chase

Smith, August 3, 1967, all in Margaret Chase Smith Library, Skowhegan, Maine (hereafter cited as MCSL).

19. On Hawkins and his thinking about Model Cities, see "Address on Model Cities: An Overview of Some Issues: Address by Robert R. Hawkins, Model Cities Administrator," February 17, 1968, MSP, box 867, folder 11, MA.

20. Portland West, *Final Evaluation Report on Model Cities in Portland, Maine: 'Improving the Quality of Life in Portland, Maine: The Final Evaluation Report of the Portland Model Cities Program. April 1975* (Washington, D.C.: GPO, 1975), in MSP, box 2481, folder 4, MA (hereafter cited as Final Report 1975); Hawkins, "Address on Model Cities."

21. See City of Portland, "Application to the Department of Housing and Urban Development for a Grant to Carry Out a Comprehensive City Demonstration Plan including "THE FIRST YEAR ACTION PROGRAM (1969) FOR THE PORTLAND WEST NEIGHBORHOOD, PORTLAND, MAINE," December 13, 1968 (hereafter cited as Portland West Action Program, 1968), MSP, box 1825, folder 4, MA.

22. See Final Report 1975. To secure even broader participation in neighborhood planning, one of the Model Cities consultants, the Urban Design Group of Newport, Rhode Island, held a "plan-in" to elicit ideas from local people. Held in St. Dominic's church hall, the program drew more than 150 people and used slides, strobe lights, and other devices to generate excitement and participation in the discussions. See "Special Attachment: A Plan-in: An Example of the Citizen Participation That Went into This Document," pt. 1, sec. 1, Portland West, Action Program, 1968.

23. *Portland West: Our Model Cities Program: Some Questions and Answers,* brochure, MSP, box 1733, folder 1, MA.

24. Weaver to Senator Margaret Chase Smith, November 16, 1967, enclosing statement announcing grant, MCSL.

25. Muskie to Casper Cowan of the Portland Renewal Authority, March 31, 1967, MSP, box 191, folder 9, MA.

26. Howard Heller to Muskie, September 22, 1967, letter enclosing "Portland's Program for Meeting the National Goals of Urban Renewal Priorities [of HUD]," September 21, 1967, MSP, box 1107, folder 8, MA.

27. "Portland's Program for Meeting the National Goals of Urban Renewal Priorities."

28. Chip to Muskie on subject of Downtown 2, November 13, 1967; William Bruce Dalton, Planning Director of Portland, to Stephen Seni, Region I, HUD, New York, October 16, 1967; Heller to Charles Horan, November 15, 1967, MSP, box 1107, folder 8, MA.

29. For example, Carleton Lane to Paul Folan, chair of PRA, September 13, 1967; Arthur Benoit to Paul Folan, September 15, 1967; and Arthur H. Benoit to Muskie, November 22, 1967, MSP, box 1107, folder 8, MA.

30. "HUD Funds Unlikely Soon for Downtown Renewal," *Maine Sunday Telegram,* April 14, 1968, MSP, box 1733, folder 2, MA.

31. Harold Loring to Muskie, April 25, 1968, MSP, box 867, folder 11; Dick Davis, Urban Development Commission of Greater Portland Chamber of Commerce, "Presentation before HUD," June 18, 1968, MSP, box 1107, folder 8; Muskie to Ray Stetson, June 11, 1969, MSP, box 1733, folder 3, all in MA; Portland Renewal Authority, *Annual Report* (1922), PDL.

32. Greater Portland Landmarks, *Portland* (1986; repr., Portland: Greater Portland Landmarks, 1999).

33. Portland West Action Program, 1968, passim; Final Report 1975; Greater Portland Landmarks, *Portland.*

34. For data on demolitions, see City Planning Board, "Housing Code Compliance Program for Portland, Maine," Planning Board Report no. 20-68, March 1968, PDL; and Planning Department (Philip Sieber), "Inventory of Housing Neighborhood Analysis and Housing Forecast," Planning Report no. 55-73, March 1973, PDL. On alley life in Washington, D.C., see James Borchert, *Alley Life in Washington: Family, Community, Religion, and Folklife in the City, 1850–1970* (Urbana: University of Illinois Press, 1980).

35. Portland West Action Program, 1968, passim. On business opposition, see Reginald LaVerdiere, LaVerdiere's Super Drug Stores, to Muskie, May 3, 1973, and Muskie to LaVerdiere, May 31, 1973, MSP, box 2171, folder 4, MA.

36. Portland West Action Program, 1968, passim. Note that historic preservation early played a role in renewal planning: see, for example, Brian G. Greenfield, "Marketing the Past: Historic Preservation in Providence, Rhode Island," in Max Page and Randall Mason, eds., *Giving Preservation a History: Histories of Historic Preservation in the United States* (New York: Routledge, 2004), 163–84.

37. Portland West Action Program, 1968, pt. 1, sec. 4, 4, MSP, file 1825, folder 4, MA.

38. John E. Menario to H. Ralph Taylor, assistant secretary, HUD, June 7, 1968, and "Housing Experiment May Be Tried Here," *Portland Evening Express,* April 26, 1968, news clipping, MSP, box 1733, folder 2, MA.

39. Final Report 1975, box 2481, folder 4, MA.

40. On Housing Opportunities, Inc., see Menario to Muskie, March 29, 1971, MSP, box 1733, folder 5, MA; Portland Renewal Authority, Portland Renewal Authority *Annual Report, 1972* (Portland, 1972), PRSC.

41. See Final Report 1975; box 2481, folder 4, MA; "Failure of Housing Opportunities," *Waterville Evening Express,* February 7, 1973, MSP, box 2171, folder 4, MA.

42. "Conservation Work in Longfellow Square and MICAH," Final Report 1975, 107, 117–18.

43. "Romney Predicts Funds Cut for Model Cities," *Portland Evening Express,* August 8, 1969, MSP, box 1106, folder 6, MA; Muskie to James Barry, regional director, HUD, February 23, 1973, MSP, box 2171, folder 3, MA; Jadine R. O'Brien, director, Portland Model Cities, to Muskie, October 10, 1973, MSP, box 2070, folder 4, MA; see also "Goodbye to Model Cities," *Portland Evening Express,* January 23, 1974, MSP, box 2070, folder 4, MA.

44. Dana A. Little and Carl E. Veazie, "Economic Review and Analysis of the Greater Portland Region: A Report to the Greater Portland Regional Planning Commission" (Public Affairs Research Center of Bowdoin College, June 1969), PDL.

45. See "Building a New Portland," *Portland: The Magazine of Greater Portland* 14 (Summer 1970): 16–17. It appears that after a forty-seven-year-long hiatus the Portland Chamber introduced a new publication. Like the old magazine it featured a list of members and advertisements, but the new one was slicker and aimed at a more general audience.

46. Urban Design Group, *Port of Portland, Maine, Development Plan: Prepared for the Greater Portland Chamber of Commerce* (Newport, R.I: Urban Design Group, 1969), in Hawthorne-Longfellow Library, Bowdoin College.

47. "Over $42 Million in New Major Building Logs '72 as Portland's Greatest Advance," *Portland Evening Express,* January 27, 1973; advertisement, "Intown Portland: Everybody's Great Place to Shop," *Portland Evening Express,* January 27, 1973; see also "Proposed Eastern Promenade Apartments," *Portland Evening Express,* January 7, 1973; City of Portland, "MAINE WAY PROJECT: Submitted to U.S. Department of Housing and Urban Development, Planning Report no. 16-71, June 1971," PRSC.
48. Greater Portland Landmarks, *Portland,* passim.
49. Earle Shettleworth Jr., interview by author, January 12, 2010. On Sills Committee, see Joseph A. Conforti, ed., *Creating Portland: History and Place in Northern New England* (Hanover, N.H.: University Press of New England, 2005), xix; for a list of founding members, see "Greater Portland Landmarks, Inc. Incorporators," in Sills Collection, box 1, Greater Portland Landmarks Archives, Portland, Maine (hereafter cited as GPLA).
50. "State of Maine: Certificate of Organization of a Corporation," for Greater Portland Landmarks, Inc., July 31, 1964, Sills Collection, GPLA; see also letters seeking new members and informing recipients about origins of GPL, GPLA; see also Elizabeth Ring, corresponding secretary, to Mrs. Phillips M. Payson, June 25, 1965, Sills Collection, GPLA; on GPL's growing membership, see Greater Portland Landmarks, "Annual Report, Greater Portland Landmarks, 1969–1970," Office Files 70–80, file 1100, GPLA.
51. William J. Murtagh, *Keeping Time: The History and Theory of Preservation in America,* rev. ed. (New York: John Wiley, 1997).
52. On GPL and Model Cities, see Greater Portland Landmarks, "Summary of Activities April 1966–1967," in Sills Collection, box 1, GPLA; Urban Design Group, for Model Cities Agency, "Portland, Maine Preservation Planning Report: Clark/Park Districts," July 1969, Sills Collection, box 1, GPLA.
53. See Greater Portland Landmarks, "Annual Report, Greater Portland Landmarks, 1969–1970," in Office Files 70s, 80s, file 1100, GPLA; Greater Portland Landmarks, "Annual Report, Greater Portland Landmarks, 1970," file 1100, GPLA; and City of Portland, Maine Way Project (June 1971), in PRSC.
54. See Greater Portland Landmarks, Board of Trustees minutes, April 27 and March 2, 1971, Office Files 70–80, file 1500, GPLA; Susan T. Sewell, President, to GPL members, March 17, 1971, Sills Collection, box 1, GPLA.
55. Report of President Peter L. Murray, GPL annual meeting, May 10, 1973, in Office Files 70s, 80s, Trustees Minutes, GPLA.
56. On the revolving fund and Hay Building, see ibid.; Joel Russ, Executive Director of GPL, to Perkins Trust, Maine National Bank, December 21, 1978; Russ to Bob Niss, *Portland Evening Express,* October 13, 1978; and Carleton G. Lane to John Menario, October 12, 1978. On Hay Block and its importance to Congress Square, see Russ to A. J. Wilson, City Manager, City of Portland, December 18, 1978, GPL Chronological File, July–December 1978, GPLA; on revolving fund and GPL strategies for rebuilding city using historic preservation, see Pamela Plumb to Herbert J. Ludwig, November 19, 1980, Chronological File July–December 1980, GPLA.
57. "Economic Impact of Investment Tax Credits for Historic Building Rehabilitation in Portland, Maine, 1976–1985," minutes of Board of Trustees of Greater Portland Landmarks, 1985–1986, Office Files 70–80, GPLA.

58. John Lovell, "Rebirth of a City: Portland Booms Back after Decades of Decay," in Albert F. Barnes, ed., *Greater Portland Celebration 350* (Portland: Gannett Books, 1984), 218. On Akers and founding of GPL, see also Grace Ha Cho, "Saving the Waterfront. Saving a Way of Life: The Battle Over Portland's Waterfront" (honors paper for Department of History, Bowdoin College, 2005), 42–43.
59. On GPL support for Old Port Exchange, see Charlton S. Smith, President, GPL, to Stuart Pennell, President, Old Port Exchange Association (15 Exchange Street), February 3, 1972, in minutes, 1971–1972, File 1500, GPLA. On tour in the Old Port, see "Upstairs Down in the Old Port, 1978," typed proof of brochure with corrections, GPLA; and Joel Russ, Executive Director, GPL, to Charles Redman, Millikin-Tomlinson Company, August 23, 1978, Chronological File, 1978, GPLA.
60. See "Upstairs Down in the Old Port" and "Upstairs Down in the Old Port 1978 Itinerary," GPLA; "Economic Impact of Investment Tax Credits for Historic Building Rehabilitation in Portland, Maine, 1976–1985," GPLA.
61. On data, see Fay, Spofford & Thorndike, Inc., Engineers, "Feasibility Study of the Development of Cargo Handling Facilities at Maine Ports," submitted to Maine Department of Transportation and Maine State Planning Office, January 1978; and "Portland Harbor," *Portland: The Magazine of the Greater Portland Chamber of Commerce* (February 1975): 20–25, PRSC.
62. See Cho, "Saving the Waterfront"; "Container Cargo Port Here Is One Man's Dream," *Portland Evening Express,* September 1, 1972.
63. "Waterfront Problems Immense," *Portland Evening Express,* July 26, 1977; "Portland, Part II: Ideas Flourishing, Action Lacking," *Portland Evening Express,* July 27, 1977; "Waterfront Busy Look Surprises," *Portland Evening Express,* July 29, 1977.
64. Portland Planning Board, Anderson Notter Associates, Inc., Consultants, *City Edges: Waterfront Improvement Program, Portland, Maine* (City of Portland, December 1975).
65. On plans for the waterfront and City Edges, see ibid. See also Joel Russ to Pamela Plumb, November 15, 1979, Chronological File, July–December 1979, GPLA; "GPL Comment on the American City Corporation Report: Development Program for Portland, Maine Waterfront," March 1982, Office Files 70s–80s, Board of Trustees minutes, May 1981–April 1982, GPLA; and "3 Plans Offered to Draw Tourists," *Portland Evening Express,* February 9, 1983.
66. Clark Irwin, "Fisherman Look for Helpful $$$," *Portland Evening Express,* July 28, 1977; and Clark Irwin, "Portland Turns to the Sea," *Portland Evening Express,* July 29, 1977.
67. Cho, "Saving the Waterfront"; "Waterfront Tide Turns," *Portland Evening Express,* May 6, 1987. 67; and John Farland, "3 Plans Offered to Draw Tourists," *Portland Evening Express,* February 9, 1983.
68. "A Field Guide to Waterfront Perspectives, *Portland Monthly* 1, no. 1 (April 1986): 30–31.
69. "Opinion by Jeffrey W. Monroe," *Portland Monthly* 1, no. 1 (April 1986): 27–29; see also "Field Guide to Waterfront Perspectives."
70. Edwin Murphy, "Waterfront Tide Turning, " *Portland Evening Express,* May 6, 1987; Cho, "Saving the Waterfront."

Conclusion

1. Chamber of Commerce of Greater Portland Region, *Port of Portland: Imagine a Great Port* (c. 1995), PRSC.
2. U.S. Bureau of the Census, *1990 Census of Population: Selected Population and Housing Characteristics, Portland, Maine,* www.census.gov/cen1990/html; U.S. Bureau of the Census, *2000 Census of Population: Selected Population and Housing Characteristics, Portland, Maine,* www.census.gov/cen2000/html; U.S. Bureau of the Census, *2010 Census of Population: Selected Population and Housing Characteristics, Portland, Maine,* www.census.gov/cen2010/html.
3. "Questions Arise over Money Paid to BIW," *Portland Press Herald,* May 9, 1982; "Uncertain Times on the Portland Waterfront," *Maine Sunday Telegram,* January 25, 2009.
4. See "Waterfront Panel Crafts Tax Plan to Fund Upkeep," *Portland Press Herald,* June 22, 2000; "Waterfront Plans Need Focused Development," *Portland Press Herald,* June 23, 2000.
5. "Uncertain Times on the Portland Waterfront," *Portland Press Herald,* January 25, 2009. On dwindling landings of fish at Fish Exchange, see *Portland Press Herald,* March 2, 2010. "In Portland, Me., A New Business Plan," *New York Times,* August 18, 2010.
6. "Portland Goes with the Flow When It Comes to Oil," *Portland Press Herald,* February 21, 2008.
7. "Portland's Port 'Very Healthy,' Director Says," *Portland Press Herald,* February 19, 2008.
8. "Uncertain Times on the Portland Waterfront," *Portland Press Herald,* January 25, 2009. The high-speed Portland-to-Yarmouth ferry, a hydrofoil, was called the CAT, see "Loss of Cat Takes Bite Out of Tourism," *Portland Press Herald,* December 19, 2009, and "Port Projects and Jobs Hinge on Stimulus Win," *Portland Press Herald,* December 10, 2009. See also "There Are More Ways Than One to Preserve Waterfront," *Portland Press Herald,* May 26, 2010; "Petition Opposes Change at Piers," *Portland Press Herald,* July 21, 2010; "Waterfront Property Owners Propose More Relaxed Zoning," *Portland Press Herald,* March 2, 2010.
9. On Bayside, "Office Proposal Set in Bayside," *Portland Press Herald,* June 20, 2000; "Deal Clears Way for Bayside Development," *Portland Press Herald,* August 16, 2005.
10. On Noyce, see "New Age Dawning for Libra Generosity," *Maine Sunday Telegram,* February 7, 2010; "Why Congress Street Hit Rock Bottom," *Portland Press Herald,* June 7, 1990; "Market in the Square," *Portland Press Herald,* June 7, 1990; "Council to Name Committee," *Portland Press Herald,* June 6, 1990. On a vital Congress Street as Historic District, see "Shops, Condos, Arts Venues, Help Keep Corridor Healthy," *Portland Press Herald,* March 16, 2009.

Index